Celebration Bar Review

Multistate Workbook 1

This book is printed for the exclusive use of
This Registered Celebration Bar Review Student
and may not be used by any other person without written permission of Celebration Bar Review. No Resale Permitted.

Table of Contents

MULTISTATE TECHNIQUES

INTRODUCTION

A working knowledge of the objectives of the Multistate Bar Examination, the skills it attempts to test, how it is drafted, the relationship of the Component parts of a Multistate question, and the limitations imposed on its authors can provide a student with a substantial advantage in understanding and passing the exam. These materials are designed to look at the Multistate Bar Examination from the examiners' point of view to help you enhance your Multistate score independent of your knowledge of the law. Obviously, there is no real substitute for knowing the law and how it works in a factual context, but these tips may help you in circumstances where you don't know the answer.

WHAT THE MULTISTATE EXAMINERS ARE TRYING TO ACCOMPLISH

The fundamental objective of the Multistate Examiners is to provide a tool to measure fairly and efficiently which law school graduates have the qualifications to be admitted to the bar and which do not.

The 200-question multiple-choice examination that is used to accomplish this objective must be of a consistent level of difficulty and the level at which the pass/fail decision is made must be achievable by a substantial majority of candidates. These limitations on the examiners lead to the first important insight into preparation for the exam, the kind of questions that really make a difference on whether you pass or fail. An adversarial relationship, which is one of the hallmarks of the legal profession exists between you and the bar examiners when you take the bar exam so that you can enter their profession. The more you know about your adversary and the rules they play by, the easier it is for you to beat them.

MARKER QUESTIONS

For years, performance of students on individual questions during their study has been compared with success or failure on the bar examination. Through an analysis of these statistics, we can identify those questions that are best able to predict performance on the exam.

In general, perhaps surprisingly, the hardest questions aren't particularly good predictors, because most of the students who passed them passed the examination. On the other hand, many of the easier questions are very good predictors.

In particular, we identified several questions where students answering them incorrectly failed the bar exam at a rate significantly higher than the usual failure rate of the overall bar exam population.

For example, one of the easiest questions given by the Multistate Examiners in the released February 1978 Exam reads as follows:

Ted frequently visited Janet, his next-door neighbor. Janet was separated from her husband, Howard. Howard resided with his mother but jointly owned the house in which Janet resided. Late one night, Ted and Janet were sitting on the bed in Janet's bedroom drinking when Howard burst through the door and told Ted, "Get out!" When Ted refused, Howard challenged him to go outside and "fight it out." Ted again refused. Howard then pulled a knife from his pocket and lunged at Ted. Ted grabbed a lamp, struck Howard on the head, and killed him. Ted is charged with murder. On a charge of murder, Ted should be found
- (A) not guilty, because Ted had as much right as Howard to be in the house.
- (B) not guilty, because Howard attacked Ted with a deadly weapon.
- (C) guilty, because Ted's presence in Janet's bedroom prompted Howard's attack.
- (D) guilty, because Ted's failure to obey Howard's order to leave the house made him a trespasser.

Of the students who participated in our Analysis, 98% correctly chose (B) as the correct answer. But of the 2% who answered this question incorrectly, 38% failed to pass the bar exam compared to a 20% failure rate overall.

SKILLS TESTED BY THE EXAMINERS

The Examiners test the following skills in the multiple-choice question format.

1. The ability to read a set of facts carefully.
2. The ability to identify the legal issue in a set of facts.
3. Knowledge of the law governing the legal issues found.

4.   The ability to apply the correct principle of substantive law to come to the correct conclusion for the right reason.

5.   The ability to distinguish between closely related principles of law which are frequently confused.

6.   The ability to make reasonable judgments on an ambiguous set of facts.

7.   The ability to understand the way in which limiting words make plausible-sounding choices wrong.

8.   The ability to guess the right answer by intelligently eliminating incorrect choices.

LIMITATIONS ON THE EXAMINERS

The Examiners are constrained in the way they construct the Multistate Bar Examination. All of the questions have to be related to the subject matter set forth in the outline in their Bulletin for Applicants. While that outline is broad and ambiguous, many years of experience with the Examination has delineated the scope of the material asked, so that you can feel confident that you do not have to go beyond the substantive texts and questions to find the important substantive law and the testable issues which are likely to appear on the Multistate Bar Examination.

The Examiners have specified their sources of authority for the correct answers. In most subjects, it is the generally accepted view of the law in the United States. Decisions of the United States Supreme Court control in Constitutional Law and Criminal Procedure, as does the Uniform Commercial Code in Sales and the Federal Rules in Evidence. In most areas, we have seen enough officially released questions so that we know what the Examiners consider to be the controlling law, and have incorporated that law into our materials. The Examiners are not in a position to change those rules absent a change in the governing law. Recent changes in the law, except U.S. Supreme Court decisions that are more than one year old, will not form the basis for correct answers to questions.

The time between the drafting of a Multistate Bar Examination question and its appearance on the examination is at least one year. After a question is initially drafted, it must be reviewed for substance by a committee responsible for that subject, and then must be reviewed by the technical exam writers working for ACT. It finally appears on an exam which is initially held for back-up in case there is a breach of security for the scheduled exam. The back-up exam is then administered as the scheduled exam during the next administration, six months later.

Therefore, the draftsperson of a question which you are taking was not aware of roughly the last two years of decisions by the United States Supreme Court at the time the question was drafted.

The Examiners have an obligation to ask fair questions. While a very careful reading of a fact pattern or item is required in order to reach the right answer, they do not in general rely on "trick" questions. Again, it is the basic, straightforward questions that determine whether you pass, not the occasional oddball or trick question. Reading too much into a question and looking for a trick lurking behind every fact will lead you to the wrong answer more often than it will lead you to the correct answer. Therefore, you should always take questions at face value.

The greatest limitation on the Examiners is that every question must have one demonstrably correct answer and three demonstrably wrong answers. When we look at the details of the construction of the questions, we will see how this limitation sometimes will give you a clue to the correct choice.

The Examiners have the obligation to administer the exam in a secure fashion. They, therefore, must prepare different versions of the exam to be given to persons sitting in close proximity to one another. There is no set order in which you will receive the 100 questions given each session. One group of candidates may get all of the long questions first and think the morning session is very difficult and another group may get easy questions at first and come to the opposite conclusion. You should not discuss the exam at lunch time and become upset because other people have a different impression of the exam than you.

ANATOMY OF A MULTISTATE QUESTION

This officially released question, illustrates the structure of a Multistate question.

ROOT OR FACT PATTERN:

Pemberton and three passengers, Able, Baker, and Charley, were injured when their car was struck by a truck owned by Mammoth Corporation and driven by Edwards. Helper, also a Mammoth employee, was riding in the truck. The issues in *Pemberton v. Mammoth* include the negligence of Edwards in driving too fast and failing to wear glasses, and of Pemberton in failing to yield the right of way.

Pemberton's counsel proffers evidence showing that shortly after the accident, Mammoth put a speed governor on the truck involved in the accident.

<table>
<tr><td>**STEM
OR CALL OF
QUESTION**</td><td colspan="3">The judge should rule the proffered evidence</td></tr>
<tr><td>**OPTIONS**</td><td></td><td></td></tr>
<tr><td>*DISTRACTER*</td><td>(A)</td><td>admissible as an admission of a party.</td></tr>
<tr><td>*DISTRACTER*</td><td>(B)</td><td>admissible as *res gestae.*</td></tr>
<tr><td>*KEY*</td><td>(C)</td><td>inadmissible for public policy reasons.</td></tr>
<tr><td>*DISTRACTER*
drawing of an</td><td>(D)</td><td>inadmissible, because it would lead to the
inference on an inference.</td></tr>
</table>

You should read the call first because it tells you what task you will be performing when choosing the correct answer, and will help focus your attention when you read the facts. Most of the time, it will be phrased in the positive asking the "best argument" or "most likely result." However, when the call of the question is in the negative, asking for the "weakest argument" or asking which of the options is "not" in a specified category, you must examine each option with the mindset that it if it is wrong, it is the correct answer.

Next, you should read the root or fact pattern, formulating the legal issue involved in those facts and recalling the principles of law or testable points which will resolve the legal issues.

Finally, you should look at each of the options and use the techniques described below to assist you in picking the correct option.

TECHNIQUES FOR PICKING THE CORRECT OPTION

THE PROCESS OF ELIMINATION

Your task in answering a Multistate question is not to find the ideal answer to the question asked, but rather to pick the best of the four options available. Many times when all the options are unattractive, your process is one of elimination. Some options can be positively eliminated because they state an incorrect proposition of law or because they do not appropriately relate to the facts.

If you can positively eliminate three choices and the remaining choice is not totally unacceptable, then you should pick it and move on to the next question.

The following question illustrates this point.

Hamilton owns a two-acre ocean-front estate known as "Doubleacre." His three neighbors - Alpha, Beta and Charlie - each own a lot without access to the ocean. Hamilton met Alpha and told him that he was interested in selling his estate for around $700,000 and that he would either sell for all cash or for part cash and part purchase money mortgage. Alpha indicated that he was interested in purchasing the property. A few days later, Alpha phoned Hamilton and informed him that he had secured the financing necessary to purchase the property. Hamilton subsequently met Beta and Charlie at the town dock and indicated to them that he was interested in selling his property and that the price would be around $700,000.

Three weeks later, Hamilton sent three identical letters to Alpha, Beta and Charlie, and did not inform any of them that the letter was being sent to all of them. The letter read as follows:

"As I have previously indicated to you, I am planning to sell Doubleacre for $700,000. I will sell either for $700,000 cash or for $200,000 cash and a promissory note for $500,000 for a term of ten years with interest at 10%. The sale is conditional upon my lawyer, Legalsmith, approving any deed which I give and any note and mortgage which I receive."
(s) Hamilton

Beta immediately drafted a letter that he delivered by messenger to Hamilton which read as follows:

"I accept your offer to purchase Doubleacre for $700,000 cash. I will close at your convenience."
(s) Beta

One day after the Beta letter was received by Hamilton, Alpha delivered a letter to Hamilton as follows:

"I reaffirm my previous offer to purchase Doubleacre for $700,000 cash. I will close at your convenience."
(s) Alpha

Shortly thereafter, Hamilton sold Doubleacre to Stranger for $700,000 cash. If Alpha sues Hamilton for breach of contract, which of the following would be Hamilton's strongest defense?

(A) The acceptance sent by Beta was prior in time to that of Alpha and terminated Alpha's power to accept.

(B) A binding contract between Hamilton and Alpha could not occur until the occurrence of the condition specified in the offer, namely, that Hamilton's lawyer approve the deed.

(C) The letter from Hamilton to Alpha did not state explicitly or by reasonable implication that Alpha could enter into a contractual relationship by manifesting an acceptance.

(D) The fact that identical letters were sent to potential buyers indicates that Hamilton did not intend that the letter be an offer.

This is a difficult question because Hamilton will probably lose and your task is to eliminate those defenses that are clearly wrong, and then pick the remaining choice which is not clearly incorrect.

(A) is clearly incorrect, since this is not a real estate brokerage contract which could be terminated without notice to the offeree.

(B) is clearly incorrect. The approval by Hamilton's lawyer would not take place until near the closing, and is at most a condition subsequent which might relieve Hamilton of performance if the buyer insisted on a deed which was unacceptable to Hamilton's lawyer. It would not prevent the formation of a contract in which the approval of the deed was a term of the contract.

(D) would be a strong argument if each of the offerees knew about the multiple addressees, because it would then be unreasonable for an addressee to expect that he had the power to form a contract.

However, the facts indicate the addressees did not know that the letter was sent to more than one person and (D) must therefore be wrong.

That leaves you with an unimpressive (C). However, it is possible to read Hamilton's letter as not manifesting an intention to create the power in the addressee to form a contract by accepting, but rather as an invitation for offers only.   Accordingly, Hamilton could argue that neither his conversation with Alpha nor his letter to Alpha should be interpreted to give Alpha the power to conclude a contract. It is therefore the correct answer. While it is likely that Hamilton would lose on that argument, the other three choices are wrong and this one is at least plausible.

ELIMINATING SOME CHOICES AND THEN GUESSING

Certain questions on the Multistate Bar Examination are hard because of the difficulty involved in distinguishing between two of the four choices when finally picking the best answer.

A common lament from students leaving the bar exam is "I could not decide between the last two choices." The positive side of that problem is that you have eliminated two of the four choices. The arithmetic of the Multistate Bar Examination makes it very likely that you will pass if you have gone about eliminating choices intelligently. If you are sure of the answer to only half of the 200 questions on the exam and can confidently eliminate two of the four choices on the remaining hundred, then you can randomly guess between the two remaining choices, and the odds are that you will get 50 of them right. Those 50, coupled with the 100 questions of which you were sure of the answer, will produce a raw score of 150 on the Multistate Bar Examination, allowing you to pass with room to spare.

An example of that partial elimination process is shown in this Evidence question:

Davis is being tried for the common-law rape of Peg by force. Davis alleges consent.
Quigley, a defense witness, testifies that he had overheard Peg invite Davis to become intimate with her. The prosecution possesses a certified copy of Quigley's three-year old conviction for arson, a crime punishable by five year's imprisonment. Without asking Quigley about the conviction on cross-examination, the prosecution offers the copy of the conviction into evidence on rebuttal. The trial judge should rule the copy of the conviction

(A)   inadmissible because the prosecution failed to call the attention of the witness to the conviction on cross-examination.
(B)   inadmissible because evidence of convictions to impeach the character of witnesses cannot be shown by extrinsic evidence
(C)   admissible only if the trial judge finds that the probative value of admitting the evidence outweighs its prejudicial effect on the accused.
(D)   admissible unless its probative value is substantially outweighed by the danger of unfair prejudice.

A student with a rudimentary knowledge of evidence should be able to quickly eliminate (A) and (B), because (A) states the rule with respect to prior inconsistent statements, not convictions, and (B) deals with limitations on extrinsic evidence not applicable to impeachment by convictions. Moreover, given the complex and precise nature of choices (C) and (D), compared to the rather simplistic issues in choices (A) and (B), you should have a sixth sense that the right choice lies between (C) and (D).

Choosing between them is difficult because it tests your knowledge of a relatively recent amendment to the Federal Rules of Evidence which relaxed the standard which must be proven by the prosecution when the character of a witness, rather than the character of the criminal defendant, is involved. However, an absolutely random guess between (C) and (D) gives you even odds of answering the question correctly.

THE DOUBLE TRUE/FALSE QUESTION

Because the form of the multiple-choice question used on the Multistate Bar Examination has four options, the double true/false question appears in many forms. In that type of question, the four options are

    (A)   proposition A is true.
    (B)   proposition B is true.
    (C)   both propositions are true.
    (D)   neither proposition is true.

The propositions are set out with roman numerals in the body of the question itself.
This type of question appeals to the Examiners because the student must judge the truth of each proposition based upon the facts set forth in the root of the question, and little time has to be spent on either the call of the question or the draftsmanship of the options.

In preparing for the exam, it is not necessary to practice on questions that combine the issues to be tested in the precise combination which they are tested on the examination. The important thing to learn is the substantive law governing the issues so that you can correctly judge if a proposition is true or false. Combining two true/false questions in a single multiple-choice question is easy if you can handle each true/false issue separately.

There are no sure rules for guessing on this type of question. Each proposition must be examined independently to determine if it is true or false. The choice of the correct option follows mechanically once that determination is made.

However, where the two propositions are closely related, the Examiner is most often trying to highlight a difference between them, and therefore very often the correct choice is one of the two choices which deals with the two propositions differently.

This is illustrated by this Property Question:

The following conveyances were made of Blackacre by O who holds title in fee simple:

1.   I.   "To A so long as the premises are used for church purposes, and if they are not so used, then to X."
II.   II.   "To B, but if the premises should not be used for church purposes, then to X.

        O retains an interest in Blackacre

(A) after conveyance I.
(B) after conveyance II.
(C) after both conveyances.
(D) after neither conveyance.

Since propositions I and II look very similar, the shrewd guess is that the examiner is trying to illustrate the difference between them and that O retains an interest after one but not the other. In fact, that is the case. Even if you do not know anything about property law and have to guess between (A) and (B), you have doubled your chances of getting the correct answer.

The statistics on this question illustrate a point made earlier. This question is extremely difficult. Less than one student in four, the result that would occur in random guessing, answered it correctly. Yet, the better students obtained the correct answer twice as often as the poor students. However, it didn't make any difference in the long run whether you got this question right or wrong because those getting it right passed the bar exam at only a slightly higher rate than those answering it incorrectly. This question, which involves the intricacies of determinable fees and the Rule Against Perpetuities is not the kind of question you spend a good deal of time on unless your objective is to obtain a very high score on the Multistate Bar Examination.

THE CORRECTLY STATED BUT INAPPLICABLE PRINCIPLE OF LAW

The task of the Examiners is to make wrong choices look good. One of the best ways to accomplish this is to write a choice which impeccably states a rule of law that is not applicable because of facts in the root of the question.

This is illustrated by the following officially released question:

Trease owned Hilltop in fee simple. By his will, he devised as follows: "Hilltop to such of my grandchildren who shall reach the age of 21; and by this provision I intend to include all grandchildren whenever born." At the time of his death, Trease had three children and two grandchildren.

Courts hold such a devise valid under the common-law Rule Against Perpetuities.
What is the best explanation of that determination?

    (A)   All of Trease's children would be measuring lives
    (B)   The rule of convenience closes the class of beneficiaries when any grandchild reaches the age of 21.
    (C)   There is a presumption that Trease intended to include only those grandchildren born prior to his death.
    (D)   There is a subsidiary rule of construction that dispositive instruments are to be interpreted so as to uphold interests, rather than to invalidate them under the Rule Against Perpetuities.

Choice (B) correctly states the rule of convenience as it applies to class gifts. However, the rule of convenience is only a rule of construction, which means that it is not applicable if the grantor has expressed a contrary intent. In this case, the will stated that Trease intended to include all grandchildren whenever born. Therefore, the rule of convenience does not apply, because the body of the question contains facts which make it inapplicable. Be wary of a perfectly stated rule of law. The Examiners usually state a rule that way only when it is not applicable.

ELIMINATION OF CHOICES BY OBSERVING THE INCONSISTENCY BETWEEN THEM AND THE FACT PATTERN

Another method the Examiners use to write appealing but wrong answers is to write a choice which sounds very plausible but is flatly contradicted by the fact pattern. In the process of reaching the correct answer, you must eliminate any choice which states a position inconsistent with the facts of the question.

This is illustrated by the following officially released question:

Trease owned Hilltop in fee simple. By his will, he devised as follows: "Hilltop to such of my grandchildren who shall reach the age of 21; and by this provision I intend to include all grandchildren, whenever born." At the time of his death Trease had three children and two grandchildren.

Which of the following additions to or changes in the facts stated in the previous paragraph would produce a violation of the common-law Rule Against Perpetuities?

    (A)   A posthumous child was born to Trease.
    (B)   Trease's will expressed the intention to include all after-born grandchildren in the gift.
    (C)   The instrument was an inter vivos conveyance rather than a will.
    (D)   Trease had no grandchildren living at the time of his death.

Choice (B) can be eliminated even if you know nothing about the Rule Against Perpetuities. The focus of the question asks what additions or changes in the preceding paragraph will cause a violation of the Rule. This choice does not represent an addition or change. Trease's will, which is set forth in the root of the question, already expresses the intent to include afterborn grandchildren. Therefore, it must be eliminated, whether or not it would cause a violation of the Rule Against Perpetuities, because it is not an "addition" or "change." It is important when answering these questions to read carefully and compare the choices to the body of the question.

THE THREE-ONE RULE

The author of a question must provide one answer that is correct and three that are not correct. Most questions in which there is a dichotomy of result, such as guilty/not guilty or admissible/inadmissible, will show two choices on each side of the general conclusion. If the question is skewed so that three choices are on one side of the general conclusion and one is on the other, the drafting of the question becomes more difficult if the correct choice is one of the three because the reasoning behind each choice must be distinct from the other choices. On the other hand, if the correct choice is the only one reaching a particular conclusion, there is no requirement to draft a reason why that choice is correct and there is no requirement that the reasoning among the three choices on the other side be clear and distinct. Therefore, the best guess in such a question is the sole choice reaching a conclusion rather than one of the other three choices.

An example of this type of question follows from Criminal Law:

A statute in State X provides: "Arson shall be punishable by a sentence of not more than ten years in state prison." X, during the daytime, went to a house in his neighborhood that was vacant because the previous owners had moved out and the new owners had not yet moved in. He put a lighted torch to the side of the house, and shortly thereafter extinguished the torch. The fire only slightly burned some of the shingles on the house. X is charged with arson. He is

   (A)   guilty.
   (B)   not guilty, because there was not sufficient burning.
   (C)   not guilty, because the house was unoccupied at the time.
   (D)   not guilty, because the activity took place during the daytime.

The "guilty" correct answer needs no explanation, and there is no requirement to distinguish between the three "not guilties" because they are all wrong.

THE DISTANCE BETWEEN CHOICES

By far the most common choice pattern is the "two-two" pattern – e.g., two choices which say that P will prevail, and two which say that D will prevail. The best way to approach this kind of question is to rely on your knowledge of the law or on your instinctive feeling as to which general conclusion is correct, then try to distinguish between the explanation following each of the general conclusions and pick the one that best justifies the conclusion.

However, if the justifications following the conclusion on the side you chose seem indistinguishable, then look at the explanations for the choices on the other side. If they are readily distinguishable, and one appears reasonable and the other incorrect, then reconsider your initial choice of a general conclusion. Remember that the Examiner is required to provide a clearly distinguishable reason why one explanation of a general conclusion is right and the other is wrong. That obligation does not exist if the general conclusion itself is wrong. If choices (A) and (B) on one side both sound extremely reasonable, and are consistent with the fact pattern and on the other side answer (C) seems clearly wrong, or is inconsistent with the fact pattern, and answer (D) sounds reasonable, then from a purely technical viewpoint, the best guess is answer (D).

This is illustrated by the following Property Question:

In 1976, Barbara was the owner of Blueacre and Gertrude was the owner of the adjoining property, Greenacre. An unpaved driveway running from the main road across a portion of Greenacre gave Gertrude access to her residence. However, Gertrude decided that it would be more convenient for her to use the paved driveway on Blueacre and, in January of 1976, Gertrude began to use this paved driveway without making any effort to obtain Barbara's consent.

Barbara died in 1977 survived by Bonnie, age 12, her sole heir. Prior to her death, Barbara had also used the paved driveway as access to Blueacre but did not discover that Gertrude was also using it.

In 1978, Bonnie's guardian discovered Gertrude's use and orally protested to Gertrude. Gertrude ignored the protest and continued to use the driveway.

In February 1991, Gertrude conveyed Greenacre to Donna, informing Donna that Gertrude had been using the paved driveway on Blueacre. Donna continued to use the driveway until the end of the year, but made no use of it during 1992 or 1993. In January of 1994, Donna decided to begin using the paved driveway again, but when she attempted to do so, she discovered that Evelyn (who had purchased Blueacre from Bonnie in 1990) had erected a fence which blocked access to Greenacre from the paved driveway.

A statute in the jurisdiction provides that: "All actions to recover possession of real property must be brought within fifteen years of the time that the cause of action accrues."

Donna is now claiming that she has acquired an easement in Blueacre, and wishes to compel Evelyn to remove the fence.

Which of the following is the most accurate statement with regard to the events following Gertrude's conveyance of Greenacre to Donna in February, 1991?

(A) The use of the driveway by Donna after her acquisition of Greenacre in 1991 will be "tacked" onto the use by Gertrude to compute the statutory prescriptive period.

(B) Donna's failure to use the driveway during 1992 and 1993 will interrupt the running of the prescriptive period, which is required to be continuous.

(C) The conveyance of Greenacre to Donna also gave her an easement in Blueacre entitling her to the use of the driveway.

(D) Donna's failure to use the driveway during 1992 and 1993 would operate as an abandonment of any rights that she may have theretofore acquired.

The difficulty with this question is that you have to go through 15 years of transactions to determine if Gertrude achieved an easement by prescription before February 1991. Choices (A) and (B) are based on the premise that no easement was obtained, whereas (C) and (D) state conclusions based upon a valid easement by prescription. While a judgment that no easement exists might be reasonable, you can tell that this is not the result envisioned by the Examiners because (A) and (B) are virtually indistinguishable if you come to the conclusion that there was no easement by prescription in 1991. If the easement had not ripened, additional prescriptive time would be tacked on, the conclusion stated by (A). However, the result suggested by (B), that non-use would interrupt the continuous nature of the possession, is also a valid conclusion if there were no easement. Therefore, (A) and (B) must both be wrong and the correct answer must be on the side where the choices are distinguishable. Choice (C) is the right answer because it gives Donna all the rights of an easement-holder, while (D) incorrectly states that she can lose those rights by a short period of non-use.

THE OPPOSITES RULE

Many times the Examiners may desire to test your knowledge of the applicability of a principle of law to a question. Then, often, two of the four choices will be phrased in terms of the applicability of that principle. The other two choices will deal with extraneous issues. When this pattern emerges, the correct answer is usually in one of the two opposites, provided the principle of law they deal with is relevant to a determination of the issue. The choice between those opposites must be made from your knowledge of the substantive law.

An example of this type of question can be found in this officially released question:

Seller and Buyer execute an agreement for the sale of real property on September 1. The jurisdiction in which the property is located recognizes the principle of equitable conversion, and has no statute pertinent to this problem.
Seller dies before closing, and his will leaves personal property to Perry and his real property to Rose. There being no breach of the agreement by either party, which of the following is correct?

  (A)   Death, an eventuality which the parties could have provided for, terminates the agreement if they did not provide otherwise.

(B)   Rose is entitled to the proceeds of the sale when it closes, because the doctrine of equitable conversion does not apply to these circumstances.
(C)   Perry is entitled to the proceeds of the sale when it closes.
(D)   Title was rendered unmarketable by Seller's death.

The fact that the issue is the effect of the doctrine of equitable conversion on the fight to the proceeds can be gleaned from the nature of the choices. (B) and (C) reach the opposite conclusion on this issue, and this narrows your choices to two. The correct answer, (C), is one of those choices.

USE OF THE CONJUNCTION "BECAUSE"

The conjunction "because" connects a conclusion with a reason for that conclusion, For an option in a Multistate question using "because" to be the correct answer, the conclusion must be correct and the reason must logically follow based upon the facts and the applicable substantive law.

For example,

(Fact Pattern 1)
Seller, the owner of Blackacre, offered in a writing, signed by him, to sell Blackacre to Buyer for $10,000 on a specific date and Buyer accepted the offer. Seller later refused to perform.
In a suit by Buyer against Seller....

In Fact Pattern 1, an option which said, "Buyer will win because the agreement was in writing" would be correct. It reaches the correct conclusion and states a valid reason both in fact and in law for that conclusion.
Note that the only requirement of the reason following the word "because" is that it logically follow the conclusion and that it be supported by the facts and the substantive law.

However, it need not be the **only** reason that supports the conclusion. For example, in Fact Pattern 1, a choice which said "Buyer will win **because** he accepted Seller's offer" would also be correct since it satisfies the two requirements of the conjunction "because": the general conclusion is correct and the reason logically follows and is supported by the facts and the law.

If either of the two requirements is **not** met, the choice is wrong. For example,

(Fact Pattern 2)

Seller, the owner of Blackacre, offered orally to sell Blackacre to Buyer for $10,000 on a specific date and Buyer accepted the offer. Seller later refused to perform.

In a suit by Buyer against Seller....
The option, "Buyer will win **because** he accepted Seller's offer" would not be correct since the conclusion is incorrect. Buyer would lose because of the absence of a writing. The fact that the reason which follows "because" logically follows and is supported by the facts is irrelevant because the conclusion is wrong.
Likewise, the option is incorrect if the reasoning does not logically follow from the facts. An option following Fact Pattern I which said, "Buyer will win **because** the doctrine of part performance takes the agreement out of the Statute of Frauds" would be incorrect, even though the conclusion is correct and the principle of law is correctly stated. The reasoning is not supported by the facts and therefore does not follow logically therefrom.

The failure of logical reasoning can apply to legal principles as well as the facts. An option Following Fact Pattern 1 which said, "Buyer will win **because** Seller's offer is admissible under the parol evidence rule" is incorrect, even though it relates to the facts of the question, because the reasoning concerning the parol evidence rule is not a legal basis for Buyer's winning.

The "because" conjunction is heavily used because it requires the applicants to determine the correct conclusion based upon their knowledge of the substantive law and also requires applicants to determine if there is a logical nexus between the conclusion and the reason stated based upon their analysis of the facts in the root of the question and their knowledge of the substantive law.

USE OF THE ADVERBS AND ADJECTIVES "ALL," "ANY," "NEVER," "ALWAYS," AND "EVERY"

In addition to the limitations imposed by the conjunctions discussed above, options can be narrowed by the use of limiting adverbs and adjectives which require that a proposition be true all of the time or none of the time. These are substantial conditions which are designed to make close choices wrong.

This is illustrated by this Evidence Question:

Which of the following statements regarding judicial notice is most accurate?

    (A)   A court may take judicial notice only when requested by one of the parties.
    (B)   Once the court takes judicial notice, the jury is required to accept as conclusive any fact judicially noticed in all proceedings.
    (C)   If a court, on its own authority, takes judicial notice of a fact, a party is not entitled to a hearing as the propriety of the action.
    (D)   Judicial notice may be taken for the first time during the appellate stages of litigation.

Choice (B) is a very popular wrong answer to this question. While the statement about the conclusive nature of the facts judicially noticed is true in civil cases, it is false in criminal cases. A jury is not required to find in accordance with judicially noticed facts in a criminal case. Therefore, it is incorrect because the choice says that such facts are true concerning **any** fact in **all** proceedings.

The same analysis must be applied to any choice involving an "all," "always," "any," or "every." Irrespective of the facts of the question, the proposition stated must be true no matter what the circumstances. Likewise, the legal principle stated in a choice including a "never" must be false no matter what the circumstances; if there are any circumstances in which the legal proposition stated is true, the choice is wrong.

TIMING

The time given you to complete a Multistate Bar Examination is ordinarily adequate, if you have practiced enough on questions to improve your speed and efficiency to the required level. The examination is broken into two 100-question segments. You are allowed three hours for each set of 100 questions – one minute and forty-eight seconds per question. However, all questions do not require the same amount of time.

You should first check the clock 15 minutes after the examination starts. By then, you should have nine questions completed. You should check at 15-minute intervals thereafter. As long as you have completed 18 questions in the first half hour, 90 in the first two and one-half hours, and 100 after two hours and forty-five minutes, your pace is right.

If you find a particularly hard question or one you do not know the answer to, make a shrewd guess within this time frame and make a note to yourself to come back if time allows. DO NOT LEAVE IT BLANK.

If you find that your natural, careful pace is faster than this, work at your faster pace, but use your extra time fruitfully on the harder questions or in thoroughly rechecking your work at the end.

If you find that you absolutely cannot finish all the questions in the allotted time, then you should skip those questions with a long fact pattern and only one question. If you follow this advice, make sure that you keep your proper place on your answer sheet by skipping the row on the answer sheet corresponding to the question you skipped. Come back to those questions at the end and do as many as you can. Then, before turning your paper in, guess at the rest. In this way, you can reduce the number of random guesses to a minimum. **Make sure that you answer every question,** even if you have not even read the question, since wrong answers do not count against you.

As you decide each correct answer, circle it in your examination book and mark the appropriate block on your answer sheet. At the pace of nine questions per 15 minutes, you should have about seven minutes left at the end. Spend that time proofreading your answer sheet, which is the only paper that will be graded. Check against the answers you circled in the book to be certain that you marked the appropriate block on your answer sheet. Make sure that there are no blanks on your answer sheet and no questions for which you have marked two answers. If you have erased, make sure that your erasure is thorough; otherwise, the computer may reject your answer because it thinks you have marked two answers. DO NOT use this time to change the answer you have already picked unless you have a very good reason to change. If you have time left after your proofreading is done, go back to the difficult questions and re-think the answers you have chosen. But even after careful thought, you should hesitate to change an answer. Do not leave any section of the examination early. Use all the time allotted to you wisely.

MULTISTATE NUTSHELLS OF LAW

The following rules of law have controlled the answers to questions on the Multistate Bar Exam. They should be committed to memory and their application understood before you take the Multistate Bar Exam.

FEDERAL JURISDICTION & CIVIL PROCEDURE

ORIGINAL JURISDICTION

"In all cases affecting ambassadors, other public ministers and consuls, and those in which a state shall be a party, the Supreme Court shall have original jurisdiction." Congress can neither add to the original jurisdiction of the Supreme Court, nor take away any of that jurisdiction.

APPELLATE JURISDICTION

The Constitution provides that in all other cases within the judicial power of the United States, "the Supreme Court shall have appellate jurisdiction, both as to law and fact, with such exceptions, and under such regulations as the Congress shall make."

CONCURRENT AND EXCLUSIVE JURISDICTION

Generally, absent express limitation or implication, federal jurisdiction is concurrent with that of the state courts

FEDERAL SUBJECT MATTER JURISDICTION

The first issue in federal jurisdiction is to determine whether the court has jurisdiction to decide the particular controversy brought before it – subject matter jurisdiction.

Federal courts have subject matter jurisdiction in: (1) suits between citizens of different states; (2) suits involving a federal question; (3) cases involving ambassadors, admiralty, and maritime jurisdiction; and (4) cases where the United States is a party.

SUPPLEMENTAL JURISDICTION

A district court generally will have supplemental jurisdiction over any claims so related to the claim upon which federal jurisdiction is founded that "they form part of the same case or controversy.

REMOVAL

A civil action brought in a state court may be removed by the defendant to the federal district court if the plaintiff could have brought the action in federal court originally

REMAND

If, at any time before final judgment, it appears that the case was removed improvidently and without jurisdiction, the federal court must remand the case to the state court, and may order the payment of just costs.

PERSONAL JURISDICTION

In addition to jurisdiction over the subject matter, a federal court must have jurisdiction over the persons or property involved in the suit. This is sometimes referred to as territorial jurisdiction or personal jurisdiction.

In personam jurisdiction gives the court power to award a judgment imposing personal liability on the defendant. It is usually the most desirable form of jurisdiction, since, in effect, the judgment attaches to the person of the defendant and follows wherever he goes

The basis for in personam jurisdiction are:

(1)   Personal service within the state;

(2)   Domicile of the defendant in the state - Domicile requires the maintenance of a residence or physical presence in the state, and the mental intent to make the state one's permanent residence;

(3)   Consent of the defendant to be sued in the state (by contract, intentional waiver of an objection, or failure to raise the objection in timely fashion);

(4)   Fictional presence of a corporation in the state ("doing business") - The key factor is the extent of business - the corporation must do business in the state not occasionally or casually, but with a fair measure of permanence and continuity; or

(5)   Long-arm jurisdiction.   .

LONG ARM JURISDICTION

Under the minimum contacts doctrine there are two bases for the assumption of jurisdiction: (1) if the cause of action arose from the defendant's activities within the state, jurisdiction would be proper; (2) if the cause of action arose from conduct outside the forum state, jurisdiction would be proper if the out-of-state defendant engaged in continuous and systematic business within the state (e.g., a permanent office or regular sales representatives).

IN REM JURISDICTION

In rem jurisdiction is based upon the physical presence of property in the state. An action in rem is not against any one party, but seeks to settle some question as to the res "against all the world"; by its judgment, the court establishes rights in the property against all potential claimants.

Two things are necessary for a state to have in rem jurisdiction: (1) the presence of the res in the state, and (2) adequate notice to persons with an interest in the res, so that they can participate in any determination.

SERVICE OF PROCESS AND NOTICE

A defendant is given notice that an action has been brought against him by the service of process (unless service by publication is appropriate). Process from federal courts can be served (1) within the state where the district court is located, or (2) outside the state, if the state in which it is sitting has a long-arm statute,

Service made after a nonresident is lured into the state under false pretenses can be invalidated. However, if a defendant is already in the state, deception may be used to deliver process (e.g., process server uses false identity to coax defendant out of hotel room).

NOTICE

Due process requires that before jurisdiction can be exercised over a person or his property, he must be given notice and an opportunity to be heard. The notice must be "reasonably calculated, under all the circumstances, to apprise interested parties of the pendency of the action and afford them an opportunity to present their objections

VENUE, FORUM NON CONVENIENS, AND TRANSFER

Venue refers to the proper place for trial of an action over which several courts could exercise jurisdiction.

The purposes of venue requirements are (1) to distribute cases within the court system, and (2) to promote convenience, by ensuring that the place of trial has some relationship with the parties or the cause of action, and it is thus not an undue burden on the parties to try the case there.

Venue in either a diversity or federal question case is proper in any district in which either:

(a)   a defendant resides, if all of the defendants reside in the same state, or

(b)   a "substantial" part of the events or property which are the basis of the claim took place.

FORUM NON CONVENIENS

The doctrine of forum non conveniens allows dismissal by a court if it would be an unfair or inconvenient forum.

Dismissal will usually be appropriate where trial in the plaintiff's chosen forum imposes a heavy burden on the defendant or the court, and where the plaintiff is unable to offer any specific reasons of convenience supporting her choice. However, dismissal is not appropriate if the alternative forum does not permit litigation of the subject matter of the dispute.

TRANSFER

If an action is commenced in the wrong district, the court shall dismiss, or if it is in the interest of justice, the court may transfer the case to any district in which it could have been brought. Transfer can be ordered only if the court in which the action was brought has subject matter jurisdiction. The case must be transferred to a district in which venue is proper, and in which the defendant is amenable to process.

Even though venue is proper in the district where an action is brought, the court may, in its discretion, transfer the suit to any district "where it might have been brought," "for the convenience of parties and witnesses, in the interest of justice."

LAW APPLIED BY THE FEDERAL COURTS

A federal court must apply the substantive law that would be applied by a state court in the state where the federal court is sitting. In instances when federal common law is applicable, it preempts state statutes and case law and must be applied by state courts as well as federal courts. A case "arising under" federal common law is a federal question case.

III. PRETRIAL PROCEDURES.

B. PLEADINGS AND AMENDED AND SUPPLEMENTAL PLEADINGS

The primary purpose of pleadings is to give fair notice to the parties of the claims and defenses in the action. Under this theory of notice pleading adopted by the Federal Rules, liberal discovery procedures, rather than the detailed pleadings of common law, are used to narrow the issues for trial. There are no technical forms of pleading, and the underlying philosophy of the Rules is that all pleadings shall be so construed as to do substantial justice. Thus, pleadings are not construed against the pleader, but are to be construed liberally. A plaintiff may base his claim on alternative or even inconsistent theories; likewise, the defendant may raise as many defenses as he has, regardless of consistency.

THE COMPLAINT

Each complaint (or other claim for relief, e.g., a counterclaim) must contain: (1) a short and plain statement of the grounds upon which the court's jurisdiction depends; (2) a short and plain statement of the claim showing that the pleader is entitled to relief; and (3) a demand for judgment for the relief to which he deems himself entitled. A party can seek both equitable relief and damages in the same action. The complaint should give the defendant fair notice of what the plaintiff's claim is and the grounds upon which it rests. The burden of pleading an issue is usually on the party who has the burden of producing evidence on that issue at trial.

Generally, the plaintiff need not plead matters on which the defendant must introduce proof. So, if a defense goes to the heart of the action, the plaintiff must plead that it does not exist –

Although the general rule is that the pleadings need only give fair notice of the claim, in certain circumstances more detailed allegations are required. Those include, 1) fraud or mistake; 2) conditions precedent; and 3) special damages.

THE ANSWER
The defendant's answer responds to the plaintiff's complaint by denying its allegations and/or by raising affirmative defenses to the allegations. The requirements as to the form of a complaint, supra, also apply to the answer.

DENIALS
General Denials
A general denial controverts all allegations in the complaint, e.g., "Defendant denies each and every allegation in Plaintiff's complaint." In federal court, a general denial is improper unless the defendant intends in good faith to contest every allegation, including jurisdictional allegations.
Specific Denials
In a specific denial, the defendant admits or denies the plaintiff's allegations paragraph by paragraph. If only a part of a paragraph is true, the defendant admits what is true and denies the remainder
If the defendant is without knowledge or information sufficient to form a belief as to the truth of an averment, she may so state in her answer, and this has the effect of a denial.
Effect of Failure To Deny
An allegation that is not denied, or that is improperly denied, is deemed to have been admitted, and is binding on the parties.

AFFIRMATIVE DEFENSES
Even if the defendant admits the allegations of the complaint, there may be additional facts which, if established, would bar the plaintiff's recovery. These are called affirmative defenses and must be raised by the defendant in the answer. An affirmative defense is waived if not raised in the answer

Counterclaims, Cross-Claims, and Third Party Claims
A counterclaim is a claim for relief against the plaintiff asserted by the defendant in her answer to the complaint. A counterclaim may seek relief exceeding in amount, or different in kind from, that sought by the plaintiff.

Compulsory Counterclaims

A defendant must assert any claim which he has against the plaintiff at the time of serving the pleading if it arises out of the transaction or occurrence that is the subject matter of the opposing party's claim and does not require for its adjudication the presence of third parties of whom the court cannot acquire jurisdiction. A counterclaim is logically related to the claim if separate trials on each of the claims would involve substantial duplication of effort and time by the parties and the courts. If a compulsory counterclaim is not asserted, it cannot be raised in a subsequent action in federal court.

Permissive Counterclaims

Any claim that does not arise out of the same transaction or occurrence as the original claim may be pleaded as a permissive counterclaim. However, the court may, for convenience, order separate trials for unrelated actions.

Cross-Claims

A cross-claim is a claim asserted by one party against a co-party. A cross-claim, like a counterclaim, should be pleaded in the answer, but is not compulsory. The co-party against whom a cross-claim is asserted must file an answer to the cross-claim. A cross-claim must "arise out of the transaction or occurrence that is the subject matter either of the original action or of a counterclaim therein, or relate to any property that is the subject matter of the original action." In determining the extent of a "transaction or occurrence", the same logical relationship test as is applied in counterclaims is used.

A defendant may file a cross-claim against a co-party who "is or may be liable to the cross-claimant for all or part" of the original plaintiff's claim.

Joinder of Additional Parties to Counterclaims And Cross-Claims

Persons other than those who are parties to the original action may be added as parties to a counterclaim or cross-claim if they are "indispensable", "necessary" or "proper" parties.

Impleader

Impleader allows a defendant to assert a claim against a third person not a party to the original action who is or may be liable to the defendant for all or part of the plaintiff's claim against the defendant. Impleader is not mandatory; the defendant may choose to assert his claim in a separate action.

Impleader is improper if the third party's liability to the defendant is direct rather than derivative. Impleader can be used to assert claims for indemnity, subrogation, contribution, or breach of warranty. Impleader is permissible when a third party "may be" liable. Thus, the third person can be made a party to the main action even though his liability to the defendant is contingent upon the defendant being found liable or being required to pay more than her share of liability.

Amended and Supplemental Pleadings

Amendment of the pleadings is liberally allowed under the Federal Rules. Amendment may be necessary if the other party has successfully challenged the sufficiency of a pleading, or if the party wishes to add claims or defenses that he had not known or had overlooked at the time of filing the original pleading.

Amendment as Of Right

A party may amend his pleading once as a matter of course (1) at any time before a responsive pleading has been served, or (2) if no responsive pleading is required and the action has not been placed on the trial calendar, within twenty days after service of his pleading.

Amendment by Leave Of Court

After expiration of the period for amendment as of right, a party may amend his pleading only by leave of court or by written consent of the adverse party. Generally, leave to amend will be denied only if amendment would cause actual prejudice to the opposing party.

Effect of Amendment

An amended pleading supersedes the original pleading. If a response to the original pleading was required, then a response to the amended pleading is also required, unless the amendment was very minor.

Relation Back Of Amendments

If a party seeks to assert a new claim in her amended pleading, a problem arises if the statute of limitations has run before the amendment. The doctrine of relation back can save the claim. Where the limitations period had run on the claim before the original pleading was filed, the claim is barred. Amendment cannot be used to circumvent the statute.

However, if the applicable limitations law allows or the new claim arose out of the conduct, transaction or occurrence set forth in the original pleading, the amendment relates back to the date of original pleading Thus, the claim would not be barred even though the statute had run between the filing of the original pleading and the filing of the amendment. Because the other party had notice within the limitations period of a claim against her arising out of the transaction, she is not prejudiced by the addition of another claim based on the same transaction. Courts are usually liberal in finding that the additional claim arose from the transaction or occurrence.

Supplemental Pleadings

A supplemental pleading merely adds to, rather than supersedes, the original pleading. A supplemental pleading may cure a defective original pleading, in the court's discretion. The court also has discretion to order a response to a supplemental pleading.

RULE 11

Every pleading, motion and other paper must be signed by at least one attorney of record in the attorney's name or by a party personally if the party is not represented by an attorney. The paper must state the attorney's or party's address, e-mail address, and telephone number.

By presenting to the court a pleading, motion, or other paper, whether by signing, filing, submitting, or later advocating it, that attorney or party certifies that to the best of that person's knowledge, information, and belief after an inquiry reasonable under the circumstances: 1) It is not being presented for any improper purpose, such as to harass, cause unnecessary delay, or needlessly increase the cost of litigation; 2) The claims, defenses, and other legal contentions are warranted by existing law or by a non-frivolous argument for extending, modifying, or reversing existing law or for establishing new law;

3) The factual contentions have evidentiary support or, if specifically so identified, will likely have evidentiary support after reasonable opportunity for further investigation or discovery; and 4) The denials of factual contentions are warranted on the evidence or, if specifically so identified, are reasonably based on belief or a lack of information.

Sanctions

If, after notice and reasonable opportunity to respond, the court determines that the Rule has been violated, the court may impose an appropriate sanction for the violation. Sanctions imposed under this rule must be limited to deter repetition of the conduct or comparable conduct by others. The sanction may include non-monetary directives, an order to pay a penalty, or, if warranted, an order directing payment of part or all of the reasonable attorney's fees and other expenses directly resulting from the violation.

JOINDER OF PARTIES AND CLAIMS

To prevent a multiplicity of suits as to the same matter, the Rules provide for bringing in other persons who have claims or who may be liable. If the connection of such a person is so close that the action should be dismissed unless he is joined, he is an "indispensable" party. If he ought to be joined if possible, he is a "necessary" party. If he can be joined or not, at the plaintiff's option, he is a "proper" party.

Compulsory Joinder

In determining a compulsory joinder question, the court must decide (1) whether a person is needed for a just adjudication, (2) whether it is feasible to join that person, and (3) if he cannot be joined, whether the action can proceed in his absence.

Persons To Be Joined If Feasible

A person is needed for a just adjudication if (1) in his absence, complete relief cannot be accorded to the existing parties, or (2) he claims an interest in the controversy and is so situated that disposition of the action in his absence may (i) as a practical matter impair or impede his ability to protect that interest or (ii) expose any of the existing parties to a substantial risk of double, multiple or inconsistent obligations by reason of his claimed interest. If a person meets this test, and he is subject to service of process and his joinder will not deprive the court of jurisdiction, he must be joined.

If Joinder Is Not Feasible

If a person is needed for a just adjudication, but cannot be made a party either because he is not subject to process or his joinder would destroy the court's jurisdiction, the court must determine whether in equity and good conscience the action should proceed without him, or whether the action should be dismissed.

In this determination, the court must consider (1) to what extent a judgment rendered in his absence would prejudice him or the existing parties; (2) whether protective provisions in the judgment decree could lessen or avoid that prejudice; (3) whether a judgment rendered in his absence would be adequate; and (4) whether the plaintiff will have an adequate remedy if the action is dismissed for non-joinder.

Permissive Joinder

A party who has some relation to the suit, although not close enough to make him necessary for "just adjudication" is a "proper" party and may be joined at the option of one of the existing parties. Two tests must be satisfied: (1) the right to relief arises out of the same transaction, occurrence, or series of transactions or occurrences, and (2) there is a question of law or fact common to all the parties to the action.

Defendants may be joined even if the claims against them are asserted severally or in the alternative.

Misjoinder and Non-Joinder

If a party has been improperly joined, the action will not be dismissed, but the party may be dropped upon motion or upon the court's initiative at any stage of the action and on such terms as are just. If a party has not been joined who should have been, he may be added. However, if he is an indispensable party who cannot be joined, the suit will be dismissed.

Joinder of Claims

A party asserting a claim (whether an original claim, counterclaim, cross-claim or third-party claim) may join with it as many claims as he has against an opposing party. Joinder of claims is never required, and each claim must have an independent basis for subject matter jurisdiction.

Interpleader

Interpleader allows a person who does not know to which of several claimants he is liable to join all the claimants in one action, and require them to litigate among themselves to determine which claim is valid. Interpleader protects the stakeholder from multiple lawsuits and possible multiple liability.

Intervention

Intervention provides a procedure whereby a nonparty can enter a lawsuit upon her own initiative to protect her interests. Intervention may be either as a matter of right or permissive.

Intervention Of Right

Intervention of right is granted when (1) a federal statute confers an unconditional right to intervene, or (2) when the applicant claims an interest relating to the property or transaction which is the subject of the action and he is so situated that the disposition of the action may as a practical matter impair or impede his ability to protect that interest, unless the applicant's interest is adequately represented by existing parties.

Permissive Intervention

If intervention of right is not available a party may still be permitted to intervene in the court's discretion. Permissive intervention may be granted if (1) a federal statute confers a conditional right to intervene, or (2) an applicant's claim or defense and the main action have a question of law or fact in common.

DISCOVERY

Discovery procedures are methods by which a party can gather information from his opponent and from witnesses to aid in the preparation of his case. In general parties may obtain discovery regarding any matter not privileged that is relevant to the claim or defense of any party. For good cause, the court may broaden the scope to include any matter relevant to the subject matter involved in the pending action.

Relevance and Admissibility

"Relevance" is given a very broad interpretation. It does not matter that the information will be inadmissible at trial as long as the information sought "appears reasonably calculated to lead to the discovery of admissible evidence."

Privilege

Discovery extends only to matter "not privileged." A matter is privileged from discovery if it would be privileged at trial under the applicable rules of evidence. The most important privileges are the privilege against self-incrimination, the attorney-client privilege, the physician-patient privilege, and the privileges protecting a confidential communication between spouses and exempting one spouse from testifying against the other.

Insurance Agreements

A party can discover the existence and contents of a liability insurance agreement. However, information concerning the insurance is not thereby made admissible. Information on the application for insurance is not discoverable.

Trial Preparation Materials
Work Product

A qualified immunity protects from discovery materials prepared for litigation. The policy underlying the "work product" immunity is the necessity for the lawyer to investigate all facets of the case and develop his theories without fear of having to disclose his strategies or information that is unfavorable to his client.

The work-product immunity extends to persons other than the attorney who are representing a party, e.g., investigators or insurers. However, the document must have been prepared "in anticipation of litigation"; documents prepared in the regular course of business are not within the work-product immunity.

Discovery of work product information may be allowed if it is otherwise unobtainable, e.g., if a witness is dead or his memory is faulty. In determining whether "undue hardship" exists, the court will consider the cost of otherwise obtaining the material, the financial resources of the party seeking it, and the likelihood that a "substantial equivalent" cannot be obtained. Absolute immunity from discovery protects "the mental impressions, conclusions, opinions or legal theories of an attorney or other representative of a party concerning the litigation."

Statements of A Party Or A Witness

A party can obtain a copy of any statement that he had previously made concerning the action or its subject matter. No showing of need is required. Likewise, a nonparty can obtain automatically a copy of any statement that she has made.

However, a party cannot obtain the statement of a witness except by a showing of necessity sufficient to overcome the qualified immunity.

Expert Information
Experts Who Will Testify

A party may through interrogatories discover the identity of each expert witness his opponent expects to call at trial, the subject matter on which the expert is expected to testify, and the substance of the facts and opinions to which the expert is expected to testify and a summary of the grounds for each opinion. Further discovery by other means (e.g., depositions) may be ordered by the court if necessary, but the party seeking discovery generally must pay the expert a reasonable fee for his time.

Experts Not Expected To Testify

However, if an expert has been retained by the opponent in anticipation of, or in preparation for, litigation and is not expected to testify at trial, facts known or opinions held by the expert are discoverable only upon a showing of exceptional circumstances under which it is impracticable for the party seeking discovery to obtain facts or opinions on the same subject by other means.

Methods of Discovery

Oral Depositions

Oral depositions are the most valuable of the discovery tools because they can be taken from any person, whether or not a party, and because they provide for examination and cross-examination of a person face-to-face without time to deliberate carefully and fashion a response. The deposing party must give reasonable notice in writing to all other parties, stating the time and place for the taking of the deposition, and the name and address of the deponent.

The subpoena may also designate documents to be brought to the deposition (subpoena duces tecum). A witness who fails to respond to a subpoena may be cited for contempt. If a deposing party fails to attend, or did not subpoena a witness who then fails to attend, he may be ordered to pay the opposing party's reasonable expenses.

A statement in a deposition is generally inadmissible as hearsay. However, it may be admitted in limited circumstances: (1) any deposition may be used by any party for contradicting or impeaching the deponent's testimony as a witness or for any other purpose permitted by the Federal Rules of Evidence (e.g., prior inconsistent statement in a deposition can be used as substantive evidence); (2) the deposition of an adverse party or of an officer, director or other agent of an adverse corporate party may be admitted for any purpose; (3) the deposition of any witness (party or nonparty) may be used for any purpose if the deponent is (a) dead; (b) more than 100 miles from the trial; (c) infirm or imprisoned and unable to testify; (d) not obtainable by subpoena; or if (e) special circumstances make it desirable in the interests of justice to use the deposition.

Depositions upon Written Questions

Depositions can also be taken upon written questions. Generally, leave of the court is not necessary except when the person being deposed is confined to prison or when the person has already been deposed. In this situation, a party's lawyer serves upon any person or party written questions she wishes to ask; the opposing party serves cross-questions upon all the parties, and redirect and re-cross questions may also be served. Because the questioner cannot effectively follow up the answers, this type of deposition is really useful only in establishing formal matters that are not complex.

Interrogatories to Parties

Interrogatories are written questions to another party, which must be answered in writing and under oath. Although interrogatories allow time to formulate careful (or even evasive) answers, they are useful for obtaining details, such as names and addresses of witnesses, or the existence of documents, and for narrowing the issues and obtaining admissions. The Rules impose a "presumptive numerical limit" on interrogatories; each party is limited to 25 interrogatories, unless leave of court is otherwise granted or the parties otherwise stipulate.

Each interrogatory must be answered separately and fully, unless it is objected to, in which case the reasons for objection must be stated. The answers are signed by the person making them and the objections are signed by the attorney making them. Generally, a party must answer based upon all the information that is within its possession and that can be reasonably obtained without undue labor and cost.

Thus, a corporation must examine its employees and records in order to answer fully. However, if the answer can be ascertained from the party's business records and the burden of ascertaining the answer is substantially the same for the propounding party as for the party interrogated, the interrogated party may specify the pertinent records and make them available for inspection and copying by the other party.

Production of Documents Or Things Or Entry On Land

A party may serve on any other party a request to produce and permit inspection and copying of any designated documents (e.g., writings, photographs, recordings or data compilations) or things, or to permit entry upon his land or property for the purpose of inspecting, testing, or sampling any tangible things.

Physical or Mental Examinations

Whenever the physical or mental condition of a party is in controversy, the court may require him to submit to an examination by a physician, psychologist, or other appropriate licensed professional.

Unlike other forms of discovery, a physical or mental examination is available only by court order upon motion by a party. A showing of "good cause" is necessary for the granting of the motion.

The party examined has an absolute right to a copy of a detailed written report of the physician or psychologist who examined him. By requesting and obtaining a report of the ordered examination, the examinee waives the physician-patient privilege as to any testimony in regard to the same mental or physical condition.

Requests for Admission

One party may serve, upon another party, written requests for the admission of the truth of any discoverable matter. The request may relate to statements or opinions of fact or of the application of law to fact, including the genuineness of any documents described in the request. Each matter must be separately set forth.

A matter is deemed admitted unless within thirty days after service of the request the party serves an answer or objection signed by the party or by his attorney. Any matter admitted is conclusively established at trial.

Sanctions for Failure To Make Or Cooperate In Discovery

Motion to Compel A Response And Award Of Expenses

Upon motion, a court can order a party or witness to answer a question at a deposition or on interrogatories, or to produce a requested document or allow a requested inspection, or to admit or deny a request to admit. If the motion is granted and the court finds that the refusal was without sufficient justification, it will require the refusing party, or the attorney advising the refusal, to pay the reasonable expenses incurred in obtaining the order, including reasonable attorney's fees.

Failure To Comply With Order

Failure to comply with a court order or subpoena may be punished by (1) an order that the matters dealt with in the original order or other designated facts will be taken as established; (2) an order striking designated claims or defenses, or prohibiting introduction of designated evidence; (3) dismissal of an action or claims or defenses, or entering of a default judgment; (4) a contempt order, including a fine, or imprisonment until a proper response is made.

ADJUDICATION WITHOUT A TRIAL
Dismissal

A plaintiff can voluntarily dismiss her action by filing a notice of dismissal at any time before the defendant serves his answer or a motion for summary judgment. Thereafter, the plaintiff can dismiss without leave of court only by filing a stipulation of dismissal signed by all parties who have appeared. After the defendant has answered or moved for summary judgment, the plaintiff can dismiss, without a stipulation, only by leave of court and upon such terms and conditions as are just. Also, the court may order the involuntary dismissal of plaintiff's action for failure to prosecute or for failure to comply with the Rules or court orders. However, dismissal is a severe sanction and is not favored.

Default Judgment

If a party against whom a claim has been asserted fails to plead or otherwise to defend, the clerk, upon affidavit or other showing, enters a default. When the plaintiff's claim is for a sum certain, the clerk can enter a default judgment for that amount plus costs, if the plaintiff presents a request and an affidavit of the amount due. No notice to the defendant is necessary. A default judgment cannot give relief different in kind or exceeding in amount that prayed for in the complaint. Rule 54(c).

Judgment On The Pleadings

After the pleadings have closed, any party may move for judgment on the pleadings. The motion challenges the legal sufficiency of the adversary's pleadings.

Summary Judgment

A motion for summary judgment allows the court to "look behind" the pleadings to determine whether any genuine issue of fact exists for trial. If not, the movant is entitled to a final judgment as a matter of law without trial.

PRETRIAL CONFERENCE AND ORDER

Except in cases exempted by local rule, the judge must enter a scheduling order no later than 120 days after filing of the complaint. The order limits the time to join other parties and to amend the pleadings, to file and hear motions, and to complete discovery, and may also deal with any other appropriate matters.

The court in its discretion may order counsel to participate in a pre-trial conference. (In some districts, pre-trial conferences are mandatory.) At the conference, the parties may clarify the issues, amend the pleadings, eliminate matters to be proved by agreeing to admissions or stipulations, identify the witnesses, determine whether issues should be referred to a master for findings, and consider the possibility of settlement or use of extrajudicial procedures to resolve the dispute.

If a party or his attorney fails to appear at a pre-trial conference, or is substantially unprepared to participate, or fails to participate in good faith, or fails to obey a pre-trial order, the judge may exclude designated claims or evidence, strike pleadings, treat the act as a contempt, or assess the expenses, including attorney's fees, caused by the noncompliance.

JURY TRIALS
RIGHT TO JURY TRIAL

The Seventh Amendment to the United States Constitution provides: In suits at common law, where the value in controversy shall exceed twenty dollars, the right of trial by jury shall be preserved, and no fact tried by a jury shall be otherwise re-examined in any Court of the United States, than according to the rules of the common law.

The Seventh Amendment guarantee creates a historical test for the right to a jury trial. There would be a right to jury trial in an action seeking damages only, but not in an action seeking specific performance only. Statutes also may explicitly grant a right to jury trial or may explicitly deny it.

However, if there is no right to jury trial, the court has discretion to summon an advisory jury (except in actions against the United States); its verdict is merely advisory and the judge still must make the findings of fact.

Where, through joinder of claims and interposition of counterclaims, the parties are asserting various claims for relief or are seeking various remedies based on the same claim, legal and equitable claims may be intertwined, with issues of fact common to both. Therefore, in all such cases, the legal claim should be tried first in order to preserve the right to jury trial.

MOTIONS

Instead of filing an answer, a defendant may file a motion, challenging the sufficiency of the pleadings: 1) Motion to Dismiss; 2) Motion for Judgment on the Pleadings; 3) Motion for More Definite Statement; or 4) Motion to Strike.

MOTIONS FOR JUDGMENTS AS A MATTER OF LAW

A trial judge enters judgment as a matter of law when a party convinces the judge that there is no evidence upon which the other party can prevail on a given issue or claim – in essence, that there is no basis upon which a jury could find a material fact and so that issue can and should be decided as a matter of law. A party may move for judgment as a matter of law any time after the opposing party has been fully heard with respect to the issue or claim, but before the case has been submitted to the jury.

The motion must state the law and facts which entitle the party to judgment as a matter of law. The court must consider the evidence in the light most favorable to the party against whom the motion is made; all legitimate inferences are drawn in the opponent's favor. The court takes into account not only the evidence favorable to the party opposing the motion but also any unfavorable evidence that the jury is required to believe

POSTTRIAL MOTIONS

Renewal Of a Motion For Judgment Of A Matter Of Law

A motion for judgment as a matter of law may be granted during a trial (as discussed supra), but is more likely to be granted after the jury returns an unsupportable verdict. A renewal of the motion after the verdict is also required; neither the trial court nor the appellate court may enter a judgment as a matter of law on its own initiative.

Motion for A New Trial

A judge has broad discretion to order a new trial as to all or part of the issues "for any of the reasons for which new trials have heretofore been granted in actions at law" (or in a nonjury action, for the reasons an equity court would have granted a rehearing).

Grounds for A New Trial

In an action tried to a jury, a new trial can be granted as to all or any of the parties on all or some of the issues of fact or law because of harmless error, the verdict is against the weight of the evidence, prejudicial misconduct, excusable lack of preparation, newly discovered evidence, errors at law or excessive or inadequate damages.

Motion To Amend Judgment

A motion to amend or alter any judgment (including a default judgment) must be served within ten days after entry of judgment. Thereafter, the judgment may be attacked only by a motion for relief from judgment, or by appeal.

JURY VERDICTS
General Verdict

The general verdict is the most commonly used. The jury merely finds for one party or the other and determines the relief to be awarded.

General Verdict with Interrogatories

To ensure that jurors correctly considered key elements in a complex case, the judge, in his discretion, may instruct the jury to return a general verdict and may also submit to the jury written interrogatories upon specific facts the decision of which is necessary to a verdict. If the answers are inconsistent with each other and one or more is likewise inconsistent with the general verdict, the court must either order further jury deliberation or a new trial.

Special Verdict

In a special verdict, the judge submits to the jury written questions susceptible of brief answers on specific factual issues. The jury writes answers to the questions, but renders no general verdict; the court renders the verdict on the basis of the answers.

JUDICIAL FINDINGS AND CONCLUSIONS

A judgment is the decree or order of the court that finally adjudicates the rights of the parties. Usually, appeal is allowed only from a final judgment. The date of entry of judgment is significant for several reasons; most importantly, it marks the starting point of the time in which to make post-trial motions or to appeal.

Except as to default judgments, every final judgment shall grant the relief to which the party is entitled, even if the party has not demanded such relief in his pleadings. In an action tried on the facts without a jury or with an advisory jury, the court must find the facts specially and state its conclusions of law separately.

CLAIM AND ISSUE PRECLUSION

Res judicata, or claim preclusion, prevents a litigant from reasserting a claim that has already been decided on the merits. Collateral estoppel, or issue preclusion, prevents a party from re-litigating an issue that has been determined in a prior suit.

Claim Preclusion (Res Judicata)

If a final, valid judgment has been rendered on the merits of a claim, the claim cannot be re-litigated. If judgment is rendered for the plaintiff, his claim is merged into the judgment and he cannot sue on it again. Similarly, if judgment is rendered for the defendant, the judgment serves as a bar to the plaintiff's suing on the claim again.

The test used to determine whether res judicata applies is the transactional test: "the claim extinguished includes all rights of the plaintiff to remedies against the defendant with respect to all or any part of the transaction, or series of connected transactions, out of which the action arose."

Res judicata applies only if the prior judgment was a final determination of the claim and was made on the merits. Hence, res judicata does not apply to interlocutory orders. Summary judgment is entitled to res judicata effect.

A judgment is deemed final even though an appeal is taken; only when the judgment is reversed or modified does its res judicata effect cease.   A judgment must be valid to have res judicata effect

Issue Preclusion (Collateral Estoppel)

If an issue was actually litigated and necessarily determined in an action, the parties to the first action (and nonparties who are in privity with parties) are estopped from re-litigating that issue in a later action. Collateral estoppel precludes re-litigation only of specific issues that actually were litigated and necessarily determined; the cause of action that raises these issues will be different in the second suit. However, if the issue arose in two different contexts, estoppel will not apply. To be binding, the issue must have been necessary to the determination in the first suit.

If two or more issues could have been the basis for the general verdict rendered, none of the issues will have collateral estoppel effect because there is no certainty as to which was necessary to the jury's determination.

APPEALS
FINAL JUDGMENT RULE

The federal courts of appeals have "jurisdiction of appeals from all final decisions of the district courts." A final decision "generally is one which ends the litigation on the merits and leaves nothing for the court to do but execute the judgment

This rule minimizes delay and expense because all alleged errors are appealed after the trial rather than in succession during the trial, and because appeal may be unnecessary if the aggrieved party wins a favorable judgment despite the errors.

During trial, most orders are not directly appealable. After trial, an order granting a new trial is not appealable; although an order denying a new trial is not appealable, the judgment itself can be appealed. Although an order may not be appealable in itself, an appeal from the final judgment may raise the erroneous order and it may then be reviewed. The exceptions to this are collateral orders and irreparable injury.

SCOPE OF REVIEW FOR JUDGE AND JURY

The appellate court reviews only matters that appear on the trial record. Evidence not introduced at trial cannot be presented on appeal.

Generally, a party may not appeal from an error at trial unless he made a timely objection at trial Review of factual determinations at trial is very limited, because the findings of the jury or judge are entitled to deference. An appellate court reviewing a jury verdict will uphold the verdict as long as it is supported by "substantial evidence." If the judge granted a judgment as a matter of law, the appellate court will reverse him only where there was substantial evidence to support a verdict contrary to the judge's.

Where the case was tried without a jury, the judge's findings of fact, whether based on oral or documentary evidence, will be set aside only if they were "clearly erroneous" and due regard must be given to the opportunity of the trial court to judge the credibility of the witnesses In areas where a judge has broad discretion, e.g., scope of discovery, the appellate court will overturn his decision only if he was clearly wrong. If the judge has made an error of law, either in instructing a jury or in stating his conclusions in a nonjury trial, the judgment will be reversed, unless the error was harmless.

CONSTITUTIONAL LAW

NATURE OF JUDICIAL REVIEW

The Federal and State Court Systems

Congress can require state courts to hear causes of action based upon federal statutes.

State governments or agencies are not citizens of a state for the purpose of federal diversity jurisdiction.

A private citizen cannot sue a state in a federal court.

A private citizen can challenge the constitutionality of a state statute in a federal court by suing a state officer to enjoin the enforcement of the statute on the ground that it is unconstitutional.

Political subdivisions of a state can be sued by citizens in federal court because they do not enjoy the protection afforded a state under the Eleventh Amendment.

Supreme Court Jurisdiction and Review

If a case has been decided by a state court on an independent state ground, there is no jurisdiction for Supreme Court review, even if the state court decides a federal issue in the case which is not essential to the decision. If, on the other hand, the state court decides a state issue on the basis of federal decisions on the same point, then the state ground is not independent and there is a basis for Supreme Court review.

A state has the right to sue another state in the United States Supreme Court on behalf of its citizens on claims affecting a multiplicity of citizens (the *parens patriae* doctrine).

There is no direct right of appeal to the Supreme Court from a federal district court decision holding an act of Congress unconstitutional.

There is no right to appeal a state court advisory opinion to the United States Supreme Court even if it involves federal constitutional issues because there is no case or controversy, as required by the United States Constitution for federal court jurisdiction.

CONGRESSIONAL CONTROL OVER JURISDICTION; ARTICLE I COURTS

Congress has control of the jurisdiction of the federal courts and can establish or abolish lower federal courts.

Congress cannot alter the jurisdiction of the Supreme Court in such a way as to interfere with the Court's essential function of preserving constitutional order.

Congress cannot interfere with inherent judicial functions in courts it has created.

Congress can set up courts pursuant to its powers under Article I of the Constitution. Judges of such courts are not constitutionally entitled to life tenure.

Due process requires that there must ultimately be a right of appeal to an Article III court from the decision of an Article I court or an administrative body.

STANDING; CASE OR CONTROVERSY

A person has standing by virtue of being a taxpayer only to challenge legislation authorizing expenditures on the basis that those expenditures contravene specific constitutional limitations on the spending power.

A mere philosophical, ethical or intellectual interest in the outcome of a case is not sufficient to qualify for standing.

Standing exists in a party that has a close relationship to the party actually injured if the injured party is unlikely to successfully assert its rights.

MOOTNESS AND RIPENESS

A case will not be dismissed for mootness if the issue is capable of repetition and will consistently evade review.

A case will be dismissed as not ripe if events which will raise material issues in the case have not yet occurred.

ABSTENTION

A federal court has discretion to abstain from deciding an issue of state law if a decision by a state court on the state issue might obviate the need for a decision on a federal constitutional issue.

A federal court will abstain from a case asking for an injunction against the enforcement of a state criminal statute if a prosecution under that statute has commenced.

JUSTICIABILITY; POLITICAL QUESTIONS

Under the political question doctrine, the United States Supreme Court will not review an issue on the merits if it determines that the Constitution places final authority to resolve the issue in another branch of government.

Burden of Proof in Constitutional Litigation

If constitutional litigation involves the strict scrutiny tier of equal protection, the denial of substantive due process rights which are highly protected, or the deprivation of the right of free speech or of freedom of religion, the state must show a compelling state need and that no less burdensome method would achieve that objective.

If constitutional litigation involves sexual discrimination, the state must show that the classification has an important governmental objective and is substantially related to achieving those objectives.

If constitutional litigation involves matters other than those described above, the plaintiff must prove that the legislation lacked a rational basis.

The state never has the burden when only lack of rational basis must be shown, and the plaintiff never has the burden when highly protected rights are involved.

SEPARATION OF POWERS

CONGRESSIONAL COMMERCE POWER

The Supremacy Clause itself is not a source of congressional power.

Congress may exercise the commerce power to regulate purely local commerce as long as it affects interstate commerce.

Congress may exercise the commerce power to regulate the conduct of private individuals with respect to racial discrimination (even though such private action could not be regulated by legislation under the Fourteenth Amendment) so long as the individual's conduct affects interstate commerce.

Congress may delegate rulemaking power to an administrative agency, but cannot reserve to itself the right to change such rules by anything short of legislation adopted by the full constitutional process.

CONGRESSIONAL TAXING AND SPENDING POWER

Through Congress's power to condition expenditures on compliance with its standards, Congress can persuade the states and individuals to adopt measures which it could not directly require through legislation.

While Congress can tax and spend for the general welfare, the General Welfare Clause is not a source of congressional regulatory power.

Congress can achieve a regulatory effect through a taxing statute as long as the statute has a revenue-raising purpose.

CONGRESSIONAL PROPERTY POWER AND POWER OVER TERRITORIES

The property power, not the commerce power, is the best source of congressional authority to regulate or dispose of property owned by the United States.

Congress holds all of the regulatory power of territories which would be possessed by the state legislature if the territory were a state.

Judges appointed to serve in the territories are not Article III judges entitled to lifetime tenure.

CONGRESSIONAL DEFENSE AND GENERAL LEGISLATIVE POWERS

Congress has the power to investigate and subpoena witnesses for the purpose of obtaining information with respect to potential legislation which it might pass.

An individual can successfully defend against a contempt of Congress charge for failing to answer a question from a congressional committee only if the witness can show that the subject matter of the questioning was beyond the power of Congress to pass potential legislation or beyond the scope of the power delegated by Congress to that committee.

CONGRESSIONAL POWER TO ENFORCE 13TH, 14TH, AND 15TH AMENDMENTS

Congress has power under the 13th Amendment to affect individual conduct but only to eradicate slavery or the effects of slavery. Pursuant to that authority, it has the power to regulate the manner in which Blacks are treated.

Congress has power under the 14th Amendment only to reach state action (or action accomplished under the color of state law) which abrogates the rights guaranteed by that Amendment.

Congress has power under the 15th Amendment to directly regulate voting procedures in the states for the purpose of eradicating procedures which affect the rights of minorities to vote or to have their vote counted.

POWERS OF THE PRESIDENT

The President is obligated to carry out legislation mandating that the President act in a specific manner.

The pardon power only extends to federal crimes.

Executive privilege is absolute with respect to defense and foreign policy matters. Confidential communications between the President and advisors in all other areas are presumptively privileged; disclosure can be required only when a specific communication is subpoenaed and a substantial governmental interest outweighs the President's interest in nondisclosure.

INTERBRANCH CHECKS ON POWER

Only the President has the right to appoint officers of the United States, and an attempted appointment by Congress or by members thereof is unconstitutional.

The Supreme Court has the right under the Constitution to decide which branch of government is vested with final authority to decide a particular matter.

While the Senate has the right to advise and consent on presidential appointments, it does not have the right to advise and consent when the President removes officers of the Executive branch.

THE RELATION OF THE NATION AND STATES

INTERGOVERNMENTAL IMMUNITIES

Absent congressional intention to the contrary, states can tax buildings leased by the federal government and contractors doing business with the federal government, as long as such tax is not discriminatory.

The federal government has the right to tax and regulate the instrumentalities and employees of state government.

AUTHORITY RESERVED TO THE STATES

A state has the right to regulate interstate commerce as long as it does not contravene an express federal policy, does not discriminate against interstate commerce, and does not unduly burden interstate commerce.

In determining the validity of a state action which burdens interstate commerce, the court will consider whether the state used the least restrictive means to achieve a legitimate state objective.

A state regulatory statute which discriminates in favor of local commerce and against out-of-state commerce is unconstitutional because of the negative implications of the Commerce Clause.

The negative implications of the Commerce Clause prevent a state from requiring that a resource of the state be sold to in-state customers only.

The negative implications of the Commerce Clause prevent a state from excluding trash from a sister state if its landfills accept in-state trash.

A state acting in a proprietary rather than a regulatory capacity may discriminate in favor of local business and against interstate commerce.

Congress has the right to expressly authorize a state to burden commerce or discriminate in favor of local commerce, even if the Supreme Court has held such burden or discrimination unconstitutional under the negative implications of the Commerce Clause. The police power is a source of state power, not a source of congressional power.

NATIONAL POWER TO OVERRIDE STATE AUTHORITY

The Supremacy Clause is the source of constitutional power for a court to hold state statutes and decisions unconstitutional because they conflict with the Constitution, laws, or treaties of the United States or acts done in furtherance of them.

If Congress has provided a comprehensive scheme of regulation in an area, Congress may be said to have occupied the field and any state regulation (even if complementary to the federal legislation) will be preempted, unless Congress's intent was to allow state regulation. Congress has the ability to permit states to operate in areas where it has legislated.

States may not enact any legislation which affects foreign policy, because foreign policy is the exclusive province of the federal government.

State legislation or decisions which are contrary to a federal policy expressed in an executive agreement are invalid.

A state or municipal law in conflict with a federal regulation dealing with standards applicable to federal offices is invalid because of the Supremacy Clause.

INDIVIDUAL RIGHTS

STATE ACTION

The activity of a state in regulating or taxing an activity does not render the activity itself "state action" subject to 14th Amendment scrutiny.

The action of any political subdivision of a state constitutes state action.

The activities of an entity in which the state has a partnership interest constitute state action.

SUBSTANTIVE DUE PROCESS

An economic regulation violates the substantive strand of the Due Process Clause if there is no rational basis for it.

Substantive due process prohibits states from limiting fundamental privacy interests, absent a showing of a compelling state need. The right to use contraceptives and the right of an extended family to live together are examples of such interests.

A state activity is no more likely to withstand constitutional challenge because it is part of the state constitution or enacted by referendum.

PROCEDURAL DUE PROCESS

Procedural due process is required only if the action of the decisionmaker constitutes state action.

An individual has a property interest in continued employment if the individual has an employment contract or tenure.

The factors in determining what process is "due" are the type of interest infringed, the likelihood of an erroneous decision, and the burden on the government in providing process.

The minimum necessary to satisfy due process is notice and an opportunity to be heard.

Criminal statutes violate due process if they are so vague that they do not inform a citizen of the conduct deemed criminal. A judicial construction of the statute can cure the vagueness with respect to future violators, but not with respect to any person charged before the decision was rendered.

EQUAL PROTECTION – REGULATION OF VOTING AND LEGISLATIVE REPRESENTATION

The Equal Protection Clause is contained in the Fourteenth Amendment and does not apply to the federal government. However, the principles of equal protection are applied to the federal government through the Due Process Clause of the Fifth Amendment.

The one man/one vote rule applies to municipal legislative bodies.

The state may impose limited residency requirements (e.g., two months) on the right to vote to assure that voters are bona fide residents.

The state may impose reasonable requirements regarding filing fees, residency, and petition signatures to achieve ballot access.

EQUAL PROTECTION – REGULATION OF SOCIAL AND ECONOMIC WELFARE

Economic regulation need only satisfy the rational basis standard.

The right to be free from poverty is not a fundamental right.

EQUAL PROTECTION – REGULATION OF OTHER INTERESTS

The right to work is not a fundamental right and the state can impose age classifications on various governmental jobs.

EQUAL PROTECTION – CLASSIFICATION BY RACE OR ALIENAGE

Neither the state nor the federal government can discriminate on the basis of race except to further a compelling state need.

A regulation or decision which classifies on the basis of race in order to remedy specific past racial discrimination is valid.

A classification based upon a racially neutral principle such as residence, which also indirectly discriminates by race, is not unconstitutional unless there is an intention to discriminate by race.

The federal government has broad discretion to discriminate on the basis of alienage in the furtherance of foreign policy. A state cannot discriminate on the basis of alienage except in elective governmental positions and non-elective governmental jobs which formulate or execute public policy.

EQUAL PROTECTION – CLASSIFICATION BY GENDER OR ILLEGITIMACY

Discrimination on the basis of gender is valid only if it serves an important governmental purpose and is substantially related to achieving that purpose.

The state cannot deny worker's compensation benefits, wrongful death benefits, or intestacy benefits based upon illegitimacy where the parent-child relationship has been adjudicated or acknowledged, but can make distinctions where proof of the relationship is difficult.

PRIVILEGES AND IMMUNITIES

The Privileges and Immunities Clause of the Fourteenth Amendment applies only to the privileges of national citizenship and is rarely if ever a valid reason for holding a statute unconstitutional.

The Privileges and Immunities Clause of Article IV of the Constitution is an alternative analysis where the state discriminates on a matter of fundamental interest in favor of its own citizens and against out-of-staters.

OBLIGATIONS OF CONTRACT; BILLS OF ATTAINDER

State legislation which impairs the obligations of a contract is invalid unless there is a valid police power reason for the legislation or unless it only alters the remedies for breach of contract and other feasible remedies are available.

Legislation, either federal or state, which withholds appropriations for a specific job as long as a named individual holds that job is a bill of attainder and unconstitutional.

FIRST AMENDMENT – FREEDOM OF RELIGION

A state has the right to regulate action based upon religious belief if there is a compelling state need.

When religious belief is the basis for resisting government rules (e.g., conscientious objector status) the courts have a right to examine the sincerity of the belief, but not the belief itself.

Courts cannot decide ecclesiastical questions to settle disputes concerning church management or property.

FIRST AMENDMENT – SEPARATION OF CHURCH AND STATE

State aid to religions is constitutional only if the activity reflects a secular purpose, it has a primary effect which neither advances nor inhibits religion, and there is no excessive entanglement between church and state.

State activity which aids all religions equally can still violate the Establishment Clause.

State laws requiring that religious theory be taught in public schools violate the Establishment Clause.

FIRST AMENDMENT – REGULATION OF CONTENT OF SPEECH

Action which is a substitute for words can be protected symbolic speech. However, even if action is intended as symbolic speech, it can be regulated to protect a legitimate government interest divorced from the content of the symbolic speech itself (e.g., burning draft cards).

All speech is protected speech for purposes of content regulation except fighting words, defamatory speech, obscene speech, and to some degree commercial speech.

Neither the state nor the federal government can regulate the content of protected speech unless it can show a compelling state need.

A compelling state need is present and the state can proscribe the content of protected speech which is directed toward inciting immediate lawless action and is likely to incite that action.

Commercial speech can be subject to reasonable governmental regulation for the protection of consumers and other legitimate government interests, but outright prohibition of commercial speech is unconstitutional.

Requiring an individual to display a message prescribed by the state is the equivalent of regulating the content of speech.

The state has an affirmative obligation to protect a speaker before an audience, but the speaker can be required to stop speaking if there is a genuine likelihood of immediate violence which the state cannot prevent.

FIRST AMENDMENT – REGULATION OF TIME, PLACE AND MANNER OF SPEECH

The state cannot completely prohibit the exercise of free speech rights in a public forum such as streets or parks, but can regulate such speech pursuant to narrowly drawn statutes conferring limited discretion on officials to ban speech at particular times and places and in particular ways, as long as the prohibition of speech does not turn on its content.

The state has the right to forbid speech near semi-public forums such as schools, libraries and courthouses to prevent interference with governmental functions.

The state has the right to prohibit the exercise of free speech rights in places closed to the public such as jails, military bases and private government offices.

Unless the regulation of speech on private property becomes state action (as in the operation of a company town), the owner of private property can regulate and prohibit the exercise of speech on that property.

FIRST AMENDMENT – OBSCENITY

Speech is obscene and subject to complete prohibition if it appeals to the prurient interest of an average person applying contemporary community standards, depicts or describes sexual activity in a patently offensive way, and taken as a whole, lacks serious literary, artistic, political or scientific value.

Child pornography is totally unprotected speech.

Communications portraying nudity or sexual activity can be regulated concerning the time, place and manner of their exhibition even if the communication is not pornographic and the regulation is content-based.

FIRST AMENDMENT - PROCEDURAL PROBLEMS

If a court has issued an injunction banning the exercise of free speech rights, the constitutional issues raised by the issuance of the injunction cannot be litigated in a contempt prosecution for violation of the injunction.

A statute which is overly broad (i.e., prohibits protected speech as well as properly regulated speech) or vague (i.e., a person of ordinary intelligence cannot distinguish permitted from prohibited activities) is unconstitutional on its face and can be successfully challenged even by those who could be regulated if the statute were clear and narrowly drawn.

An individual is entitled to notice and a hearing before an injunction is granted limiting the time, place and manner of his expression, unless there is a genuine emergency justifying an ex parte application.

FIRST AMENDMENT - FREEDOM OF ASSOCIATION; LICENSE OR BENEFITS BASED UPON FIRST AMENDMENT RIGHTS

A public employee's freedom of speech with respect to matters of public concern cannot be infringed unless the employer's interest in operating the public service outweighs the employee's interest in expressing the employee's political views.

A public employee who has joined a subversive organization cannot be dismissed from public employment unless the employer can prove that the employee would have been dismissed even if the employee had not exercised the right of freedom of association by joining the organization.

CONTRACTS AND SALES

FORMATION OF CONTRACTS

OFFERS

A communication is an offer for a bilateral contract if it sets forth a proposed exchange of promises in such a manner that the person to whom it is directed reasonably believes that he can enter into a binding contract by accepting those terms.

The person selling goods at auction is not bound by the highest bid unless he advertises the auction as "without reserve," in which case placing the goods at auction is making an offer to the highest bidder.

ACCEPTANCE

At common law, an offer can only be accepted by the offeree agreeing, before the offer is revoked, to all of its terms in the time and manner specified by the offeror (or in a reasonable time and in a reasonable manner, if the offeror did not specify the manner of acceptance).

Unless the offeror specifically states that his offer may be accepted by silence or the course of dealings between the parties indicates that the offer will be accepted if the offeree does nothing, silence will not operate as an acceptance.

Under the UCC, a valid contract is formed if the offeree accepts the offer, even if he proposes different or additional terms. Between merchants, the different or additional terms become part of the contract if they do not materially alter the offer and the offeror does not object.

Under the UCC, a seller can accept an offer either by a promise to sell the goods requested by the buyer or by shipping conforming goods in accordance with the offer.

REVOCATION OF OFFERS

At common law, an offer is generally revocable even if the offer says it will remain open for a specified time. At common law, an offer is irrevocable for the time specified only if an option contract is formed, i.e., if the offeree has given consideration to the offeror in exchange for the offeror's agreement to keep the offer open.

Under the UCC, a "firm offer" cannot be revoked before the expiration date. Such a "firm offer" can only be made by a merchant, must state in writing that the offer is irrevocable until a date certain, and cannot remain irrevocable for more than three months.

An offer for a unilateral contract is irrevocable by the offeror if the offeree has, with the knowledge of the offeror, started substantial performance.

An offer is revoked if the notice of revocation is communicated to the offeree in any manner before the offer is accepted. The notice of revocation can be any communication which fairly indicates to the offeree that the offeror has withdrawn the offer.

In a real estate brokerage transaction where the owner makes an offer for a unilateral contract which the broker accepts by producing a buyer ready, willing and able to buy at the listing price, the offer is automatically revoked by the seller's acceptance of an offer to purchase the property from a buyer not produced by the broker.

An offer for a contract which would fall within the statute of frauds can be revoked orally.

If the offeror dies before the offer is accepted, it is revoked. However, if the offer is accepted, then death does not terminate the obligations of the contract.

REJECTION

If the offeree rejects an offer or makes a counter-offer, the original offer is terminated and cannot thereafter be accepted, even if the time for expiration of the offer has not yet occurred.

If the offeror has made an offer which he permits to be accepted in part, acceptance of part can be considered a rejection of the remainder.

An inquiry in response to an offer ("Would you consider a lesser price?") is not a rejection.

MISTAKE, FRAUD, AND DURESS

A contract can be avoided on the grounds of unilateral mistake if the mistake was so obvious that the offeree should have known of the mistake at the time he accepted the offer.

If each of the parties innocently has a different understanding of the meaning of the words of the agreement, then there is no contract.

A party has the right to rescind a contract if it was entered into in reliance on an untrue material fact.

INDEFINITENESS AND ABSENCE OF TERMS

If the price term is missing in a UCC transaction, there is a contract at a reasonable price.

CAPACITY TO CONTRACT

A minor can disaffirm a contract, even one that has been completed, within a reasonable time of reaching the age of majority.

IMPLIED-IN-FACT CONTRACTS; QUASI CONTRACTS

If a person accepts services from someone in the business of providing those services, there is an implied-in-fact contract to pay for the reasonable value of those services.

If necessary services are rendered to a person at a time when he lacks the mental capacity to request such services, (e.g., he is unconscious at the time medical services are rendered), there is an implied-in-law contract to pay for them.

A quasi contract exists when there is no enforceable contractual relationship between the parties, but one party has conferred a benefit on the other not intended to be gratuitous. The party conferring the benefit is entitled to collect the fair value of the services rendered.

A party does not have the right to sue in *quantum meruit* for a benefit conferred if there is an enforceable right to sue under a contract.

PRE-CONTRACTUAL LIABILITY BASED UPON DETRIMENTAL RELIANCE

If a subcontractor submits an offer to perform a subcontract to a contractor knowing that the contractor will rely on that offer when making a bid to the contracting authority, then under the doctrine of promissory estoppel, the subcontractor may not revoke his offer until the contractor has had an opportunity to accept, if the contractor is the successful bidder.

CONSIDERATION

BARGAIN AND EXCHANGE

The concept of bargain is the essence of consideration. If a party asks for something that he wants, even though it does not directly benefit him, and promises something in return, there is valid bargained-for consideration.

An illusory promise, one which gives the party the unilateral right to do anything they want, is not valid consideration.

A gift contingent on a minor condition which is not bargained for by the donor, such as "I will give you a birthday present if you come down and pick it up," does not amount to a contract supported by consideration.

ADEQUACY OF CONSIDERATION

The value of what a party promises or requests is irrelevant for purposes of determining if there is valid consideration.

If a party to a contract performs the promise he makes, he is entitled to enforce the contract according to its terms, even if he is getting far more than he has given.

MORAL OBLIGATIONS; DETRIMENTAL RELIANCE

One party's promise to make a gift is enforceable under the doctrine of promissory estoppel if (1) the donor-promisor knows that the promise will induce substantial reliance on the part of the promisee, and (2) failure to enforce the promise will cause substantial hardship.

A service which has already been gratuitously rendered is not valid consideration for a later promise to pay for that service.

A promise in writing to pay a debt which is barred by the statute of limitations is enforceable according to its terms without new consideration.

MODIFICATION OF CONTRACTS; PREEXISTING DUTY RULE

In a **non**-UCC contract, consideration is required to support a modification. In a UCC contract, consideration is **not** required to support a modification.

If each side to an existing contract modifies its rights and obligations in exchange for modification of the rights of the party(ies) on the other side, there is consideration.

If the parties agree to rescind an executory (i.e., uncompleted) contract, consideration is found in the mutual agreements to give up rights under the contract.

The agreement to perform an act which a person is already legally obligated to perform is not valid consideration.

COMPROMISE AND SETTLEMENT OF CLAIMS

Forbearance (a promise not to assert a legal right) is valid consideration if the person seeking to enforce the contract reasonably believes that he has a valid legal claim.

OUTPUT AND REQUIREMENTS CONTRACTS

Output or requirements contracts are generally valid.

They are enforceable for the actual amount of the output or requirements as long as those amounts are not unreasonably disproportionate to the expectations of the parties at the time the contract was formed.

Output and requirements contracts are specifically enforceable if the nonbreaching party will have difficulty in obtaining substitute performance.

THIRD-PARTY BENEFICIARY CONTRACTS

INTENDED BENEFICIARIES

Intended beneficiaries are those persons who have a right to sue on a third-party beneficiary contract because the original contracting parties either explicitly or implicitly intended to benefit them.

If the third-party beneficiary contract is designed to satisfy an obligation of the promisee to the third party, the third-party beneficiary does not give up his rights against the promisee until such time as the promisor renders performance to the third-party beneficiary.

INCIDENTAL BENEFICIARIES

An incidental beneficiary, a person that the original contracting parties did not intend to benefit, has no right to enforce a third-party beneficiary contract.

MODIFICATION OF THE THIRD-PARTY BENEFICIARY'S RIGHTS

The promisor and promisee of a third-party beneficiary contract can modify their contract to the detriment of the intended beneficiary only until the beneficiary either assents to the contract at a party's request, sues on the contract, or changes her position in reliance on it.

ENFORCEMENT BY THIRD PARTY

The third party need not provide consideration to be able to sue on a third-party beneficiary contract.

The promisor of a third-party beneficiary contract has a valid defense in a suit by the intended beneficiary if the promisee fails to perform his obligations to the promisor.

ASSIGNMENT AND DELEGATION

ASSIGNMENT OF RIGHTS

The benefits of a UCC contract are assignable even if the contract prohibits assignment.

The benefits of a contract can be assigned without the assignee becoming bound to perform the obligations of the contract.

An assignee takes rights under the contract subject to any defenses which the contracting party has against the assignor.

If a party to a contract is notified of the assignment of rights under that contract, the contracting party cannot raise against the assignee rights against the assignor which accrue after notice of the assignment.

DELEGATION OF DUTIES

A contract is not delegable if the party wishing to delegate possesses unique characteristics such that the performance rendered by a delegatee would vary materially from that bargained for.

A contract is also not delegable if the contract specifically prohibits it.

The party delegating duties (the delegator) remains liable on the contract as a surety for the performance of the delegatee, the party now principally liable on the contract.

STATUTE OF FRAUDS

CONTRACT CANNOT BE PERFORMED WITHIN ONE YEAR

In determining if a contract can be performed within one year, measure from the time of the making of the contract to the time prescribed for the end of performance, not just the time when performance will take place.

A personal services contract for more than a year is within the statute of frauds despite the fact that the contract would be prematurely terminated if the personal service supplier died within the year.

A contract for life is not within the statute of frauds because death could occur within a year, which would be the natural termination of the contract.

SURETYSHIP

An oral promise to pay the debt of another is usually unenforceable because of the statute of frauds. However, if a person agrees to pay the debt of another for the primary purpose of furthering his own goals, rather than those of the debtor, the statute of frauds will not prevent enforcement of the promise.

SALE OF GOODS

Contracts for the sale of goods for $500 or more must satisfy the statute of frauds, unless they are specially manufactured goods and not suitable for sale to others in the ordinary course of business. . (Note that the most recent revision of UCC §2-201 increases this triggering amount to $5,000, but as of 2006 no U.S. state has adopted revised Section 201.)

The statute of frauds is satisfied to the extent that there is part performance.

The statute of frauds with respect to the sale of goods does not apply where the goods have been received and accepted.

The statute of frauds with respect to the sale of goods is satisfied in a contract between merchants where one merchant sends a written, signed memorandum of the transaction sufficient to bind him to the contract and the receiving merchant does not object within ten days.

In a UCC contract, a memorandum satisfies the statute of frauds if it indicates there is a contract, it contains a description of the goods and the quantity, and is signed. It need not contain the price.

A modification of a UCC contract, if it involves a sale of goods for more than $500, requires compliance with the statute of frauds.

LAND CONTRACTS

In a contract for the sale of land, the memorandum required to satisfy the statute of frauds must contain the price.

A real estate brokerage contract is not within the statute of frauds.

PAROL EVIDENCE RULE

PAROL EVIDENCE RULE

Parol evidence is admissible to show that there is a condition precedent to a contract's coming into existence.

Parol evidence is admissible to explain an ambiguity.

Parol evidence is admissible to show that the parties used words in a nontraditional manner or spoke in code.

Parol evidence is admissible to prove a mistake in reducing the terms of an oral agreement to writing.

In a UCC contract, a provision which requires subsequent modifications be in writing is valid. In a **non**-UCC contract, a provision requiring that subsequent modifications be in writing is **in**valid.

Except in a UCC contract requiring subsequent amendments to be in writing, evidence of an oral modification subsequent to the making of a written contract is admissible.

INTERPRETATION OF CONTRACTS

Achieving the intent of the parties is the overriding principle of contract interpretation.

The past course of dealing of the parties is important evidence in interpreting a contract.

CONDITIONS

EXPRESS CONDITIONS

A party seeking to sue on a contract must either show compliance with an express condition, or that the other party was in bad faith with respect to the condition, thereby excusing its performance.

If a contract contains a condition that performance must be satisfactory to the purchaser, that satisfaction will be judged by an objective standard, unless the contract involves personal taste, in which case the performance must be subjectively satisfactory to the purchaser (limited only by the purchaser's obligation to exercise good faith).

CONSTRUCTIVE CONDITIONS OF EXCHANGE

Unless otherwise specified, each party must perform its obligations under the contract to be able to demand performance from the other side. Such mutual conditions precedent are constructive conditions of exchange.

DIVISIBLE CONTRACTS; INSTALLMENT CONTRACTS

If a contract is divisible, then performance of one divisible portion permits the plaintiff to demand performance from the defendant for that divisible portion, even if the plaintiff is in breach with respect to another divisible portion.

The fact that a construction contract requires periodic payments does not make it a divisible contract.

Under the UCC, if a contract is determined to be an installment contract, the buyer can reject a nonconforming shipment only if it substantially impairs the value of the installment and cannot be cured.

Under a UCC installment contract, a breach with respect to one installment is a breach of the total contract only if the nonconformity substantially impairs the value of the entire contract.

IMMATERIAL BREACH AND SUBSTANTIAL PERFORMANCE

Under the common law, the plaintiff can sue for breach of contract if she has substantially performed the contract, even if there is an immaterial (nonwilful) breach.

Under the UCC, except for an installment contract, the seller must tender the correct number of conforming goods at the time specified in the contract or the buyer can reject the goods without liability. However, the seller has a limited right to "cure" after a nonconforming tender.

CONSTRUCTIVE CONDITION OF COOPERATION

A condition of cooperation is implied into every contract. A party who wrongfully hinders the other party's performance breaches the contract.

OBLIGATIONS OF GOOD FAITH AND FAIR DEALING

Each party to a contract has an implied duty to cooperate with the other party in achieving the objects of the contract. Failure of the plaintiff to discharge that implied duty is a defense in a suit on the contract.

SUSPENSION OR EXCUSE OF CONDITIONS BY WAIVER, ELECTION

Waiver occurs when a party affirmatively represents that it will not act on a known right. If the other party relies on the waiver to its detriment, the waiver becomes irrevocable.

REMEDIES

ANTICIPATORY REPUDIATION; DEMAND FOR ASSURANCES

Under the UCC, when a party has reasonable grounds for insecurity, he may demand adequate assurances from the other party and suspend his performance until he receives them.

If a party repudiates a contract before the time for performance, the other party may treat the repudiation as a total breach, seek performance elsewhere, and sue for breach.

If the nonrepudiating party has not canceled the contract or materially changed position, the repudiating party may retract the repudiation, providing he gives adequate assurances. The nonrepudiating party then has no right to sue for breach.

RISK OF LOSS; RIGHTS OF BONA FIDE PURCHASERS

The seller shifts the risk of loss to the buyer when he completes his delivery obligation for conforming goods. If the contract is FOB seller's place of business, the delivery obligation is completed by placing conforming goods on a common carrier with arrangements that they be shipped to the buyer.

If the contract is FOB buyer's place of business, the delivery obligation is completed when the goods are delivered to buyer's place of business; the seller retains the risk of loss during transit.

If the seller ships nonconforming goods on a shipment or a destination contract, she retains the risk of loss until the goods are accepted.

If the buyer rightfully revokes acceptance of the goods, the risk of loss is on the seller to the extent that the goods are not covered by buyer's insurance.

If the buyer breaches or repudiates the contract before the risk of loss passes to him, the risk of loss is on the buyer for a commercially reasonable time to the extent that the loss is not covered by seller's insurance.

SELLER'S REMEDIES IN THE EVENT OF BUYER'S BREACH

The seller may sell the goods in a commercially reasonable manner and collect the difference between the contract price and the sales price, plus incidental damages.

If the difference between the sales price and the contract price does not reasonably reflect the seller's damage because he has an unlimited supply of the goods, then the measure of damage is the seller's profit, the difference between his production cost for the goods and the contract price.

The seller may sue for the contract price if the goods cannot be sold in the seller's ordinary course of business.

BUYER'S REMEDIES IN THE EVENT OF SELLER'S BREACH

The buyer may seek specific performance and replevin the goods where they are unique (and in other special circumstances).

The buyer may seek damages – the difference between the market price and the contract price.

The buyer may cover, that is, purchase the goods elsewhere and collect the difference between the cover price and the contract price.

MEASURE OF DAMAGES

The usual contract measure of damages is the amount which will put the nonbreaching party in the position it would have been in had the contract been performed – the amount of unreimbursed money expended on the contract plus the profit which it would have made on the contract.

If expectancy damages are too speculative, the nonbreaching party may seek reliance damages – the amount expended by him to perform the contract.

CONSEQUENTIAL DAMAGES; LIQUIDATED DAMAGES; SPECIFIC PERFORMANCE

Consequential damages are limited to those damages which were reasonably foreseeable.

Liquidated damages are only collectible if the liquidated amount is reasonable either in respect to the amount of damages which the parties anticipated at the time of making the contract, or in respect to the actual damages incurred.

Both the buyer and the seller are entitled to sue for specific performance of enforceable land contracts.

RESTITUTION DAMAGES

If a party is prevented from suing on the contract because the contract is unenforceable or because he has breached the contract, he is entitled to collect restitution damages in *quantum meruit*, measured by the fair value of the benefit conferred on the other party.

IMPOSSIBILITY AND FRUSTRATION

At common law, the excuse of impossibility applies when the subject matter of the contract is destroyed or a party to a personal service contract dies.

Under the UCC doctrine of impracticability, performance is excused when (1) goods identified to the contract are destroyed, (2) performance becomes illegal, or (3) performance is prevented by a nonforeseeable event the nonoccurrence of which was a basic assumption of the contract.

CRIMINAL LAW AND PROCEDURE

HOMICIDE CRIMES

MURDER – INTENTIONAL KILLINGS

A mercy killing is murder because it is an intentional killing, even if the victim asks the person to kill him.

A person who sets up a mechanical device which kills a person is guilty of the crime which would have been committed if the person had personally set off the device intentionally.

If a person takes steps to make substantially certain that an event will occur, he has intended the act even if he subjectively does not desire that the result occur.

MURDER – INTENT TO DO GREAT BODILY HARM

If a person commits an act which would not ordinarily inflict fatal injury, but would likely cause great bodily harm, and the victim dies, that person is guilty of murder, even if the victim died because of a peculiar medical condition.

An intent to do great bodily harm can be inferred from the use of a weapon to inflict bodily injury.

FELONY MURDER

A defendant is not guilty of felony murder unless he is guilty of the commission or attempted commission of the underlying felony.

A defendant is not guilty of felony murder if the commission of the felony has not yet begun or is completed at the time the death occurs.

A co-conspirator of the felon who actually commits the killing is not guilty of felony murder if the killing was beyond the scope of the conspiracy.

The felonies of manslaughter or assault and battery cannot be the underlying felony for felony murder.

If a third party kills a cofelon in the course of a felony, the surviving felon is not guilty of felony murder because the killing is justifiable homicide.

ABANDONED OR MALIGNANT HEART MURDER

Firing bullets in a confined space or through a wall, or playing russian roulette, is abandoned heart murder if a death results.

Deliberately and unjustifiably driving a car onto a crowded sidewalk would constitute abandoned heart murder if a death results.

DEGREES OF MURDER

A homicide accompanied by malice in the form of a deliberate intentional killing is first-degree murder.

A death in the course of the serious common law felonies of Mayhem, Rape, Sodomy, Burglary, Arson, Kidnapping, Escape and Robbery is first-degree murder ("felony murder").

A murder accompanied by malice in the form of intent to do great bodily harm is usually second-degree murder.

A murder accompanied by malice in the form of a depraved heart is second-degree murder.

VOLUNTARY MANSLAUGHTER

To reduce a murder crime to voluntary manslaughter, there must be adequate provocation to inflame a reasonable person into the heat of passion and the defendant must have actually been in such a state. A violent battery, spousal adultery, mutual affray and an illegal arrest are adequate provocation. The killing must also take place in a time frame where the passions of a reasonable person would not have cooled and the passion of the defendant must not in fact have cooled.

A murder crime can be reduced to manslaughter if the defendant had a defense (e.g., a right to defend himself or another), but used that defense imperfectly (e.g., by employing excessive force).

If the defendant would only have been guilty of voluntary manslaughter if she had killed A, she is only guilty of voluntary manslaughter if she shoots at A, misses him and kills V.

INVOLUNTARY MANSLAUGHTER

A death occurring in the course of willful, wanton conduct is involuntary manslaughter.

A death occurring in the course of a misdemeanor malum in se is involuntary manslaughter.

A person under a duty to aid another person because of a contractual or family relationship is guilty of involuntary manslaughter if a death occurs because of unreasonable failure to give that aid. However, a person under no duty can unreasonably refuse to give aid without any criminal liability.

SELF-DEFENSE AND DEFENSE OF OTHERS

An aggressor does not have the right of self-defense, unless he attacked with nondeadly force and is met with deadly force, or unless he completely ends his aggression and makes that known to the person attacked.

A person committing a felony does not have the right of self-defense.

An individual has the right to use deadly force to apprehend a felon committing a dangerous felony or to prevent a dangerous felony from being committed. Only nondeadly force can be used if the crime is a misdemeanor.

Force is classified as deadly or nondeadly by its likelihood to cause death, not whether death in fact occurred.

A belief that the person defended has the right of self-defense is a defense in a criminal prosecution, even if the person defended does not in fact have the right of self-defense (e.g., because he was the aggressor). (To avoid liability in tort, though, the person defended must have **actually** had a right to self-defense.)

A person does not have the right to use self-defense to avoid being arrested by a police officer.

If an individual has a perfect right of self-defense but, in the exercise of that right, kills the wrong person, the homicide is still excused.

OTHER DEFENSES TO HOMICIDE CRIMES

Defense of property is not sufficient to justify the use of deadly force.

A killing commanded by the law, such as an execution or killing on the battlefield in time of war is not murder because it is a justifiable homicide.

Duress relates to coercion by a human force, whereas necessity relates to coercion by nonhuman elements. Duress and necessity cannot be defenses to a homicide crime, but can be defenses to an underlying felony, which would then be a defense to felony murder.

OTHER CRIMES

LARCENY

The specific intent necessary for larceny is not present if the defendant intends to return the property at the time he committed the trespassory taking.

If the defendant intended to return the property, the fact that it was not returned because it was unintentionally destroyed does not transform the intent into an intent to steal. However, an intent to destroy is equivalent to an intent to steal.

If possession is obtained by fraud, the crime is larceny by trick, not embezzlement.

The trespassory act necessary for larceny can be committed by an innocent agent of the defendant.

A person with title to property can be guilty of larceny if he wrongfully takes that property from a person rightfully in possession.

A lower-level employee in possession of the goods of an employer, or a bailee who breaks the bulk of the goods bailed, does not have a sufficient possessory interest to have the taking of those goods constitute embezzlement.

EMBEZZLEMENT

Embezzlement only occurs when a person rightfully gains possession of another's property and then converts it to his own use.

OBTAINING PROPERTY BY FALSE PRETENSES

To be guilty of obtaining property by false pretenses, the victim must give up title to property in reliance on a false representation of material fact by the defendant.

The defendant's honest belief that the representation is true prevents the defendant from having the specific intent necessary for the crime of obtaining property by false pretenses, even if the belief is unreasonable.

RECEIVING STOLEN GOODS

A belief that the goods were not stolen is a defense to the crime of receiving stolen goods.

If the goods are not in fact stolen goods, the defendant cannot be convicted of receiving stolen goods even if he believes that the goods are stolen.

ROBBERY

Larceny is an essential element of (and merges into the more serious crime of) robbery when all of the elements of robbery are found.

The battery which constitutes the force employed in a robbery merges into the more serious crime of robbery.

The use of force or intimidation to retain possession of property already stolen is not robbery.

The threat to use force in the future is the threat necessary for extortion, not robbery.

BURGLARY

In order to be guilty of burglary, the defendant must have the specific intent to commit a felony on the premises at the moment of the entering.

Burglary is committed if the defendant breaks and enters a part of a dwelling house, even if he does not break and enter when he first enters the dwelling.

The breaking and entering need not occur simultaneously.

The breaking and entering necessary for burglary are present if entry is obtained by fraud.

A person cannot be guilty of burglary for breaking and entering into his own home.

Defendant is guilty of burglary even if not successful in completing the intended felony.

ASSAULT AND BATTERY

The defendant never has the obligation to retreat if he is using nondeadly force as a defense to an assault or battery.

RAPE

Consent to intercourse is not a defense if the victim's assent to the act performed is procured through fraud which obscures the fact that intercourse is taking place.

An underage female who engages in intercourse cannot be held guilty of conspiracy to commit statutory rape or as an accessory to statutory rape.

KIDNAPPING AND ARSON

Demand for a ransom is not an element of simple kidnapping.

A person cannot be guilty of the common law crime of arson for burning his own house.

A minimal burning of part of the dwelling house is all that is required for arson, but the burning of the contents alone is not sufficient.

INCHOATE CRIMES

ATTEMPTS

To be guilty of the crime of attempt, the defendant must intend to commit the crime which she is attempting.

If the act which the defendant intended to accomplish is not a crime, the defendant is not guilty of an attempt even if he thinks he has committed a crime.

If the defendant is successful in his attempt and commits the substantive crime, there is no separate crime of attempt; the attempt and the crime merge.

CONSPIRACY

A co-conspirator is guilty of the substantive crimes committed by any other co-conspirator during the course of the conspiracy and within the scope of the conspiracy.

If a co-conspirator withdraws from the conspiracy and informs his co-conspirators of the withdrawal, he is not guilty of the substantive crimes committed by the conspirators after the withdrawal, but is guilty of the conspiracy crime.

An overt act is not necessary to complete the conspiracy crime at common law, but is required today for federal conspiracy crimes and is required in some states.

The impossibility of accomplishing the object of the conspiracy is not a defense to conspiracy, but there is no conspiracy if the parties mistakenly believe that the lawful object of the conspiracy is a crime.

A person is not a conspirator unless he combines with another human being to commit an unlawful act or a lawful act by unlawful means. Persons who do not have the requisite intent to qualify as a conspirator do not count as that other person.

A person is not a conspirator if he does not intend to combine to commit a crime. For example, a person is not a conspirator if he intends to combine only to do something which he believes is legal.

A person is not guilty of conspiracy if he combines with another person who is essential to the commission of the substantive crime (e.g., adultery).

Conspiracy does not merge into the substantive offense.

SOLICITATION

If the party solicited agrees to commit the crime, there is a conspiracy and the crime of solicitation is merged into it.

PARTIES TO CRIMES

To be guilty as an accomplice, the person must know that the principal is committing a crime and must intend to help the principal.

If the act being committed by the principal is not in fact a crime, the accessory is not guilty despite his intent to help with an illegal act.

Presence at the scene of the crime plus encouragement of the principal to commit the crime is sufficient for accomplice liability.

GENERAL PRINCIPLES

GENERAL INTENT CRIMES

To be guilty of a general intent crime, the intent to accomplish the act must coincide with the doing of the act.

If a person desires a result and that result occurs, even through an unexpected means, the person has intended the act for purposes of the criminal law.

SPECIFIC INTENT CRIMES

To be guilty of a specific intent crime, the defendant must have the required specific intent at the time he is accomplishing the specific act.

STRICT LIABILITY

The doing of the actus reus is all that is required for the defendant to be guilty of a strict liability crime.

Specifically forbidding an agent to perform an illegal act is not a defense for a principal if performing that act constitutes a strict liability offense.

To be guilty of an **attempt** to commit a strict liability offense, the defendant must have the specific intent to commit the offense.

MISTAKE OF FACT

A reasonable mistake of fact is a defense to a general intent crime.

A reasonable or unreasonable mistake of fact which prevents the specific intent from being formed is a valid defense to a specific intent crime.

MISTAKE OF LAW

A mistake of law is not a defense to a general intent crime, but a mistake of law which prevents the specific intent from being formed is a defense to a specific intent crime.

INSANITY

A mental illness which causes delusions will not create the defense of insanity under the *M'Naghten* test if the individual knows what he is doing and knows that it is a crime. The irresistible impulse test is not part of the *M'Naghten* test of insanity.

INTOXICATION

In a specific intent crime, intoxication is a defense if the intoxication prevents the defendant from forming the required specific intent.

Intoxication can prevent the formation of the malice necessary to constitute first-degree murder and reduce the crime to second-degree murder, but not to manslaughter.

CAUSATION

If a person mortally wounds a victim, but death occurs from a totally independent cause, that person is not guilty of murder.

Improper medical treatment resulting in death is within the scope of the risk when an individual causes bodily harm. Therefore, lack of causation is not a defense to a homicide crime if there was the required intent or misconduct.

JUSTIFICATION

A police officer is justified in using deadly force to apprehend a person who it reasonably appears is either committing or escaping from a dangerous felony. The use of deadly force to arrest a person for a nondangerous felony or any misdemeanor is not justified.

A person assisting a police officer is justified in using the same force that a police officer would be justified in using.

CONSTITUTIONAL PROTECTIONS

ARREST

Except in the case of hot pursuit, a warrant is required to arrest an individual in his home.

A police officer has the right to arrest without a warrant outside of the home if he has probable cause to believe that the arrestee committed a misdemeanor in the presence of the officer or committed a felony.

DEFINITION OF A SEARCH

A search involves government intrusion into space or activities where an individual has a reasonable expectation of privacy.

An individual has a reasonable expectation of privacy in his person, his home (including the curtilage), in his desk and file cabinets in a private office at work, and in containers for personal effects.

An individual only has standing to object to searches which violate his own reasonable expectation of privacy.

The Fourth Amendment rules apply only to searches by government authorities or those acting under their express direction. It does not apply to searches by private individuals.

An individual does not have a reasonable expectation of privacy in his financial records in the hands of a third party.

If property is in plain view from a place where a law enforcement officer has a lawful right to be, there is no search.

SEARCH INCIDENT TO A VALID ARREST

If the arrest is invalid, or the search is made before there is a valid ground to arrest, then the evidence obtained by the search is inadmissible.

A search incident to an arrest must be essentially contemporaneous with the arrest and only of the area within the arrestee's immediate control.

CONSENT SEARCHES

The consent given by an individual to search his own property must be voluntary, but the suspect need not be warned that he need not give consent.

A third party can give valid consent to search areas over which he has joint access.

A hotel manager cannot validly consent to the search of rooms in the hotel which are rented to guests.

AUTOMOBILE SEARCHES

The random stopping of automobiles without any probable cause constitutes an invalid search. However, stops of all vehicles at a fixed checkpoint are permissible.

Once an automobile is stopped with probable cause, the entire automobile (including the trunk and containers in the automobile) may be searched. The search need not take place immediately.

The police may stop a car and search containers within the car if they have probable cause as to the containers.

OTHER WARRANTLESS SEARCHES

A search at a border (or the functional equivalent thereof) does not require probable cause or a warrant.

A regulatory search does not require probable cause.

A "stop and frisk" is permitted only if there is a suspicion of criminality and may extend only to a "pat down" search. If the "pat down" uncovers an object which may be a weapon, an intrusive search may be made for weapons.

SEARCHES PURSUANT TO A SEARCH WARRANT

A search warrant can only be issued by a neutral and detached magistrate on the basis of probable cause.

Probable cause can be based on the totality of the circumstances and does not require evidence on both the basis for the search and the reliability of the informant.

The warrant must state with particularity the place to be searched and the objects of the search.

If a magistrate grants a search warrant, and the police execute it believing in good faith that it is valid, the property seized pursuant to the search is admissible.

COERCED CONFESSIONS

If a confession is coerced, even by a private individual, then it is inadmissible for any purpose. However, if improperly admitted, such admission is subject to the harmless error rule.

MIRANDA

Miranda only applies when the suspect is interrogated while he is in custody.

Interrogation can take the form of behavior by the police likely to induce the defendant to make a statement.

If the defendant exercises his *Miranda* rights by demanding a lawyer, no further questioning can take place until a lawyer is present and the defendant agrees to interrogation after consultation with his lawyer.

If a defendant agrees to submit to interrogation, he can be questioned about more subjects than the crime which is the primary object of the police interrogation.

If evidence is inadmissible substantively because of a *Miranda* violation, it is nevertheless admissible to impeach.

LINEUPS AND OTHER FORMS OF IDENTIFICATION

There is a right to counsel at a lineup only after the criminal process has commenced.

If the likelihood of a proper identification is so remote or the lineup is so prejudicial that it offends due process standards, then both testimony about the lineup identification and a subsequent in-court identification are inadmissible.

RIGHT TO COUNSEL

A defendant has the right to counsel in all felonies and all misdemeanors for which he is actually incarcerated.

An individual has the right to act as his own counsel and, if he does, he cannot later complain that he was denied his right to counsel.

A defendant has the right to counsel for one appeal.

The defendant has been deprived of effective assistance of counsel if his attorney has a conflict of interest because he is also representing a co-defendant.

PUBLIC TRIAL; FAIR CONDUCT BY THE PROSECUTOR

Even if both the prosecutor and defendant want a private trial, the public has a right to a public trial. A trial must be public unless there is either a substantial likelihood of prejudice to the defendant or a need to limit access to ensure an orderly proceeding.

A prosecutor has the obligation to disclose to the defendant all exculpatory material known to or in the possession of the prosecutor's office.

JURY TRIAL; SPEEDY TRIAL

The right to speedy trial does not commence to run until the defendant is charged with the crime.

The defendant is not denied the right to a speedy trial solely by the passage of time. There must also be prejudice to the defendant.

The defendant is entitled to be tried by a jury if the period of incarceration can exceed six months.

The defendant is entitled to be tried by a jury chosen from a venire in which there is no systematic racial exclusion. Neither the defendant nor the prosecutor may systematically exclude individuals of one race from the jury by peremptory challenges.

The jury need consist of only six persons. However, if the jury consists of only six persons, the verdict must be unanimous. If the jury consists of twelve persons, a nine-person verdict is constitutional.

CONFRONTATION; SEVERANCE; STANDARD OF PROOF

The confrontation clause is satisfied if the defendant had the right to cross-examine the witness at a pretrial hearing and there is a valid excuse for the witness's absence from the trial.

If the statement of one defendant is admissible against the confessor, but also implicates a co-defendant and is inadmissible against the co-defendant, the court must either excise the offending portions of the statement or grant a severance.

The prosecution must prove all elements of the offense beyond a reasonable doubt. However, the state can place upon the defendant the obligation to plead affirmative defenses and prove them by a preponderance of the evidence.

FAIR TRIAL - POST-TRIAL STAGE

The appellate court may constitutionally order a new trial if the verdict is against the weight of the evidence.

A defendant's criminal record is admissible after the verdict, for purposes of deciding the appropriate sentence.

DOUBLE JEOPARDY

Jeopardy attaches in a criminal jury trial when the jury is sworn, and in a jury-waived trial, when the first witness begins to testify.

Double jeopardy does not apply when the judge declares a mistrial to benefit the defendant or the appellate court orders a new trial as the result of the defendant's appeal.

The prosecution can only appeal a judgment if a victory for the prosecution will not result in a retrial.

COLLATERAL ESTOPPEL

If issues are litigated in one criminal case between the prosecution and the defendant, they cannot be relitigated in a separate criminal case between the same parties.

EVIDENCE

PRESENTATION OF EVIDENCE

PERSONAL KNOWLEDGE

Every witness (except an expert witness and a witness testifying to admissible hearsay) must testify from first-hand knowledge.

LEADING AND ARGUMENTATIVE QUESTIONS

Leading questions are not permitted on direct examination until a witness's memory is exhausted, but are permissible on cross-examination.

An argumentative question (e.g., one that starts "Don't you know that . . .") is inadmissible even on cross-examination.

REFRESHING RECOLLECTION

Present memory refreshed occurs when the witness's memory is revived (e.g., by reference to a document). The witness then testifies to what he remembers. The rules regarding hearsay and admissibility of writings are inapplicable.

On the other hand, past recollection recorded occurs when a witness has made a written record on a matter while his memory was fresh, and his memory of that matter is exhausted and cannot be revived. The document itself, which comes within a hearsay exception, is read to the jury and must satisfy the requirements for admissibility of a writing.

If a witness brings written documents with him while testifying, opposing counsel can examine them as a matter of right in the course of cross-examination.

OBJECTIONS AND OFFERS OF PROOF

Hearsay evidence which would be inadmissible at trial is admissible before a judge hearing evidence on a preliminary question of fact.

An offer of proof is required only when an objection to a question is sustained. The party must state for the record what the answer to the question would be, if known.

To preserve an issue for appeal, counsel must object to the admissibility of evidence at the time it is offered.

LAY OPINIONS AND EXPERT WITNESSES

A layperson can testify in the form of opinion with respect to matters on which laypersons are competent to form opinions, if the opinion is based upon personal knowledge and is helpful to an understanding of the testimony.

A lay witness cannot testify on matters on which only experts are qualified to give opinions, even if the layperson's opinion is based upon first-hand knowledge.

An expert witness need not testify from personal knowledge, but instead may draw inferences from facts presented to him and may rely on the opinions of other experts if to do so is customary in the field of expertise.

An expert witness can be cross-examined about specific instances in his background which bear on his qualification as an expert.

Except for the mental state of a criminal defendant, an expert witness can give an opinion on the ultimate issue in a case.

QUALIFICATIONS AND COMPETENCE OF WITNESSES

The Federal Rules of Evidence require that a federal court apply the state's rule on matters of competency of witnesses and privilege if state law provides the basis for decision in the federal court (as it would in diversity cases).

JUDICIAL NOTICE

A jury in a criminal case is not bound to take as true matters which have been judicially noticed.

CROSS-EXAMINATION

If the opposing party is deprived of his opportunity to cross-examine a witness, the remedy is to strike the direct examination.

If part of a document is admitted in evidence by one party, the opposing party has the right to introduce any other part of the same document which ought in fairness be considered with the part already in evidence, even if such evidence would otherwise be inadmissible.

An out-of-court declarant whose statement is admissible hearsay may be impeached in the same manner as an in-court witness.

PRIOR INCONSISTENT STATEMENTS

A prior inconsistent statement is admissible only to impeach unless it comes within an exception to the hearsay rule or it was given under oath, in which case it is admissible to prove the matter asserted.

Extrinsic evidence of a prior inconsistent statement is inadmissible to impeach credibility unless the attention of the witness is called to the statement.

BIAS

Unless the witness admits the fact relating to bias on cross-examination, extrinsic evidence can be introduced to prove bias.

If offered to prove bias, usually inadmissible evidence (such as insurance coverage and other criminal convictions) is admissible.

IMPEACHMENT – CONVICTIONS

Prior convictions of a person can only be introduced to impeach credibility after that person has testified.

Evidence of convictions for juvenile crimes and for misdemeanors not involving dishonesty or false statement are always inadmissible to impeach credibility.

The party proffering a witness can anticipate impeachment of the witness through the use of prior convictions by introducing the convictions against the witness on direct examination.

The court must admit **any** conviction involving dishonesty or false statement against **any** witness, as long as the conviction is recent (i.e., less than 10 years old).

The court may admit a recent conviction of the **criminal defendant** for a crime punishable by death or at least one year imprisonment only if the impeaching party first shows that the probative value of the conviction outweighs its prejudicial effect. The court must admit a recent conviction of a **witness (other than the accused)** for a nonfraud crime punishable by death or at least one year imprisonment unless the objecting party shows that the prejudicial effect of the impeachment **substantially** outweighs the probative value of the evidence.

A conviction more than 10 years old can only be admitted against **any** witness only if the impeaching party first shows that the probative value of the conviction substantially outweighs its prejudicial effect.

IMPEACHMENT – PRIOR BAD ACTS

Evidence of bad acts which show fraudulent conduct can be inquired into on cross-examination to impeach credibility, but extrinsic evidence of such conduct cannot be introduced.

IMPEACHMENT – REPUTATION FOR VERACITY

Character can be attacked either by opinion evidence or by reputation evidence.

The character of a witness for truthfulness cannot be introduced until that character trait has been attacked.

IMPEACHMENT BY CONTRADICTION

Extrinsic evidence cannot be used to contradict a witness on a collateral matter.

REHABILITATION AND REDIRECT EXAMINATION

Testimony on redirect examination must relate to those matters asked on cross-examination.

A witness's credibility can be rehabilitated only with respect to the manner in which it has been attacked. For example, evidence of good character can only be presented if the witness's character has been attacked.

PRESUMPTIONS

If the party seeking the benefit of a presumption introduces evidence from which the jury can find the basic fact giving rise to the presumption, the party against whom the presumption operates must introduce evidence contradicting the presumed fact or face a directed verdict against him on that fact.

PRIVILEGES AND EXCLUSIONS

HUSBAND-WIFE COMMUNICATIONS

There are two separate marital privileges, with distinct rules. Under the first, a witness-spouse can refuse to testify in a criminal prosecution of the defendant-spouse, but the defendant-spouse cannot keep the witness-spouse off the stand. With respect to this rule, the parties must be married at the time of trial.

The second applies to confidential communications between individuals who are at the time of the communication married to each other. The privilege with respect to such communications survives divorce. The presence of third parties capable of understanding the conversation destroys the confidentiality necessary for this spousal privilege.

ATTORNEY-CLIENT PRIVILEGE

The privilege only applies to confidential communications between a client and an attorney for the purpose of obtaining legal advice.

The privilege applies even if the attorney is not in fact hired by the client.

The privilege applies even if the individual consulted is not an attorney, if the client reasonably believed that he was.

The presence of third parties reasonably necessary for either the attorney or the client to perform their duties does **not** destroy the confidentiality necessary for the privilege.

If two clients consult one lawyer, communications in the presence of both clients and the lawyer are privileged in any suit with a third party, but are not privileged in a suit between the clients.

The privilege is inapplicable if the purpose of the communication was to commit future fraud or future criminal conduct.

The privilege is inapplicable if the client or a disciplinary body calls the attorney's conduct into question and the attorney must reveal the confidential communication to defend herself.

Turning over preexisting documents to an attorney does not make them privileged, but a letter to an attorney seeking legal advice is privileged.

PHYSICIAN-PATIENT PRIVILEGE

The physician-patient privilege is a statutory privilege by which the patient can prevent the disclosure of confidential communications made to a physician, and the disclosure of observations made by him. The confidential nature of the communications or observations is not destroyed by the presence of third persons necessary to the performance of the physician's duties. The privilege is waived if the patient introduces evidence on his physical condition, or sues the physician.

SELF-INCRIMINATING STATEMENTS

The privilege against self-incrimination is a testimonial privilege and does not empower a defendant to refuse to turn over nontestimonial items such as bodily, handwriting, or voice samples.

The privilege against self-incrimination (except for cases where the *Miranda* rule concerning confessions is applicable) operates prospectively, and does not give a defendant the power to suppress a statement already made.

A defendant who testifies on a preliminary matter in a criminal case does **not** waive his right to refuse to testify in the case itself, and cannot be cross-examined in the preliminary hearing on matters beyond the scope of the preliminary hearing.

Admissions of ownership for purposes of asserting standing in a hearing on a motion to suppress evidence are not admissible in the criminal trial.

The government, by granting use and derivative use immunity, can compel testimony despite the privilege against self-incrimination.

SUBSEQUENT SAFETY MEASURES

Evidence of subsequent remedial measures is not admissible to prove negligence or culpable conduct, but is admissible to prove ownership or control.

OFFERS OF SETTLEMENT; PAYMENT OF MEDICAL EXPENSES

An offer to compromise a disputed claim **and all statements made in such a context** are not admissible to prove liability.

However, an offer in compromise is admissible if it is accepted and the party is suing in contract to enforce it.

An offer in compromise cannot qualify as such until the other party has made a claim so that a dispute exists.

An offer to pay or the payment of medical expenses is likewise not admissible to show liability. However, a statement made in connection with an offer to pay medical expenses **is** admissible.

An offer to plea bargain and statements made in connection therewith are not admissible at a subsequent trial.

If the criminal process has not begun, a statement made in an attempt to avoid criminal liability (for example, an offer to pay for goods which were stolen) is admissible at a subsequent trial.

OTHER PRIVILEGES

Other privileges, recognized in some jurisdictions, include a priest-penitent privilege, a social worker-client privilege, and privileges not to disclose one's vote, a newsperson's sources and government secrets.

RELEVANCY AND ITS COUNTERWEIGHTS

PROBATIVE VALUE

Evidence of a rape victim's sexual conduct is admissible only if it involves other sexual conduct with the alleged perpetrator or the alleged victim's sexual conduct with a person other than the defendant at the time of the alleged rape **and** the judge determines that the probative value of the evidence outweighs its prejudicial effect.

USE OF CHARACTER TO PROVE ACTIONS

Evidence of a character trait to show propensity to act in accordance with that trait is **always** inadmissible in a civil case.

The defense in a criminal case can prove, by either opinion or reputation evidence, character traits of the criminal defendant which are inconsistent with the alleged criminal activity. After the defendant introduces such evidence, the prosecution can rebut with similar character evidence.

The prosecution cannot initiate the proof of character in a criminal case, except to prove the peaceful nature of the victim in a homicide case where the defendant has raised the defense of self-defense.

EVIDENCE OF OTHER CRIMES

Evidence of other crimes is admissible only to prove identity, motive, notice, opportunity, plan or similar relevant facts in a criminal case. Conviction of the other crime need **not** be proven.

HABIT, CUSTOM AND ROUTINE PRACTICE

Evidence of regularized conduct which can be characterized as a habit is admissible to prove conduct in accordance with that habit.

SIMILAR HAPPENINGS AND TRANSACTIONS

Evidence of similar events or circumstances is not admissible to prove the relevant event unless the probative value is compelling.

EXPERIMENTAL AND SCIENTIFIC EVIDENCE

Evidence of a scientific test which fairly represents a relevant event is admissible even if the opposing party had no notice of the test and did not participate in it.

DEMONSTRATIVE EVIDENCE

The judge has wide discretion in deciding whether and in what form to allow demonstrative evidence. The judge may exclude demonstrative evidence as unduly inflammatory, even if it is relevant.

WRITINGS AS EVIDENCE

AUTHENTICATION; PROOF OF SIGNATURES

Objects which do not have any identifying characteristics must be authenticated by proving a chain of custody from the point at which the object became relevant to the time of trial.

A photograph is admissible upon testimony that it fairly and accurately depicts a relevant event. The photographer is not required to so testify; any witness may testify.

A telephone voice of an individual is authenticated by testimony either that the witness recognized the voice, or that the witness called the number listed to that individual and the call was answered by a person identifying himself as that individual. A telephone voice of an individual is **not** authenticated if the witness does not recognize the voice and the person **calls the witness** and identifies himself.

A lay witness cannot testify to the genuineness of a signature solely on the basis of comparing the signature in question to an admittedly genuine signature, but a handwriting expert can.

Familiarity with a signature by a witness, even at a distant time, is all that is required to authenticate the signature.

BEST EVIDENCE RULE

Secondary evidence used to prove a collateral matter is admissible despite the best evidence rule.

The best evidence rule does not require the production of a written record of an event if the witness can testify about that event from first-hand knowledge.

HEARSAY

DEFINITION OF HEARSAY

An out-of-court statement is not hearsay if you do not have to believe the statement is true for it to be relevant in the lawsuit.

Nonverbal conduct is hearsay **only** if the person intended to make an assertive statement by the conduct.

EVIDENCE USED CIRCUMSTANTIALLY AS NONHEARSAY

Out-of-court statements which are only used circumstantially - not to prove the truth of the matter asserted - are not hearsay. Examples of this include statements admitted to show: (1) the knowledge or state of mind of either the declarant or the recipient of the statement, when such is relevant to a case, (2) the declarant's lack of credibility, or (3) the meaning to the parties of the words involved in a statement.

NONHEARSAY - PRIOR INCONSISTENT STATEMENT GIVEN UNDER OATH

If a witness testifies on the stand, a prior inconsistent statement by the witness given under oath subject to the penalty of perjury is admissible substantively to contradict the witness.

If the prior inconsistent statement was not made under oath subject to the penalty of perjury, it is only admissible to impeach. If the witness is not on the stand, a prior statement can be admissible under the former testimony exception to the hearsay rule, if the necessary requirements are met (the declarant is unavailable, etc.).

NONHEARSAY - PRIOR CONSISTENT STATEMENT

An out-of-court statement consistent with testimony on the witness stand is admissible substantively for the purpose of showing that the testimony given on the witness stand is not a recent contrivance when the opposing party has impeached credibility by use of a prior inconsistent statement.

An out-of-court statement consistent with testimony on the witness stand is admissible substantively to rebut an inference of bias if the consistent statement was made prior to the time that the reason for the bias occurred.

NONHEARSAY - PRIOR OUT-OF-COURT IDENTIFICATION BY WITNESS AT TRIAL

A prior identification by a witness is admissible if the witness is on the stand and testifying subject to cross-examination.

NONHEARSAY - ADMISSIONS BY PARTY

An out-of-court statement of a party is admissible, even though it was in his interest at the time he made it, and even though he had no personal knowledge of the facts contained in it.

In addition to the statement of a party, his actions which are inconsistent with the position he is taking in a case are admissible against him.

NONHEARSAY - ADOPTIVE ADMISSIONS

Likewise, statements made by others which a party has adopted through his actions are admissions. This most commonly occurs when a party remains silent when a statement is made in his presence which he would deny if it were false. Such statements are not admissible when a defendant is entitled to his *Miranda* rights. A party may adopt a statement without knowing its precise nature if he indicates that its author is a reliable person.

NONHEARSAY - VICARIOUS ADMISSIONS

Statements made by an authorized agent, a partner, or a predecessor in title are admissible.

NONHEARSAY - STATEMENT BY EMPLOYEE

The statement of an employee while still employed concerning matters within the scope of his employment is an admission against his employer, even if the employee was not specifically authorized to speak for the employer.

NONHEARSAY - STATEMENT MADE BY A CONSPIRATOR

Admissions made by one co-conspirator are only admissible against another co-conspirator if made during the course of the conspiracy. A conspiracy ends with the arrest of the co-conspirators.

INADMISSIBLE HEARSAY

Evidence which is hearsay and does not come within any hearsay exception is inadmissible.

HEARSAY EXCEPTION – PRIOR TESTIMONY

Statements made in contemplation of impending death, declarations against interest, former testimony, and statements of personal and family history require unavailability. Other hearsay exceptions do not.

A witness who is available but refuses to answer questions or claims the privilege against self-incrimination is "unavailable" for purposes of the Rule 804 hearsay exceptions.

If prior testimony is offered in a case where the parties are not identical to the case in which the witness testified, the prior testimony is admissible only if the opposing attorney in the first trial had an opportunity and the same motive for cross-examination as the party against whom the statement is offered in the second trial.

HEARSAY EXCEPTION – DECLARATION AGAINST INTEREST

When the out-of-court declarant is unavailable, a statement made by him which was contrary to the declarant's pecuniary or proprietary interest and which would likely subject him to criminal or tort liability, or which would likely render invalid a claim which he might possess, is admissible as an exception to the hearsay rule, provided that it was against his or her interest at the time that it was made. If the statement is offered to exonerate a criminal defendant by showing that the out-of-court declarant committed the crime, the evidence must be corroborated.

HEARSAY EXCEPTION – STATEMENT MADE WITH KNOWLEDGE OF IMPENDING DEATH

A statement of impending death is admissible only in civil cases and criminal homicide prosecutions. The death of the declarant is not required (only unavailability).

HEARSAY EXCEPTION – PRESENT SENSE IMPRESSIONS AND EXCITED UTTERANCES

A present sense impression must be more contemporaneous with the prompting event than an excited utterance, but does not require an **exciting** event.

A witness may testify to a present sense impression stated by the declarant without having been in a position to observe the facts related by the declarant.

HEARSAY EXCEPTION – STATEMENTS OF MENTAL OR PHYSICAL CONDITION

The present mental state exception can be used to prove actions in accordance with that mental state.

Statements of **present** physical condition are admissible if made to anyone. Statements of **past** physical condition are admissible only if made to a doctor or the like for purposes of medical diagnosis.

HEARSAY EXCEPTION – PAST RECOLLECTION RECORDED

The declarant must be on the witness stand for either a past recollection recorded or a nonhearsay statement of prior identification to be admissible.

HEARSAY EXCEPTION – BUSINESS RECORDS

The business record exception is not applicable to a business record made in preparation for a lawsuit.

HEARSAY EXCEPTION – TEXTBOOKS

Where the learned treatise exception applies, the passage in the learned treatise is admitted substantively. However, the treatise itself cannot be admitted as an exhibit.

The learned treatise exception is available only after the opposing expert testifies and the proponent establishes the authority of the treatise. The opposing expert need not admit to the authority of the treatise, but some expert must establish its qualifications.

OTHER EXCEPTIONS

Family records and reputation concerning family history are admissible to prove family relationships. If the declarant is unavailable, his own statement concerning his personal history is admissible.

Documents more than 20 years old in proper custody come within the ancient documents exception to the hearsay rule.

PROPERTY

THE ESTATE SYSTEM

FEE SIMPLE DETERMINABLE AND FEE SIMPLE SUBJECT TO CONDITION SUBSEQUENT

The interest created in the grantor after a **fee simple determinable** ("to X so long as the premises are used for church purposes") is a **possibility of reverter**.

The interest created in the grantor after a **fee simple subject to a condition subsequent** ("to X but if alcoholic beverages are served on the premises, then the grantor has a right to reenter") is a **right of entry for condition broken**.

A fee simple determinable or fee simple subject to a condition subsequent are the only devices which will allow a seller who retains no land to control the use of the property.

The interest created in a third person after a fee simple determinable or a fee simple subject to a condition subsequent is an **executory interest** which is subject to the Rule Against Perpetuities. Unless that interest must vest or fail within the period of the Rule (lives in being plus 21 years) it is void.

FUTURE INTERESTS

If an interest is created in a third party in the same instrument as the prior possessory interest and can take in possession upon the termination of the prior interest it is a remainder.

A remainder is contingent if there is a condition precedent to its becoming possessory or the holders are unascertained.

A remainder is vested if it can take whenever and however the previous estate terminates. The persons taking are ascertained and there is no condition precedent to their taking.

If the named vested remainderman dies before the life tenant, his devisees take his interest if he leaves a will. His heirs take if he dies intestate.

If there is a class gift (a gift to children or grandchildren) afterborn members of the class can join the class until the class closes. If the grantor does not indicate otherwise, the class closes at the time any member of the class is capable of taking possession of the gift.

If there is a remainder to the children of a living person and one or more children are in existence, then during the prior estate the interest in the children is "subject to open," or "subject to partial divestment."

A future interest can be alienated prior to its becoming possessory.

The interest in the "heirs" of a living person is contingent, because heirs cannot be determined until the person's death.

LIFE ESTATES

Any remainderman (including a contingent remainderman) can enjoin a life tenant from committing waste.

The holder of an interest after a qualified fee simple determinable or fee simple subject to a condition subsequent cannot enjoin the holder of the fee simple for waste.

If there is a mortgage on property at the time it is conveyed to a life tenant and a remainderman, the life tenant is responsible for interest and current real estate taxes, and the remainderman is responsible for paying the principal.

THE RULE AGAINST PERPETUITIES

A child conceived but not born at the time of the commencement of the Rule will be considered a life in being.

The Rule Against Perpetuities does not apply to interests in the grantor (reversions, possibilities of reverter, or rights of entry for condition broken) or vested remainders.

The time for determining lives in being when the conveyance is by will is at the death of the testator.

The time for determining lives in being when the conveyance is by inter vivos deed is at the time of the conveyance.

The time for determining lives in being when the conveyance is by irrevocable inter vivos trust is at the time of the conveyance. If the trust is revocable, it is at the time that the power to revoke terminates (either on the death of the testator or earlier if the power to revoke is relinquished).

The Rule Against Perpetuities invalidates rights of first refusal which might not be exercised within the period of the Rule.

Under the common-law Rule Against Perpetuities, any person is irrebuttably presumed capable of having children until death.

If the Rule Against Perpetuities invalidates the interest of one member of a class, the disposition to the entire class is invalid.

If an interest is invalid because of the Rule Against Perpetuities, the disposition is construed with the invalid gift deleted.

If there is no ultimate disposition in a will because of an invalid disposition, then the testator's heirs take.

If there is an incomplete disposition by conveyance because of an invalidity, then the grantor or his heirs have a reversion.

RESTRAINTS ON ALIENATION

A right of first refusal which only requires the seller to sell at market value is not an invalid restraint on alienation.

A prohibition of a grantee's right to alienate property or a provision forfeiting an interest if the grantee attempts to alienate is invalid.

The owner of property can by contract restrict his own right to alienate property.

COTENANCIES BETWEEN HUSBAND AND WIFE

The conveyance of one spouse's interest in a tenancy by the entirety to a third party is invalid and creates no property interest in the third party.

A conveyance to two persons who are not married to each other as tenants by the entirety creates a joint tenancy.

CONVERSION OF JOINT TENANCIES INTO TENANCIES IN COMMON

The granting of a mortgage by one joint tenant does not transform the tenancy into a tenancy in common in a state adopting the lien theory of mortgages, but it does in a title theory state.

If two joint tenants die simultaneously, the estate of each takes one half.

A conveyance by all joint tenants of an undivided portion of their interest to a third party does <u>not</u> destroy the joint tenancy between them in the portion they retain.

CHARACTERISTICS OF COTENANCIES

A cotenant who makes improvements to property cannot charge his cotenants for contribution for the cost of the improvements.

A cotenant who occupies the property owes no rent to his fellow cotenants.

Persons owning property as joint tenants or tenants in common have an inalienable right to partition. Tenants by the entirety have no right to partition.

RIGHTS AND LIABILITIES OF ADJOINING LANDOWNERS

An abutting landowner has an absolute duty of lateral support to his neighbor's land in its natural state, and a duty to avoid negligence regardless.

RIGHTS IN LAND

EXPRESS EASEMENTS

An easement is overburdened if it is used to benefit land other than the dominant estate.

Non-use alone is insufficient to terminate an easement.

An easement by grant must be in writing and signed by the grantor to be valid.

An easement by grant must be recorded in order to bind bona fide purchasers of the benefited land.

An appurtenant easement is automatically transferred with the dominant estate.

A person cannot alienate his interest in an appurtenant easement separate from the alienation of the dominant estate.

The holder of an easement has the right to make repairs to property such as pipes and roads which are associated with the easement.

A person cannot have an easement on land which he owns in fee simple.

If the holder of the dominant estate acquires title to the servient estate, the easement is destroyed by merger and is not reinstated by a later conveyance of the servient estate.

If the owner of an interest in land induces another person to substantially rely on the fact that the owner will not assert his property right, the owner will be prevented from later asserting that right by reason of estoppel.

EASEMENTS BY IMPLICATION AND NECESSITY

An easement by necessity or implication can only be created at the time of the division of a commonly owned parcel.

An easement created by necessity ends when the necessity ends, but the end of the reason for creating an express easement does not terminate an express easement.

An easement for light and air does **not** arise by necessity or implication.

EASEMENTS BY PRESCRIPTION

An easement by prescription need not be recorded to be effective against purchasers.

The scope of an easement by prescription depends upon the scope of the use during the prescriptive period.

Once an easement by prescription ripens with the passage of the appropriate time, continuous use of the easement is not necessary to maintain it.

If use is with the permission of the owner, then no prescriptive rights accrue. If nothing is said, then the use is adverse.

The adverse use of the property need not be exclusive to obtain an easement by prescription.

PROFITS

A person who holds an exclusive profit a prendre has the right to apportion it.

A profit a prendre can be unlimited in time and is created in the same manner as an express easement.

FIXTURES

A tenant has the right to remove personal property which he attached to the real estate, even though the property might otherwise be characterized as a fixture (real estate).

A person having an estate of uncertain duration (e.g., a life estate) who plants crops on that land can enter the land and remove the crops at the end of the growing season.

COVENANTS

The person who imposes a covenant which runs with the land cannot enforce that covenant against a subsequent purchaser unless he is still the owner of some land which was owned by him at the time he imposed the covenant.

For a deed covenant to be enforceable against a subsequent owner of the property restricted, the original parties must have intended that it apply to subsequent owners, the subsequent owners must have actual or record notice of the restriction, and the subject matter of the restriction must touch and concern the land.

The recording by a grantee of a deed containing a covenant running with the land is a satisfactory substitute for a memorandum signed by the grantee, and the defense that the covenant is unenforceable because of the Statute of Frauds is invalid.

COMMON SCHEMES

If the grantor consistently imposes similar covenants on a group of lots in a subdivision, he has created a common scheme and the owner of any lots burdened by the restrictions can sue the owner of any other lot to enforce the restrictions.

If the grantor imposes similar covenants on a group of lots in a subdivision, he has created a common scheme and can be required to impose similar restrictions on all remaining lots in the subdivision, even if he has not promised in writing that he will do so.

CHOICE OF PROPERTY DEVICES

The most useful property device to control the use of land, which does not seriously affect the marketability of title, is usually an easement. However, if the marketability of title is not an issue, a qualified estate is the most certain form of control.

VENDOR AND PURCHASER

STATUTE OF FRAUDS

A written brokerage listing agreement is not a memorandum sufficient to satisfy the Statute of Frauds.

Payment of the purchase price by the buyer is not sufficient part performance to take an oral agreement out of the Statute of Frauds.

A written memorandum is necessary to change co-ownership from one form to another.

EQUITABLE CONVERSION

In a jurisdiction which recognizes equitable conversion, the risk of loss is on the buyer from the time that a binding purchase and sale agreement is executed.

If a purchase and sale agreement is executed in a jurisdiction which recognizes equitable conversion, the buyer's interest is immediately an interest in realty and the seller's interest is immediately an interest in the proceeds (i.e., personalty).

TIME OF CLOSING

If time is of the essence, then the seller and the buyer must each be prepared to close on the date specified in the agreement or each are in default.

MARKETABLE TITLE

Restrictions imposed by zoning ordinances do not render title unmarketable.

The fact that a buyer would be exposed to nonfrivolous litigation is sufficient to render title unmarketable.

An adverse possessor whose title has not been confirmed in a judicial proceeding does not have marketable title.

SURVIVAL OF COVENANTS IN THE PURCHASE AND SALE AGREEMENT

If a purchase and sale agreement is consummated by the delivery of a deed, covenants contained in the purchase and sale agreement are no longer enforceable unless the agreement specifically states that they survive the closing.

MORTGAGES

A person who purchases at a mortgage foreclosure takes free of any encumbrances placed on the land subsequent to the mortgage which is being foreclosed.

If the mortgagor sells property without paying off the mortgage and the buyer agrees to assume and pay the mortgage, the buyer is primarily liable and the mortgagor is only secondarily liable on the mortgage note.

If the mortgagor sells property without paying off the mortgage and the buyer takes subject to the mortgage (i.e., without agreeing to pay the debt), the buyer is not liable for any deficiency judgment on the mortgage note, but can lose the property through foreclosure if he does not pay the mortgage.

If a deed (rather than a mortgage) is given to secure the payment of a debt, the deed is an equitable mortgage. Parol evidence can be used to prove that the deed was intended to be a mortgage.

If there is an equitable mortgage, the grantor/mortgagor can require a reconveyance of the property upon payment of the debt unless the grantee/mortgagee has conveyed the property to a bona fide purchaser.

A mortgage foreclosure is not effective against a junior encumbrance unless notice is given to the holder of the encumbrance.

A purchase money mortgage (a mortgage from the grantee to the grantor to secure part of the purchase price) which is recorded immediately after the deed, takes precedence over any other liens on the property.

MORTGAGES AND OTHER SECURITY DEVICES

A deed which is absolute on its face, but was intended only to convey a security interest, can be reformed by a court into an equitable mortgage, as long as a bona fide purchaser does not now hold title.

Other security devices, such as installment sales contracts, will be treated as a mortgage by a court. The usual procedures required for foreclosure and redemption will be applied.

TITLE

ADVERSE POSSESSION

Open, notorious and exclusive possession by one cotenant for the statutory period will not establish adverse possession unless the other cotenant was ousted at the beginning of that period.

Joint possession with the rightful owner interrupts the adverse possessor's exclusive possession. Adverse possession must start all over again after the rightful owner leaves.

If adverse possession commences against a competent adult, the subsequent ownership by a minor or a person with a disability does not interrupt the statutory period.

It is possible to obtain title by adverse possession to airspace by projections from a structure which overhang another's property.

Transfer of ownership by the true owner does not interrupt the running of the period of adverse possession.

Transfer of rights from one adverse possessor to a subsequent adverse possessor does not interrupt the running of the period of adverse possession.

DELIVERY AND VALIDITY OF A DEED

A forged deed is a nullity conveying no title.

The time of the transfer of title dates back to the time when the deed was delivered into a commercial escrow if the transaction is consummated.

If the owner of property delivers a valid deed to a grantee, title is transferred to the grantee even though the deed is not recorded.

The subsequent redelivery of the original deed from the grantee to the grantor does not retransfer title to the grantor. A new deed signed by the grantee is required for that retransfer.

A grantee who receives a warranty deed does not have to be a bona fide purchaser to sue his grantor for a breach of a warranty.

If the grantee of a validly delivered deed objects to owning the property, title has not been transferred because the grantee has not accepted the deed.

DESCRIPTION OF PROPERTY

Any description of property which describes the property deeded with reasonable certainty is sufficient to make the deed effective. A reference to a survey or plan is sufficient, even if the survey or plan is not recorded. In cases of ambiguity, parol evidence is admissible to clarify the parties' intent. A deed which does not sufficiently describe the property, even after consideration of parol evidence, is invalid.

Where there is a conflict, a description of the property by monuments prevails over a description of the property by distances.

COVENANTS OF TITLE

A quitclaim deed contains no covenants. A warranty deed usually contains both present and future covenants. Future covenants run with the land, while present covenants do not. Thus, the grantee may sue only the immediate grantor for breach of a present covenant (such as the covenant against encumbrances). Present covenants are also breached, if at all, at the time of conveyance.

The covenant of quiet enjoyment (a future covenant) is breached only when the grantee is ousted from possession of (even part of) the land.

ESTOPPEL BY DEED

If a person grants an interest in land which he does not own by a warranty deed to a grantee, the grantee automatically becomes the owner of that interest as soon as the grantor acquires it, because of estoppel by deed.

RECORDING SYSTEM

Recording is not required for an effective transfer of interests between the parties to the transaction.

If the owner of property delivers a deed to a grantee and he records immediately, and the owner then delivers a deed of the same property to a subsequent grantee, the subsequent grantee loses because he has (constructive) notice of the prior deed.

If the owner of property deeds first to one grantee and then to a second grantee, the issue of which grantee prevails does not turn on whether the first grantee is a bona fide purchaser. That inquiry is relevant only with respect to the second grantee.

A deed which is recorded out of order in the chain of title is not constructive notice to a subsequent bona fide purchaser.

TYPES OF RECORDING SYSTEMS

In a notice jurisdiction, the subsequent grantee cuts off the interest of the prior grantee who fails to record if the subsequent grantee is a bona fide purchaser.

In a race-notice jurisdiction, the subsequent grantee cuts off the interest of the prior grantee who fails to record if the subsequent grantee is a bona fide purchaser and records prior to the first grantee.

CHARACTERISTICS OF A BONA FIDE PURCHASER

A person who takes a conveyance in satisfaction of a prior debt is a purchaser.

A person need not actually search title in the registry to be a bona fide purchaser.

Even though a donee is not a purchaser, the donee can sell to a bona fide purchaser who will prevail over a prior grantee.

Persons who take title in a chain where there is a forged deed or where the record owner has lost title by adverse possession are not protected by the recording system.

If the subsequent grantee has actual knowledge of the deed to the prior grantee, he cannot prevail even if the prior grantee's deed is not properly recorded.

LANDLORD-TENANT RELATIONSHIP

A tenant is liable to pay rent during the term even if he has assigned his interest in the leasehold.

A tenant who is denied the beneficial use of the property by the landlord and who moves out is not liable to pay the rent on the theory that he was constructively evicted.

TYPES OF TENANCIES

A periodic tenancy is terminated by notice (from either the landlord or the tenant) before the beginning of a rental period terminating the tenancy at the end of that period.

A term for years is terminated at the end of the term without notice by either party.

ASSIGNMENT AND SUBLETTING OF TENANCIES

An assignee is obligated to pay rent during the time that he possesses the leasehold property, but is not obligated to pay rent if he further assigns his leasehold interest.

Only if the landlord, tenant, and assignee enter into a novation, is the tenant no longer liable for the rent.

When a tenant validly assigns a lease, the assignee and the landlord (or the landlord's successors) are bound by all of the covenants in the lease, such as a covenant to pay taxes or a covenant giving the tenant a right to purchase the property.

A covenant against assignment does not prevent a tenant from subletting the property and vice versa.

INTENTIONAL TOR[T]

ASSAULT

Intent to cause app[...]
Contact or intent to actua[...]

Words alone are not [...]
intent to act.

There is a privilege [...]
defense, defense of othe[...]
as long as the actor rea[...]
conduct, even if there wa[...]

BATTERY

The plaintiff must [...]
harmful or offensive (4)[...]

There is a privilege to use any assault or reasonable battery in self defense, defense of others, and to eject trespassers. These privileges exist as long as the actor reasonably believed the circumstances called for the conduct, even if there was a mistake.

FALSE IMPRISONMENT

The plaintiff need not resist confinement to have an action for false imprisonment.

The imprisonment must be (1) intentional and (2) without consent to be actionable.

A shopkeeper has a privilege to reasonably detain someone reasonably suspected of shoplifting.

The plaintiff must have been aware of the confinement.

Any reasonable exist or alternate route confinement defeats the cause of action.

utes false imprisonment. The fact that
mit the crime does not automatically give

ND

be used to gain entry, but consent (even implied
t the cause of action.

a privilege to trespass in emergency situations and to protect
property, but the trespasser must pay for any damage done by
ass.

TRESPASS TO CHATTELS AND CONVERSION

Both trespass to chattels and conversion require an intentional interference with the personal property of another. However, like trespass to land, the defendant need not know that the trespass was wrongful for it to be actionable. The defendant need only intend to commit the act which constitutes the trespass.

Only a **substantial** interference with personal property can be the basis for an action of conversion. If the defendant has substantially damaged or lost the personal property or if the defendant refuses to return it after demand has been made, the plaintiff can bring an action for conversion to recover the value of the personal property at the time that the defendant first asserted dominion over it. Any lesser interference with personal property is only the basis for a trespass to chattels action to recover damages for the harm done to the chattel and the plaintiff's lost use of the chattel.

INTENTIONAL INFLICTION OF EMOTIONAL DISTRESS

The defendant's conduct must be extreme and outrageous such that it would be substantially certain to cause severe emotional distress in a person of normal sensitivities. However, the defendant can also be held liable if he knows of the victim's peculiar sensitivities.

Bystanders can recover for emotional distress resulting from an intentional tort to family member only if the defendant knew the bystander was a witness.

NUISANCE

A nuisance exists when the defendant's use of neighboring land unreasonably interferes with the use and enjoyment of the plaintiff's land.

A defendant can be held liable for nuisance even if the offending use is not negligent.

PRIVATE NUISANCE

If there is an actual physical invasion of the plaintiff's land, the cause of action is for trespass, rather than nuisance.

Which use commenced first is a factor to be considered in deciding whether a particular use is a nuisance, but it is not dispositive. (That is, one can "move to the nuisance" and still enjoin it or recover damages in some cases.)

The fact that a particular use is permitted by the applicable zoning regulations does not establish that it is not a nuisance, although it is some proof that the use is reasonable.

Some courts will deny any judgment for plaintiff if the defendant's use of the land is socially useful. Other courts will award damages, but will refuse to enjoin such a use.

PUBLIC NUISANCE

A nuisance is a private nuisance if it interferes with only one neighbor's use and enjoyment of his land. That neighbor has a cause of action for private nuisance.

A nuisance is a public nuisance if it interferes with the use and enjoyment of several neighboring parcels. In general, only the relevant political subdivision (city, county, etc.) has the right to sue for a public nuisance. However, a private plaintiff can sue for public nuisance if the harm to that plaintiff from the nuisance is different in kind from the harm to the public (or if a statute gives the neighbor a private cause of action).

STRICT LIABILITY

PRODUCTS LIABILITY – STRICT LIABILITY OF MANUFACTURERS

A supplier (i.e., a seller or manufacturer) of a product is strictly liable if (1) the product was defective when it left the party's hands and (2) that defect causes the plaintiff harm.

Foreseeable users and even bystanders may recover under a strict liability theory.

Assumption of the risk is a defense in strict products liability actions, but not contributory negligence.

Exercise of utmost care by the defendant in manufacturing or handling the product will not defeat plaintiff's strict liability claim.

Misuse by the plaintiff is not a defense, unless that misuse was unforeseeable.

Alteration of the product after it left the defendant's hands can defeat the plaintiff's strict liability action.

An assembler is liable for the defective parts included in its finished product.

Unavoidably unsafe drugs (including blood) are the basis of strict liability only if the supplier does not notify the physician of the potential dangers.

PRODUCTS LIABILITY – STRICT LIABILITY OF SUBCONTRACTORS AND VENDORS

The manufacturer of a defective component is liable for the defective parts included in the finished product.

ABNORMALLY DANGEROUS ACTIVITIES

There is strict liability for any harm which results from a use of land which (1) is not common to the area, and (2) presents a serious risk of harm even if undertaken with due care.

In such a case, the plaintiff need not show that the defendant's conduct of the abnormally dangerous activity was negligent to recover.

ANIMALS

Owners of wild animals are strictly liable for the harm cause by them; owners of domesticated animals are only liable for their own negligence regarding the animals.

NEGLIGENCE

RISK AND DUTY

Generally, one has a duty to act reasonably, but one usually does not have a duty to rescue someone from a danger that he or she did not create. Only the creator of the peril or a close family member (usually a parent) has any duty to rescue someone in danger.

Once one undertakes to rescue, though, one has a duty to act with reasonable care. This is called the Good Samaritan doctrine.

One who has acted negligently is liable not only to direct victims of his negligence, but anyone who undertakes to rescue persons in peril from the defendant's negligence. A defendant who endangers only himself is also liable for his negligence to anyone who tries to rescue him from his own misconduct.

GENERAL STANDARD OF CONDUCT

The usual standard of care is that of a reasonable adult in the circumstances.

Evidence of custom is admissible to establish due care in a particular circumstance or field, but is not binding on the jury.

A manufacturer is not liable (in negligence) if the manufacturer used reasonable care in inspecting component parts assembled into a finished product.

STATUTORY STANDARD OF CONDUCT

Violation of a regulatory statute or ordinance is "negligence per se" (absolute proof of negligence) or some proof of negligence – depending upon the jurisdiction's rule – if the statute or ordinance was promulgated to avoid the harm that resulted. There must also be a causal connection between the violation and the harm.

The fact that the defendant has complied with statutes and ordinances is usually not proof that there was no negligence.

Licensing statutes are irrelevant to the proof of negligence.

The fact that the defendant is guilty of negligence per se does not mean that the plaintiff's own negligence will not defeat or diminish his recovery.

Under "guest statutes," the driver of a car is only liable to a passenger in his car for gross negligence.

STANDARD OF CONDUCT OF CLASSES OF PERSONS

Children under the age of seven are presumed incapable of negligence as a matter of law. (However, children can be held guilty of intentional torts.)

A minor may usually be held to a lower standard of care, but if the minor is engaged in an adult activity (e.g., driving), an adult standard of care will be applied.

Parents can be held liable for the torts of their child only if the parents are guilty of negligence in raising or supervising the child, or the child is acting as an agent of the parents.

METHOD OF PROVING FAULT

Proof of subsequent repairs is not admissible to prove negligence (but may be used to prove other matters, such as control).

Violations of regulatory statutes can be used to prove negligence. (See above.)

Prior misconduct cannot be used to prove negligence unless the misconduct rises to the level of habit.

Negligence need not be proven by direct evidence, but can be proved by inference or circumstantial evidence. (See below.)

However, negligence must be established by a preponderance of the evidence. It must be shown that there is a probability (not merely a possibility) that the defendant was negligent and such negligence caused the plaintiff's harm.

Expert testimony will be required only where the jury cannot determine based on their everyday knowledge and experience whether the defendant was negligent or whether the defendant's negligence was the cause of the plaintiff's harm.

Prior accidents (or lack of prior accidents) is admissible to prove that a situation or condition was negligent (or not negligent) only if the situation or condition was the same in the prior incidents. Regardless, the lack of prior accidents may be admissible solely to prove that the defendant had no notice of the dangerous condition.

RES IPSA LOQUITUR

The plaintiff can prevail without direct proof of the defendant's negligence if he can prove (or the circumstances alone indicate) that he would not have been harmed if the defendant had not been negligent. The plaintiff need only show that it is more likely than not that the defendant was negligent (and that there is a causal connection to the plaintiff's harm).

Res ipsa loquitur is irrelevant if there is direct evidence that the defendant was negligent.

The defendant can defeat a res ipsa loquitur case against him by showing that it is just as likely that someone else's negligence caused the plaintiff's harm.

CAUSATION

The test of factual causation is "but for," i.e., the plaintiff's harm would not have occurred if not for the defendant's negligence.

The chain of causation is broken by a **superseding** intervening cause. However, the defendant is liable for any harm which would have occurred if not for the superseding cause.

A foreseeable intervening cause is not superseding. An unlawful or negligent act may be foreseeable.

Once a plaintiff has recuperated from an injury by the defendant, the defendant is not liable for subsequent injuries just because they would not have happened if not for the plaintiff's weakened condition from the first injury.

Even if there is factual causation, there must be proximate cause (i.e., the plaintiff's harm must not be too remote). A cause cannot be the "proximate" cause unless it is also the factual cause.

Where two or more independent defendants are responsible for the plaintiff's harm, each is generally ultimately liable only for the part of plaintiff's harm for which he is responsible. However, the plaintiff can recover all of his damages from the defendants if their combined negligence causes more harm than their actions alone would have caused (or even if, alone, their actions would not have caused **any** harm).

CONTRIBUTION AMONG JOINT TORTFEASORS

Contribution is available between joint tortfeasors no matter what the relative degrees of fault. Contribution allows a defendant who was held liable to recover a pro rata share of his liability from his joint tortfeasors.

A negligent defendant is only entitled to contribution (not complete indemnification) from a joint tortfeasor.

INDEMNITY OF ONE TORTFEASOR TO ANOTHER

A right of indemnification exists when a non-negligent defendant has been held vicariously liable (i.e., for the negligence of another, e.g., a servant). The non-negligent defendant has the right to recover all of the amount for which he was held liable from the negligent party.

NEGLIGENCE LIABILITY OF OWNERS AND OCCUPIERS OF LAND

At common law, a business invitee was owed a duty of reasonable care. A licensee (social guest) was only owed a duty to warn of dangers known to the owner or occupant but not obvious to the licensee. A trespasser was only owed a duty to avoid gross negligence or wanton, willful misconduct.

The doctrine of "attractive nuisance" only applies if the landowner or occupant has reason to know both that children might come onto the land and that the nuisance might be dangerous to them. Then, the landowner owes a duty of reasonable care to the infant trespasser(s). It is not necessary that the children be attracted onto the land **by** the nuisance.

NEGLIGENT INFLICTION OF MENTAL DISTRESS

A plaintiff can recover for negligent infliction of mental distress only if (a) he experiences some actual physical harm from the defendant's negligence, (b) he is within the zone of danger, or (c) he witnesses harm to a family member.

The plaintiff can only recover if the defendant's conduct was sufficient to cause emotional distress in a person of normal sensitivities. Once this objective test is met, the plaintiff can recover for any emotional harm, even if it is unusual.

VICARIOUS LIABILITY

Employers are liable for the torts of their servants committed within the scope of their employment. An intentional tort is within the scope of employment if it was committed to further the master's business.

A plaintiff who is injured by a servant may sue the servant and/or the employer.

JOINT ENTERPRISE LIABILITY

When two parties enter into a joint enterprise, they are liable for each other's torts within the scope of the joint enterprise activity.

LIABILITY FOR INDEPENDENT CONTRACTORS AND NONDELEGABLE DUTIES

Generally, the employer of an independent contractor is not liable for the torts of the independent contractor. An employee is an independent contractor – as opposed to a servant (see above) – if the employer does not control the employee's performance.

However, an employer is liable for ultrahazardous activity (e.g., blasting) undertaken by an independent contractor. There is said to be a nondelegable duty to see that such activity is performed properly.

An employer of an independent contractor can also be held liable for his negligence in hiring an unfit contractor.

ASSUMPTION OF RISK

A plaintiff's cause of action is defeated by assumption of the risk only if he had actual, subjective knowledge of the risk and voluntarily assumed it.

CONTRIBUTORY NEGLIGENCE AND LAST CLEAR CHANCE

Under a contributory (as opposed to comparative) negligence rule, any negligence on the part of the plaintiff would bar his recovery against the defendant. However, in some jurisdictions, a negligent plaintiff could still recover if the defendant had the last clear chance to avoid the accident.

The contributory negligence of another party will not be attributed to the plaintiff, even if the parties are related. However, under most wrongful death statutes, the contributory negligence of either the decedent or the beneficiaries will bar recovery.

COMPARATIVE NEGLIGENCE

Under a comparative negligence statute, the negligence of the plaintiff will not defeat the plaintiff's cause of action, but her recovery will be reduced by her share of the negligence.

Under a "pure" comparative negligence statute, the plaintiff will recover no matter how negligent she was. Under a "hybrid" comparative negligence statute, she will recover only if her negligence was equal to or less than the combined negligence of the other parties.

Comparative negligence does not change the rule of joint and several liability between joint tortfeasors. A plaintiff can recover all of his damages (minus his share of the negligence) from one defendant; that defendant will then have to seek contribution from the joint tortfeasor (based on the joint tortfeasor's share of the negligence).

ELEMENTS OF TORT DAMAGE

Expert testimony is usually required to prove future medical expenses.

A defendant is liable for all of the damages proximately caused by his negligence, even if the defendant's particular damages were unforeseeable.

PRODUCTS LIABILITY – CLAIMS IN NEGLIGENCE

Contributory negligence is a defense in a products liability action based on negligence.

Exercise of due care by the defendant in manufacturing or handling the product **will** defeat plaintiff's products liability claim in negligence.

DEFAMATION

Material is defamatory if it would lower the person's esteem in the eyes of a reputable segment of the community.

LIBEL

Some jurisdictions treat libel per se and libel per quod differently. Libel per se is that which is libelous on its face. Libel per quod is that which is libelous only when taken in conjunction with facts known by those to whom the libel is published. These jurisdictions allow recovery for libel per quod only if there are "special" (i.e., actual monetary) damages.

There must be a publication – meaning that the defendant must intend or allow that at least one person (other than the defamer and defamed) receive and understand the statement (even if they didn't believe it).

A public official or figure must prove "malice" – that the defendant acted with knowledge of falsity or reckless disregard for the truth – in order to recover for defamation (or invasion of privacy).

Any other plaintiff must at least prove negligence to recover for defamation.

SLANDER

The common law rule is that a plaintiff suing for slander must show special damages unless the slander constitutes slander per se (charging the plaintiff with a crime, a loathsome disease, sexual misconduct or business incompetence).

DEFENSES

Truth is an absolute defense in a defamation action (and a "false light" privacy action).

PRIVILEGES

There is no defamation if the statement was privileged. Relevant statements made in court hearings are absolutely privileged. (A perjury action not a defamation action, is the proper action for lies stated in court.) All other privileged statements (those made by an employer to another employer about an employee, statements in administrative hearings) are only protected by a qualified privilege. Such qualified privileges can be overcome if the statement was made with knowledge that it was false or with reckless disregard for its truth.

CONSTITUTIONAL PROBLEMS

A public official or figure must prove "actual malice" to recover for defamation. "Actual malice" requires that the plaintiff prove that the defendant either knew that the information was false, or acted with reckless disregard for its truth or falsity.

Even private persons must show at least negligence to recover against a media defendant.

PRIVACY

Publication is not required for the tort of intentional intrusion upon seclusion.

Truth is not a defense to the torts of invasion of privacy (except "false light" publicity).

Newsworthiness is a defense to the torts of invasion of privacy.

Publishing information in the public record cannot generally be the basis for a privacy tort.

A defendant can be held liable for giving unreasonable publicity to the plaintiff's private life if the material published would be highly offensive to a reasonable person and is not of legitimate public concern (i.e., newsworthy).

A defendant can be held liable for false light publicity even if the material published is complimentary (as long as it is untrue).

DECEIT

In order to be deceit, there must usually be an affirmative misrepresentation. Silence is a misrepresentation only when the defendant had some legal (e.g., fiduciary) duty to disclose.

A statement of opinion is not an actionable misrepresentation.

> **Please Note:** Over the past couple of years, the multistate examiners have revised the manner in which MBE questions are asked on the exam. However, the previous exams included in this workbook do not include the revised language. On the MBE, the following changes should be anticipated in the format of questions:
>
> 1. Questions will no longer be presented in the "K-Type" format (i.e., Answer A says Statement I is true, II & III are false, Answer B says Statements I, II and III are all true, etc.)
>
> 2. Questions will no longer use proper nouns, common nouns will be used instead (i.e., a painter might encounter a contract problem rather than "Painter" or "Pete Painter").
>
> 3. Questions will include all of the facts necessary to answer the question in the fact pattern, not hypothetical facts in the multiple choice answers (i.e., hypothetical facts will not be introduced in the multiple choice answers by using the words "if" or "then" in the answers followed by new information).
>
> 4. Questions will only include quotations when it is part of a statute or a contract necessary to the legal issue being examined.

5. Questions will no longer use an answer choice such as "None of the above" or "All of the above".

In our view, these changes do not reduce the predictive value of the following test. It continues to accurately predict actual MBE performance and we strongly suggest you complete the test and listen to the MBE Workshop lecture for answer explanations. In addition, you should be aware of the changes in question format and will see those types of questions in the 2006 (MBE IV) practice exam found elsewhere in the course.

FEBRUARY, 1991 MULTISTATE BAR EXAM

(MBE I)

DO NOT TURN THIS PAGE UNTIL YOU ARE INSTRUCTED TO DO SO
OR ARE READY TO BEGIN THE TEST.

AM Book
Time– 3 hours

Directions: Each of the questions or incomplete statements below is followed by four suggested answers or completions. You are to choose the best of the stated alternatives. Answer all questions according to the generally accepted view, except where otherwise noted.

For the purposes of this test, you are to assume that Articles 1 and 2 of the Uniform Commercial Code have been adopted. You are also to assume relevant application of Article 9 of the UCC concerning fixtures. The Federal Rules of Evidence are deemed to control. The terms "Constitution," "constitutional," and "unconstitutional" refer to the federal Constitution unless indicated to the contrary. You are also to assume that there is no applicable community property law, no guest statute, and no No–Fault Insurance Act unless otherwise specified. In negligence cases, if fault on the claimant's part is or may be relevant, the statement of facts for the particular question will identify the contributory or comparative negligence rule that is to be applied.

1. Walter, a 16–year–old, purchased an educational chemistry set manufactured by Chemco.

Walter invited his friend and classmate, Peter, to assist him in a chemistry project. Referring to a library chemistry book on explosives and finding that the chemistry set contained all of the necessary chemicals, Walter and Peter agreed to make a bomb. During the course of the project, Walter carelessly knocked a lighted Bunsen burner into a bowl of chemicals from the chemistry set. The chemicals burst into flames, injuring Peter. In a suit by Peter against Chemco, based on strict liability, Peter will

(A)   prevail, if the chemistry set did not contain a warning that its contents could be combined to form dangerous explosives.
(B)   prevail, because manufacturers of chemistry sets are engaged in an abnormally dangerous activity.
(C)   not prevail, because Walter's negligence was the cause in fact of Peter's injury.
(D)   not prevail, if the chemistry set was as safe as possible, consistent with its educational purposes, and its benefits exceeded its risks.

2. On August 1, Geriatrics, Inc., operating a "lifetime care" home for the elderly, admitted Ohlster, who was 84 years old, for a trial period of two months.

On September 25, Ohlster and Geriatrics entered into a written lifetime care contract with an effective commencement date of October 1. The full contract price was $20,000, which, as required by the terms of the contract, Ohlster prepaid to Geriatrics on September 25. Ohlster died of a heart attack on October 2.

In a restitutionary action can the administratrix of Ohlster's estate, a surviving sister, recover on behalf of the estate either all or part of the $20,000 paid to Geriatrics on September 25?

(A)   Yes, because Geriatrics would otherwise be unjustly enriched
(B)   Yes, under the doctrine of frustration of purpose.
(C)   No, because Ohlster's life span and the duration of Geriatrics' commitment to him was a risk assumed by both parties.
(D)   No, but only if Geriatrics can show that between September 25 and Ohlster's death it rejected, because of its commitment to Ohlster, an application for lifetime care from another elderly person.

3. While walking home one evening, Harold, an off-duty police officer, was accosted by Jones, a stranger. Jones had been drinking and mistakenly thought Harold was a man who was having an affair with his wife. Intending to frighten Harold but not to harm him, Jones pulled out a knife, screamed obscenities, and told Harold he was going to kill him. Frightened and reasonably believing Jones was going to kill him and that using deadly force was his only salvation Harold took out his service revolver and shot and killed Jones. Harold is charged with murder.

Harold's claim of self-defense should be

(A)   sustained, because Harold reasonably believed Jones was planning to kill him and that deadly force was required.
(B)   sustained, because the killing was in hot blood upon sufficient Provocation.
(C)   denied, because Jones did not in fact intend to harm Harold and Harold was incorrect in believing that he did.
(D)   denied, because Harold was not defending his home and had an obligation to retreat or to repel with less than deadly force.

4. Anna entered a hospital to undergo surgery and feared that she might not survive. She instructed her lawyer by telephone to prepare a deed conveying Blackacre, a large tract of undeveloped land, as a gift to her nephew, Bernard, who lived in a distant state. Her instructions were followed, and, prior to her surgery, she executed a document in a form sufficient to constitute a deed of conveyance.

The deed was recorded by the lawyer promptly and properly as she instructed him to do. The recorded deed was returned to the lawyer by the land record office. Anna in fact, recovered from her surgery and the lawyer returned the recorded deed to her.

Before Anna or the lawyer thought to inform Bernard of the conveyance, Bernard was killed in an auto accident. Bernard's will left all of his estate to a satanic religious cult. Anna was very upset at the prospect of the cult's acquiring Blackacre.

The local taxing authority assessed the next real property tax bill on Blackacre to Bernard's estate.

Anna brought an appropriate action against Bernard's estate and the cult to set aside the conveyance to Bernard.

If Anna loses, it will be because

(A)   the gift of Blackacre was *inter vivos* rather than *causa mortis.*
(B)   the showing of Bernard's estate as the owner of Blackacre on the tax rolls supplied what otherwise would be a missing essential element for a valid conveyance.
(C)   disappointing Bernard's devisee would violate the religious freedom provisions of the First Amendment to the Constitution.

(D)   delivery of the deed is presumed from the recording of the deed.

5. In a prosecution of Doris for murder, the government seeks to introduce a properly authenticated note written by the victim that reads: "Doris did it." In laying the foundation for admitting the note as a dying declaration, the prosecution offered an affidavit from the attending physician that Doris knew she was about to die when she wrote the note.

The admissibility of the note as a dying declaration is

(A)   a preliminary fact question for the judge, and the judge must not consider the affidavit.
(B)   a preliminary fact question for the judge, and the judge may properly consider the affidavit.
(C)   a question of weight and credibility for the jury, and the jury must not consider the affidavit
(D)   a question of weight and credibility for the jury, and the jury may Properly consider the affidavit.

6. As Paul, a bartender, was removing restraining wire from a bottle of champagne produced and bottled by Winery, Inc., the plastic stopper suddenly shot out of the bottle. The stopper struck and injured Paul's eye.

Paul had opened other bottles of champagne, and occasionally the stoppers had shot out with great force, but Paul had not been injured.

Paul has brought an action against Winery, Inc., alleging that the bottle that caused Ms injury was defective and unreasonably dangerous because its label did not warn that the stopper might suddenly shoot out during opening. The state has merged contributory negligence and unreasonable assumption of risk into a pure comparative fault system that is applied in strict products liability actions.

If the jury finds that the bottle was defective and unreasonably dangerous because it lacked a warning, will Paul recover a judgment in his favor?

(A)   No, if the jury finds that a legally sufficient warning would not have prevented Paul's injury.

(B)   No, if a reasonable bartender would have realized that a stopper could eject from the bottle and hit his eye.

(C)   Yes, with damages reduced by the percentage of any contributory fault on Paul's part.

(D)   Yes, with no reduction in damages, because foreseeable lack of caution is the reason for requiring a warning.

7. Swatter, a baseball star, contracted with the Municipal Symphony Orchestra, Inc. to perform for $5,000 at a children's concert as narrator of "Peter and the Wolf." Shortly before the concert, Swatter became embroiled in a highly publicized controversy over whether he had cursed and assaulted a baseball fan. The orchestra canceled the contract out of concern that attendance might be adversely affected by Swatter's appearance.

Swatter sued the orchestra for breach of contract. His business agent testified without contradiction that the cancellation had resulted in Swatter's not getting other contracts for performances and endorsements.

The trial court instructed the jury, in part, as follows: "If you find for the plaintiff, you may award damages for losses which at the time of contracting could reasonably have been foreseen by the defendant as a probable result of its breach. However, the law does not permit recovery for the loss of prospective profits of a new business caused by breach of contract."

On Swatter's appeal from a jury verdict for Swatter, and judgment thereon, awarding damages only for the $5,000 fee promised by the orchestra, the judgment will probably be

(A)   affirmed, because the trial court stated the law correctly.

(B) affirmed because the issue of damages for breach of contract was solely a jury question.

(C) reversed, because the test for limiting damages is what the breaching party could reasonably have foreseen at the time of the breach.

(D) reversed, because under the prevailing modern view, lost profits of a new business are recoverable if they are established with reasonable certainly.

8. Road Lines is an interstate bus company operating in a five-state area. A federal statute authorizes the Interstate Commerce Commission (ICC) to permit interstate carriers to discontinue entirely any unprofitable route. Road Lines applied to the ICC for permission to drop a very unprofitable route through the sparsely populated Shaley Mountains. The ICC granted that permission even though Road Lines provided the only public transportation into the region.

Foley is the owner of a mountain resort in the Shaley Mountains, whose customers usually arrived on vehicles operated by Road Lines. After exhausting all available federal administrative remedies, Foley filed suit against Road Lines in the trial court of the state in which the Shaley Mountains are located to enjoin the discontinuance by Road Lines of its service to that area. Foley alleged that the discontinuance of service by Road Lines would violate a statute of that state prohibiting common carriers of persons from abandoning service to communities having no alternate form of public transportation.

The state court should

(A) dismiss the action, because Foley lacks standing to sue.

(B) direct the removal of the case to federal court, because, this suit involves a substantial federal question.

(C) hear the case on its merits and decide for Foley because, on these facts, a federal agency is interfering with essential state functions.

(D) hear the case on its merits and decide for Road Lines, because a valid federal law preempts the state statute on which Foley relies.

9. Shore decided to destroy his dilapidated building in order to collect the insurance money. He hired Parsons to burn down the building. Parsons broke into the building and carefully searched it to make sure no one was inside. He failed, however, to see a vagrant asleep in an office closet. He started a fire.

The building was destroyed, and the vagrant died from burns a week later.

Two days after the fire, Shore filed an insurance claim in which he stated that he had no information about the cause of the fire.

If Shore is guilty of felony-murder, it is because the vagrant's death occurred in connection with the felony of

(A) arson.
(B) fraud.
(C) conspiracy.
(D) burglary.

10. Plaintiff challenged the constitutionality of a state tax law, alleging that it violated the equal protection clauses of both the United States Constitution and the state constitution. The state supreme court agreed and held the tax law to be invalid. It said: "We hold that this state tax law violates the equal protection clause of the United States Constitution and also the equal protection clause of the state Constitution because we interpret that provision of the state constitution to contain exactly the same prohibition against discriminatory legislation as is contained in the equal protection clause of the Fourteenth Amendment to the United States Constitution."

The state sought review of this decision in the United States Supreme Court, alleging that the state supreme court's determination of the federal constitutional issue was incorrect.

How should the United States Supreme Court dispose of the case if it believes that this interpretation of the federal Constitution by the state supreme court raises an important federal question and is incorrect on the merits?

(A) Reverse the state supreme court decision because the equal protection clause of a state constitution must be construed by the state supreme court in a manner that is congruent with the meaning of the equal protection clause of the federal Constitution.
(B) Reverse the state supreme court decision with respect to the equal protection clause of the federal Constitution and remand the case to the state supreme court for further proceedings, because the state and federal constitutional issues are so intertwined that the federal issue must be decided so that this case may be disposed of properly.
(C) Refuse to review the decision of the state supreme court, because it is based on an adequate and independent ground of state law.
(D) Refuse to review the decision of the state supreme court, because a state government may not seek review of decisions of its own courts in the United States Supreme Court.

11. A federal statute prohibits the construction of nuclear energy plants in this country without a license from the Federal Nuclear Plant Siting Commission. The statute provides that the Commission may issue a license authorizing the construction of a proposed nuclear energy plant 30 days after the Commission makes a finding that the plant will comply with specified standards of safety, technological and commercial feasibility, and public convenience. In a severable provision, the Commission's enabling statute also provides that the Congress, by simple majorities in each house, may veto the issuance of a particular license by the Commission if such a veto occurs within 30 days following the required Commission finding.

Early last year, the Commission found that Safenuke, Inc., met all statutory requirements and, therefore, voted to issue Safenuke, Inc., a license authorizing it to construct a nuclear energy plant. Because they believed that the issuance of a license to Safenuke, Inc., was not in accord with the applicable statutory criteria, a majority of each of the two houses of Congress voted, within the specified 30-day period, to veto the license. On the basis of that veto, the Commission refused to issue the license. Subsequently, Safenuke, Inc., sued the Commission in an appropriate federal district court, challenging the constitutionality of the Commission's refusal to issue the license.

In this suit, the court should hold the congressional veto of the license of Safenuke, Inc., to be

(A) invalid, because any determination by Congress that particular agency action does not satisfy statutory criteria violates Article III, Section I of the Constitution because it constitutes the performance of a judicial function by the legislative branch.

(B) invalid, because Article I, Section 7 of the Constitution has been interpreted to mean that any action of Congress purporting to alter the legal rights of persons outside of the legislative branch must be presented to the President for his signature or veto.

(C) valid, because Congress has authority under the commerce clause to regulate the construction of nuclear energy plants.

(D) valid, because there is a compelling national interest in the close congressional supervision of nuclear plant siting in light of the grave dangers to the public health and safety that are associated with the operation of such plants.

Questions 12-14 are based on the following fact situation.

A jurisdiction has the following decisional law on questions of principal and accomplice liability:

CASE A: Defendant, a hardware store owner, sold several customers an item known as a "SuperTrucker," which detects police radar and enables speeders to avoid detection. When one of the devices broke down and the speeder was arrested, he confessed that he often sped, secure in the knowledge that his "SuperTrucker" would warn him of police radar in the vicinity. Held: Defendant guilty as an accomplice to speeding.

H:P

CASE B: Defendant told Arnold that Defendant had stored some stereo equipment in a self-storage locker. He gave Arnold a key and asked Arnold to pick up the equipment and deliver it to Defendant's house. Arnold complied, and removed the equipment from the locker, using the key. In fact, the equipment belonged to Defendant's neighbor, whose locker key Defendant had found in the driveway. Held: Defendant guilty as an accomplice to burglary.

A: P

CASE C: Tooley, a city council member, accepted a bribe from Defendant in exchange for his vote on Defendant's application for a zoning variance. A statute prohibits the taking of bribes by public officials. Held: Defendant not guilty as an accomplice to Tooley's violation of the bribery statute.

NG

CASE D: Defendant, an innkeeper, sometimes let his rooms to prostitutes, whom he knew to be using the rooms to ply their trade. He charged the prostitutes the same price as other guests at his inn. Held: Defendant not guilty as an accomplice to prostitution.

NG

12. Lipsky, a college student, purchased narcotics from Speed, whom he believed to be a "street person" but who was in fact an undercover police agent. Lipsky has been charged as an accomplice to the sale of narcotics.

He should be

(A)   convicted on the authority of Case A.
(B)   convicted on the authority of Case B.
(C)   acquitted on the authority of Case C.
(D)   acquitted on the authority of Case D.

13. In this jurisdiction, conviction for statutory rape requires proof of the defendant's knowledge that the victim is underage. Howard, who knew that Sarah was underage, encouraged George, who was unaware of Sarah's age, to have sex with Sarah.

Howard has been charged as an accomplice to statutory rape.

He should be

(A)   convicted on the authority of Case A.
(B)   convicted on the authority of Case B.
(C)   acquitted on the authority of Case C.
(D)   acquitted on the authority of Case D.

14. Larson, a plastic surgeon, agreed to remove the fingerprints from the hands of "Fingers" Malloy, whom Larson knew to be a safecracker. Larson charged his usual hourly rate for the operation. Afterward, Malloy burglarized a bank safe and was convicted of burglary.

Charged with burglary, Larson should be

(A)   convicted on the authority of Case A.
(B)   convicted on the authority of Case B.
(C)   acquitted on the authority of Case C.
(D)   acquitted on the authority of Case D.

15. Able and Baker are students in an advanced high school Russian class. During an argument one day in the high school cafeteria, in the presence of other students, Able, in Russian, accused Baker of taking money from Able's locker.

In a suit by Baker against Able based on defamation, Baker will

(A)   prevail, because Able's accusation constituted slander per se.
(B)   prevail, because the defamatory statement was made in the presence of third persons.
(C)   not prevail, unless Able made the accusation with knowledge of falsity or reckless disregard of the truth.
(D)   not prevail, unless one or more of the other students understood Russian.

16. Congressional hearings determined that the use of mechanical power hammers is very dangerous to the persons using them and to persons in the vicinity of the persons using diem. As a result, Congress enacted a statute prohibiting the use of mechanical power hammers on all construction projects in the United States. Subsequently, a study conducted by a private research firm concluded that nails driven by mechanical power hammers have longer-lasting joining power than hand-driven nails. After learning about this study, the city council of the city of Green enacted an amendment to its building safety code requiring the use of mechanical power hammers in the construction of all buildings intended for human habitation.

This amendment to the city of Green's building safety code is

(A)   unconstitutional, because it was enacted subsequent to the federal statute.
(B)   unconstitutional, because it conflicts with the provisions of the federal statute.
(C)   constitutional, because the federal statute does not expressly indicate that it supersedes inconsistent state or local laws.
(D)   constitutional, because the long-term safety of human habitations justifies some additional risk to the people engaged in their construction.

Questions 17-18 are based on the following fact situation.

Under a written agreement Superpastries, Inc., promised to sell its entire output of baked buns at a specified unit price to Bonnie's Buns, Inc., a retailer, for one year. Bonnie's Buns promised not to sell any other supplier's baked buns.

17. For this question only, assume the following facts. Shortly after making the contract, and before Superpastries had tendered any buns, Bonnie's Buns decided that the contract had become undesirable because of a sudden, sharp decline in its customers' demand for baked buns. It renounced the agreement and Superpastries sues for breach of contract.

Which of the following will the court probably decide?

(A)   Bonnie's Buns wins, because mutuality of obligation was lacking in that Bonnie's Buns made no express promise to buy any of Superpastries' baked buns.
(B)   Bonnie's Buns wins, because the agreement was void for indefiniteness of quantity and total price for the year involved.
(C)   Superpastries wins, because Bonnie's Buns' promise to sell at retail Superpastries' baked buns exclusively, if it sold any such buns at all, implied a promise to use its best efforts to sell Superpastries' one-year output of baked buns.
(D)   Superpastries wins, because under the applicable law both parties to a sale-of-goods contract impliedly assume the risk of price and demand fluctuations.

18. For this question only, assume the following facts. The parties' contract included a provision for termination by either party at any time upon reasonable notice. After six months of performance on both sides, Superpastries, claiming that its old bun-baker had become uneconomical and that it could not afford a new one, dismantled the bun-baker and began using the space for making dog biscuits.

Superpastries' output of baked buns having ceased, Bonnie's Buns sued for breach of contract. Bonnie's Buns moves for summary judgment on liability, and Superpastries moves for summary judgment of dismissal.

Which of the following should the court rule?

(A)   Summary judgment for Bonnie's Buns, because as a matter of law Superpastries could not discontinue production of baked buns merely because it was losing money on that product.

(B)   Summary judgment for Superpastries, because its cessation of baked-bun production and Bonnie's Buns' awareness thereof amounted as a matter of law to valid notice of termination as permitted by the contract.

(C)   Both motions denied, because there are triable issues of fact as to whether Superpastries gave reasonable notice of termination or whether its losses from continued production of baked buns were sufficiently substantial to justify cessation of production.

(D)   Both motions denied: Superpastries may legally cease production of baked buns, but under the circumstances it must share with Bonnie's Buns its profits from the manufacture of dog biscuits until the end of the first year.

19. Dirk is on trial for the brutal murder of Villas. Dirk's first witness, Wesley, testified that in her opinion Dirk is a peaceful and nonviolent person. The prosecution does not cross-examine Wesley, who is then excused from further attendance.

Which one of the following is INADMISSIBLE during the prosecution's rebuttal?

(A)   Testimony by Wesley's former employer that Wesley submitted a series of false expense vouchers two years ago.

(B)   Testimony by a police officer that Dirk has a long-standing reputation in the community as having a violent temper.

(C)   Testimony by a neighbor that Wesley has a long-standing reputation in the community as an untruthful person.

(D)   Testimony by Dirk's former cell mate that he overheard Wesley offer to provide favorable testimony if Dirk would pay her $5,000.

20. Amos owned Greenfield, a tract of land. His friend Bert wanted to buy Greenfield and offered $20,000 for it. Amos knew that Bert was insolvent, but replied, "As a favor to you as an old friend, I will sell Greenfield to you for $20,000, even though it is worth much more, if you can raise the money within one month."

Bert wrote the following words, and no more, on a piece of paper: "I agree to sell Greenfield for $20,000." Amos then signed the piece of paper and gave it to Bert. Three days later, Amos received an offer of $40,000 for Greenfield. He asked Bert if he had raised the $20,000. When Bert answered, "Not yet," Amos told him that their deal was off and that he was going to accept the $40,000 offer.

The next week, Bert secured a bank commitment to enable him to purchase Greenfield. Bert immediately brought an appropriate action against Amos to compel Amos to convey Greenfield to him. The following points will be raised during the course of the trial.

I.   The parol evidence rule.
II.   Construction of the contract as to time of performance.
III.   Bert's ability to perform.
Which will be relevant to a decision in favor of Bert?

(A)   I only.
(B)   I and II only.
(C)   II and III only.
(D)   I, II, and III.

21. Modality City has had a severe traffic problem on its streets. As a result, it enacted an ordinance prohibiting all sales to the public of food or other items by persons selling directly from trucks, cars, or other vehicles located on city streets. The ordinance included an inseverable grandfather provision exempting from its prohibition vendors who, for 20 years or more, have continuously sold food or other items from such vehicles located on the streets of Modality City.

Northwind Ice Cream, a retail vendor of ice cream products, qualifies for this exemption and is the only food vendor that does. Yuppee Yogurt is a business similar to Northwind, but Yuppee has been selling to the public directly from trucks located on the streets of Modality City only for the past ten years. Yuppee filed suit in an appropriate federal district court to enjoin enforcement of this ordinance on the ground that it denies Yuppee the equal protection of the laws.

In this case, the court will probably rule that the ordinance is

(A)   constitutional, because it is narrowly tailored to implement the city's compelling interest in reducing traffic congestion and, therefore, satisfies the strict scrutiny test applicable to such cases.
(B)   constitutional, because its validity is governed by the rational basis test, and the courts consistently defer to economic choices embodied in such legislation if they are even plausibly justifiable.

(C)   unconstitutional, because the nexus between the legitimate purpose of the ordinance and the conduct it prohibits is so tenuous and its provisions are so underinclusive that the ordinance fails to satisfy the substantial relationship test applicable to such cases.

(D)   unconstitutional, because economic benefits or burdens imposed by legislatures on the basis of grandfather provisions have consistently been declared invalid by courts as per se violations of the equal protection clause of the Fourteenth Amendment.

Questions 22-23 are based on the following fact situation.

Doe, the governor of State, signed a death warrant for Rend, a convicted murderer. Able and Baker are active opponents of the death penalty. At a demonstration protesting the execution of Rend, Able and Baker carried large signs that stated, "Governor Doe – Murderer." Television station XYZ broadcast news coverage of the demonstration, including pictures of the signs carried by Able and Baker.

22. If Governor Doe asserts a defamation claim against XYZ, will Doe prevail?

(A)   Yes, because the signs would cause persons to hold Doe in lower esteem.

(B)   Yes, if Doe proves that XYZ showed the signs with knowledge of falsity or reckless disregard of the truth that Doe had not committed homicide.

(C)   No, unless Doe proves he suffered pecuniary loss resulting from harm to his reputation proximately caused by the defendants' signs.

(D)   No, if the only reasonable interpretation of the signs was that the term "murderer" was intended as a characterization of one who would sign a death warrant.

23. If Doe asserts against XYZ a claim for damages for intentional infliction of emotional distress, will Doe prevail?

(A)   Yes, if the broadcast showing the signs caused Doe to suffer severe emotional distress.

(B)   Yes, because the assertion on the signs was extreme and outrageous.

(C)   No, unless Doe suffered physical harm as a consequence of the emotional distress caused by the signs.

(D)   No, because XYZ did not publish a false statement of fact with "actual malice."

Questions 24-25 are based on the following fact situation.

On July 18, Snowco, a shovel manufacturer, received an order for the purchase of 500 snow shovels from Acme, Inc., a wholesaler.

Acme had mailed the purchase order on July 15. The order required shipment of the shovels no earlier than September 15 and no later than October 15. Typed conspicuously across the front of the order form was the following: "Acme, Inc., reserves the right to cancel this order at any time before September 1." Snowco's mailed response, saying "We accept your order," was received by Acme on July 21.

24. As of July 22, which of the following is an accurate statement as to whether a contract was formed?

(A) No contract was formed, because of Acme's reservation of the right to cancel.

(B) No contract was formed, because Acme's order was only a revocable offer.

(C) A contract was formed, but prior to September 1, it was terminable at the will of either party.

(D) A contract was formed, but prior to September 1, it was an option contract terminable only at the will of Acme.

25. For this question only, assume the following facts. Acme did not cancel the order, and Snowco shipped the shovels to Acme on September 15. When the shovels, conforming to the order in all respects, arrived on October 10, Acme refused to accept them.

Which of the following is an accurate statement as of October 10 after Acme rejected the shovels?

(A) Acme's order for the shovels, even if initially illusory, became a binding promise to accept and pay for them.

(B) Acme's order was an offer that became an option after shipment by Snowco.

(C) Acme's right to cancel was a condition subsequent, the failure of which resulted in an enforceable contract.

(D) In view of Acme's right to cancel its order prior to September 1, the shipment of the shovels on September 15 was only an offer by Snowco.

26. A federal statute prohibits the sale or resale, in any place in this country, of any product intended for human consumption or ingestion into the human body that contains designated chemicals known to cause cancer, unless the product is clearly labeled as dangerous. The constitutionality of this federal statute may most easily be justified on the basis of the power of Congress to

(A) regulate commerce among the states.

(B) enforce the Fourteenth Amendment.

(C) provide for the general welfare.

(D) promote science and the useful arts.

27. A federal statute enacted pursuant to the powers of Congress to enforce the Fourteenth Amendment and to regulate commerce among the states prohibits any state from requiring any of its employees to retire from state employment solely because of their age. The statute expressly authorizes employees required by a state to retire from state employment solely because of their age to sue the state government in federal district court for any damages resulting from that state action. On the basis of this federal statute, Retiree sues State X in federal district court. State X moves to dismiss the suit on the ground that Congress lacks authority to authorize such suits against a state.

Which of the following is the strongest argument that Retiree can offer in opposition to the state's motion to dismiss this suit?

(A)   When Congress exercises power vested in it by the Fourteenth Amendment and/or the commerce clause, Congress may enact appropriate remedial legislation expressly subjecting the states to private suits for damages in federal court.

(B)   When Congress exercises power vested in it by any provision of the Constitution, Congress has unlimited authority to authorize private actions for damages against a state.

(C)   While the Eleventh Amendment restrains the federal judiciary, that amendment does not limit the power of Congress to modify the sovereign immunity of the states.

(D)   While the Eleventh Amendment applies to suits in federal court by citizens of one state against another state, it does not apply to such suits by citizens against their own states.

28. At a country auction, Powell acquired an antique cabinet that he recognized as a "Morenci," an extremely rare and valuable collector's item. Unfortunately, Powell's cabinet had several coats of varnish and paint over the original finish. Its potential value could only be realized if these layers could be removed without damaging the original finish. Much of the value of Morenci furniture depends on the condition of a unique oil finish, the secret of which died with Morenci, its inventor.
A professional restorer of antique furniture recommended that Powell use *Restorall* to remove the paint and varnish from the cabinet. Powell obtained and read a sales brochure published by Restorall, Inc., which contained the following statement: "This product will renew all antique furniture. Will not damage original oil finishes."

Powell purchased some *Restorall* and used it on his cabinet, being very careful to follow the accompanying instructions exactly. Despite Powell's care, the original Morenci finish was irreparably damaged. When finally refinished, the cabinet was worth less than 20% of what it would have been worth if the Morenci finish had been preserved.

If Powell sues Restorall, Inc., to recover the loss he has suffered as a result of the destruction of the Morenci finish, will Powell prevail?

(A)   Yes, unless no other known removal technique would have preserved the Morenci finish.

(B)   Yes, if the loss would not have occurred had the statement in the brochure been true.

(C)   No, unless the product was defective when sold by Restorall, Inc.

(D)   No, if the product was not dangerous to persons.

29. Two adjacent, two-story, commercial buildings were owned by Simon. The first floors of both buildings were occupied by various retail establishments. The second floors were rented to various other tenants. Access to the second floor of each building was reached by a common stairway located entirely in Building 1. While the buildings were being used in this manner, Simon sold Building 1 to Edward by warranty deed which made no mention of any rights concerning the stairway. About two years later Simon sold Building 2 to Dennis. The stairway continued to be used by the occupants of both buildings. The stairway became unsafe as a consequence of regular wear and tear. Dennis entered upon Edward's building and began the work of repairing the stairway. Edward demanded that Dennis discontinue the repair work and vacate Edward's building. When Dennis refused, Edward brought an action to enjoin Dennis from continuing the work.

Judgment should be for

(A)   Edward, because Dennis has no rights in the stairway.

(B)   Edward, because Dennis's rights in the stairway do not extend beyond the normal life of the existing structure.

(C)   Dennis, because Dennis has an easement in the stairway and an implied right to keep the stairway in repair.

(D)   Dennis, because Dennis has a right to take whatever action is necessary to protect himself from possible tort liability to persons using the stairway.

30. Hydro-King, Inc., a high-volume, pleasure-boat retailer, entered into a written contract with Zuma, signed by both parties, to sell Zuma a power boat for $12,000.

4ways

no liq included

The manufacturer's price of the boat delivered to Hydro-King was $9,500. As the contract provided, Zuma paid Hydro-King $4,000 in advance and promised to pay the full balance upon delivery of the boat. The contract contained no provision for liquidated damages. Prior to the agreed delivery date, Zuma notified Hydro-King that he would be financially unable to conclude the purchase; and Hydro-King thereupon resold the same boat that Zuma had ordered to a third person for $12,000 cash.

P=2,500

If Zuma sues Hydro-King for restitution of the $4,000 advance payment, which of the following should the court decide?

(A)   Zuma's claim should be denied, because, as the party in default, he is deemed to have lost any right to restitution of a benefit conferred on Hydro-King.

(B)   Zuma's claim should be denied, because, but for his repudiation, Hydro-King would have made a profit on two boat-sales instead of one.

lost profits

(C)   Zuma's claim should be upheld in the amount of $4,000 minus the amount of Hydro-King's lost profit under its contract with Zuma.

(D)   Zuma's claims should be upheld in the amount of $3,500 ($4,000 minus $500 as statutory damages under the UCC).

31. Deeb was charged with stealing furs from a van. At trial, Wallace testified she saw Deeb take the furs.

The jurisdiction in which Deeb is being tried does not allow in evidence lie detector results. On cross-examination by Deeb's attorney, Wallace was asked, "The light was too dim to identify Deeb, wasn't it?" She responded, "I'm sure enough that it was Deeb that I passed a lie detector test administered by the police." Deeb's attorney immediately objects and moves to strike.

The trial court should

(A)   grant the motion, because the question was leading.

(B)   grant the motion, because the probative value of the unresponsive testimony is substantially outweighed by the danger of unfair prejudice.

(C)   deny the motion, because it is proper rehabilitation of an impeached witness.

(D)   deny the motion, because Deeb's attorney "opened the door" by asking the question.

32. Park sued Officer Dinet for false arrest. Dinet's defense was that, based on a description he heard over the police radio, he reasonably believed Park was an armed robber.

Police radio dispatcher Brigg, reading from a note, had broadcast the description of an armed robber on which Dinet claims to have relied.

The defendant offers the following items of evidence:

I.   Dinet's testimony relating the description he heard.
II.   Brigg's testimony relating the description he read over the radio.
III.   The note containing the description Brigg testifies he read over the radio.

Which of the following are admissible on the issue of what description Dinet heard?

(A)   I and II only.
(B)   I and III only.
(C)   II and III only.
(D)   I, II, and III.

33. Aris was the owner in fee simple of adjoining lots known as Lot 1 and Lot 2. He built a house in which he took up residence on Lot 1. Thereafter, he built a house on Lot 2, which he sold, house and lot, to Baker. Consistent with the contract of sale and purchase, the deed conveying Lot 2 from Aris to Baker contained the following clause:

"In the event Baker, his heirs or assigns, decide to sell the property hereby conveyed and obtain a purchaser ready, willing, and able to purchase Lot 2 and the improvements thereon on terms and conditions acceptable to Baker, said Lot 2 and improvements shall be offered to Aris, his heirs or assigns, on the same terms and conditions. Aris, his heirs or assigns, as the case may be, shall have ten days from said offer to accept said offer and thereby to exercise said option."

Three years after delivery and recording of the deed and payment of the purchase price, Baker became ill and moved to a climate more compatible with his health. Baker's daughter orally offered to purchase the premises from Baker at its then fair market value. Baker declined his daughter's offer but instead deeded Lot 2 to his daughter as a gift.
Immediately thereafter, Baker's daughter sold Lot 2 to Charles at the then fair market value of Lot 2. The sale was completed by the delivery of deed and payment of the purchase price. At no time did Baker or his daughter offer to sell Lot 2 to Aris.

Aris learned of the conveyance to Baker's daughter and the sale by Baker's daughter to Charles one week after the conveyance of Lot 2 from Baker's daughter to Charles. Aris promptly brought an appropriate action against Charles to enforce rights created in him by the deed of Aris to Baker.

B\ D
D

C

Aris tendered the amount paid by Charles into the court for whatever disposition the court deemed proper. The common-law Rule Against Perpetuities is unmodified by statute.

Which of the following will determine whether Aris will prevail?

I.   The parol evidence rule.
II.   The Statute of Frauds.
III.   The type of recording statute of the jurisdiction in question.
IV.   The Rule Against Perpetuities.

(A)   I only.
(B)   IV only.
(C)   I and IV only.
(D)   II and III only.

34. Perez sued Dawson for damages arising out of an automobile collision. At trial, Perez called Minter, an eyewitness to the collision. Perez expected Minter to testify that she had observed Dawson's automobile for five seconds prior to the collision and estimated Dawson's speed at the time of the collision to have been 50 miles per hour. Instead, Minter testified that she estimated Dawson's speed to have been 25 miles per hour.
Without finally excusing Minter as a witness, Perez then called Wallingford, a police officer, to testify that Minter had told him during his investigation at the

P v D

accident scene that Dawson "was doing at least 50."

Wallingford's testimony is

(A)   admissible as a present sense impression.
(B)   admissible to impeach Minter.
(C)   inadmissible, because Perez may not impeach his own witness.
(D)   inadmissible, because it is hearsay not within any exception.

35. After waiting until all the customers had left, Max entered a small grocery store just before closing time. He went up to the lone clerk in the store and said, "Hand over all the money in the cash register or you will get hurt." The clerk fainted and struck his head on the edge of the counter. As Max went behind the counter to open the cash register, two customers entered the store. Max ran out before he was able to open the register drawer.

On this evidence Max could be convicted of

(A)   robbery.
(B)   assault and robbery.
(C)   attempted robbery.
(D)   assault and attempted robbery.

lesser included

36. Palko is being treated by a physician for asbestosis, an abnormal chest condition that was caused by his on-the-job handling of materials containing asbestos. His physician has told him that the asbestosis is not presently cancerous, but that it considerably increases the risk that he will ultimately develop lung cancer.

Palko brought an action for damages, based on strict product liability, against the supplier of the materials that contained asbestos. The court in this jurisdiction has ruled against recovery of damages for negligently inflicted emotional distress in the absence of physical harm.

If the supplier is subject to liability to Palko for damages, should the award include damage for emotional distress he has suffered arising from his knowledge of the increased risk that he will develop lung cancer?

(A)   No, because Palko's emotional distress did not cause his physical condition.

(B)   No, unless the court in this jurisdiction recognizes a cause of action for an increased risk of cancer.

(C)   Yes, because the supplier of a dangerous product is strictly liable for the harm it causes.

(D)   Yes, because Palko's emotional distress arises from bodily harm caused by his exposure to asbestos.

37. Dalton is on trial for burglary. During cross examination of Dalton, the prosecutor wants to inquire about Dalton's earlier conviction for falsifying a credit application.

Which of the following facts concerning the conviction would be the best reason for the trial court's refusing to allow such examination?

(A)   Dalton was released from prison 12 years ago.

(B)   Dalton was put on probation rather than imprisoned.

(C)   It was for a misdemeanor rather than a felony.

(D)   It is on appeal.

Questions 38-39 are based on the following fact situation.

Police received information from an undercover police officer that she had just seen two men (whom she described) in a red pickup truck selling marijuana to schoolchildren near the city's largest high school.

A few minutes later, two police officers saw a pickup truck fitting the description a half block from the high school. The driver of the truck matched the description of one of the men described by the undercover officer.

The only passenger was a young woman who was in the truck but police observed her get out and stand at a nearby bus stop. They stopped the truck and searched the driver. In the pocket of the driver's jacket, the police found a small bottle of pills that they recognized as narcotics. They then broke open a locked toolbox attached to the flatbed of the truck and found a small sealed envelope inside. They opened it and found marijuana. They also found a quantity of cocaine in the glove compartment.

After completing their search of the driver and the truck, the police went over to the young woman and searched her purse. In her purse, they found a small quantity of heroin. Both the driver and the young woman were arrested and charged with unlawful possession of narcotics.

38. If the driver moves to suppress the use as evidence of the marijuana and cocaine found in the search of the truck, the court should

(A)   grant the motion as to both the marijuana and the cocaine.
(B)   grant the motion as to the marijuana but deny it as to the cocaine.
(C)   deny the motion as to the marijuana but grant it as to the cocaine.

(D)   deny the motion as to both the marijuana and the cocaine.

39. If the young woman moves to suppress the use as evidence of the heroin, the court should

(A)   grant the motion, because she did not fit the description given by the informant and her mere presence does not justify the search.
(B)   grant the motion, because the police should have seized her purse and then obtained a warrant to search it.
(C)   deny the motion, because she had been a passenger in the truck and the police had probable cause to search the truck.
(D)   deny the motion, because she was planning to leave the scene by bus and so exigent circumstances existed.

40. Len owned two adjoining parcels known as Lot 1 and Lot 2. Both parcels fronted on Main Street and abutted a public alley in the rear. Lot 1 was improved with a commercial building that covered all of the Main Street frontage of Lot 1; there was a large parking lot on the rear of Lot 1 with access from the alley only.

Fifteen years ago, Len leased Lot 1 to Tenny for 15 years. Tenny has continuously occupied Lot 1 since that time.

Thirteen years ago, without Len's permission, Tenny began to use a driveway on Lot 2 as a better access between Main Street and the parking lot than the alley.

2003 [handwritten]

Eight years ago, Len conveyed Lot 2 to Owen and five years ago, Len conveyed Lot 1 to Tenny by a deed that recited "together with all the appurtenances."

2008 [handwritten]
L – O [handwritten]

Until last week, Tenny continuously used the driveway over Lot 2 to Tenny's parking lot in the rear of Lot 1.

2013 [handwritten]
L – T [handwritten]

Last week Owen commenced construction of a building on Lot 2 and blocked the driveway used by Tenny. Tenny has commenced an action against Owen to restrain him from blocking the driveway from Main Street to the parking lot at the rear of Lot 1.

The period of time to acquire rights by prescription in the jurisdiction is ten years.

If Tenny loses, it will be because

easement by prescription [handwritten]

(A)   Len owned both Lot 1 and Lot 2 until eight years ago.
(B)   Tenny has access to the parking lot from the alley.
(C)   mere use of an easement is not adverse possession.
(D)   no easement was mentioned in the deed from Len to Owen.

41. Dewar, a developer, needing a water well on one of his projects, met several times about the matter with Waterman, a well driller. Subsequently, Waterman sent Dewar an unsigned typewritten form captioned "WELL DRILLING PROPOSAL" and stating various terms the two had discussed but not agreed upon, including a "proposed price of $5,000." The form concluded, "'This proposal will not become a contract until signed by you [Dewar] and then returned to and signed by me [Waterman]."

Dewar signed the form and returned it to Waterman, who neglected to sign it but promptly began drilling the well at the proposed site on Dewar's project. After drilling for two days, Waterman told Dewar during one of Dewar's daily visits that he would not finish unless Dewar would agree to pay twice the price recited in the written proposal. Dewar refused, Waterman quit, and Dewar hired Subbo to drill the well to completion for a price of $7,500.

In an action by Dewar against Waterman for damages, which of the following is the probable decision?

(A)   Dewar wins, because his signing of Waterman's form constituted an acceptance of an offer by Waterman.

(B)   Dewar wins, because Waterman's commencement of performance constituted an acceptance by Waterman of an offer by Dewar and an implied promise by Waterman to complete the well.

(C)   Waterman wins, because he never signed the proposal as required by its terms.

(D)   Waterman wins, because his commencement of performance merely prevented Dewar from revoking his offer, made on a form supplied by Waterman and did not obligate Waterman to complete the well.

42. In an action brought against Driver by Walker's legal representative, the only proofs that the legal representative offered on liability were that: (1) Walker, a pedestrian, was killed instantly while walking on the shoulder of the highway; (2) Driver was driving the car that struck Walker; and (3) there were no living witnesses to the accident other than Driver, who denied negligence.

Assume the jurisdiction has adopted a rule of pure comparative negligence.

If, at the end of the plaintiff's case, Driver moves for a directed verdict, the trial judge should

(A)   grant the motion, because the legal representative has offered no specific evidence from which reasonable jurors may

conclude that Driver was negligent.

(B)   grant the motion, because it is just as likely that Walker was negligent as that Driver was negligent.

(C)   deny the motion, unless Walker was walking with his back to traffic, in violation of the state highway code.

(D)   deny the motion, because, in the circumstances, negligence on the part of Driver may be inferred.

43. Smith joined a neighborhood gang. At a gang meeting, as part of the initiation process, the leader ordered Smith to kill Hardy, a member of a rival gang. Smith refused, saying he no longer wanted to be part of the group. The leader, with the approval of the other members, told Smith that he had become too involved with the gang to quit and that they would kill him if he did not accomplish the murder of Hardy. The next day Smith shot Hardy to death while Hardy was sitting on his motorcycle outside a restaurant.

Smith is charged with first-degree murder. First-degree murder is defined in the jurisdiction as the intentional premeditated killing of another. Second-degree murder is all other murder at common law.

If Smith killed Hardy because of the threat to his own life, Smith should be found

"only if"

W v. D

(A)   not guilty, because of the defense of duress.

(B)   not guilty, because of the defense of necessity.

(C)   guilty of first-degree murder.

(D)   guilty of second-degree murder.

Questions 44 –45 are based on the following fact situation.

Ohner and Planner signed a detailed writing in which Planner, a landscape architect, agreed to landscape and replant Ohner's residential property in accordance with a design prepared by Planner and incorporated in the writing. Ohner agreed to pay $10,000 for the work upon its completion. Ohner's spouse was not a party to the agreement, and had no ownership interest in the premises.

44. For this question only, assume the following facts. Shortly before the agreement was signed, Ohner and Planner orally agreed that the writing would not become binding on either party unless Ohner's spouse should approve the landscaping design.

If Ohner's spouse disapproves the design and Ohner refuses to allow Planner to proceed with the work, is evidence of the oral agreement admissible in Planner's action against Ohner for breach of contract?

(A)   Yes, because the oral agreement required approval by a third party.

(B)   Yes, because the evidence shows that the writing was intended to take effect only if the approval occurred.

(C)   No, because the parol evidence rule bars evidence of a prior oral agreement even if the latter is consistent with the terms of a partial integration.

(D)   No, because the prior oral agreement contradicted the writing by making the parties' duties conditional.

45. For this question only, assume the following facts. At Ohner's insistence, the written Ohner–Planner agreement contained a provision that neither party would be bound unless Ohner's law partner, an avid student of landscaping, should approve Planner's design. Before Planner commenced the work, Ohner's law partner, in the presence of both Ohner and Planner, expressly disapproved the landscaping design. Nevertheless Ohner ordered Planner to proceed with the work, and Planner reluctantly did so. When Planner's performance was 40% complete, Ohner repudiated his duty, if any, to pay the contract price or any part thereof.

If Planner now sues Ohner for damages for breach of contract, which of the following concepts best supports Planner's claim?

(A)   Substantial performance.
(B)   Promissory estoppel.
(C)   Irrevocable waiver of condition.
(D)   Unjust enrichment.

[handwritten margin note: lack of consid. / restitution]

46. A federal law provides that all motor vehicle tires discarded in this country must be disposed of in facilities licensed by the federal Environmental Protection Agency. Pursuant to this federal law, and all proper federal procedural requirements, that agency has adopted very strict standards for the licensing of such facilities. As a result, the is cost of disposing of tires in licensed facilities substantial. The state of East Dakota has a very large fleet of motor vehicles, including trucks used to support state-owned commercial activities and police cars. East Dakota disposes of used tires from both kinds or vehicles in a state-owned and -operated facility. This state facility is unlicensed, but its operation in actual practice meets most of the standards imposed by the federal Environmental Protection agency on facilities it licenses to dispose of tires.

Consistent with United States Supreme Court precedent, may the state of East Dakota continue to dispose of its used tires in this manner?

(A)   No, because a state must comply with valid federal laws

that regulate matters affecting interstate commerce.
(B)   No, because some of the tires come from vehicles that are used by the state solely in its commercial activities.
(C)   Yes, because some of the tires come vehicles that are used by the state in the performance of core state governmental functions such as law enforcement.
(D)   Yes, because the legitimate needs of the federal government are satisfied by the fact that the unlicensed state disposal scheme meets, in actual practice, most of the federal standards for the licensing of such facilities.

47. Arnold and Beverly owned a large tract of land, Blackacre, in fee simple as joint tenants with rights of survivorship. While Beverly was on an extended safari in Kenya, Arnold learned that there were very valuable coal deposits within Blackacre, but he made no attempt to inform Beverly. Thereupon, Arnold conveyed interest in Blackacre to his wife, Alice, who reconveyed that interest to Arnold. The common-law joint tenancy is unmodified by statute.

[handwritten margin note: sacred JT]

Shortly thereafter, Arnold was killed in an automobile accident. His will, which was duly probated, specifically devised his one-half interest in Blackacre to Alice.

[handwritten note: A·B / A]

Beverly then returned from Kenya and learned what had happened. Beverly brought an appropriate action against Alice, who claimed a one-half interest in Blackacre, seeking a declaratory judgment that she, Beverly, was the sole owner of Blackacre.

In this action, who should prevail?

(A) Alice, because Arnold and Beverly were tenants in common at the time of Arnold's death.
(B) Alice, because Arnold's will severed the joint tenancy.
(C) Beverly, because the joint tenancy was reestablished by Alice's reconveyance to Arnold.
(D) Beverly, because Arnold breached his fiduciary duty as her joint tenant.

48. Dent operates a residential rehabilitation center for emotionally disturbed and ungovernable children who have been committed to his custody by their parents or by juvenile authorities. The center's purpose is to modify the behavior of the children through a teaching program carried out in a family-like environment. Though the children are not permitted to leave the center without his permission, there are no bars or guards to prevent them from doing so. It has been held in the state where the center is located that persons having custody of children have the same duties and responsibilities that they would have if they were the parents of the children.

Camden, aged 12, who had been in Dent's custody for six months, left the center without permission. Dent became aware of Camden's absence almost immediately, but made no attempt to locate him or secure his return, though reports reached him that Camden had been seen in the vicinity. Thirty-six hours after Camden left the center, Camden committed a brutal assault upon Pell, a five-year-old child, causing Pell to suffer extensive permanent injury.

If an action is brought against Dent on behalf of Pell to recover damages for Pell's injuries, will Pell prevail?

P v D

(A) No, because parents are not personally liable for their child's intentional torts.
(B) Yes, if Camden was old enough to be liable for battery.
(C) Yes, because Camden was in Dent's custody.
(D) No, unless Dent knew or had reason to know that Camden had a propensity to attack younger children.

49. Deetz was prosecuted for homicide. He testified that he shot in self-defense. In rebuttal, Officer Watts testified that he came to the scene in response to a telephone call from Deetz.

Watts offers to testify that he asked, 'What is the problem here, sir?" and Deetz replied, "I was cleaning my gun and it went off accidentally."

The offered testimony is

(A)   admissible, as an excited utterance.
(B)   admissible, to impeach Deetz and as evidence that he did not act in self-defense.
(C)   inadmissible, because of Deetz's privilege against self-incrimination.
(D)   inadmissible, because it tends to exculpate without corroboration.

50. Landco owns and operates a 12-story apartment building containing 72 apartments, 70 of which are rented. Walker has brought an action against Landco alleging that while he was walking along a public sidewalk adjacent to Landco's apartment building a flower pot fell from above and struck him on the shoulder, causing extensive injuries. The action was to recover damages for those injuries.
If Walker proves the foregoing facts and offers no other evidence explaining the accident, will his claim survive a motion for directed verdict offered by the defense?

(A)   Yes, because Walker was injured by an artificial rendition of the premises while using an adjacent public way.

(B)   Yes, because such an accident does not ordinarily happen in the absence of negligence.
(C)   No, if Landco is in no better position than Walker to explain the accident.
(D)   No, because there is no basis for a reasonable inference that Landco was negligent.

51. At the time of his death last week, Test owned Blackacre, a small farm. By his duly probated will, drawn five years ago, Test did the following:

(1)   devised Blackacre "to Arthur for the life of Baker, then to Casper";
(2)   gave "all the rest residue and remainder of my Estate, both real and personal, to my friend Fanny."

At his death, Test was survived by Arthur, Casper, Sonny (Test's son and sole heir), and Fanny. Baker had died a week before Test.

Title to Blackacre is now in

(A)   Arthur for life, remainder to Casper.
(B)   Casper, in fee simple.
(C)   Sonny, in fee simple.
(D)   Fanny, in fee simple.

A, C B

W v L

Questions 52-53 are based on the following fact situation.

Gyro, an expert in lifting and emplacing equipment atop tall buildings, contracted in a signed writing to lift and emplace certain air-conditioning equipment atop Tower's building. An exculpatory clause in the contract provided that Gyro would not be liable for any physical damage to Tower's building occurring during installation of the air-conditioning equipment. There was also a clause providing for per diem damages if Gyro did not complete performance by a specified date and a clause providing that "time is of the essence." Another clause provided that any subsequent agreement for extra work under the contract must be in writing and signed by both parties.

With ample time remaining under the contract for commencement and completion of his performance, Gyro notified Tower that he was selling his business to Copter, who was equally expert in lifting and emplacing equipment atop tall buildings, and that Copter had agreed to "take over the Gyro-Tower contract."

52. If Tower refuses to accept Copter's services, which of the following clauses in the Gyro-Tower contract will best support Tower's contention that Gyro's duties under the contract were not delegable without Tower's consent?

(A)   The exculpatory clause.
(B)   The liquidated damage clause.
(C)   The "time is of the essence" clause.
(D)   The extra-work clause.

53. For this question only, assume that Tower orally agreed with Gyro to accept Copter's services and that Copter performed on time but negligently installed the wrong air-conditioning equipment.

Will Tower succeed in an action against Gyro for damages for breach of contract?

(A)   Yes, because Tower did not agree to release Gyro from liability under the GyroTower contract.
(B)   Yes, because Tower received no consideration for the substitution of Copter for Gyro.
(C)   No, because by accepting the substitution of Copter for Gyro, Tower effected a novation, and Gyro was thereby discharged of his duties under the Gyro-Tower contract.
(D)   No, because the liquidated damage clause in the Gyro-Tower contract provided only for damages caused by delay in performance.

54. Allen owned Grecnacre in fee simple of record on January 10. On that day, Maria loaned Allen $50,000 and Allen mortgaged Greenacre to Maria as security for the loan. The mortgage was recorded on January 18.

Allen conveyed Greenacre to Barnes for a valuable consideration on January 11. Maria did not know of this, nor did Barnes know of the mortgage to Maria, until both discovered the facts on January 23, the day on which Barnes recorded Allen's deed.

The recording act of the jurisdiction provides: "No unrecorded conveyance or mortgage of real property shall be good against subsequent purchasers for value without notice, who shall first record." There is no provision for a period of grace and there is no other relevant statutory provision.

Maria sued Barnes to establish that her mortgage was good against Greenacre.

The court should decide for

(A)   Barnes, because he paid valuable consideration without notice before Maria recorded her mortgage.
(B)   Barnes, because Maria's delay in recording means that she is estopped from asserting her priority in time.

(C)   Maria, because Barnes did not record his deed before her mortgage was recorded.
(D)   Maria, because after the mortgage to her, Allen's deed to Barnes was necessarily subject to her mortgage.

55. Frank owned two adjacent parcels, Blackacre and Whiteacre. Blackacre fronts on a poor unpaved public road, while Whiteacre fronts on Route 20, a paved major highway. Fifteen years ago, Frank conveyed to his son, Sam, Blackacre "together with a right-of-way 25 feet wide over the east side of Whiteacre to Route 20." At that time, Blackacre was improved with a ten-unit motel.

Ten years ago, Frank died. His will devised Whiteacre "to my son, Sam, for life, remainder to my daughter, Doris." Five years ago, Sam executed an instrument in the proper form of a deed purporting to convey Blackacre and Whiteacre to Joe in fee simple. Joe then enlarged the motel to 12 units. Six months ago, Sam died and Doris took possession of Whiteacre. She brought an appropriate action to enjoin Joe from using the right-of-way.

In this action, who should prevail?

(A)   Doris, because merger extinguished the easement.

(B)   Doris, because Joe has overburdened the easement.
(C)   Joe, because he has an easement by necessity.
(D)   Joe, because he has the easement granted by Frank to Sam.

56. Park sued Dunlevy for copyright infringement for using in Dunlevy's book some slightly disguised house plans on which Park held the copyright. Park is prepared to testify that he heard Dunlevy's executive assistant for copyright matters say that Dunlevy had obtained an advance copy of the plans from Park's office manager. *P v. D*

Park's testimony is
(A)   admissible as reporting a statement of an employee of a party opponent.
(B)   admissible as a statement of a coconspirator.
(C)   inadmissible, because it is hearsay not within any exception.
(D)   inadmissible, because there is no showing that the assistant was authorized to speak for Dunlevy.

57. Congress enacted a statute providing grants of federal funds for the restoration and preservation of courthouses that were built before 1900 and are still in use. The statute contains an inseverable condition requiring that any courthouse restored with the aid of such a grant must be equipped with ramps and other facilities necessary to accommodate physically handicapped people.

A law of the state of Blue requires public buildings in Blue to have ramps and other facilities for handicapped people. It exempts from those requirements any building that is more than 70 years old if the State Board of Architects finds that the installation of such facilities would destroy the architectural integrity of the building.

The Red County Courthouse in the state of Blue was built in 1895 and is still in use. It does not contain ramps or other special facilities for handicapped people. The State Board of Architects has determined that the installation of those facilities would destroy the architectural integrity of the building. Nevertheless, the County Board of Red County applies for a federal grant to restore and preserve that county's courthouse.

If the County Board of Red County restores the Red County Courthouse with the aid of a federal restoration and preservation grant, is the board bound to install ramps and other facilities for handicapped people in that building?

(A) Yes, because Congress may impose reasonable conditions related to the public welfare on grants of federal funds to public bodies when the public bodies are free to accept or reject the grants.

(B) Yes, because the rights of handicapped and disabled people are fundamental rights that take precedence, as a constitutional matter, over considerations of architectural integrity.

(C) No, because the Constitution does not authorize the federal government to direct the actions of the states or any of their political subdivisions with respect to matters affecting their own governmental buildings.

(D) No, because any acceptance of this condition by the Red County Board of Supervisors would, as a matter of law, be considered to be under duress.

58. Arnold decided to destroy an old warehouse that he owned because the taxes on the structure exceeded the income that he could receive from it. He crept into the building in the middle of the night with a can of gasoline and a fuse and set the fuse timer for 30 minutes. He then left the building. The fuse failed to ignite, and the building was not harmed.

Arson is defined in this jurisdiction as "The intentional burning of any building or structure of another, without the consent of the owner." Arnold believed, however, that burning one's own building was arson, having been so advised by his lawyer.

Has Arnold committed attempted arson?

(A) Yes, because factual impossibility is no defense.

(B) Yes, because a mistake of law even on the advice of an attorney is no defense.

(C) No, because his mistake negated a necessary mental state.

(D) No, because even if his actions had every consequence he intended, they would not have constituted arson.

59. "Look-alike drugs" is the term used to describe nonprescription drugs that took like narcotic drugs and are sold on the streets as narcotic drugs. After extensive hearings, Congress concluded that the sale of look-alike-drugs was widespread in this country and was creating severe health and law enforcement problems. To combat these problems, Congress enacted a comprehensive statute that regulates the manufacture, distribution, and sale of all nonprescription drugs in the United States.

Which of the following sources of constitutional authority can most easily be used to justify the authority of Congress to enact this statute?

(A)   The spending power.
(B)   The commerce clause.
(C)   The general welfare clause.
(D)   The enforcement powers of the Fourteenth Amendment.

60. After several well-publicized deaths caused by fires in products made from highly flammable fabrics, the state of Orange enacted a statute prohibiting "the manufacture or assembly of any product in this state which contains any fabric that has not been tested and approved for flame retardancy by the Zetest Testing Company." The Zetest Testing Company is a privately owned and operated business located in Orange.

For many years, Fabric Mill, located in the state of Orange, has had its fabric tested for flame retardancy by the Alpha Testing Company, located in the state of Green. Alpha Testing Company is a reliable organization that uses a process for testing and approving fabrics for flame retardancy identical in all respects to that used by the Zetest Testing Company.

Because Fabric Mill wishes to continue to have its fabric tested solely by Alpha Testing Company, Fabric Mill files an action in Orange state court challenging the constitutionality of the Orange statute as applied to its circumstances.

In this suit, the court should hold the statute to be

(A)   constitutional, because it is reasonably related to the protection of the reputation of the fabric industry located in the state of Orange.
(B)   constitutional, because it is a legitimate means of protecting the safety of the public.
(C)   unconstitutional, because it denies to Fabric Mill the equal protection of the laws.
(D)   unconstitutional, because it imposes an unreasonable burden on interstate commerce.

61. Peter and Donald were in the habit of playing practical jokes on each other on their respective birthdays. On Peter's birthday, Donald sent Peter a cake containing an ingredient that he knew had, in the past, made Peter very ill. After Peter had eaten a piece of the cake, he suffered severe stomach pains and had to be taken to the hospital by ambulance. On the way to the hospital, the ambulance driver suffered a heart attack, which caused the ambulance to swerve from the road and hit a tree. As a result of the collision, Peter suffered a broken leg.

In a suit by Peter against Donald to recover damages for Peter's broken leg, Peter will

(A)   prevail, because Donald knew that the cake would be harmful or offensive to Peter.

(B)   prevail, only if the ambulance driver was negligent.

(C)   not prevail, because Donald could not reasonably be expected to foresee injury to Peter's leg.

(D)   not prevail, because the ambulance driver's heart attack was a superseding cause of Peter's broken leg.

62. Decker, charged with armed robbery of a store, denied that he was the person who had robbed the store, In presenting the state's case, the prosecutor seeks to introduce evidence that Decker had robbed two other stores in the past year.

This evidence is

(A)   admissible, to prove a pertinent trait of Decker's character and Decker's action in conformity therewith.

(B)   admissible, to prove Decker's intent and identity.

(C)   inadmissible, because character must be proved by reputation or opinion and may not be proved by specific acts.

(D)   inadmissible, because its probative value is substantially outweighed by the danger of unfair prejudice.

63. Twenty-five years ago, Seller conveyed Blackacre to Buyer by a warranty deed. Seller at that time also executed and delivered an instrument in the proper form of a deed purporting to convey Whiteacre to Buyer. Seller thought she had title to Whiteacre but did not; therefore, no title passed by virtue of the Whiteacre deed. Whiteacre consisted of three acres of brushland adjoining the west boundary of Blackacre. Buyer has occasionally hunted rabbits on Whiteacre, but less often than annually. No one else came on Whiteacre except occasional rabbit hunters.

Twenty years ago, Buyer planted a row of evergreens in the vicinity of the opposite (east) boundary of Blackacre and erected a fence just beyond the evergreens to the east. In fact both the trees and the fence were placed on Greenacre, owned by Neighbor, which bordered the east boundary of Blackacre. Buyer was unsure of the exact boundary, and placed the trees and the fence in order to establish his rights up to the fence. The fence is located ten feet within Greenacre.

Now, Buyer has had his property surveyed and the title checked and has learned the facts.

The period of time to acquire title by adverse possession in the jurisdiction is 15 years.

Buyer consulted his lawyer, who properly advised that, in an appropriate action, Buyer would probably obtain title to

(A) Whiteacre but not to the ten-foot strip of Greenacre.
(B) the ten-foot strip of Greenacre but not to Whiteacre.
(C) both Whiteacre and the ten-foot strip of Greenacre.
(D) neither Whiteacre nor the ten-foot strip of Greenacre.

Questions 64-65 are based on the following fact situation.

Elda, the aged mother of Alice and Barry, both adults, wished to employ a live-in companion so that she might continue to live in her own home. Elda, however, had only enough income to pay one-half of the companion's $2,000 monthly salary. Learning of their mother's plight, Alice and Barry agreed with each other in a signed writing that on the last day of January and each succeeding month during their mother's lifetime, each would give Elda $500. Elda then hired the companion.

Alice and Barry made the agreed payments in January, February, and March. In April, however, Barry refused to make any payment and notified Alice and Elda that he would make no further payments.

64. Will Elda succeed in an action for $500 brought against Barry after April 30?

(A) Yes, because by making his first three payments, Barry confirmed his intent to contract.
(B) Yes, because Elda is an intended beneficiary of a contract between Alice and Barry.
(C) No, because a parent cannot sue her child for breach of a promise for support.
(D) No, because Alice and Barry intended their payments to Elda to be gifts.

65. For this question only, assume that there is a valid contract between Alice and Barry and that Elda has declined to sue Barry.

Will Alice succeed in an action against Barry in which she asks the court to order Barry to continue to make his payments to Elda under the terms of the Alice-Barry contract?

(A) Yes, because Alice's remedy at law is inadequate.
(B) Yes, because Alice's burden of supporting her mother will be increased if Barry does not contribute his share.
(C) No, because a court will not grant specific performance of a promise to pay money.
(D) No, because Barry's breach of contract has caused no economic harm to Alice.

66. Mom owned Blackacre, a two-family apartment house on a small city lot not suitable for partition-in-kind.

Upon Mom's death, her will devised Blackacre to "my sons, Joe and John."

A week ago, Ken obtained a money judgment against Joe, and properly filed the judgment in the county where Blackacre is located. A statute in the jurisdictions provides: any judgment properly filed shall, for ten years from filing, be a lien on the real property then owned or subsequently acquired by any person against whom the judgment is rendered.

Joe needed cash, but John did not wish to sell Blackacre. Joe commenced a partition action against John and Ken.

Assume that the court properly ordered a partition by judicial sale.

After the sale, Ken's judgment will be a lien on

(A)   all of Blackacre.
(B)   only a one-half interest in Blackacre.
(C)   all of the proceeds of sale of Blackacre.
(D)   only the portion of the proceeds of sale due Joe.

67. Suspecting that Scott had slain his wife, police detectives persuaded one of Scott's employees to remove a drinking glass from Scott's office so that it could be used for fingerprint comparisons with a knife found near the body. The fingerprints matched. The prosecutor announced that he would present comparisons and evidence to the grand jury. Scott's lawyer immediately filed a motion to suppress the evidence of the fingerprint comparisons to bar its consideration by the grand jury, contending that the evidence was illegally acquired.

The motion should be

(A)   granted, because, if there was no probable cause, the grand jury should not consider the evidence.
(B)   granted, because the employee was acting as a police agent and his seizure of the glass without a warrant was unconstitutional.
(C)   denied, because motions based on the exclusionary rule are premature in grand jury proceedings.
(D)   denied, because the glass was removed from Scott's possession by a private citizen and not a police officer.

Questions 68–70 are based on the following fact situation.

Dora, who was eight years old, went to the grocery store with her mother. Dora pushed the grocery cart while her mother put items into it. Dora's mother remained near Dora at all times. Peterson, another customer in the store, noticed Dora pushing the cart in a manner that caused Peterson no concern.

A short time later, the cart Dora was pushing struck Peterson in the knee, inflicting serious injury.

68. If Peterson brings an action, based on negligence, against the grocery store, the store's best defense will be that

(A) a store owes no duty to its customers to control the use of its shopping carts.

(B) a store owes no duty to its customers to control the conduct of other customers.

(C) any negligence of the store was not the proximate cause of Peterson's injury.

(D) a supervised child pushing a cart does not pose an unreasonable risk to other customers.

69. If Peterson brings an action, based on negligence, against Dora's mother, will Peterson prevail?

(A) Yes, if Dora was negligent.

(B) Yes, because Dora's mother is responsible for any harm caused by Dora.

(C) Yes, because Dora's mother assumed the risk of her child's actions.

(D) Yes, if Dora's mother did not adequately supervise Dora's actions.

70. If Peterson brings an action, based on negligence, against Dora, Dora's best argument in defense would be that

(A) Dora exercised care commensurate with her age, intelligence, and experience

(B) Dora is not subject to tort liability

(C) Dora was subject to parental supervision.

(D) Peterson assumed the risk that Dora might hit Peterson with the cart.

71. Adam entered into a valid written contract to sell Blackacre, a large tract of land, to Betsy. At that time, Blackacre was owned by Adam's father, Fred; Adam had no title to Blackacre and was not the agent of Fred.

After the contract was executed and before the scheduled closing date, Fred died intestate leaving Adam as his sole heir. Shortly thereafter, Adam received an offer for Blackacre that was substantially higher than the purchase price in the contract with Betsy.

Adam refused to close with Betsy although she was ready, willing, and able to close pursuant to the contract.

Betsy brought an appropriate action for specific performance against Adam.

In that action, Betsy should be awarded

(A)   nothing, because Adam had no authority to enter into the contract with Betsy.

(B)   nothing, because the doctrine of afteracquired title does not apply to executory contracts.

(C)   judgment for specific performance, because Adam acquired title prior to the scheduled closing.

(D)   judgment for specific performance, to prevent unjust enrichment of Adam.

72. Dayton operates a collection agency. He was trying to collect a $400 bill for medical services rendered to Pratt by Doctor.

Dayton went to Pratt's house and when Martina, Pratt's mother, answered the door, Dayton told Martina he was there to collect a bill owed by Pratt. Martina told Dayton that because of her illness, Pratt had been unemployed for six months, that she was still ill and unable to work, and that she would pay the bill as soon as she could. Dayton, in a loud voice, demanded to see Pratt and said that if he did not receive payment immediately, he would file a criminal complaint charging her with fraud. Pratt, hearing the conversation, came to the door. Dayton, in a loud voice, repeated his demand for immediate payment and his threat to use criminal process.

If Pratt asserts a claim against Dayton, based on infliction of emotional distress, will Pratt Prevail?

(A)   Yes, if Pratt suffered severe emotional distress as a result of Dayton's conduct.

(B)   Yes, unless the bill for medical services was valid and past due.

(C)   No, unless Pratt suffered physical harm as a result of Dayton's conduct.

(D)   No, if Dayton's conduct created no risk of physical harm to Pratt.

73. Public schools in the state of Green are financed in large part, by revenue derived from real estate taxes imposed by each school district on the taxable real property located in that district. Public schools also receive other revenue from private gifts, federal grants, student fees, and local sales taxes.

For many years, Green has distributed additional funds, which come from the state treasury to local school districts in order to equalize the funds available on a per-student basis for each public school district. These additional funds are distributed on the basis of a state statutory formula that considers only the number of students in each public school district and the real estate tax revenue raised by that district. The formula does not consider other revenue received by a school district from different sources.

The school boards of two school districts, together with parents and schoolchildren in those districts, bring suit in federal court to enjoin the state from allocating the additional funds from the state treasury to individual districts pursuant to this formula. They allege that the failure of the state, in allocating this additional money, to take into account a school district's sources of revenue other than revenue derived from taxes levied on real estate located there violates the equal protection clause of the Fourteenth Amendment. The complaint does not allege that the allocation of the additional state funds based on the current statutory formula has resulted in a failure to provide minimally adequate education to any child.

Which of the following best describes the appropriate standard by which the court should review the constitutionality of the state statutory funding formula?

(A)   Because classifications based on wealth are inherently suspect, the state must demonstrate that the statutory formula is necessary to vindicate a compelling state interest.

(B)   Because the statutory funding formula burdens the fundamental right to education, the state must demonstrate that the formula is necessary to vindicate a compelling state interest.

(C)   Because no fundamental right or suspect classification is implicated in this case, the plaintiffs must demonstrate that the funding allocation formula bears no rational relationship to any legitimate state interest.

(D)   Because the funding formula inevitably leads to disparities among the school districts in their levels of total funding, the plaintiffs must only demonstrate that the funding formula is not substantially related to the furtherance of an important state interest.

74. A car driven by Dan entered land owned by and in the possession of Peter, without Peter's permission.

Which, if any, of the following allegations, without additional facts, would provide a sufficient basis for a claim by Peter against Dan?

I. Dan intentionally drove his car onto Peter's land.
II. Dan negligently drove his car onto Peter's land.
III. Dan's car damaged Peter's land.

(A)   I only.
(B)   III only.
(C)   I, II, or III
(D)   Neither I, II, nor III.

75. In which of the following cases is Morrow most likely to be convicted if she is charged with receiving stolen property?

(A)   Morrow bought a car from Aster, who operates a used car lot. Before the purchase, Aster told Morrow that the car had been stolen, which was true. Unknown to Morrow, Aster is an undercover police agent who is operating the lot in cooperation with the police in exchange for leniency in connection with criminal charges pending against him.

(B)   Morrow bought a car from Ball. Before the purchase, Ball told Morrow that the car was stolen. Ball had stolen the car with the help of Eames, who, unknown to Morrow or Ball, was an undercover police agent who feigned cooperation with Ball in the theft of the car.

(C)   Morrow bought a car from Cooper. Before the purchase, Cooper told Morrow that the car was stolen. Unknown to Morrow, Cooper had stolen the car from a parking lot and had been caught by the police as he was driving it away. He agreed to cooperate with the police and carry through with his prearranged sale of the car to Morrow.

(D)   Morrow bought a car from Dixon. Before the purchase, Dixon told Morrow that the car was stolen. Unknown to Morrow, Dixon was in fact the owner of the car but had reported it to the police as stolen and had collected on a fraudulent claim of its theft from his insurance company.

76. Barrel, a retailer of guns in State X, U.S.A., received on June 1 the following signed letter from Slidebolt, a gun wholesaler in another state: "We have just obtained 100 of the assault rifles you inquired about and can supply them for $250 each. We can guarantee shipment no later than August 1."

On June 10, Slidebolt sold and delivered the same rifles to another merchant for $300 each. Unaware of that transaction, Barrel on the morning of June 11 mailed Slidebolt a letter rejecting the latter's offer, but, changing his mind an hour later, retrieved from his local post office the letter of rejection and immediately dispatched to Slidebolt a letter of acceptance, which Slidebolt received on June 14.

On June 9, a valid federal statute making the interstate sale of assault rifles punishable as a crime had become effective, but neither Barrel nor Slidebolt was aware until June 15 that the statute was already in effect.

As between Barrel and Slidebolt, which of the following is an accurate statement?

(A)   No contract was formed, because Slidebolt's June 10 sale of the rifles to another merchant revoked the offer to Barrel.

(B)   If a contract was formed, it is voidable because of mutual mistake.

(C)   If a contract was formed, it is unenforceable because of supervening impracticability.

(D)   No contract was formed because Barrel's June 11 rejection was effective on dispatch.

77. Palmco owns and operates a beachfront hotel. Under a contract with City to restore a public beach, Dredgeco placed a large and unavoidably dangerous stonecrushing machine on City land near Palmco's hotel. The machine creates a continuous and intense noise that is so disturbing to the hotel guests that they have canceled their hotel reservations in large numbers, resulting in a substantial loss to Palmco.

Palmco's best chance to recover damages for its financial losses from Dredgeco is under the theory that the operation of the stone-crushing machine constitute

(A)   an abnormally dangerous activity.

(B)   a private nuisance.

(C)   negligence.

(D)   a trespass.

78. The constitution of State X authorizes a five-member state reapportionment board to redraw state legislative districts every ten years. In the last state legislative reapportionment, the board, by a unanimous vote, divided the greater Green metropolitan area, composed of Green City and several contiguous townships, into three equally populated state legislative districts.

The result of that districting was that 40% of the area's total black population resided in one of those districts, 45% of the area's total black population resided in the second of those districts, and 15% resided in the third district.

Jones is black, is a registered voter, and is a resident of Green City. Jones brings suit in an appropriate court against the members of the state reapportionment board, seeking declaratory and injunctive relief that would require the boundary lines of the state legislative districts in the greater Green metropolitan area to be redrawn. His only claim is that the current apportionment violates the Fifteenth Amendment and the equal protection clause of the Fourteenth Amendment because it improperly dilutes the voting power of the blacks who reside in that area.

If no federal statute is applicable, which of the following facts, if proven, would most strongly support the validity of the action of the state reapportionment board?

(A)　　In drawing the current district lines, the reapportionment board precisely complied with state constitutional requirements that state legislative districts be compact and follow political subdivision boundaries to the maximum extent feasible.

(B)　　The reapportionment board was composed of three white members and two black members and both of the board's black members were satisfied that its plan did not improperly dilute the voting power of the blacks who reside in that area.

(C)　　Although the rate of voter registration among blacks is below that of voter registration among whites in the greater Green metropolitan area, two black legislators have been elected from that area during the last 15 years.

(D)　　The total black population of the greater Green metropolitan area amounts to only 15% of the population that is required to comprise a single legislative district.

79. Paulsen Corporation sued Dorr for ten fuel oil deliveries not paid for. Dorr denied that the deliveries were made. At trial Paulsen calls its office manager, Wicks, to testify that Paulsen employees always record each delivery in duplicate, give one copy to the customer, and place the other copy in Paulsen's files; that he (Wicks) is the custodian of those files; and that his examination of the files before coming to court revealed that the ten deliveries were made. Wicks's testimony that the invoices show ten deliveries is

(A)　　admissible, because it is based on regularly kept business records.

(B)　　admissible, because Wicks has first-hand knowledge of the contents of the records.

(C)　　inadmissible, because the records must be produced in order to prove their contents.

(D)　　inadmissible, because the records are self-serving.

80. Dan entered the police station and announced that he wanted to confess to a murder. The police advised Dan of the Miranda warnings, and Dan signed a written waiver. Dan described the murder in detail and pinpointed the location where a murder victim had been found a few weeks before. Later, a court-appointed psychiatrist determined that Dan was suffering from a serious mental illness that interfered with his ability to make rational choices and to understand his rights and that the psychosis had induced his confession.

Dan's confession is

(A)　　admissible, because there was no coercive police conduct in obtaining Dan's statement.

(B)　　admissible, because Dan was not in custody.

(C)   inadmissible, because Dan's confession was a product of his mental illness and was therefore involuntary.

(D)   inadmissible, because under these circumstances, there was no valid waiver of Miranda warnings.

81. Leaseco owned Blackacre, a tract of 100 acres. Six years ago, Leaseco leased a one-acre parcel, Oneacre, located in the northeasterly corner of Blackacre, for a term of 30 years, to Eatco. Eatco intended to and did construct a fast-food restaurant on Oneacre.

The lease provided that:

1. Eatco was to maintain Oneacre and improvements thereon, to maintain full insurance coverage on Oneacre, and to pay all taxes assessed against Oneacre.

2. Leaseco was to maintain the access roads and the parking lot areas platted on those portions of Blackacre that adjoined Oneacre and to permit the customers of Eatco to use them in common with the customers of the other commercial users of the remainder of Blackacre.

3. Eatco was to pay its share of the expenses for the off-site improvements according to a stated formula.

Five years ago, Leaseco sold Oneacre to Jones, an investor; the conveyance was made subject to the lease to Eatco. However, Jones did not assume the obligations of the lease and Leaseco retained the remainder of Blackacre. Since that conveyance five years ago, Eatco has paid rent to Jones.

Eatco refused to pay its formula share of the offsite improvement costs as provided in the lease. Leaseco brought an appropriate action against Eatco to recover such costs.

The most likely outcome would be in favor of

(A)   Leaseco, because the use of the improvements by the customers of Eatco imposes an implied obligation on Eatco.

(B)   Leaseco, because the conveyance of Oneacre to Jones did not terminate Eatco's covenant to contribute.

(C)   Eatco, because the conveyance of Oneacre to Jones terminated the privity of estate between Leaseco and Eatco.

(D)   Eatco, because Jones, as Eatco's landlord, has the obligation to pay the maintenance costs by necessary implication.

82. While Patty was riding her horse on what she thought was a public park the owner of a house next to the path approached her, shaking a stick and shouting, "Get off my property." Unknown to Patty, the path on which she was riding crossed the private property of the shouting owner.

When Patty explained that she thought the path was a public trail, the man cursed her, approached Patty's horse, and struck the horse with the stick. As a result of the blow, the horse reared, causing Patty to fear that she would fall. However, Patty managed to stay on the horse, and then departed. Neither Patty nor the horse suffered bodily harm.

If Patty brings an action for damages against the property owner, the result should be for

(A) Patty, for trespass to her chattel property.
(B) Patty, for battery and assault.
(C) the defendant, because Patty suffered no physical harm.
(D) the defendant, because he was privileged to exclude trespassers from his property.

83. Five years ago, Sally acquired Blackacre, improved with a 15-year-old dwelling. This year Sally listed Blackacre for sale with Bill, a licensed real estate broker. Sally informed Bill of several defects in the house that were not readily discoverable by a reasonable inspection, including a leaky basement, an inadequate water supply, and a roof that leaked. Paul responded to Bill's advertisement, was taken by Bill to view Blackacre, and decided to buy it. Bill saw to it that the contract specified the property to be "as is" but neither Bill nor Sally pointed out the defects to Paul, who did not ask

about the condition of the dwelling.

After closing and taking possession, Paul discovered the defects, had them repaired, and demanded that Sally reimburse him for the cost of the repairs. Sally refused and Paul brought an appropriate action against Sally for damages.

If Sally wins, it will be because

(A) Sally fulfilled the duty to disclose defects by disclosure to Bill.
(B) the contract's "as is" provision controls the rights of the parties.
(C) Bill became the agent of both Paul and Sally and thus knowledge of the defects was imputed to Paul.
(D) the seller of a used dwelling that has been viewed by the buyer has no responsibility toward the buyer.

84. In which of the following situations would a court applying common-law doctrine be most likely to convict Defendant of the crime charged, despite Defendant's mistake?

(A) Defendant was charged with bigamy. He married his neighbor four years after her husband was reported missing at sea. The rescued husband returns alive.

A state statute provides that a person is presumed dead after five years of unexplained absence. Defendant believed the statutory period was three years.

(B)   Defendant was charged with murder after he shot and killed a man who had extorted money from him. Defendant mistakenly thought the victim had raised his hand to shoot, when, in fact, the victim was shaking his fist at Defendant to frighten him.

(C)   Defendant was charged with assault with intent to rape a woman who he mistakenly believed had agreed to have sexual intercourse with him.

(D)   Defendant was charged with burglary. He had broken into an office where he once worked and had taken a typewriter that he erroneously believed had been given to him before he was fired.

Questions 85-86 are based on the following fact situation.

Spender owed Midas $1,000, plus interest at 8% until paid, on a long-overdue promissory note, collection of which would become barred by the statute of limitations on June 30. On the preceding April 1, Spender and Midas both signed a writing in which Spender promised to pay the note in full on the following December 31, plus interest at 8% until that date, and Midas promised not to sue on the note in the meantime. Midas, having received some advice from his nonlawyer brother-in-law, became concerned about the legal effect of the April 1 agreement.

On May 1, acting pro se as permitted by the rules of the local small claims court, he filed suit to collect the note.

85. Assuming that there is no controlling statute, is the April 1 agreement an effective defense for Spender?

(A)   Yes, because Spender's promise to pay interest until December 31 was consideration for Midas's promise not to sue.

(B)   Yes, because the law creates a presumption that Spender relied on Midas's promise not to sue.

(C)   No, because there was no consideration for Midas's promise not to sue, in that Spender was already obligated to pay $1,000 plus interest at 8% until the payment date.

(D)   No, because Spender's April 1 promise is enforceable with or without consideration.

86. For this question only, assume that on January 2 of the following year Midas's suit has not come to trial, Spender has not paid the note, Midas has retained a lawyer, and the lawyer, with leave of court, amends the complaint to add a second count to enforce the promise Spender made in the April 1 agreement.

Does the new count state a claim upon which relief can be granted?

(A) Yes, because Spender's failure to pay the note, plus interest, on December 31 makes Midas's breach of promise not to sue before that date no longer material.

(B) Yes, because Spender's April 1 promise is enforceable by reason of his moral obligation to pay the debt.

(C) No, because such relief would undermine the policy of the statute of limitations against enforcement of stale claims.

(D) No, because Spender's April 1 promise was lawfully conditioned upon Midas's forbearing to sue prior to December 31.

87. Which of the following acts by the United States Senate would be constitutionally IMPROPER?

(A) The Senate decides, with the House of Representatives, that a disputed state ratification of a proposed constitutional amendment is valid.

(B) The Senate determines the eligibility of a person to serve as a senator.

(C) The Senate appoints a commission to adjudicate finally a boundary dispute between two states.

(D) The Senate passes a resolution calling on the President to pursue a certain foreign policy.

88. While driving his car, Plaintiff sustained injuries in a three-car collision. Plaintiff sued the drivers of the other two cars, D-1 and D-2, and each defendant crossclaimed against the other for contribution. The jurisdiction has adopted a rule of pure comparative negligence and allows contribution based upon proportionate fault. The rule of joint and several liability has been retained.

40 v. 30 + 30

The jury has found that Plaintiff sustained damages in the amount of $100,000, and apportioned the causal negligence of the parties as follows: Plaintiff 40%, D-1 30%, and D-2 30%.

How much, if anything, can Plaintiff collect from D-1, and how much, if anything, can D-1 then collect from D-2 in contribution?

(A) Nothing, and then D-1 can collect nothing from D-2.

(B) $30,000, and then D-1 can collect nothing from D-2.

(C) $40,000, and then D-1 can collect $10,000 from D-2.

(D) $60,000, and then D-1 can collect $30,000 from D-2.

89. Pater and his adult daughter, Carmen, encountered Tertius, an old family friend, on the street. Carmen said to Tertius, "How about lending me $1,000 to buy a used car? I'll pay you back with interest one year from today."

Pater added, "And if she doesn't pay it back as promised, I will." Tertius thereupon wrote out and handed to Carmen his personal check, payable to her, for $1,000, and Carmen subsequently used the funds to buy a used car. When the debt became due, both Carmen and Pater refused to repay it, or any part of it.

In an action by Tertius against Pater to recover $1,000 plus interest, which of the following statements would summarize Pater's best defense?

(A)   He received no consideration for his conditional promise to Tertius.
(B)   His conditional promise to Tertius was not to be performed in less than a year from the time it was made.
(C)   His conditional promise to Tertius was not made for the primary purpose of benefiting himself (Pater).
(D)   The loan by Tertius was made without any agreement concerning the applicable interest rate.

90. Hal and Wan owned Blackacre as joint tenants, upon which was situated a two-family house. Hal lived in one of the two apartments and rented the other apartment to Tent. Hal got in a fight with Tent and injured him. Tent obtained and properly filed a judgment for $10,000 against Hal.

H. W
(H)   T

The statute in the jurisdiction reads: Any judgment properly filed shall, for ten years from filing, be a lien on the real property then owned or subsequently acquired by any person against whom the judgment is rendered.

Wan, who lived in a distant city, knew nothing of Tent's judgment. Before Tent took any further action, Hal died. The common-law joint tenancy is unmodified by statute.

Wan then learned the facts and brought an appropriate action against Tent to quiet title to Blackacre.

The court should hold that Tent has

(A)   a lien against the whole of Blackacre, because he was a tenant of both Hal and Wan at the time of the judgment.
(B)   a lien against Hal's undivided one-half interest in Blackacre, because his judgment was filed prior to Hal's death.
(C)   no lien, because Wan had no actual notice of Tent's judgment until after Hal's death.
(D)   no lien, because Hal's death terminated the interest to which Tent's lien attached.

91. In litigation on a federal claim, Plaintiff had the burden of proving that Defendant received a notice.

Plaintiff relied on the presumption of receipt by offering evidence that the notice was addressed to Defendant, properly stamped, and mailed. Defendant, on the other hand, testified that she never received the notice.

Which of the following is correct?

(A)   The jury must find that the notice was received.
(B)   The jury may find that the notice was received.
(C)   The burden shifts to Defendant to persuade the jury of nonreceipt.
(D)   The jury must find that the notice was not received, because the presumption has been rebutted and there is uncontradicted evidence of nonreceipt.

92. In a medical malpractice suit by Payne against Dr. Dock, Payne seeks to introduce a properly authenticated photocopy of Payne's hospital chart. The chart contained a notation made by a medical resident that an aortic clamp had broken during Payne's surgery. The resident made the notation in the regular course of practice, but had no personal knowledge of the operation, and cannot remember which of the operating physicians gave him the information.
The document is

(A)   admissible as a record of regularly conducted activity.
(B)   admissible as recorded recollection.

(C)   inadmissible as a violation of the best evidence rule.
(D)   inadmissible, because it is hearsay within hearsay.

93. Parr sued Davis for damages for physical injuries allegedly caused by Davis's violation of the federal civil rights law. The incident occurred wholly within the state of Chippewa but the case was tried in federal court. The Chippewa state code says, "The common-law privileges are preserved intact in this state."

At trial, Davis called Dr. Webb, Parr's physician, to testify to confidential statements made to him by Parr in furtherance of medical treatment for the injuries allegedly caused by Davis. Parr objects, claiming a physician-patient privilege.

The court should apply

(A)   state law and recognize the claim of privilege.
(B)   federal law and recognize the claim of privilege.
(C)   state law and reject the claim of privilege.
(D)   federal law and reject the claim of privilege.

P v. D
Dr. w

94. Kathy, a two-year-old, became ill with meningitis. Jim and Joan, her parents, were members of a group that believed fervently that if they prayed enough, God would not permit their child to die. Accordingly, they did not seek medical aid for Kathy and refused all offers of such aid. They prayed continuously. Kathy died of the illness within a week.

Jim and Joan are charged with murder in a common-law jurisdiction.

Their best defense to the charge is that

(A) they did not intend to kill or to harm Kathy.
(B) they were pursuing a constitutionally protected religious belief.
(C) Kathy's death was not proximately caused by their conduct.
(D) they neither premeditated nor deliberated.

95. In a prosecution of Dahle for assault, Wharton is called to testify that the victim, Valerian, had complained to Wharton that Dahle was the assailant.

Wharton's testimony is most likely to be admitted if Wharton is

(A) a doctor, whom Valerian consulted for treatment.
(B) a minister, whom Valerian consulted for counseling.

State v. D

(C) Valerian's husband, whom she telephoned immediately after the event.
(D) a police officer, whom Valerian called on instructions from her husband.

Questions 96-97 are based on the following fact situation.

Betty Bower, an adult, asked Jeff Geetus to lend her $ 1,000. Geetus replied that he would do so only if Bower's father, Cash, would guarantee the loan. At Bower's request, Cash mailed a signed letter to Geetus: "If you send $1,000 to my daughter, I will repay it if she doesn't." On September 15, Geetus, having read Cash's letter, lent $1,000 to Bower, which Bower agreed to repay in installments of $100 plus accrued interest on the last day of each month beginning October 31. Cash dies on September 16. Later that same day, unaware of Cash's death Geetus mailed a letter to Cash advising that he had made the $1,000 loan to Bower on September 15.

Bower did not pay the installments due on October 31, November 30, or December 31, and has informed Geetus that she will be unable to make repayments in the foreseeable future.

96. On January 15, Geetus is entitled to a judgment against Bower for which of the following amounts?

(A)   Nothing, because if he sues before the entire amount is due, he will be splitting his cause of action.

(B) $300 plus the accrued interest, because Bower's breach is only a partial breach.

(C) $1,000 plus the accrued interest, because Bower's unexcused failure to pay three installments is a material breach

(D) $1,000 plus the accrued interest, because the failure to pay her debts as they come due indicates that Bower is insolvent and Geetus is thereby entitled to accelerate payment of the debt.

97. For this question only, assume that Bower's entire debt is due and that she has failed to repay any part of it.

In an action by Geetus against Cash's estate for $1,000 plus accrued interest, which of the following, if any, will serve as (an) effective defense(s) for Cash's estate?

I. There was no consideration to support Cash's promise, because he did not receive any benefit.
II. Cash died before Geetus accepted his offer.
III. Cash died before Geetus notified him that his offer had been accepted.

(A)   I only.

(B)   II only.
(C)   I and III only.
(D)   Neither I nor II nor III.

98. At Darrow's trial for stealing an automobile, Darrow called a character witness, Goode, who testified that Darrow had an excellent reputation for honesty. In rebuttal, the prosecutor calls Wick to testify that he recently saw Darrow cheat on a college examination.

This evidence should be

(A)   admitted, because Darrow has "opened the door" to the prosecutor's proof of character evidence.
(B)   admitted, because the cheating involves "dishonesty or false statement."
(C)   excluded, because it has no probative value on any issue in the case.
(D)   excluded, because Darrow's cheating can be inquired into only on cross-examination of Goode.

99. The Federal Family Film Enhancement Act assesses an excise tax of 10% on the price of admission to public movie theaters when they show films that contain actual or simulated scenes of human sexual intercourse.

Which of the following is the strongest argument against the constitutionality of this federal act?

(A)   The act imposes a prior restraint on the freedom of speech protected by the First Amendment.

(B)   The act is not rationally related to any legitimate national interest.

(C.)   The act violates the equal protection concepts embodied in the due process clause of the Fifth Amendment because it imposes a tax on the price of admission to view certain films and not on the price of admission to view comparable live performances.

(D)   The act imposes a tax solely on the basis of the content of speech without adequate justification and, therefore, it is prohibited by the freedom of speech clause of the First Amendment.

100.   Desmond fell while attempting to climb a mountain, and lay unconscious and critically injured on a ledge that was difficult to reach. Pearson, an experienced mountain climber, was himself seriously injured while trying to rescue Desmond. Pearson's rescue attempt failed, and Desmond died of his injuries before he could be reached.

Pearson brought an action against Desmond's estate for compensation for his injuries. In this jurisdiction, the traditional common-law rules relating to contributory negligence and assumption of risk remain in effect.

Will Pearson prevail in his action against Desmond's estate?

(A)   Yes, if his rescue attempt was reasonable

(B)   Yes, because the law should not discourage attempts to assist persons in helpless peril.

(C)   No, unless Desmond's peril arose from his own failure to exercise reasonable care.

(D)   No, because Pearson's rescue attempt failed and therefore did not benefit Desmond.

STOP

IF YOU FINISH BEFORE TIME IS CALLED, CHECK YOUR WORK ON THIS TEST

101. At a party for coworkers at Defendant's home, Victim accused Defendant of making advances toward his wife. Victim and his wife left the party. The next day at work, Defendant saw Victim and struck him on the head with a soft drink bottle, Victim fell into a coma and died two weeks after the incident.

This jurisdiction defines aggravated assault as an assault with any weapon or dangerous implement and punishes it as a felony. It defines murder as the unlawful killing of a person with malice aforethought or in the course of an independent felony.

Defendant may be found guilty of murder

(A)   only if the jury finds that Defendant intended to kill Victim.
 (B)   only if the jury finds that Defendant did not act in a rage provoked by Victim's accusations.
(C)   if the jury finds that Defendant intended either to kill or to inflict serious bodily harm.
(D)   if the jury finds that the killing occurred in the course of an aggravated assault.

102. As a result of an accident at the NPP nuclear power plant, a quantity of radioactive vapor escaped from the facility and two members of the public were exposed to excessive doses of radiation. According to qualified medical opinion, that exposure will double the chance that these two persons will ultimately develop cancer. However, any cancer that might be caused by this exposure will not be detectable for at least ten years. If the two exposed persons do develop cancer, it will not be possible to determine whether it was caused by this exposure or would have developed in any event.

If the exposed persons assert a claim for damages against NPP shortly after the escape of the radiation, which of the following questions will NOT present a substantial issue?

(A)   Will the court recognize that the plaintiffs have suffered a present legal injury?
(B)   Can the plaintiffs prove the amount of their damages?
(C)   Can the plaintiffs prove that any harm they may suffer was caused by this exposure?
(D)   Can the plaintiffs prevail without presenting evidence of specific negligence on the part of NPP?

103. A city ordinance makes the city building inspector responsible for ensuring that all buildings in that city are kept up to building code standards, and requires the inspector to refer for prosecution all known building code violations.

Another ordinance provides that the city building inspector may be discharged for "good cause." The building inspector took a newspaper reporter through a number of run-down buildings in a slum neighborhood. After using various epithets and slurs to describe the occupants of these buildings, the building inspector stated to the reporter: "I do not even try to get these buildings up to code or to have their owners prosecuted for code violations because if these buildings are repaired, the people who live in them will just wreck them again." The reporter published these statements in a story in the local newspaper. The building inspector admitted he made the statements.

On the basis of these statements, the city council discharged the building inspector.
Is the action of the city council constitutional?

(A)   Yes, because the statements demonstrate that the building inspector has an attitude toward a certain class of persons that interferes with the proper performance of the obligations of his job.

(B)   Yes, because the building inspector is a government employee and a person holding such a position may not make public comments inconsistent with current governmental policy.

(C)   No, because the statements were lawful comments on a matter of public concern.

(D)   No, because the statements were published in a newspaper that is protected by the First and Fourteenth Amendments.

104. In preparation for a mountain-climbing expedition, Alper purchased the necessary climbing equipment from Outfitters, Inc., a retail dealer in sporting goods. A week later, Alper fell from a rock face when a safety device he had purchased from Outfitters malfunctioned because of a defect in its manufacture. Thereafter, Rollins was severely injured when he tried to reach and give assistance to Alper on the ledge to which Alper had fallen. Rollins's injury was not caused by any fault on his own part.

If Rollins brings an action against Outfitters, Inc., to recover damages for his injuries, will Rollins prevail?

(A)   No, unless Outfitters could have discovered the defect by a reasonable inspection of the safety device.

(B)   No, because Rollins did not rely on the representation of safety implied from the sale of the safety device by Outfitters.

(C)   Yes, unless Alper was negligent in failing to test the safety device.

(D)   Yes, because injury to a person in Rollins's position was foreseeable if the safety device failed.

105. Pitt sued Dill for damages for back injuries received in a car wreck. Dill disputed the damages and sought to prove that Pitt's disability, if any, resulted from a childhood horseback riding accident. Pitt admitted the childhood accident, but contended it had no lasting effect.

Pitt calls Dr. Webb, an orthopedist who had never examined Pitt, and poses to Webb a hypothetical question as to the cause of the disability that omits any reference to the horseback riding accident. The question was not provided to opposing counsel before trial.

The best ground for objecting to this question would be that

(A)   Webb lacked firsthand knowledge concerning Pitt's condition.
(B)   the hypothetical question omitted a clearly significant fact.
(C)   hypothetical questions are no longer permitted.
(D)   sufficient notice of the hypothetical question was not given to opposing counsel before trial.

106. Daggett was prosecuted for murder of Vales, whose body was found one morning in the street near Daggett's house. The state calls Witt, a neighbor, to testify that during the night before the body was found he heard Daggett's wife scream, "You killed him! You killed him!"

Witt's testimony is

(A)   admissible as a report of a statement of belief
(B)   admissible as a report of an excited utterance.
(C)   inadmissible, because it reports a privileged spousal communication.
(D)   inadmissible on spousal immunity grounds, but only if the wife objects.

107. Orin owned in fee simple Blueacre, a farm of 300 acres. He died and by will duly admitted to probate devised Blueacre to his surviving widow, Wilma, for life with remainder in fee simple to his three children, Cindy, Clara, and Carter. All three children survived Orin.

At the time of Orin's death, there existed a mortgage on Blueacre that Orin had given ten years before to secure a loan for the purchase of the farm. At his death, there remained unpaid $40,000 in principal, payable in installments of $4,000 per year for the next ten years. In addition, there was due interest at the rate of 10% per annum, payable annually with the installment of principal.

Wilma took possession and out of a gross income of $50,000 per year realized $25,000 net after paying all expenses and charges except the installment of principal and interest due on the mortgage.

Carter and Cindy wanted the three children, including Clara, to each contribute one-third of the amounts needed to pay the mortgage installments. Clara objected, contending that Wilma should pay all of these amounts out of the profits she had made in operation of the farm. When foreclosure of the mortgage seemed imminent, Clara sought legal advice.

If Clara obtained sound advice relating to her rights, she was told that
(A) her only protection would lie in instituting an action for partition to compel the sale of the life estate of Wilma and to obtain the value of Clara's one-third interest in remainder.
(B) she could obtain appropriate relief to compel Wilma personally to pay the sums due because the income is more than adequate to cover these amounts.
(C) she could be compelled personally to pay her share of the amounts due because discharge of the mortgage enhances the principal.
(D) she could not be held personally liable for any amount but that her share in remainder

could be lost if the mortgage installments are not paid.

Questions 108-109 are based on the following fact situation.

Tune Corporation, a radio manufacturer, and Bill's Comex, Inc., a retailer, after extensive negotiations entered into a final, written agreement in which Tune agreed to sell and Bill's agreed to buy all of its requirements of radios, estimated at 20 units per month, during the period January 1, 1988, and December 31, 1990, at a price of $50 per unit. A dispute arose in late December, 1990, when Bill's returned 25 undefective radios to Tune for fall credit after Tune had refused to extend the contract for a second three-year period.

In an action by Tune against Bill's for damages due to return of the 25 radios, Tune introduces the written agreement, which expressly permitted the buyer to return defective radios for credit but was silent as to return of undefective radios for credit. Bill's seeks to introduce evidence that during the three years of the agreement it had returned, for various reasons, 125 undefective radios, for which Tune had granted full credit. Tune objects to the admissibility of this evidence.

108. The trial court will probably rule that the evidence proffered by Bill's is

(A)   inadmissible, because the evidence is barred by the parol evidence rule.

(B)   inadmissible, because the express terms of the agreement control when those terms are inconsistent with the course of performance.

(C)   admissible, because the evidence supports an agreement that is not within the relevant statute of frauds.

(D)   admissible, because course-of-performance evidence, when available, is considered the best indication of what the parties intended the writing to mean.

109. For this question only, assume the following facts. When Bill's returned the 25 radios in question, it included with the shipment a check payable to Tune for the balance admittedly due on all other merchandise sold and delivered to Bill's. The check was conspicuously marked, "Payment in full for all goods sold to Bill's to date." Tune's credit manager, reading this check notation and knowing that Bill's had also returned the 25 radios for full credit, deposited the check without protest in Tune's local bank account. The canceled check was returned to Bill's a week later.

Which of the following defenses would best serve Bill's?

(A)   Tune's deposit of the check and its return to Bill's after payment estopped Tune thereafter to assert that Bill's owed any additional amount.

(B)   By depositing the check without protest and with knowledge of its wording, Tune discharged any remaining duty to pay on the part of Bill's.

(C)   By depositing the check without protest and with knowledge of its wording, Tune entered into a novation discharging any remaining duty to pay on the part of Bill's.

(D)   The parties' good-faith dispute over return of the radios suspended the duty of Bill's, if any, to pay any balance due.

110. Plaintiff was a passenger in a car that was struck in the rear by a car driven by First. The collision resulted from First's negligence in failing to keep a proper lookout. Plaintiff's physician found that the collision had aggravated a mild osteoarthritic condition in her lower back and had brought on similar, but new, symptoms in her neck and upper back.

Six months after the first accident, Plaintiff was a passenger in a car that was struck in the rear by a car driven by Second.

The collision resulted from Second's negligence in failing to keep a proper lookout.

Plaintiff's physician found that the second collision had caused a general worsening of Plaintiff's condition, marked by a significant restriction of movement and muscle spasms in her back and neck. The physician believes Plaintiff's worsened condition is permanent, and he can find no basis for apportioning responsibility for her present worsened condition between the two automobile collisions.

Plaintiff brought an action for damages against First and Second. At the close of Plaintiff's evidence, as outlined above, each of the defendants moved for a directed verdict in his favor on the ground that Plaintiff had failed to produce evidence on which the jury could determine how much damage each defendant had caused. The jurisdiction adheres to the common-law rules regarding joint and several liability.

Plaintiff's best argument in opposition to the defendants' motions would be that the defendants are jointly and severally liable for Plaintiff's entire harm, because

(A)   the wrongdoers, rather than their victim, should bear the burden of the impossibility of apportionment.

(B)   the defendants breached a common duty that each of them owed to Plaintiff.

(C)   each of the defendants was the proximate cause in fact of all of Plaintiff's damages.

(D)   the defendants are joint tortfeasors who aggravated Plaintiff's preexisting condition.

1:55

111. Adam had promised Bob that, if at any time Adam decided to sell his summer cottage property known as Blackacre, he would give Bob the opportunity to purchase Blackacre.

At a time when Bob was serving overseas with the United States Navy, Adam decided to sell Blackacre and spoke to Barbara, Bob's mother. Before Bob sailed, he had arranged for Barbara to become a joint owner of his various bank accounts so that Barbara would be able to pay his bills when he was gone. When she heard from Adam, Barbara took the necessary funds from Bob's account and paid Adam $20,000, the fair market value of Blackacre. Adam executed and delivered to Barbara a deed in the proper form purporting to convey Blackacre to Bob. Barbara promptly and properly recorded the deed.

Shortly thereafter, Barbara learned that Bob had been killed in an accident at sea one week before the delivery of the deed.

Bob's Last Will, which has now been duly probated, leaves his entire estate to First Church. Barbara is the sole heir-at-law of Bob.
There is no statute dealing with conveyances to dead persons.

Title to Blackacre is now in

(A)   First Church.
(B)   Barbara.
(C)   Adam free and clear.
(D)   Adam, subject to a lien to secure $20,000 to Bob's estate.

112. Darby was prosecuted for sexually abusing his 13-year-old stepdaughter, Wendy. Wendy testified to Darby's conduct. On cross-examination, defense counsel asks Wendy, "Isn't it true that shortly before you complained that Darby abused you, he punished you for maliciously ruining some of his phonograph records?"

The question is

(A)   proper, because it relates to a possible motive for Wendy to accuse Darby falsely.
(B)   proper, because Wendy's misconduct is relevant to her character for veracity.
(C)   improper, because the incident had nothing to do with Wendy's truthfulness.
(D)   improper, because it falls outside the scope of direct examination.

113. David entered the county museum at a time when it was open to the public, intending to steal a Picasso etching. Once inside, he took what he thought was the etching from an unlocked display case and concealed it under his coat. However, the etching was a photocopy of an original that had been loaned to another museum. A sign over the display case containing the photocopy said that similar photocopies were available free at the entrance. David did not see the sign.

Burglary in the jurisdiction is defined as "entering a building unlawfully with the intent to commit a crime."

David is guilty of

(A)   burglary and larceny.
(B)   burglary and attempted larceny.
(C)   larceny.
(D)   attempted larceny.

114. Insurance is provided in the state of Shoshone only by private companies. Although the state insurance commissioner inspects insurance companies for solvency, the state does not regulate their rates or policies.

An insurance company charges higher rates for burglary insurance to residents of one part of a county in Shoshone than to residents of another section of the same county because of the different crime rates in those areas.

Foster is a resident of that county who was charged the higher rate by the insurance company because of the location of her residence. Foster sues the insurance company, alleging that the differential in insurance rates unconstitutionally denies her the equal protection of the laws.

Will Foster's suit succeed?

(A)   Yes, because the higher crime rate in Foster's neighborhood demonstrates that the county police are not giving persons who reside there the equal protection of the laws.

(B)   Yes, because the insurance rate differential is inherently discriminatory.

(C)   No, because the constitutional guarantee of equal protection of the laws is not applicable to the actions of these insurance companies.

(D)   No, because there is a rational basis for the differential in insurance rates.

Questions 115-116 are based on the following fact situation.

Jack, a bank teller, was fired by Morgan, the president of the bank. Jack decided to take revenge against Morgan, but decided against attempting it personally, because he knew Morgan was protected around the clock by bank security guards. Jack knew that Chip had a violent temper and was very jealous. Jack falsely told Chip that Chip's wife, Elsie, was having an affair with Morgan. Enraged, Chip said, "What am I going to do?" Jack said, "If it were my wife, I'd just march into his office and blow his brains out." Chip grabbed a revolver and rushed to the bank. He walked into the bank, carrying the gun in his hand. One of the security guards, believing a holdup was about to occur, shot and killed Chip.

115. If charged with murder of Chip, Jack should be found

(A)   guilty, based upon extreme recklessness.

(B)   guilty, based upon transferred intent.

(C)   not guilty, because he did not intend for Chip to be shot by the security guard.

(D)   not guilty, because he did not shoot Chip and he was not acting in concert with the security guard.

116. If charged with attempted murder of Morgan, Jack should be found

(A)   guilty, because he intended to kill Morgan and used Chip to carry out his plan.

(B)   guilty, because he was extremely reckless as to Morgan.

(C)   not guilty, because Morgan was never in imminent danger of being killed.

(D)   not guilty, because Chip, if successful, would be guilty of no more than manslaughter and an accessory cannot be guilty of a higher crime than the principal.

117. The National AIDS Prevention and Control Act is a new, comprehensive federal statute that was enacted to deal with the public health crisis caused by the AIDS virus. Congress and the President were concerned that inconsistent lower court rulings with respect to the constitutionality, interpretation, and application of the statute might adversely affect or delay its enforcement and, thereby, jeopardize the public health. As a result, they included a provision in the statute providing that all legal challenges concerning those matters may be initiated only by filing suit directly in the United States Supreme Court.

The provision authorizing direct review of the constitutionality, interpretation, or application of this statute only in the United States Supreme Court is

(A)   constitutional, because it is authorized by the Article I power of Congress to enact all laws that are "necessary and proper" to implement the general welfare.

(B)   constitutional, because Article III provides that the jurisdiction of the United States Supreme Court is subject to such exceptions and such regulations as Congress shall make.

(C)   unconstitutional, because it denies persons who wish to challenge this statute the equal protection of the laws by requiring them to file suit in a court different from that in which persons who wish to challenge other statutes may file suit.

(D)   unconstitutional, because it is inconsistent with the specification in Article III of the original jurisdiction of the United States Supreme Court.

118. Miller was indicted in a state court in January 1985 for a robbery and murder that occurred in December 1982. He retained counsel, who filed a motion to dismiss on the ground that Miller had been prejudiced by a 25-month delay in obtaining the indictment. Thereafter, Miller, with his counsel, appeared in court for arraignment and stated that he wished to plead guilty.

The presiding judge asked Miller whether he understood the nature of the charges, possible defenses, and maximum allowable sentences. Miller replied that he did, and the judge reviewed all of those matters with him.

He then asked Miller whether he understood that he did not have to plead guilty. When Miller responded that he knew that, the judge accepted the plea and sentenced Miller to 25 years.

Six months later, Miller filed a motion to set aside his guilty plea on each of the following grounds.
Which of these grounds provides a constitutional basis for relief?

(A)   The judge did not rule on his motion to dismiss before accepting the guilty plea.
(B)   The judge did not determine that Miller had robbed and killed the victim.
(C)   The judge did not determine whether Miller understood that he had a right to jury trial.
(D)   The judge did not determine whether the prosecutor's file contained any undisclosed exculpatory material.

119. Sally told Michael she would like to have sexual intercourse with him and that he should come to her apartment that night at 7 p.m. After Michael arrived, he and Sally went into the bedroom. As Michael started to remove Sally's blouse, Sally said she had changed her mind. Michael tried to convince her to have intercourse with him, but after ten minutes of her sustained refusals, Michael left the apartment. Unknown to Michael, Sally was 15 years old. Because she appeared to be older, Michael believed her to be about 18 years old.

A statute in the jurisdiction provides: "A person commits rape in the second degree if he has sexual intercourse with a girl, not his wife, who is under the age of 16 years."

If Michael is charged with attempting to violate this statute, he is

(A)   guilty, because no mental state is required as to the element of age.
(B)   guilty, because he persisted after she told him she had changed her mind.
(C)   not guilty, because he reasonably believed she had consented and voluntarily withdrew after she told him she had changed her mind.
(D)   not guilty, because he did not intend to have intercourse with a girl under the age of 16.

Questions 120-121 are based on the following fact situation.

Alice entered into a contract with Paul by the terms of which Paul was to paint Alice's office for $1,000 and was required to do all of the work over the following weekend so as to avoid disruption of Alice's business.

2:15

120. For this question only, assume the following facts. If Paul had started to paint on the following Saturday morning, be could have finished before Sunday evening. However, he stayed home that Saturday morning to watch the final game of the World Series on TV and did not start to paint until Saturday afternoon. By late Saturday afternoon, Paul realized that he had underestimated the time it would take to finish the job if he continued to work alone. Paul phoned Alice at her home and accurately informed her that it was impossible to finish the work over the weekend unless he hired a helper. He also stated that to do so would require an additional charge of $200 for the work. Alice told Paul that she apparently had no choice but to pay "whatever it takes" to get the work done as scheduled.

Paul hired Ted to help finish the painting and paid Ted $200. Alice has offered to pay Paul $1,000. Paul is demanding $1,200.

How much is Paul likely to recover

(A) $1,000 only, because Alice received no consideration for her promise to pay the additional sum.
(B) $1,000 only, because Alice's promise to pay "whatever it takes" is too uncertain to be enforceable.

(C) $1,200, in order to prevent Alice's unjust enrichment.
(D) $1,200, because the impossibility of Paul's completing the work alone discharged the original contract and a new contract was formed.

121. For this question only, assume the following facts. Paul commenced work on Saturday morning, and had finished half the painting by the time he quit work for the day. That night, without the fault of either party, the office building was destroyed by fire.

Which of the following is an accurate statement?

(A)   Both parties' contractual duties are discharged, and Paul can recover nothing from Alice.
(B)   Both parties' contractual duties are discharged, but Paul can recover in quasi-contract from Alice.
(C)   Only Paul's contractual duty is discharged, because Alice's performance (payment of the agreed price) is not impossible.
(D)   Only Paul's contractual duty is discharged, and Paul can recover his reliance damages from Alice.

122. The state of Erehwon has a statute providing that an unsuccessful candidate in a primary election for a party's nomination for elected public office may not become a candidate for the same office at the following general election by nominating petition or by write-in votes.

Sabel sought her party's nomination for governor in the May primary election. After losing in the primary, Sabel filed nominating petitions containing the requisite number of signatures to become a candidate for the office of governor in the following general election. The chief elections officer of Erehwon refused to certify Sabel's petitions solely because of the above statute. Sabel then filed suit in federal district court challenging the constitutionality of this Erehwon statute.

As a matter of constitutional law, which of the following is the proper burden of persuasion in this suit?

(A)   Sabel must demonstrate that the statute is not necessary to achieve a compelling state interest.

(B)   Sabel must demonstrate that the statute is not rationally related to a legitimate state interest.

(C)   The state must demonstrate that the statute is the least restrictive means of achieving a compelling state interest.

(D)   The state must demonstrate that the statute is rationally related to a legitimate state interest.

123. Rohan executed and delivered a promissory note and a mortgage securing the note to Acme Mortgage Company, which was named as payee in the note and as mortgagee in the mortgage. The note included a statement that the indebtedness evidenced by the note was "subject to the terms of a contract between the maker and the payee of the note executed on the same day" and that the note was "secured by a mortgage of even date." The mortgage was promptly and properly recorded. Subsequently, Acme sold the Rohan note and mortgage to XYZ Bank and delivered to XYZ Bank a written assignment of the Rohan note and mortgage. The assignment was promptly and properly recorded. Acme retained possession of both the note and the mortgage in order to act as collecting agent. Later, being short of funds, Acme sold the note and mortgage to Peterson at a substantial discount. Acme executed a written assignment of the note and mortgage to Peterson and delivered to him the note, the mortgage, and the assignment.

Peterson paid value for the assignment without actual knowledge of the prior assignment to XYZ Bank and promptly and properly recorded his assignment. The principal of the note was not then due, and there had been no default in payment of either interest or principal.

If the issue of ownership of the Rohan note and mortgage is subsequently raised in an appropriate action by XYZ Bank to foreclose, the court should hold that

(A)   Peterson owns both the note and the mortgage.
(B)   XYZ Bank owns both the note and the mortgage.
(C)   Peterson owns the note and XYZ Bank owns the mortgage.
(D)   XYZ Bank owns the note and Peterson owns the mortgage.

124. In order to provide funds for a system of new major airports near the ten largest cities in the United States, Congress levies a tax of $25 on each airline ticket issued in the United States. The tax applies to every airline ticket, even those for travel that does not originate in, terminate at, or pass through any of those ten large cities.

As applied to the issuance in the United States of an airline ticket for travel between two cities that will not be served by any of the new airports, this tax is

(A)   constitutional, because Congress has broad discretion in choosing the subjects of its taxation and may impose taxes on subjects that have no relation to the purpose for which those tax funds will be expended.
(B)   constitutional, because an exemption for the issuance of tickets for travel between cities that will not be served by the new airports would deny the purchasers of all other tickets the equal protection of the laws.
(C)   unconstitutional, because the burden of the tax outweighs its benefits for passengers whose travel does not originate in, terminate at, or pass through any of the ten largest cities.
(D)   unconstitutional, because the tax adversely affects the fundamental right to travel.

125. Stoven, who owned Craigmont in fee simple, mortgaged Craigmont to Ulrich to secure a loan of $100,000. The mortgage was promptly and properly recorded. Stoven later mortgaged Craigmont to Martin to secure a loan of $50,000. The mortgage was promptly and properly recorded. Subsequently, Steven conveyed Craigmont to Fritsch. About a year later, Fritsch borrowed $100,000 from Zorn, an elderly widow, and gave her a mortgage on Craigmont to secure repayment of the loan.

Zorn
S - U 100

S - M 500

S → F

Zorn did not know about the mortgage held by Martin. The understanding between Fritsch and Zorn was that Fritsch would use, the $100,000 to pay off the mortgage held by Ulrich and that Zorn would, therefore, have a first mortgage on Craigmont. Zorn's mortgage was promptly and properly recorded. Fritsch paid the $100,000 received from Zorn to Ulrich and obtained and recorded a release of the Ulrich mortgage.

The $50,000 debt secured by the Martin mortgage was not paid when it was due, and Martin brought an appropriate action to foreclose, joining Stoven, Fritsch, and Zorn as defendants and alleging that Martin's mortgage was senior to Zorn's mortgage on Craigmont.

If the court rules that Zorn's mortgage is entitled to priority over Martin's mortgage, which of the following determinations are necessary to support that ruling?

I   Ulrich's mortgage was originally senior to Martin's mortgage.
II.   Zorn is entitled to have Ulrich's mortgage revived for her benefit, and Zorn is entitled to be subrogated to Ulrich's original position as senior mortgagee.
III.   There are no countervailing equities in favor of Martin.

(A)   I and II only.
(B)   I and III only.
(C)   II and III only.

(D)   I, II, and III.

126. Paul sued Dyer for personal injuries sustained when Dyer's car hit Paul, a pedestrian. Immediately after the accident, Dyer got out of his car, raced over to Paul, and said, "Don't worry, I'll pay your hospital bill."

Paul's testimony concerning Dyer's statement is

(A)   admissible, because it is an admission of liability by a party opponent.
(B)   admissible, because it is within the excited utterance exception to the hearsay rule.
(C)   inadmissible to prove liability, because it is an offer to pay medical expenses.
(D)   inadmissible, provided that Dyer kept his promise to pay Paul's medical expenses.

127. One evening, Parnell had several drinks and then started to drive home. As he was proceeding down Main Boulevard, an automobile pulled out of a side street to his right. Parnell's car struck this automobile broadside. The driver of the other car was killed as a result of the collision. A breath analysis test administered after the accident showed that Parnell satisfied the legal definition of intoxication.

If Parnell is prosecuted for manslaughter, his best chance for acquittal would be based on an argument that

(A) the other driver was contributorily negligent.

(B) the collision would have occurred even if Parnell had not been intoxicated.

(C) because of his intoxication he lacked the *mens rea* needed for manslaughter.

(D) driving while intoxicated requires no *mens rea* and so cannot be the basis for misdemeanor manslaughter.

128. Seisin and Vendee, standing on Greenacre, orally agreed to its sale and purchase for $5,000, and orally marked its bounds as "that line of trees down there, the ditch that intersects them the fence on the other side, and that street on the fourth side."

In which of the following is the remedy of reformation most appropriate?

(A) As later reduced to writing, the agreement by clerical mistake included two acres that are actually beyond the fence.

(B) Vendee reasonably thought that two acres beyond the fence were included in the oral agreement but Seisin did not. As later reduced to writing, the agreement included the two acres.

(C) Vendee reasonably thought that the price orally agreed upon was $4,500, but Seisin did not. As later reduced to writing, the agreement said $5,000.

(D) Vendee reasonably thought that a dilapidated shed backed up against the fence was to be tom down and removed as part of the agreement, but Seisin did not. As later reduced to writing, the agreement said nothing about the shed.

129. Airco operates an aircraft maintenance and repair business serving the needs of owners of private airplanes. Flyer contracted with Airco to replace the engine in his plane with a more powerful engine of foreign manufacture. Airco purchased the replacement engine through a representative of the manufacturer and installed it in Flyer's plane. A short time after it was put into use, the new engine failed, and the plane crashed into a warehouse owned by Landers, destroying the warehouse and its contents. Airco was guilty of no negligence in the procurement, inspection, or installation of the engine. The failure of the engine was caused by a defect that would not be disclosed by inspection and testing procedures available to an installer. There was no negligence on the part of Flyer, who escaped the disabled plane by parachute.

Landers recovered a judgment for damages from Flyer for the destruction of his warehouse and its contents, and Flyer has asserted a claim against Airco to recover compensation on account of that liability.

In that action, Flyer will recover

(A)   full compensation, because the engine was defective.

(B)   no compensation, because Airco was not negligent.

(C)   contribution only, because Airco and Flyer were equally innocent.

(D)   no compensation, because Lander's judgment established Flyer's responsibility to Landers.

130. To encourage the growth of its population the state of Axbridge established a program that awarded $1,000 to the parents of each child born within the state, provided that at the time of the child's birth the mother and father of the newborn were citizens of the United States.

The Lills are aliens who are permanent residents of the United States and have resided in Axbridge for three years. When their first child was born two months ago, they applied for and were denied the $1,000 award by Axbridge officials on the sole ground that they are not citizens of the United States.

The Lills filed suit in federal court contending that their exclusion from the award program was unconstitutional. Assume no statute addresses this question.

In this case, the court should hold that the exclusion of aliens from the Axbridge award program is

(A)   constitutional, because the Tenth Amendment reserves to the states plenary authority over the spending of state funds.

(B)   constitutional, because Axbridge has a legitimate interest in encouraging the growth of its population and a rational legislature could believe that families in which both parents are United States citizens are more likely to stay in Axbridge and contribute to its future prosperity than those in which one or both of the parents are aliens.

(C)   unconstitutional, because strict scrutiny governs judicial review of such state classifications based on alienage, and Axbridge cannot demonstrate that this classification is necessary to advance a compelling state interest.

(D)   unconstitutional, because state classifications based on alienage are impermissible unless explicitly authorized by an act of Congress.

2:35

131. While driving at a speed in excess of the statutory limit Dant negligently collided with another car, and the disabled vehicle blocked two of the highway's three northbound lanes. When Page approached the scene two minutes later, he slowed his car to see if he could help those involved in the collision. As he slowed, he was rear-ended by a vehicle driven by Thomas. Page, who sustained damage to his car and was seriously injured, brought an action against Dant to recover damages. The jurisdiction adheres to the traditional common-law rules pertaining to contributory negligence.

If Dant moves to dismiss the action for failure to state a claim upon which relief may be granted, should the motion be granted?

(A)   Yes, because it was Thomas, not Dant, who collided with Page's car and caused Page's injuries.

(B)   Yes, if Page could have safely passed the disabled vehicles in the traffic lane that remained open.

(C)   No, because a jury could find that Page's injury arose from a risk that was a Continuing consequence of Dant's negligence.

(D)   No, because Dant was driving in excess of the statutory limit when he negligently caused the first accident.

132. Olin owned Blueacre, a valuable tract of land located in York County. Olin executed a document in the form of a warranty deed of Blueacre, which was regular in all respects except that the only language designating the grantees in each of the granting and *habendum* clauses was: "The leaders of all the Protestant Churches in York County." The instrument was acknowledged as required by statute and promptly and properly recorded. Olin told his lawyer, but no one else, that he had made the conveyance as he did because he abhorred sectarianism in the Protestant movement and because he thought that the leaders would devote the asset to lessening sectarianism.
Olin died suddenly and unexpectedly a week later, leaving a will that bequeathed and devised his entire estate to Plum. After probate of the will became final and the administration on Olin's estate was closed, Plum instituted an appropriate action to quiet title to Blueacre and properly served as defendant each Protestant church situated in the county.

The only evidence introduced consisted of the chain of title under which Olin held, the probated will, the recorded deed, the fact that no person knew about the deed except Olin and his lawyer, and the conversation Olin had with his lawyer described above.

In such action, judgment should be for

(A)   Plum, because there is inadequate identification of grantees in the deed.
(B)   Plum, because the state of the evidence would not support a finding of delivery of the deed.
(C)   the defendants, because a deed is *prima facie* valid until rebutted.
(D)   the defendants, because recording established delivery *prima facie* until rebutted.

133. Old City police officers shot and killed Jones's friend as he attempted to escape arrest for an armed robbery he had committed. Jones brought suit in federal district court against the Old City Police Department and the city police officers involved, seeking only a judgment declaring unconstitutional the state statute under which the police acted. That newly enacted statute authorized the police to use deadly force when necessary to apprehend a person who has committed a felony. In his suit, Jones alleged that the police would not have killed his friend if the use of deadly force had not been authorized by the statute.
The federal district court should

(A)   decide the case on its merits, because it raises a substantial federal question.
(B)   dismiss the action, because it involves a nonjusticiable political question.
(C)   dismiss the action, because it does not present a case or controversy.
(D)   dismiss the action, because the Eleventh Amendment prohibits federal courts from deciding cases of this type.

134. Dooley and Melville were charged with conspiracy to dispose of a stolen diamond necklace. Melville jumped bail and cannot be found. Proceeding to trial against Dooley alone, the prosecutor calls Wixon, Melville's girlfriend, to testify that Melville confided to her that "Dooley said I still owe him some of the money from selling that necklace."

Wixon's testimony is

(A)   admissible as evidence of a statement by party-opponent Dooley.
(B)   admissible as evidence of a statement against interest by Melville.
(C)   inadmissible, because Melville's statement was not in furtherance of the conspiracy.

J v. PD + G

(D) inadmissible, because Melville is not shown to have firsthand knowledge that the necklace was stolen.

135. Pocket, a bank vice president, took substantial kickbacks to approve certain loans that later proved worthless. Upon learning of the kickbacks, Dudd, the bank's president, fired Pocket, telling him, "If you are not out of this bank in ten minutes, I will have the guards throw you out bodily." Pocket left at once.

If Pocket asserts a claim against Dudd based on assault, will Pocket prevail?
(A) No, because the guards never touched Pocket.
(B) No, because Dudd gave Pocket ten minutes to leave.
(C) Yes, if Dudd intended to cause Pocket severe emotional distress.
(D) Yes, because Dudd threatened Pocket with a harmful or offensive bodily contact.

136. Lee contracted with Mover, an interstate carrier, to ship household goods from the state of Green to his new home in the state of Pink. A federal statute provides that all liability of an interstate mover to a shipper for loss of or damage to the shipper's goods in transit is governed exclusively by the contract between them. The statute also requires the mover to offer a shipper at least two contracts with different levels of liability.

In full compliance with that federal statute, Mover offered Lee a choice between two shipping agreements that provided different levels of liability on the pail of Mover. The more expensive contract provided that Mover was fully liable in case of loss or damage. The less expensive contract limited Mover's liability in case of loss or damage to less than full value. Lee voluntarily signed the less expensive contract with Mover, fixing Mover's liability at less than the full value of the shipment.

Mover's truck was involved in an accident in the state of Pink. The accident was entirely a product of the negligence of Mover's driver. Lee's household goods were totally destroyed. In accordance with the contract, Mover reimbursed Lee for less than the full value of the goods. Lee then brought suit against Mover under the tort law of the state of Pink claiming that he was entitled to be reimbursed for the full value of the goods. Mover filed a motion to dismiss.

In this suit, the court should

(A) dismiss the case, because the federal statute governing liability of interstate carriers is the supreme law of the land and preempts state tort law.

(B) dismiss the case, because the contractual relationship between Lee and Mover is governed by the obligation of contracts clause of the Constitution.

(C) deny the motion to dismiss, because the full faith and credit clause of the Constitution requires that state tort law be given effect.

(D) deny the motion to dismiss, because it is unconstitutional for a federal statute to authorize Mover to contract out of any degree of liability for its own negligence.

137. John asked Doris to spend a weekend with him at his apartment and promised her they would get married on the following Monday. Doris agreed and also promised John that she would not tell anyone of their plans. Unknown to Doris, John had no intention of marrying her. After Doris came to his apartment, John told Doris he was going for cigarettes. He called Doris's father and told him that he had his daughter and would kill her if he did not receive $100,000. John was arrested on Sunday afternoon when he went to pick up the $100,000. Doris was still at the apartment and knew nothing of John's attempt to get the money.

John is guilty of

(A) kidnapping.
(B) attempted kidnapping.

(C) kidnapping or attempted kidnapping but not both.

(D) neither kidnapping nor attempted kidnapping.

138. Metro City operates a cemetery pursuant to a city ordinance. The ordinance requires the operation of the city cemetery to be supported primarily by revenues derived from the sale of cemetery lots to individuals. The ordinance further provides that the purchase of a cemetery lot entitles the owner to perpetual care of the lot, and entitles the owner to erect on the lot, at the owner's expense, a memorial monument or marker of the owner's choice, subject to certain size restrictions. The Metro City ordinance requires the city to maintain the cemetery, including mowing the grass, watering flowers, and plowing snow, and provides for the expenditure of city tax funds for such maintenance if revenues from the sale of cemetery lots are insufficient. Although cemetery lots are sold at full fair market value, which includes the current value of perpetual care, the revenue from the sale of such lots has been insufficient in recent years to maintain the cemetery. As a result, a small amount of city tax funds has also been used for that purpose.

A group of Metro City taxpayers brings suit against Metro City challenging the constitutionality of the city ordinance insofar as it permits the owner of a cemetery lot to erect a religious memorial monument or marker on his or her lot.

Is this suit likely to be successful?

(A)　No, because only a small amount of city tax funds has been used to maintain the cemetery.

(B)　No, because the purpose of the ordinance is entirely secular, its primary effect neither advances nor inhibits religion, and it does not foster an excessive government entanglement with religion.

(C)　Yes, because city maintenance of any religious object is a violation of the establishment clause of the First Amendment as incorporated into the Fourteenth Amendment.

(D)　Yes, because no compelling governmental interest justifies authorizing private persons to erect religious monuments or markers in a city-operated cemetery.

139. In a civil action for personal injury, Payne alleges that he was beaten up by Dabney during an altercation in a crowded car. Dabney's defense is that he was not the person who hit Payne.

To corroborate his testimony about the cause of his injuries, Payne seeks to introduce,

through the hospital records custodian, a notation in a regular medical record made by an emergency room doctor at the hospital where Payne was treated for his injuries. The notation is: "Patient says he was attacked by Dabney."

The notation is

(A)　inadmissible, unless the doctor who made the record is present at trial and available for cross-examination.

(B)　inadmissible as hearsay not within any exception.

(C)　admissible as hearsay within the exception for records of regularly conducted activity.

(D)　admissible as a statement made for the purpose of medical diagnosis or treatment.

140. Dexter was tried for the homicide of a girl whose strangled body was found beside a remote logging road with her hands taped together. After Dexter offered evidence of alibi, the state calls Wilma to testify that Dexter had taped her hands and tried to strangle her in the same location two days before the homicide but that she escaped.

The evidence is

(A)　admissible, as tending to show Dexter is the killer.

(B)　admissible, as tending to show Dexter's violent nature.

P v P

(C)   inadmissible, because it is improper character evidence.
(D)   inadmissible, because it is unfairly prejudicial.

141. Fruitko, Inc., ordered from Orchard, Inc., 500 bushels of No. 1 Royal Fuzz peaches, at a specified price, "for prompt shipment." Orchard promptly shipped 500 bushels, but by mistake shipped No. 2 Royal Fuzz peaches instead of No. 1. The error in shipment was caused by the negligence of Orchard's shipping clerk.

Which of the following best states Fruitko's rights and duties upon delivery of the peaches?

(A)   Orchard's shipment of the peaches was a counteroffer and Fruitko can refuse to accept them.
(B)   Orchard's shipment of the peaches was a counteroffer but, since peaches are perishable, Fruitko, if it does not want to accept them, must reship the peaches to Orchard in order to mitigate Orchard's losses.
(C)   Fruitko must accept the peaches because a contract was formed when Orchard shipped them.
(D)   Although a contract was formed when Orchard shipped the peaches, Fruitko does not have to accept them.

142. Blackacre was a tract of 100 acres retained by Byron, the owner, after he had developed the adjoining 400 acres as a residential subdivision. Byron had effectively imposed restrictive covenants on each lot in the 400 acres. Chaney offered Byron a good price for a five-acre tract located in a comer of Blackacre far away from the existing 400-acre residential subdivision. Byron conveyed the five-acre tract to Chaney and imposed the same restrictive covenants on the five-acre tract as he had imposed on the lots in the adjoining 400 acres. Byron further covenanted that when he sold the remaining 95 acres of Blackacre he would impose the same restrictive covenants in the deed or deeds for the 95 acres. Byron's conveyance to Chaney was promptly and properly recorded.

However, shortly thereafter, Byron conveyed the remaining 95 acres to Dart for $100,000 by a deed that made no mention of any restrictive covenants. Dart had no actual knowledge of the restrictive covenants in Chaney's deed. Dart now proposes to build an industrial park which would violate such restrictive covenants if they are applicable.

The recording act of the jurisdiction provides "No conveyance or mortgage of real property shall be good against subsequent purchasers for value and without notice unless the same be recorded according to law."

In an appropriate action by Chaney to enforce the restrictive covenants against Dart's 95-acre tract, if Dart wins it will be because

(A)   the deed imposing the restrictions was not in the chain of title for the 95 acres when Dart bought.
(B)   the disparity in acreage means that the covenant can only be personal to Byron.
(C)   negative reciprocal covenants are not generally recognized.
(D)   a covenant to impose restrictions is an illegal restraint on alienation.

143. A grand jury indicted Alice on a charge of arson, and a valid warrant was issued for her arrest. Paul, a police officer, arrested Alice and informed her of what the warrant stated. However, hoping that Alice might say something incriminating, he did not give her Miranda warnings. He placed her in the back seat of his patrol car and was driving her to the police station when she said, "Look, I didn't mean to burn the building; it was an accident. I was just burning some papers in a wastebasket."
At the station, after being given Miranda warnings, Alice stated she wished to remain silent and made no other statements.

Alice moved to suppress the use of her statement to Paul as evidence on two grounds: first, that the statement was acquired without giving Miranda warnings, and second, that the police officer had deliberately elicited her incriminating statement after she was in custody.

As to Alice's motion to suppress, the court should

(A)   deny the motion.
(B)   grant the motion only on the basis of the first ground stated.
(C)   grant the motion only on the basis of the second ground stated.
(D)   grant the motion on either ground.

144. Debtor's $1,000 contractual obligation to Aunt was due on July 1. On the preceding June 15, Aunt called Niece and said, "As my birthday gift to you, you may collect on July 1 the $1,000 Debtor owes me." Aunt also called Debtor and told him to pay the $1,000 to Niece on July 1. On July 1, Debtor, saying that he did not like Niece and wouldn't pay anything to her, paid the $1,000 to Aunt, who accepted it without objection.

Will Niece succeed in an action for $1,000 against Debtor?

(A)   Yes, because Aunt had effectively assigned the $1,000 debt to her.
(B)   Yes, because Aunt's calls to Niece and Debtor effected a novation.

(C)   No, because Aunt's acceptance of the $1,000, without objection, was in effect the revocation of a gratuitous assignment.

(D)   No, because Debtor cannot be compelled to render performance to an assignee whom he finds personally objectionable.

Questions 145-146 are based on the following fact situation.

Dooley was a pitcher for the City Robins, a professional baseball team. While Dooley was throwing warm-up pitches on the sidelines during a game, he was continuously heckled by some spectators seated in the stands above the dugout behind a wire mesh fence. On several occasions, Dooley turned and looked directly at the hecklers with a scowl on his face, but the heckling continued. Dooley wound up as though he was preparing to pitch in the direction of his catcher; however the ball traveled from his hand at high speed, at a 90-degree angle from the line to the catcher and directly toward the hecklers in the stands. The ball passed through the wire mesh fence and struck Patricia, one of the hecklers.

Patricia brought an action for damages against Dooley and the City Robins, based upon negligence and battery. The trial court directed a verdict for the defendants on the battery count. The jury found for the defendants on the negligence count because the jury determined that Dooley could not foresee that the ball would pass through the wire mesh fence.

Patricia has appealed the judgments on the battery counts, contending that the trial court erred in directing verdicts for Dooley and the City Robins.

145. On appeal, the judgment entered on the directed verdict in Dooley's favor on the battery claim should be

(A)   affirmed, because the jury found on the evidence that Dooley could not foresee that the ball would pass through the fence.

(B)   affirmed, if there was evidence that Dooley was mentally ill and that his act was the product of his mental illness.

(C)   reversed and the case remanded, if a jury could find on the evidence that Dooley intended to cause the hecklers to fear being hit.

(D)   reversed and the case remanded, because a jury could find that Dooley's conduct was extreme and outrageous, and the cause of physical harm to Patricia.

146. For this question only, assume that, on appeal, the court holds that the question of whether Dooley committed a battery is a jury issue.

The judgment entered on the directed verdict in favor of the City Robins should then be

(A)   reversed and the case remanded, because a jury could find the City Robins vicariously liable for a battery committed by Dooley in the course of his employment.

(B)   reversed and the case remanded, only if a jury could find negligence on the part of the Robins' management.

(C)   affirmed, because an employer is not vicariously liable for a servant's battery.

(D)   affirmed, if Dooley's act was a knowing violation of team rules.

147. The School Board of the city of Rulb issued a rule authorizing public school principals to punish, after a hearing, students who engage in violations of the board's student behavior code. According to the rule, violators of the behavior code may be punished in a variety of ways including being required to sit in designated school confinement rooms during all school hours, with their hands clasped in front of them, for a period of up to 15 school days.

Teddy, a fifth grade student in Rulb Elementary School, was charged with placing chewed bubble gum on a classmate's chair, a violation of the student behavior code. He had never violated the code before and was otherwise an attentive and well-behaved student. After a hearing on the charges, Teddy's principal determined that Teddy had violated the behavior code in the manner charged, and ordered Teddy to spend the next 15 school days in the school confinement room with his hands clasped in front of him. Teddy's parents file suit in federal court challenging, solely on constitutional grounds, the principal's action in ordering Teddy to spend the next 15 school days in the school confinement room with his hands clasped in front of him.

Which of the following arguments would be most helpful to Teddy's parents in this suit?

(A)   Because the school board rule limits the freedom of movement of students and subjects them to bodily restraint, it denies them a privilege and immunity of citizenship guaranteed them by Article IV, Section 2.

(B)   Because the school board rule is substantially overbroad in relation to any legitimate purpose, it constitutes a facial violation of the equal protection clause of the Fourteenth Amendment.

(C)   Because application of the school and board rule in this case denies the student freedom of movement and subjects him to bodily restraint in a manner grossly disproportionate to his offense and circumstances, it violates the due process clause of the Fourteenth Amendment.

(D)   Because the school board rule is enforced initially by administrative rather than judicial proceedings, it constitutes a prohibited bill of attainder.

148. Davidson and Smythe were charged with burglary of a warehouse. They were tried separately. At Davidson's trial, Smythe testified that he saw Davidson commit the burglary. While Smythe is still subject to recall as a witness, Davidson calls Smythe's cellmate, Walton, to testify that Smythe said, "I broke into the warehouse alone because Davidson was too drunk to help."

This evidence of Smythe's statement is

(A)   admissible as a declaration against penal interest.
(B)   admissible as a prior inconsistent statement.
(C)   inadmissible, because it is hearsay not within any exception.

(D)   inadmissible, because the statement is not clearly corroborated.

149. On March 1, Hotz Apartments, Inc., received from Koolair, Inc., a letter offering to sell Hotz 1,200 window air conditioners suitable for the apartments in Hotz's buildings. The Koolair offer stated that it would remain open until March 20, but that Hotz's acceptance must be received on or before that date. On March 16, Hotz posted a letter of acceptance. On March 17, Koolair telegraphed Hotz to advise that it was revoking the offer. The telegram reached Hotz on March 17, but Hotz's letter did not arrive at Koolair's address until March 21.

As of March 22, which of the following is a correct statement?

(A)   The telegram revoking the offer was effective upon receipt.
(B)   The offer was revocable at any time for lack of consideration.
(C)   The mail was the only authorized means of revocation.
(D)   Under the terms of Koolair's offer, Hotz's attempted acceptance was ineffective.

150. Dieter parked her car in violation of a city ordinance that prohibits parking within ten feet of a fire hydrant. Because Grove was driving negligently, his car sideswiped Dieter's parked car.

Plaintiff, a passenger in Grove's car, was injured in the collision. If Plaintiff asserts a claim against Dieter to recover damages for his injuries, basing his claim on Dieter's violation of the parking ordinance, will Plaintiff prevail?

(A)   Yes, because Dieter was guilty of negligence *per se.*
(B)   Yes, if Plaintiff would not have been injured had Dieter's car not been parked where it was.
(C)   No, because Dieter's parked car was not an active or efficient cause of Plaintiffs injury.
(D)   No, if prevention of traffic accidents was not a purpose of the ordinance.

151. Owen owned Greenacre, a tract of land in fee simple. By warranty deed he conveyed Greenacre to Lafe for life "and from and after the death of Lafe to Rem, her heirs and assigns."

Subsequently Rem died, devising all of her estate to Dan. Rem was survived by Hannah, her sole heir-at-law.

Shortly thereafter Lafe died, survived by Owen, Dan, and Hannah.

Title to Greenacre now is in

(A)   Owen, because the contingent remainder never vested and Owen's reversion was entitled to possession immediately upon Lafe's death.

(B)   Dan, because the vested remainder in Rem was transmitted by her will.
(C)   Hannah, because she is Rem's heir.

(D)   either Owen or Hannah, depending upon whether the destructibility of contingent remainders is recognized in the applicable jurisdiction.

152. A statute of the state of Illinois declares that after five years of continuous service in their positions all state employees, including faculty members at the state university, are entitled to retain their positions during "good behavior." The statute also contains a number of procedural provisions. Any state employee who is dismissed after that five-year period must be given reasons for the dismissal before it takes effect. In addition, such an employee must, upon request, be granted a post-dismissal hearing before an administrative board to seek reinstatement and back pay. The statute precludes any other hearing or opportunity to respond to the charges. That post-dismissal hearing must occur within six months after the dismissal takes effect.

The burden of proof at such a hearing is on the state, and the board may uphold the dismissal only if it is supported by a preponderance of the evidence.

An employee who is dissatisfied with a decision of the Board after a hearing may appeal its decision to the state courts. The provisions of this statute are inseverable.

A teacher who had been employed continuously for seven years as a faculty member at the state university was dismissed. A week before the dismissal took effect, she was informed that she was being dismissed because of a charge that she accepted a bribe from a student in return for raising the student's final grade in her course. At that time she requested an immediate hearing to contest the propriety of her dismissal.

Three months after her dismissal, she was granted a hearing before the state administrative board. The board upheld her dismissal, finding that the charge against her was supported by a preponderance of the evidence presented at the hearing.

The faculty member did not appeal the decision of the state administrative board to the Illinois state courts. Instead, she sought a declaratory judgment in federal district court to the effect that the state statute prescribing the procedures for her dismissal is unconstitutional.
In this case, the federal district court should

(A)   dismiss the suit, because a claim that a state statute is unconstitutional is not ripe for adjudication by a federal court until all judicial remedies in state courts provided for by state law have been exhausted.

(B)   hold the statute unconstitutional, because the due process clause of the Fourteenth Amendment requires a state to demonstrate beyond a reasonable doubt the facts constituting good cause for termination of a state employee.

(C)   hold the statute unconstitutional, because a state may not ordinarily deprive an employee of a property interest in a job without giving the employee an opportunity for some kind of a pre-dismissal hearing to respond to the charges against that employee.

(D)   hold the statute constitutional, because the due process clause of the Fourteenth Amendment entitles state employees who have a right to their jobs during good behavior only to a statement of reasons for their dismissal and an opportunity for a post-dismissal hearing.

153. Dorfman's dog ran into the street in front of Dorfman's home and began chasing cars. Peterson, who was driving a car on the street, swerved to avoid hitting the dog, struck a telephone pole, and was injured.

If Peterson asserts a claim against Dorfman, will Peterson prevail?

(A)   Yes, because Dorfman's dog was a cause in fact of Peterson's injury.

(B)   Yes, if Dorfman knew his dog had a propensity to chase cars and did not restrain it.

(C)   No, because a dog is a domestic animal.

(D)   No, unless a statute or ordinance made it unlawful for the owner to allow a dog to be unleashed on a public street.

154. Dower, an inexperienced driver, borrowed a car from Puder, a casual acquaintance, for the express purpose of driving it several blocks to the local drug store. Instead, Dower drove the car, which then was worth $12,000, 100 miles to Other City. While Dower was driving in Other City the next day, the car was hit by a negligently driven truck and sustained damage that will cost $3,000 to repair. If repaired, the car will be fully restored to its former condition.

If Puder asserts a claim against Dower based on conversion, Puder should recover a judgment for

(A) $12,000
(B) $3,000
(C) $3,000 plus damages for the loss of the use of the car during its repair.
(D)   nothing, unless Dower was negligent and his negligence was a substantial cause of the collision.

155. Miller's, a department store, had experienced a growing incidence of shoplifting. At the store's request, the police concealed Best, a woman who was a detective, at a vantage point above the women's apparel fitting rooms where she could see into these rooms, where customers tried on clothes. Detective Best saw Davis enter a fitting room, stuff a dress into her pocketbook, leave the fitting room, and start for the street door. By prearranged signal, Best notified another police officer near the door, who detained Davis as Davis started to go out into the street. Davis was placed under arrest, and the dress was retrieved from her purse. Davis is charged with shoplifting.

Her motion to prevent the introduction of the dress into evidence will be

(A)   granted, because the police should have secured a search warrant to search her bag.

(B)   granted, because a customer has a reasonable expectation of privacy while using a department store fitting room.

(C)   denied, because the search and seizure were made incident to a valid arrest based on probable cause.

(D)   denied, because Detective Best could see into the room and thus Davis's activities were legitimately in plain view.

Questions 156-157 are based on the following fact situation.

Pam and Dora own adjoining lots in the central portion of a city. Each of their lots had an office building. Dora decided to raze the existing building on her lot and to erect a building of greater height. Dora has received all governmental approvals required to pursue her project.

There is no applicable statute or ordinance (other than those dealing with various approvals for zoning, building, etc.).

156. After Dora had torn down the existing building, she proceeded to excavate deeper. Dora used shoring that met all local, state, and federal safety regulations, and the shoring was placed in accordance with those standards.

Pam notified Dora that cracks were developing in the building situated on Pam's lot. Dora took the view that any subsidence suffered by Pam was due to the weight of Pam's building, and correctly asserted that none would have occurred had Pam's soil been in its natural state. Dora continued to excavate.

The building on Pam's lot did suffer extensive damage, requiring the expenditure of $750,000 to remedy the defects.

Which of the following is the best comment concerning Pam's action to recover damages from Dora?

(A)   Dora is liable, because she removed necessary support for Pam's lot.

(B)   Dora cannot be held liable simply upon proof that support was removed, but may be held liable if negligence is proved.

(C)   Once land is improved with a building, the owner cannot invoke the common-law right of lateral support.

(D)   Dora's only obligation was to satisfy all local, state, and federal safety regulations.

157. Assume that no problems with subsidence or other misadventures occurred during construction of Dora's new building. However, when it was completed, Pam had discovered that the shadow created by the new higher building placed her building in such deep shade that her ability to lease space was diminished and that the rent she could charge and the occupancy rate were substantially lower. Assume that these facts are proved in an appropriate action Pam instituted against Dora for all and any relief available.

Which of the following is the most appropriate comment concerning this lawsuit?

(A)   Pam is entitled to a mandatory injunction requiring Dora to restore those existing with the prior building insofar as the shadow is concerned.

(B)   The court should award permanent damages, in lieu of an injunction, equal to the present value of all rents lost and loss on rents for the reasonable life of the building.

(C)   The court should award damages for losses suffered to the date of trial and leave open recovery of future damages.

(D)   Judgment should be for Dora, because Pam has no cause of action.

158. Deland operates a bank courier service that uses armored trucks to transport money and securities. One of Deland's armored trucks was parked illegally, too close to a street intersection. Pilcher, driving his car at an excessive speed skidded into the armored truck while trying to make a turn. The truck was not damaged, but Pilcher was injured.

Pilcher has brought an action against Deland to recover damages for his loss resulting from the accident. The jurisdiction follows a pure comparative negligence rule.

In this action, Pilcher should recover

(A)   nothing, because Deland was not an active or efficient cause of Pilcher's loss.

(B)   nothing, if Deland was less negligent than Pilcher.

(C)   his entire loss, reduced by a percentage that reflects the negligence attributed to Pilcher.

(D)   his entire loss, because Deland's truck suffered no damage.

159. Roberts, a professional motorcycle rider, put on a performance in a privately owned stadium during which he leaped his motorcycle over 21 automobiles. Spectators were charged $5 each to view the jump and were prohibited from using cameras.

However, the local television station filmed the whole event from within the stadium without the knowledge or consent of Roberts and showed the film in its entirety on the evening newscast that day. Roberts thereafter brought suit to recover damages from the station for the admittedly unauthorized filming and broadcasting of the act. The television station raised only constitutional defenses.

The court should

(A)   hold against Roberts, because the First and Fourteenth Amendments authorize press coverage of newsworthy entertainment events.

(B)   hold against Roberts, because under the First and Fourteenth Amendments news broadcasts are absolutely privileged.

(C)   find the station liable, because its action deprives Roberts of his property without due process.

(D)   find the station liable, because the First and Fourteenth Amendments do not deprive an entertainer of the commercial value of his or her performances.

160. Stirrup, a rancher, and Equinox, a trainer of horses, signed the following writing: "For $5,000, Stirrup will sell to Equinox a gray horse that Equinox may choose from among the grays on Stirrup's ranch."

Equinox refused to accept delivery of a gray horse timely tendered by Stirrup or to choose among those remaining, on the ground that during their negotiations Stirrup had orally agreed to include a saddle, worth $100, and also to give Equinox the option to choose a gray or a brown horse. Equinox insisted on one of Stirrup's brown horses, but Stirrup refused to part with any of his browns or with the saddle as demanded by Equinox.

If Equinox sues Stirrup for damages and seeks to introduce evidence of the alleged oral agreement, the court probably will

(A)   admit the evidence as to both the saddle and the option to choose a brown horse.

(B)   admit the evidence as to the saddle but not the option to choose a brown horse.

(C)   admit the evidence as to the option to choose a brown horse but not the promise to include the saddle.

(D)   not admit any of the evidence.

161. Testator, whose nephew Bypast was his only heir, died leaving a will that gave his entire estate to charity.

Bypast, knowing full well that Testator was of sound mind all of his life, and having no evidence to the contrary, nevertheless filed a suit contesting Testator's will on the ground that Testator was incompetent when the will was signed. Craven, Testator's executor, offered Bypast $5,000 to settle the suit, and Bypast agreed.

If Craven then repudiates the agreement and the foregoing facts are proved or admitted in Bypast's suit against Craven for breach of contract, is Bypast entitled to recover under the prevailing view?

(A)   Yes, because the Bypast–Craven agreement was a bargained-for exchange.

(B)   Yes, because the law encourages the settlement of disputed claims.

(C)   No, because Bypast did not bring the will contest in good faith.

(D)   No, because an agreement to oust the court of its jurisdiction to decide a will contest is contrary to public policy.

162. Parker sues Dix for breach of a promise made in a letter allegedly written by Dix to Parker. Dix denies writing the letter.

Which of the following would NOT be a sufficient basis for admitting the letter into evidence?

(A)   Testimony by Parker that she is familiar with Dix's signature and recognizes it on the letter.

(B)   Comparison by the trier of fact of the letter with an admitted signature of Dix.

(C)   Opinion testimony of a nonexpert witness based upon familiarity acquired in order to authenticate the signature.

(D)   Evidence that the letter was written in response to one written by Parker to Dix.

Questions 163-164 are based on the following fact situation.

Green contracted in a signed writing to sell Greenacre, a 500-acre tract of farmland, to Farmer. The contract provided for exchange of the deed and purchase price of $500,000 in cash on January 15. Possession was to be given to Farmer on the same date. On January 15, Green notified Farmer that because the tenant on Greenacre wrongfully refused to quit the premises until January 30, Green would be unable to deliver possession of Greenacre until then, but he assured Farmer that he would tender the deed and possession on that date. When Green tendered the deed and possession on January 30, Farmer refused to accept either, and refused to pay the $500,000.

Throughout the month of January, the market value of Greenacre was $510,000, and its fair monthly rental value was $5,000.

163.   Will Green probably succeed in an action against Farmer for specific performance?

(A)   Yes, because the court will excuse the delay in tender on the ground that there was a temporary impossibility caused by the tenant's holding over.

(B)   Yes, because time is ordinarily not of the essence in a land-sale contract.

(C)   No, because Green breached by failing to tender the deed and possession on January 15.

(D)   No, because Green's remedy at law for monetary relief is adequate.

164. For this question only, make the following assumptions. On January 30, Farmer accepted a conveyance and possession of Greenacre and paid the $500,000 purchase price, but notified Green that he was reserving any rights he might have to damages caused by Green's breach. Farmer intended to use the land for raising cattle and had entered into a contract for the purchase of 500 head of cattle to be delivered to Greenacre on January 15. Because he did not have possession of Greenacre on that date, he had to rent another pasture at a cost of $2,000 to graze the cattle for 15 days. Green had no reason to know that Farmer intended to use Greenacre for raising cattle or that he was purchasing cattle to be grazed on Greenacre.

In an action by Farmer against Green for damages, Farmer is entitled to recover

(A)   nothing, because by paying the purchase price on January 30, he waived whatever cause of action he may have had.

(B)   nominal damages only, because the market value of the land exceeded the contract price.

(C) $2,500 only (the fair rental value of Greenacre for 15 days).

(D) $2,500 (the fair rental value of Greenacre for 15 days), plus $2,000 (the cost of grazing the cattle elsewhere for 15 days).

165. Able, owner of Blackacre and Whiteacre, two adjoining parcels, conveyed Whiteacre to Baker and covenanted in the deed to Baker that when he, Able, sold Blackacre he would impose restrictive covenants to prohibit uses that would compete with the filling station that Baker intended to construct and operate on Whiteacre. The deed was not recorded.

Baker constructed and operated a filling station on Whiteacre and then conveyed Whiteacre to Dodd, who continued the filling station use. The deed did not refer to the restrictive covenant and was promptly and properly recorded.

Able then conveyed Blackacre to Egan, who knew about Able's covenant with Baker to impose a covenant prohibiting the filling station use but nonetheless completed the transaction when he noted that no such covenant was contained in Able's deed to him. Egan began to construct a filling station on Blackacre. Dodd brought an appropriate action to enjoin Egan from using Blackacre for filling station purposes.

If Dodd prevails, it will be because

(A)   Egan had actual knowledge of the covenant to impose restrictions.

(B)   Egan is bound by the covenant because of the doctrine of negative reciprocal covenants.

(C)   business-related restrictive covenants are favored in the law.

(D)   Egan has constructive notice of the possibility of the covenant resulting from the circumstances.

166. While walking on a public sidewalk, Anson was struck by a piece of lumber that fell from the roof of Bruce's house. Bruce had hired Chase to make repairs to his roof, and the lumber fell through negligence on Chase's part.

If Anson brings an action against Bruce to recover damages for the injury caused to him by Chase's negligence, will Anson prevail?

(A)   Yes, under the *res ipsa loquitur* doctrine.

(B)   Yes, if Chase's act was a breach of a nondelegable duty owed by Bruce to Anson.

(C)   No, if Chase was an independent contractor rather than Bruce's servant.

(D)   No, if Bruce exercised reasonable care in hiring Chase to do the repair work.

167. Owen contracted to sell Vacantacre to Perry. The written contract required Owen to provide evidence of marketable title of record, specified a closing date, stated that "time is of the essence," and provided that at closing, Owen would convey by warranty deed. Perry paid Owen $2,000 earnest money toward the $40,000 purchase price.

The title evidence showed that an undivided one-eighth interest in Vacantacre was owned by Alice. Perry immediately objected to title and said he would not close on Owen's title. Owen responded, accurately, that Alice was his daughter who would be trekking in Nepal until two weeks after the specified closing date. He said that she would gladly deed her interest upon her return, and that meanwhile his deed warranting title to all of Vacantacre would fully protect Perry. Owen duly tendered his deed but Perry refused to close.

Perry brought an appropriate action to recover the $2,000 earnest money promptly after the specified closing date. Owen counterclaimed for specific performance, tendering a deed from himself and Alice, who had by then returned.

The court will hold for

(A)   Owen, because Alice's deed completing the transfer was given within a reasonable time.

(B)   Owen, because his warranty deed would have given Perry adequate interim protection.

(C)   Perry, because Owen's title was not marketable and time was of the essence.

(D) Perry, because under the circumstances the earnest money amount was excessive.

168. A statute provides: A person commits the crime of rape if he has sexual intercourse with a female, not his wife, without her consent.

Dunbar is charged with the rape of Sally. At trial, Sally testifies to facts sufficient for a jury to find that Dunbar had sexual intercourse with her, that she did not consent, and that the two were not married. Dunbar testifies in his own defense that he believed that Sally had consented to sexual intercourse and that she was his common-law wife.

At the conclusion of the case, the court instructed the jury that in order to find Dunbar guilty of rape, it must find beyond a reasonable doubt that he had sexual intercourse with Sally without her consent.

The court also instructed the jury that it should find the defendant not guilty if it found either that Sally was Dunbar's wife or that Dunbar reasonably believed that Sally had consented to the sexual intercourse, but that the burden of persuasion as to these issues was on the defendant.

The jury found Dunbar guilty, and Dunbar appealed, contending that the court's instructions on the issues of whether Sally was his wife and whether he reasonably believed she had consented violated his constitutional rights Dunbar's constitutional rights were

(A) violated by the instructions as to both issues.
(B) violated by the instruction as to whether Sally was his wife, but not violated by the instruction on belief as to consent.
(C) violated by the instruction on belief as to consent, but not violated by the instruction as to whether Sally was his wife.
(D) not violated by either part of the instructions.

169. Star, who played the lead role in a television soap opera, was seriously injured in an automobile accident caused by Danton's negligent driving. As a consequence of Star's injury, the television series was canceled, and Penn, a supporting actor, was laid off.

In an action against Danton, can Penn recover for his loss of income attributable to the accident?

(A) Yes, because Danton's negligence was the cause in fact of Penn's loss.
(B) Yes, unless Penn failed to take reasonable measures to mitigate his loss.
(C) No, unless Danton should have foreseen that by injuring

Star he would cause harm to
Penn.
(D)   No, because Danton's
liability does not extend to
economic loss to Penn that arises
solely from physical harm to Star.

170. On December 1, Broker
contracted with Collecta to sell
her one of a certain type of rare
coin for $12,000, delivery and
payment to occur on the next
March 1. To fulfill that contract,
and without Collecta's
knowledge, Broker contracted on
January 1 to purchase for
$10,000 a specimen of that type
coin from Hoarder, delivery and
payment to occur on February 1.
The market price of such coins
had unexpectedly fallen to
$8,000 by February 1, when
Hoarder tendered the coin and
Broker repudiated.

On February 25, the market in
such coins suddenly reversed and
had stabilized at $12,000 on
March 1. Broker, however, had
failed to obtain a specimen of the
coin and repudiated his
agreement with Collecta when
she tendered the $12,000 agreed
price on March 1.

Later that day, after learning by
chance of Broker's dealing with
Collecta, Hoarder telephoned
Collecta and said: "Listen, Broker
probably owes me at least
$2,000 in damages for refusing
wrongfully to buy my coin for
$10,000 on February 1 when the
market was down to $8,000. But
I'm in good shape in view of the

market's recovery since then, and
I think you ought to get after the
so-and-so."

If Collecta immediately sues
Broker for his breach of the
Broker-Hoarder contract, which
of the following will the court
probably decide?

(A)   Broker wins, because
Collecta, if a beneficiary at all of
the Broker-Hoarder contract, was
only an incidental beneficiary.
(B)   Broker wins, because as of
March 1 neither Hoarder nor
Collecta had sustained any
damage from Broker's
repudiation of both contracts.

(C)   Collecta wins, because she
was an intended beneficiary of
the Broker-Hoarder contract,
under which damages for
Broker's repudiation became
fixed on February 1.
(D)   Collecta wins, because she
took an effective assignment of
Hoarder's claim for damages
against Broker when Hoarder
suggested that Collecta "get after
the so-and-so."

171. In a prosecution of Dale for
murdering Vera, Dale testified
that the killing had occurred in
self defense when Vera tried to
shoot him. In rebuttal, the
prosecution seeks to call Walter,
Vera's father, to testify that the
day before the killing Vera told
Walter that she loved Dale so
much she could never hurt him.

Walter's testimony is

(A)   admissible within the hearsay exception for statements of the declarant's then existing state of mind.
(B)   admissible, because Vera is unavailable as a witness.
(C)   inadmissible as hearsay not within any exception.
(D)   inadmissible, because Vera's character is not an issue.

172. For an agreed price of $20 million, Bildko, Inc., contracted with Venture to design and build on Venture's commercial plot a 15-story office building.

In excavating for the foundation and underground utilities, Bildko encountered a massive layer of granite at a depth of 15 feet. By reasonable safety criteria, the building's foundation required a minimum excavation of 25 feet. When the contract was made, neither Venture nor Bildko was aware of the subsurface granite, for the presence of which neither party had hired a qualified expert to test.

Claiming accurately that removal of enough granite to permit the construction as planned would cost him an additional $3 million and a probable net loss on the contract of $2 million, Bildko refused to proceed with the work unless Venture would promise to pay an additional $2.5 million for the completed building.

If Venture refuses and sues Bildko for breach of contract, which of the following will the court probably decide?

(A)   Bildko is excused under the modern doctrine of supervening impossibility, which includes severe impracticability.
(B)   Bildko is excused, because the contract is voidable on account of the parties' mutual mistake concerning an essential underlying fact.
(C)   Venture prevails, because Bildko assumed the risk of encountering subsurface granite that was unknown to Venture.

(D)   Venture prevails, unless subsurface granite was previously unknown anywhere in the vicinity of Venture's construction site.

173. Owen owned Greenacre in fee simple. The small house on Greenacre was occupied, with Owen's oral permission, rent-free, by Able, Owen's son, and Baker, a college classmate of Able. Able was then 21 years old.

Owen, by properly executed instrument, conveyed Greenacre to "my beloved son, Able, his heirs and assigns, upon the condition precedent that he earn a college degree by the time he reaches the age of 30.

If, for any reason, he does not meet this condition, then Greenacre shall become the sole property of my beloved daughter, Anna, her heirs and assigns." At the time of the conveyance, Able and Baker attended a college located several blocks from Greenacre. Neither had earned a college degree.

One week after the delivery of the deed to Able, Able recorded the deed and immediately told Baker that he, Able, was going to begin charging Baker rent since "I am now your landlord." There is no applicable statute.

Able and Baker did not reach agreement, and Able served the appropriate notice to terminate whatever tenancy Baker had. Able then sought, in an appropriate action, to oust Baker.

Who should prevail?

(A) Able, because the conveyance created a fee simple subject to divestment in Able.
(B) Able, because Owen's conveyance terminated Baker's tenancy.
(C) Baker, because Owen's permission to occupy preceded Owen's conveyance to Able.
(D) Baker, because Baker is a tenant of Owen, not of Able.

174. Owens owned Whiteacre, a dwelling house situated on a two-acre lot in an area zoned for single-family residential uses only. Although it was not discernible from the outside, Whiteacre had been converted by Owens from a single-family house to a structure that contained three separate apartments, in violation of the zoning ordinance. Further, the conversion was in violation of the building code.

Owens and Peters entered into a valid written contract for the purchase and sale of Whiteacre. The contract provided that Owens was to convey to Peters a marketable title. The contract was silent as to zoning. Peters had fully inspected Whiteacre.

Prior to the closing, Peters learned that Whiteacre did not conform to the zoning ordinance and refused to close although Owens was ready, willing, and able to perform his contract obligations. Owens brought an appropriate action for specific performance against Peters.

In that action, Owens should
(A) win, because Owens was able to convey marketable title.
(B) win, because Peters was charged with knowledge of the zoning ordinance prior to entering the contract.
(C) lose, because the illegal conversion of Whiteacre creates the risk of litigation.
(D) lose, because the illegal conversion of Whiteacre was done by Owens rather than by a predecessor.

Questions 175-176 are based on the following fact situation.

Morten was the general manager and chief executive officer of the Woolen Company, a knitting mill. Morten delegated all operational decision making to Crouse, the supervising manager of the mill. The child labor laws in the jurisdiction provide, "It is a violation of the law for one to employ a person under the age of 17 years for full-time labor."

Without Morten's knowledge, Crouse hired a number of 15- and 16-year-olds to work at the mill full time. He did not ask their ages and they did not disclose them. Crouse could have discovered their ages easily by asking for identification, but he did not do so because he was not aware of the law and believed that company policy was to hire young people.

175. If the statute is interpreted to create strict liability and Crouse is charged with violating it, Crouse is

(A)   guilty, because he should have inquired as to the ages of the children.
(B)   guilty, because he hired the children.
(C)   not guilty, because in law the Woolen Company, not Crouse, is the employer of the children.
(D)   not guilty, because he believed he was following company policy and was not aware of the violation.

176. If the statute is interpreted to create strict liability and Morten is convicted of violating it, his contention that his conviction would violate the federal Constitution is

(A)   correct, because it is a violation of due process to punish without a voluntary act.
(B)   correct, because criminal liability is personal and the Woolen Company is the employer of the children, not Morten.
(C)   incorrect, because regulatory offenses are not subject to due process limitations.
(D)   incorrect, because he was in a position to exercise control over the hiring of employees for Woolen Company.

177. Ann's three-year-old daughter, Janet, was killed in an automobile accident. At Ann's direction, Janet's body was taken to a mausoleum for internment. Normally, the mausoleum's vaults are permanently sealed with marble plates secured by "tamperproof' screws. After Janet's body was placed in the mausoleum, however, only a fiberglass panel secured by caulking compound covered her vault. About a month later, Janet's body was discovered in a cemetery located near the mausoleum.

It had apparently been left there by vandals who had taken it from the mausoleum.

As a result of this experience, Ann suffered great emotional distress.

If Ann sues the mausoleum for the damages arising from her emotional distress, will she prevail?

(A) No, because Ann experienced no threat to her own safety.

(B) No, unless the mausoleum's behavior was extreme and outrageous.

(C) Yes, if the mausoleum failed to use reasonable care to safeguard the body.

(D) Yes, unless Ann suffered no physical harm as a consequence of her emotional distress.

178. Wastrel, a notorious spendthrift who was usually broke for that reason, received the following letter from his Uncle Bullion, a wealthy and prudent man: "I understand you're in financial difficulties again. I promise to give you $5,000 on your birthday next month, but you'd better use it wisely or you'll never get another dime from me." Wastrel thereupon signed a contract with a car dealer to purchase a $40,000 automobile and to make a $5,000 down payment on the day after his birthday.

If Wastrel sues Bullion for $5,000 after the latter learned of the car-purchase contract and then repudiated his promise, which of the foregoing is Bullion's best defense?

(A) A promise to make a gift in the future is not enforceable.

(B) Reliance by the promisee on a promise to make a future gift does not make the promised gift is substantially equivalent to the promisee's loss by reliance.

(C) Reliance by the promisee on a promise to make a future gift does not make the promise enforceable unless that reliance also results in an economic benefit to the promisee.

(D) Reliance by the promisee on a promise to make a future gift does not make the promise enforceable unless injustice can be avoided only by such enforcement.

179. Congress passed a bill prohibiting the President from granting a pardon to any person who had not served at least one-third of the sentence imposed by the court which convicted that person. The President vetoed the bill claiming that it was unconstitutional. Nevertheless, Congress passed it over his veto by a two-thirds vote of each house.

This act of Congress is

(A)   constitutional, because it was enacted over the President's veto by a two-thirds vote of each house.
(B)   constitutional, because it is a necessary and proper means of carrying out the powers of Congress.

(C)   unconstitutional, because it interferes with the plenary power of the President to grant pardons.
(D)   unconstitutional, because a Presidential veto based upon constitutional grounds may be overridden only with the concurrence of three-fourths of the state legislatures.

180. Defendant is on trial for the crime of obstructing justice by concealing records subpoenaed May 1 in a government investigation. The government calls Attorney to testify that on May 3, Defendant asked him how to comply with the regulations regarding the transfer of records to a safe-deposit box in Mexico.

The testimony of Attorney is

(A)   privileged, because it relates to conduct outside the jurisdiction of the United States.
(B)   privileged, because an attorney is required to keep the confidences of his clients.
(C)   not privileged, provided Attorney knew of the concededly illegal purpose for which the advice was sought.

(D)   not privileged, whether or not Attorney knew of the concededly illegal purpose for which the advice was sought.

181. Prad entered Drug Store to make some purchases. As he was searching the aisles for various items, he noticed a display card containing automatic pencils. The display card was on a high shelf behind a cashier's counter. Prad saw a sign on the counter that read, "No Admittance, Employees Only."

Seeing no clerks in the vicinity to help him Prad went behind the counter to get a pencil. A clerk then appeared behind the counter and asked whether she could help him. He said he just wanted a pencil and that he could reach the display card himself. The clerk said nothing further. While reaching for the display card, Prad stepped sideways into an open shaft and fell to the basement, ten feet below. The clerk knew of the presence of the open shaft, but assumed incorrectly that Prad had noticed it.

Prad sued Drug Store to recover damages for the injuries he sustained in the fall. The jurisdiction has adopted a rule of pure comparative negligence, and it follows traditional common-law rules governing the duties of a land possessor.

Will Prad recover a judgment against Drug Store?

(A)   No, because Prad was a trespasser.

(B)   No, unless Prad's injuries resulted from the defendant's willful or wanton misconduct.

(C)   Yes, because the premises were defective with respect to a public invitee.

(D)   Yes, if the clerk had reason to believe that Prad was unaware of the open shaft.

182. A statute in the jurisdiction defines murder in the first degree as knowingly killing another person after deliberation. Deliberation is defined as "cool reflection for any length of time no matter how brief." Murder in the second degree is defined as "all other murder at common law except felony-murder." Felony-murder is murder in the third degree. Manslaughter is defined by the common-law law.

At 2 a.m., Duncan held up an all-night liquor store using an assault rifle. During the holdup, two police cars with flashing lights drove up in front of the store. In order to create a situation where the police would hesitate to come into the store (and thus give Duncan a chance to escape out the back) Duncan fired several rounds through the front window of the store. Duncan then ran out the back but upon discovering another police car there, surrendered quietly.

One of the shots he fired while in the store struck and killed a burglar who was stealing items from a closed store across the street.

The most serious degree of criminal homicide Duncan is guilty of is

(A)   murder in the first degree.
(B)   murder in the second degree.
(C)   murder in the third degree.
(D)   manslaughter.

183. Denn is on trial for arson. In its case in chief, the prosecution offers evidence that Denn had secretly obtained duplicate insurance from two companies on the property that burned and that Denn had threatened to kill his ex-wife if she testified for the prosecution.

The court should admit evidence of

(A)   Denn's obtaining duplicate insurance only.
(B)   Denn's threatening to kill his ex-wife only.
(C)   both Denn's obtaining duplicate insurance and threatening to kill his ex-wife.
(D)   neither Denn's obtaining duplicate insurance nor threatening to kill his ex-wife.

184. In the course of a bank holdup, Robber fired a gun at Guard.

Guard drew his revolver and returned the fire. One of the bullets fired by Guard ricocheted, striking Plaintiff.

If Plaintiff asserts a claim against Guard based upon battery, will Plaintiff prevail?

(A)   Yes, unless Plaintiff was Robber's accomplice.
(B)   Yes, under the doctrine of transferred intent.
(C)   No, if Guard fired reasonably in his own defense.
(D)   No, if Guard did not intend to shoot Plaintiff.

Questions 185-186 are based on the following fact situation.

Mural, a wallpaper hanger, sent Gennybelle, a general contractor, this telegram:

Will do all paperhanging on new Doctors' Building, per owner's specs, for $14,000 if you accept within reasonable time after main contract awarded.
                /s/ Mural

Three other competing hangers sent Gennybelle similar bids in the respective amounts of $18,000, $19,000, and $20,00. Gennybelle used Mural's $14,000 figure in preparing and submitting her own sealed bid on Doctors' Building. Before the bids were opened, Mural truthfully advised Gennybelle that the former's telegraphic sub-bid had been based on a $4,000 computational error and was therefore revoked. Shortly thereafter, Gennybelle was awarded the Doctors' Building construction contract and subsequently contracted with another paperhanger for a price of $18,000. Gennybelle now sues Mural to recover $4,000.

185. Which of the following, if proved, would most strengthen Gennybelle's prospect of recovery?

(A)   After Mural's notice of revocation, Gennybelle made a reasonable effort to subcontract with another paperhanger at the lowest possible price.
(B)   Gennybelle had been required by the owner to submit a bid bond and could not have withdrawn or amended her bid on the main contract without forfeiting that bond.
(C)   Mural was negligent in erroneously calculating the amount of his sub-bid.
(D)   Gennybelle dealt with all of her subcontractors in good faith and without seeking to renegotiate (lower) the prices they had bid.

186. Which of the following, if proved, would best support Mural's defense?

(A)   Gennybelle gave Mural no consideration for an irrevocable sub-bid.

(B)   Mural's sub-bid expressly requested Gennybelle's acceptance after awarding of the main contract.

(C)   Even after paying $18,000 for the paperhanging, Gennybelle would make a net profit of $100,000 on the Doctors' Building contract.

(D)   Before submitting her own bid, Gennybelle had reason to suspect that Mural had made a computational mistake in figuring his sub-bid.

187. Roberta Monk, a famous author, had a life insurance policy with Drummond Life Insurance Company. Her son, Peter, was beneficiary. Roberta disappeared from her residence in the city of Metropolis two years ago and has not been seen since. On the day that Roberta disappeared, Sky Airlines Flight 22 left Metropolis for Rio de Janeiro and vanished; the plane's passenger list included a Roberta Rector.

Peter is now suing Drummond Life Insurance Company for the proceeds of his mother's policy. At trial, Peter offers to testify that his mother told him that she planned to write her next novel under the pen name of Roberta Rector.

Peter's testimony is

(A)   admissible as circumstantial evidence that Roberta Monk was on the plane.

(B)   admissible as a party admission, because Roberta and Peter Monk are in privity with each other.

(C)   inadmissible, because Roberta Monk has not been missing more than seven years.

(D)   inadmissible, because it is hearsay not within any exception.

188. Jones and Smith, who were professional rivals, were attending a computer industry dinner where each was to receive an award for achievement in the field of data processing. Smith engaged Jones in conversation and expressed the opinion that if they joined forces, they could do even better. Jones replied that she would not consider Smith as a business partner and when Smith demanded to know why, told him that he, Smith, was incompetent.

The exchange was overheard by Brown, who attended the dinner. Smith suffered emotional distress but no pecuniary loss.

If Smith asserts a claim against Jones based on defamation, will Smith prevail?

(A)   No, because Smith suffered no pecuniary loss.

(B)   No, because Jones's statement was made to Smith and not to Brown.

(C)   No, unless Jones should have foreseen that her statement would be overheard by another person.

(D)   No, unless Jones intended to cause Smith emotional distress.

189. Ozzie owned and occupied Blackacre, which was a tract of land improved with a one-family house. His friend Victor orally offered Ozzie $50,000 for Blackacre, the fair market value, and Ozzie accepted. Because they were friends, they saw no need for attorneys or written contracts and shook hands on the deal. Victor paid Ozzie $5,000 down in cash and agreed to pay the balance of $45,000 at an agreed closing time and place.

Before the closing, Victor inherited another home and asked Ozzie to return his $5,000. Ozzie refused, and, at the time set for the closing, Ozzie tendered a good deed to Victor and declared his intention to vacate Blackacre the next day. Ozzie demanded that Victor complete the purchase. Victor refused. The fair market value of Blackacre has remained $50,000.

In an appropriate action brought by Ozzie against Victor for specific performance, if Ozzie loses, the most likely reason will be that

(A)   the agreement was oral.

O → V -85K

(B)   keeping the $5,000 is Ozzie's exclusive remedy.
(C)   Victor had a valid reason for not closing.
(D)   Ozzie remained in possession on the day set for the closing.

190. Small retailers located in the state of Yellow are concerned about the loss of business to certain large retailers located nearby in bordering states.

In an effort to deal with this concern, the legislature of Yellow enacted a statute requiring all manufacturers and wholesalers who sell goods to retailers in Yellow to do so at prices that are no higher than the lowest prices at which they sell them to retailers in any of the states that border Yellow. Several manufacturers and wholesalers who are located in states bordering Yellow and who sell their goods to retailers in those states and in Yellow bring an action in federal court to challenge the constitutionality of this statute.

Which of the following arguments offered by these plaintiffs is likely to be most persuasive in light of applicable precedent?

The state statute
(A)   deprives them of their property or liberty without due process of law.

(B) imposes an unreasonable burden on interstate commerce.

(C) deprives them of a privilege or immunity of national citizenship.

(D) denies them the equal protection of the laws.

191. The Pinners, a retired couple, had lived in their home in a residential neighborhood for 20 years when the Darleys moved into the house next door and built a swimming pool in the back yard. The four young Darley children frequently played in the pool after school. They often were joined by other neighborhood children. The Pinners were in the habit of reading and listening to classical music in the afternoons. Sometimes they took naps. The boisterous sounds of the children playing in the pool disturbed the Pinners' customary enjoyment of quiet afternoons.
In the Pinners' nuisance action for damages against the Darleys, the Pinners should

(A) prevail, if the children's noise constituted a substantial interference with the Pinners' use and enjoyment of their home.

(B) prevail, because the Pinners' interest in the quiet enjoyment of their home takes precedence in time over the Darleys' interests.

(C) not prevail, unless the noise constituted a substantial and unreasonable disturbance to persons of normal sensibilities.

(D) not prevail, because the children's interest in healthy play has priority over the Pinners' interest in peace and quiet.

192. Which of the following items of evidence is LEAST likely to be admitted without a supporting witness?

(A) In a libel action, a copy of a newspaper purporting to be published by Defendant Newspaper Publishing Company.

(B) In a case involving contaminated food, a can label purporting to identify the canner as Defendant Company.

(C) In a defamation case, a document purporting to be a memorandum from the Defendant Company president to "All Personnel," printed on Defendant's letterhead.

(D) In a case involving injury to a pedestrian, a pamphlet on stopping distances issued by the State Highway Department.

Questions 193-194 are based on the following fact situation.

For several weeks Mater, a wealthy, unemployed widow, and Nirvana Motors, Inc., negotiated unsuccessfully over the purchase price of a new Mark XX Rolls-Royce sedan, which, as Nirvana knew, Mater wanted her son Dilbert to have as a wedding gift.

On April 27, Nirvana sent Mater a signed, dated memo saying, "If we can arrive at the same price within the next week, do we have a deal?" Mater wrote "Yes" and her signature at the bottom of this memo and delivered it back to Nirvana on April 29.

On May 1, Mater wrote Nirvana a signed letter offering to buy "one ~offer~ new Mark XX Rolls-Royce sedan, with all available equipment, for $180,000 cash on delivery not later than June 1." By coincidence, Nirvana wrote Mater a signed letter on May 1 offering to sell her "one new Mark XX Rolls-Royce sedan, with all available equipment, for $180,000 cash on delivery not later than June 1." These letters crossed in the mails and were respectively received and read by Mater and Nirvana on May 2.

193. If Mater subsequently asserts and Nirvana denies that the parties had a binding contract on May 3, which of the following most persuasively supports Mater's position?

(A)   A sale-of-goods contract may be made in any manner sufficient to show agreement, even though the moment of its making is undetermined.
(B)   A sale-of-goods contract does not require that an acceptance be a mirror image of the offer.
(C)   With respect both to the making of an agreement and the requirement of consideration,
identical cross-offers are functionally the same as an offer followed by a responsive acceptance.
(D)   Since Nirvana was a merchant in the transaction and Mater was not, Nirvana is estopped to deny that the parties' correspondence created a binding contract.

194. For this question only, assume the following facts. On May 4, Mater and Nirvana Motors both signed a single document evidencing a contract for the sale by Nirvana to Mater, "as a wedding gift for Mater's son Dilbert," a new Mark XX Rolls-Royce sedan under the same terms as previously stated in their correspondence. On May 5, Mater handed Dilbert a carbon copy of this document. In reliance on the prospective gift, Dilbert on May 20 sold his nearly new Cheetah (an expensive sports car) to a dealer at a "bargain" price of $50,000 and immediately informed Mater and Nirvana that he had done so.

On May 25, however, Mater and Nirvana Motors by mutual agreement rescinded in a signed writing "any and all agreements heretofore made between the undersigned parties for the sale and purchase of a new Mark XX Rolls-Royce sedan."

Later that day, Nirvana sold for $190,000 cash to another buyer the only new Mark XX Rolls-Royce that it had in stock or could readily obtain elsewhere. On June 1, Dilbert tendered $180,000 in cash to Nirvana Motors and demanded delivery to him "within a reasonable time" of a new Mark XX Rolls-Royce sedan with all available equipment.

Nirvana rejected the tender and denied any obligation.

If Dilbert sues Nirvana for breach of contract, which of the following will the court probably decide?

(A) Dilbert wins, because his rights as an assignee for value of the May 4 Mater-Nirvana contract cannot be cut off by agreement between the original parties.

(B) Dilbert wins, because his rights as a third-party intended beneficiary became vested by his prejudicial reliance in selling his Cheetah on May 20.

(C) Nirvana wins, because Dilbert, if an intended beneficiary at all of the Mater -Nirvana contract, was only a donee beneficiary.

(D) Nirvana wins, because it reasonably and prejudicially relied on its contract of mutual rescission with Mater by selling the only readily available new Mark XX Rolls-Royce sedan to another buyer.

195. A federally owned and operated office building in the state of West Dakota is heated with a new, pollution-free heating system. However, in the coldest season of the year, this new system is sometimes insufficient to supply adequate heat to the building. The appropriation statute providing the money for construction of the new heating system permitted use of the old, pollution-generating system when necessary to supply additional heat.

When the old heating system operates (only about two days in any year), the smokestack of the building emits smoke that exceeds the state of West Dakota's pollution-control standards.

May the operators of the federal office building be prosecuted successfully by West Dakota authorities for violating that state's pollution control standards?

(A) Yes, because the regulation of pollution is a legitimate state police power concern.

(B) Yes, because the regulation of pollution is a joint concern of the federal Government and the state and, therefore, both of them may regulate conduct causing pollution.

(C)   No, because the operations of the federal government are immune from state regulation in the absence of federal consent.

(D)   No, because the violations of the state Pollution-control standards involved here are so *de minimis* that they are beyond the legitimate reach of state law.

196. Jones, who was driving his car at night, stopped the car and went into a nearby tavern for a drink. He left the car standing on the side of the road, projecting three feet into the traffic lane. The lights were on and his friend, Peters, was asleep in the back seat. Peters awoke, discovered the situation, and went back to sleep. Before Jones returned, his car was hit by an automobile approaching from the rear and driven by Davis. Peters was injured.
Peters sued Davis and Jones jointly to recover the damages he suffered resulting from the accident. The jurisdiction has a pure comparative negligence rule and has abolished the defense of assumption of risk. In respect to other issues, the rules of the common law remain in effect.

Peters should recover

(A)   nothing, if Peters was more negligent than either Davis or Jones.

(B)   nothing, unless the total of Davis's and Jones's negligence was greater than Peters's.

(C)   from Davis and Jones, jointly and severally, the amount of damages Peters suffered reduced by the percentage of the total negligence that is attributed to Peters.

(D)   from Davis and Jones, severally, a percentage of Peters's damages equal to the percentage of fault attributed to each of the defendants.

197. Under the rule allowing exclusion of relevant evidence because its probative value is substantially outweighed by other considerations, which of the following is NOT to be considered?

(A)   The jury may be confused about the appropriate application of the evidence to the issues of the case.

(B)   The evidence is likely to arouse unfair prejudice on the part of the jury.

(C)   The opponent is surprised by the evidence and not fairly prepared to meet it.

(D)   The trial will be extended and made cumbersome by hearing evidence of relatively trivial consequence.

198. On June 1, Buyem, Inc., a widget manufacturer, entered into a written agreement with Mako, Inc., a tool maker in which Mako agreed to produce and sell to Buyem 12 sets of newly designed dies to be delivered August 1 for the price of $50,0000 payable ten days after delivery.

P v. D+J

Encountering unexpected expenses in the purchase of special alloy steel required for the dies, Mako advised Buyem that production costs would exceed the contract price; and on July I Buyem and Make signed a modification to the June 1 agreement increasing the contract price to $60,000.

After timely receipt of 12 sets of dies conforming to the contract specifications, Buyem paid Mako $50,000 but refused to pay more.

Which of the following concepts of the Uniform Commercial Code, dealing expressly with the sale of goods, best supports an action by Mako to recover $10,000 for breach of Buyem's July 1 promise?

(A)   Bargained-for exchange.
(B)   Promissory estoppel.
(C)   Modification of contracts without consideration.
(D)   Unconscionability in the formation of contracts.

199. Smith is a new lawyer who has three clients, all of whom are indigent. To improve the appearance of his office, he decided to purchase some new furniture and to pay for it out of future earnings. Wearing an expensive suit borrowed from a friend, Smith went to a furniture store and asked to purchase on credit a desk and various other items of furniture. Smith told the store owner that he was a very able lawyer with a growing practice and that he expected to do very well in the future. The store owner agreed to sell him the items on credit, and Smith promised to make monthly payments of $800.

Smith has never had an income from his practice of more than $150 a month. Smith's business did not improve, and he did not make any payments to the furniture store. After three months, the store owner repossessed the items.

If Smith is charged with obtaining property by false pretenses, his best argument for being NOT guilty would be that

(A)   even if he misled the store owner, he intended to pay for the items.
(B)   he did not misrepresent any material fact.
(C)   the store owner got his property back and so suffered no harm.
(D)   the store owner could have asked for payment in full at the time of the purchase.

200. Twenty years ago, Test, who owned Blackacre, a one-acre tract of land, duly delivered a deed of Blackacre "to School District so long as it is used for school purposes." The deed was promptly and properly recorded. Five years ago, Test died leaving Sonny as his only heir but, by his duly probated will, he left "all my Estate to my friend Fanny."

Last month, School District closed its school on Blackacre and for valid consideration duly executed and delivered a quitclaim deed of Blackacre to Owner, who planned to use the- land for commercial development.

S → O

Owner has now brought an appropriate action to quiet title against Sonny, Fanny, and School District.

The only applicable statute is a provision in the jurisdiction's probate code which provides that any property interest which is descendible is devisable.

In such action, the court should find that title is now in

(A)   Owner.
(B)   Sonny.
(C)   Fanny.
(D)   School District.

STOP
IF YOU FINISH BEFORE TIME IS CALLED, CHECK YOUR WORK ON THIS TEST

T → S

T → F

CONVERSION TABLE OF RAW TO SCALED SCORES

RAW SCORE	SCALED SCORE	RAW SCORE	SCALED SCORE	RAW SCORE	SCALED SCORE	RAW SCORE	SCALED SCORE
80	101	100 **13.6%**	121	120 **55.6%**	140	140	159
81	102	101	122	121 **58.2%**	141	141 **91.8%**	160
82	103	102	123	122	142	142 **92.6%**	161
83	104	103	124	123	143	143	162
84	105	104	125	124	144	144	163
85	106	105	126	125	145	145	164
86	107	106 **23.5%**	127	126	146	146	165
87	108	107 **25.3%**	128	127 **71.1%**	147	147	166
88	109	108	129	128 **73.1%**	148	148 **96.5%**	167
89	110	109	130	129	149	149 **97.0%**	168
90	111	110	131	130	150	150	169
91	112	111	132	131	151	151	170
92	113	112	133	132	152	152	171
93	114	113 **38.6%**	134	133	153	153	172
94	115	114 **41.0%**	135	134 **83.5%**	153	154	173
95	116	115	136	135 **85.0%**	154	155 **98.9%**	173
96	117	116	137	136	155	156 **99.0%**	174
97	118	117	138	137	156	157	175
98	119	118 **50.0%**	138	138	157	158	176
99	120	119	139	139	158	159 **99.5%**	177

Find your raw score in the unshaded boxes above. The column to the right will show you the scaled score assigned to that raw score when this Exam was actually administered in February, 1991. The bold figures present the percentile ranking of that raw score as determined by the National Conference of Bar Examiners. For example, a raw score of 118 was the average score on this Exam when it was actually administered.

MEAN SCORES

Constitutional Law	21 (70%)	Contracts and Sales	27 (67%)	Criminal Law and Procedure	18 (60%)
Evidence	20 (67%)	Property	17 (59%)	Torts	25 (62%)
Total (Raw)	128 (58%)	Total (Scaled)	138		

The scores shown above are the mean scores on each subject and the Exam overall as reported by the National Conference of Bar Examiners. The first number is the raw score. The second number is the percentage of total correct in that subject that that raw score represents. For example, the mean score on the Constitutional Law questions on this exam was 21 (out of 30), which means that the average person got 70% of the Constitutional Law questions right. Bear in mind, though, that the "mean" score is not the same as the "passing" score. In fact, in all jurisdictions, the mean score is higher than the score required to pass. The mean scores shown above are scores to shoot for -- a score that will absolutely guarantee your passing the Multistate Bar Exam. You can pass the bar with a lower score than that shown above.

ANSWER KEY (1–150)

1.(D)	26.	(A)	51.	(B)	76.	(B)(C)	101.	(C)	126.(C)	
2.(C)	27.	(A)	52.	(A)	77.	(B)	102.	(D)	127.(B)	
3.(A)	28.	(B)	53.	(A)	78.	(A)	103.	(A)	128.(A)	
4.(D)	29.	(C)	54.	(C)	79.	(C)	104.	(D)	129.(A)	
5.(B)	30.	(C)	55.	(D)	80.	(A)	105.	(B)	130.(C)	
6.(A)	31.	(B)	56.	(A)	81.	(B)	106.	(B)	131.(C)	
7.(D)	32.	(D)	57.	(A)	82.	(B)	107.	(D)	132.(A)	
8.(D)	33.	(B)	58.	(D)	83.	(B)	108.	(D)	133.(C)	
9.(A)	34.	(B)	59.	(B)	84.	(A)	109.	(B)	134.(B)	
10.(B)	35.	(C)	60.	(D)	85.	(A)	110.	(A)	135.(B)	
11.(B)	36.	(D)	61.	(A)	86.	(D)	111.	(All)	136.(A)	
12.(C)	37.	(A)	62.	(D)	87.	(C)	112.	(A)	137.(D)	
13.(B)	38.	(D)	63.	(B)	88.	(D)	113.	(C)	138.(B)	
14.(A)	39.	(A)	64.	(B)	89.	(C)	114.	(C)	139.(B)	
15.(D)	40.	(A)	65.	(A)	90.	(D)	115.	(A)	140.(A)	
16.(B)	41.	(B)	66.	(D)	91.	(B)	116.	(A)	141.(D)	
17.(C)	42.	(D)	67.	(C)	92.	(A)	117.	(D)	142.(A)	
18.(C)	43.	(C)	68.	(D)	93.	(D)	118.	(C)	143.(A)	
19.(A)	44.	(B)	69.	(D)	94.	(A)	119.	(D)	144.(C)	
20.(D)	45.	(C)	70.	(A)	95.	(C)	120.	(A)	145.(C)	
21.(B)	46.	(A)	71.	(C)	96.	(B)	121.	(B)	146.(A)	
22.(D)	47.	(A)	72.	(A)	97.	(D)	122.	(C)	147.(C)	
23.(D)	48.	(D)	73.	(C)	98.	(D)	123.	(B)	148.(B)	
24.(A)	49.	(B)	74.	(A)	99.	(D)	124.	(A)	149.(D)	
25.(A)	50.	(D)	75.	(B)	100.	(C)	125.	(D)	150.(D)	

**Note, #99, correct answer is (D) as noted above. The lecture mistakenly states that (B) is correct.

ANSWER KEY (151–200)

151.(B)	176. (D)	51.
152.(C)	177. (C)	52.
153.(B)	178. (D)	53.
154.(A)	179. (C)	54.
155.(B)	180. (D)	55.
156.(B)	181. (D)	56.
157.(D)	182. (B)	57.
158.(C)	183. (C)	58.
159.(D)	184. (C)	59.
160.(B)	185. (B)	60.
161.(C)	186. (D)	61.
162.(C)	187. (A)	62.
163.(B)	188. (C)	63.
164.(C)	189. (A)	64.
165.(A)	190. (B)	65.
166.(B)	191. (C)	66.
167.(C)	192. (C)	67.
168.(B)	193. (A)	68.
169.(D)	194. (B)	69.
170.(A)	195. (C)	70.
171.(A)	196. (C)	71.
172.(C)	197. (C)	72.
173.(D)	198. (C)	73.
174.(C)	199. (A), (B)	74.
175.(B)	200. (C)	75.

91 MULTISTATE BAR EXAM

II)

DO NOT TURN THIS PAGE UNTIL YOU ARE INSTRUCTED TO DO SO
OR ARE READY TO BEGIN THE TEST.

Time-3 hours

Directions: Each of the questions or incomplete statements below is followed by four suggested answers or completions. You are to choose the best of the stated alternatives. Answer all questions according to the generally accepted view, except where otherwise noted.

For the purposes of this test, you are to assume that Articles 1 and 2 of the Uniform Commercial Code have been adopted. You are also to assume relevant application of Article 9 of the UCC concerning fixtures. The Federal Rules of Evidence are deemed to control. The terms "Constitution," "constitutional," and "unconstitutional" refer to the federal Constitution unless indicated to the contrary. You are also to assume that there is no applicable community property law, no guest statute, and no No-Fault Insurance Act unless otherwise specified. In negligence cases, if fault on the claimant's part is or may be relevant, the statement of facts for the particular question will identify the contributory or comparative negligence rule that is to be applied.

1. By warranty deed, Marta conveyed Blackacre to Beth and Christine "as joint tenants with right of survivorship." Beth and Christine are not related. Beth conveyed all her interest to Eugenio by warranty deed and subsequently died intestate. Thereafter, Christine conveyed to Darin by warranty deed.

    There is no applicable statute, and the jurisdiction recognizes the common-law joint tenancy.

    Title to Blackacre is in
    (A)   Darin.
    (B)   Marta.
    (C)   Darin and Eugenio.
    (D)   Darin and the heirs of Beth.

2. Peavey was walking peacefully along a public street when he encountered Dorwin, who he had never seen before. Without provocation or warning, Dorwin picked up a rock and struck Peavey with it. It was later established that Dorwin was mentally ill and suffered recurrent hallucinations.

    If Peavey asserts a claim against Dorwin based on battery, which of the following, if supported by evidence, will be Dorwin's best defense?
    (A)   Dorwin did not understand that his act was wrongful.
    (B)   Dorwin did not desire to cause harm to Peavey.
    (C)   Dorwin did not know that he was striking a person.
    (D)   Dorwin thought Peavey was about to attack him.

3. Penstock owned a large tract of land on the shore of a lake. Drury lived on a stream that ran along one boundary of Penstock's land and into the lake. At some time in the past, a channel had been cut across Penstock's land from the stream to the lake at a point some distance from the mouth of the stream. From where Drury lived, the channel served as a convenient shortcut to the lake. Erroneously believing that the channel was a public waterway, Drury made frequent trips through the channel in his motorboat. His use of the channel caused no harm to the land through which it passed.

If Penstock asserts a claim for damages against Drury based on trespass, which of the following would be a correct disposition of the case?

(A) Judgment for Penstock for nominal damages, because Drury intentionally used the channel.

(B) Judgment for Drury, if he did not use the channel after learning of Penstock's ownership claim.

(C) Judgment for Drury, because he caused no harm to Penstock's land.

(D) Judgment for Drury, because when he used the channel he believed it was a public waterway.

Questions 4–5 are based on the following fact situation.

Structo contracted with Bailey to construct for $500,000 a warehouse and an access driveway at highway level. Shortly after commencing work on the driveway, which required for the specified level some excavation and removal of surface material, Structo unexpectedly encountered a large mass of solid rock.

4. For this question only, assume the following facts. Structo informed Bailey (accurately) that because of the rock the driveway as specified would cost at least $20,000 more than figured, and demanded for that reason a total contract price of $520,000. Since Bailey was expecting warehousing customers immediately after the agreed completion date, he signed a writing promising to pay the additional $20,000. Following timely completion of the warehouse and driveway, which conformed to the contract in all respects, Bailey refused to pay Structo more than $500,000.

What is the maximum amount to which Structo is entitled?

(A) $500,000, because there was no consideration for Bailey's promise to pay the additional $20,000.

(B) $500,000, because Bailey's promise to pay the additional $20,000 was exacted under duress.

(C) $520,000, because the modification was fair and was made in the light of circumstances not anticipated by the parties when the original contract was made.

(D) $520,000, provided that the reasonable value of Structo's total performance was that much or more.

5. For this question only, assume the following facts. Upon encountering the rock formation, Structo, instead of incurring additional costs to remove it, built the access driveway over the rock with a steep grade down to the highway. Bailey, who was out of town for several days, was unaware of this nonconformity until the driveway had been finished. As built, it is too steep to be used safely by trucks or cars, particularly in the wet or icy weather frequently occurring in the area. It would cost $30,000 to tear out and rebuild the driveway at highway level. As built, the warehouse, including the driveway, has a fair market value of $550,000. Bailey has paid $470,000 to Structo, but refuses to pay more because of the nonconforming driveway, which Structo has refused to tear out and rebuild.

If Structo sues Bailey for monetary relief, what is the maximum amount Structo is entitled to recover?

(A) $30,000, because the fair market value of the warehouse and driveway "as is" exceeds the contract price by $50,000 (more than the cost of correcting the driveway).

(B) $30,000, because Structo substantially performed and the cost of correcting the driveway would involve economic waste.

(C) $30,000, minus whatever amount Structo saved by not building the driveway at the specified level.

(D) Nothing, because Bailey is entitled to damages for the cost of correcting the driveway.

6. Larson was charged with the murder of a man who had been strangled and whose body was found in some woods near his home. Larson suffers from a neurological problem that makes it impossible for him to remember an occurrence for longer than 48 hours.

After Larson was charged, the police visited him and asked if they might search his home. Larson consented. The police found a diary written by Larson. An entry dated the same day as the victim's disappearance read, "Indescribable excitement. Why did no one ever tell me that killing gave such pleasure to the master?"

Larson was charged with murder. His attorney has moved to exclude the diary from evidence on the ground that its admission would violate Larson's privilege against self-incrimination. Counsel has also argued that Larson could not give informed consent to the search because more than 48 hours had passed since the making of the entry and hence he could not remember the existence of the incriminating entry at the time he gave his consent. There is no evidence that the police officers who secured Larson's consent to the search were aware of his memory impairment.
With regard to the diary, the court should

(A) admit it, because Larson's consent was not obtained by intentional police misconduct and Larson was not compelled to make the diary entry.
(B) admit it, pursuant to the good-faith exception to the exclusionary rule.
(C) exclude it, because Larson was not competent to consent to a search.
(D) exclude it, because use of the diary as evidence would violate Larson's privilege against self-incrimination.

7. In contract litigation between Pixley and Dill, a fact of consequence to the determination of the action is whether Pixley provided Dill with a required notice at Dill's branch office "in the state capital." Pixley introduced evidence that he gave notice at Dill's office in the city of Capitan. Although Capitan is the state's capital, Pixley failed to offer proof of that fact.

Which of the following statements is most clearly correct with respect to possible judicial notice of the fact that Capitan is the state's capital?

(A) The court may take judicial notice even though Pixley does not request it.

(B) The court may take judicial notice only if Pixley provides the court with an authenticated copy of the statute that designates Capitan as the capital.

(C) If the court takes judicial notice, the burden of persuasion on the issue of whether Capitan is the capital shifts to Dill.

(D) If the court takes judicial notice, it should instruct the jury that it may, but is not required to, accept as conclusive the fact that Capitan is the capital.

8. A statute of the state of East Dakota requires each insurance company that offers burglary insurance policies in the state to charge a uniform rate for such insurance to all of its customers residing within the same county in that state. So long as it complies with this requirement, a company is free to charge whatever rate the market will bear for its burglary insurance policies.

An insurance company located in the state of East Dakota files suit in federal district court against appropriate East Dakota state officials to challenge this statute on constitutional grounds. The insurance company wishes to charge customers residing within the same county in East Dakota rates for burglary insurance policies that will vary because they would be based on the specific nature of the customer's business, on its precise location, and on its past claims record.

In this suit, the court should

(A) hold the statute unconstitutional, because the statute deprives the insurance company of its liberty or property without due process of law.

(B) hold the statute unconstitutional, because the statute imposes an undue burden on interstate commerce.

(C) hold the statute constitutional, because the statute is a reasonable exercise of the state's police power.

(D)   abstain from ruling on the merits of this case until the state courts have had an opportunity to pass on the constitutionality of this state statute.

9.   Dawson was charged with felony murder because of his involvement in a bank robbery. The evidence at trial disclosed that Smith invited Dawson to go for a ride in his new car, and after a while asked Dawson to drive. As Smith and Dawson drove around town, Smith explained to Dawson that he planned to rob the bank and that he needed Dawson to drive the getaway car. Dawson agreed to drive to the bank and to wait outside while Smith went in to rob it. As they approached the bank, Dawson began to regret his agreement to help with the robbery. Once there, Smith got out of the car. As Smith went out of sight inside the bank, Dawson drove away and went home. Inside the bank, Smith killed a bank guard who tried to prevent him from leaving with the money. Smith ran outside and, finding that his car and Dawson were gone, ran down an alley. He was apprehended a few blocks away. Dawson later turned himself in after hearing on the radio that Smith had killed the guard.

The jurisdiction has a death penalty that applies to felony murder.
Consistent with the law and the Constitution, the jury may convict Dawson of

(A)   felony murder and impose the death penalty.
(B)   felony murder but not impose the death penalty.
(C)   bank robbery only.
(D)   no crime.

10.   In an automobile negligence action by Popkin against Dwyer, Juilliard testified for Popkin. Dwyer later called Watts, who testified that Juilliard's reputation for truthfulness was bad.

On cross-examination of Watts, Popkin's counsel asks, "Isn't it a fact that when you bought your new car last year, you made a false affidavit to escape paying the sales tax?"

This question is

(A)   proper, because it will indicate Watt's standard of judgment as to reputation for truthfulness.
(B)   proper, because it bears on Watt's credibility.
(C)   improper, because character cannot be proved by specific instances of conduct.

(D)   improper, because one cannot impeach an impeaching witness.

11.   David built in his backyard a garage that encroached two feet across the property line onto property owned by his neighbor, Prudence. Thereafter, David sold his property to Drake. Prudence was unaware, prior to David's sale to Drake, of the encroachment of the garage onto her property. When she thereafter learned of the encroachment, she sued David for damages for trespass.

In this action, will Prudence prevail?

(A)   No, unless David was aware of the encroachment when the garage was built.
(B)   No, because David no longer owns or possesses the garage.
(C)   Yes, because David knew where the garage was located, whether or not he knew where the property line was.
(D)   Yes, unless Drake was aware of the encroachment when he purchased the property.

12.   Poole sued Darrel for unlawfully using Poole's idea for an animal robot as a character in Darrell's science fiction movie. Darrel admitted that he had received a model of an animal robot from Poole, but he denied that it had any substantial similarity to the movie character. After the model had been returned to Poole, Poole destroyed it.

In order for Poole to testify to the appearance of the model, Poole

(A)   must show that he did not destroy the model in bad faith.
(B)   must give advance notice of his intent to introduce the oral testimony.
(C)   must introduce a photograph of the model if one exists.
(D)   need do none of the above, because the "best evidence rule" applies only to writings, recordings, and photographs.

13.   Lanny, the owner of Whiteacre in fee simple, leased Whiteacre to Teri for a term of ten years by properly executed written instrument. The lease was promptly and properly recorded. It contained an option for Teri to purchase Whiteacre by tendering $250,000 as purchase price any time "during the term of this lease." One year later, Teri, by a properly executed written instrument, purported to assign the option to Oscar, expressly retaining all of the remaining term of the lease.

The instrument of assignment was promptly and properly recorded.

Two years later, Lanny contracted to sell Whiteacre to Jones and to convey a marketable title "subject to the rights of Teri under her lease." Jones refused to close because of the outstanding option assigned to Oscar.

Lanny brought an appropriate action against Jones for specific performance.

If judgment is rendered in favor of Lanny, it will be because the relevant jurisdiction has adopted a rule on a key issue as to which various state courts have split.

Which of the following identifies the determinative rule or doctrine upon which the split occurs, and states the position favorable to Lanny?

(A) In a contract to buy, any form of "subject to a lease" clause that fail: to mention expressly an existing option means that the seller is agreeing to sell free and clear of any option originally included in the lease.

(B) Marketable title can be conveyed so long as any outstanding option not mentioned in the purchase contract has not yet been exercised.

(C) Options to purchase by lessees are subject to the Rule Against Perpetuities.

(D) Options to purchase contained in a lease cannot be assigned separately from the lease.

14. Daniel and a group of his friends are fanatical basketball fans who regularly meet at each others' homes to watch basketball games on television. Some of the group are fans of team A, and others are fans of team B. When the group has watched televised games between these two teams, fights sometimes have broken out among the group. Despite this fact, Daniel invited the group to his home to watch a championship game between teams A and B.

During the game, Daniel's guests became rowdy and antagonistic. Fearing that they would begin to fight, and that a fight would damage his possessions, Daniel asked his guests to leave. They refused to go and soon began to fight. Daniel called the police, and Officer was sent to Daniel's home. Officer sustained a broken nose in his efforts to stop the fighting.

Officer brought an action against Daniel alleging that Daniel was negligent in inviting the group to his house to watch this championship game. Daniel has moved to dismiss the complaint.

The best argument in support of this motion would be that

(A)   a rescuer injured while attempting to avert a danger cannot recover damages from the endangered person.

(B)   a police officer is not entitled to a recovery based upon the negligent conduct that created the need for the officer's professional intervention.

(C)   as a matter of law, Daniel's conduct was not the proximate cause of Officer's injury.

(D)   Daniel did not owe Officer a duty to use reasonable care, because Officer was a mere licensee on Daniel's property.

15.   In a prosecution of Drew for forgery, the defense objects to the testimony of West, a government expert, on the ground of inadequate qualifications. The government seeks to introduce a letter from the expert's former criminology professor, stating that West is generally acknowledged in his field as well qualified.

On the issue of the expert's qualifications, the letter may be considered by

(A)   the jury, without regard to the hearsay rule.

(B)   the judge, without regard to the hearsay rule.

(C)   neither the judge nor the jury, because it is hearsay not within any exception.

(D)   both the judge and the jury, because the letter is not offered for a hearsay purpose.

Questions 16-17 are based on the following fact situation.

Responding to County Is written advertisement for bids, Tyres was the successful bidder for the sale of tires to County for County's vehicles. Tyres and County entered into a signed, written agreement that specified, "It is agreed that Tyres will deliver all tires required by this agreement to County, in accordance with the attached bid form and specifications, for a one-year period beginning September 1, 1990" Attached to the agreement was a copy of the bid form and specifications. In the written advertisement to which Tyres had responded, but not in the bid form, County had stated, "Multiple awards may be issued if they are in the best interests of County."

No definite quantity of tires to be bought by County from Tyres was specified in any of these documents.

In January 1991, Tyres learned that County was buying some of its tires from one of Tyres's competitors. Contending that the Tyres-County agreement was a requirements contract, Tyres sued County for the damages caused by County's buying some of its tires from the competitor.

16. If County defends by offering proof of the advertisement concerning the possibility of multiple rewards, should the court admit the evidence?

   (A) Yes, because the provision in the written agreement, "all tires required by this agreements" is ambiguous.
   (B) Yes, because the advertisement was in writing.
   (C) No, because of the parol evidence rule.
   (D) No, because it would make the contract illusory.

17. If the court concludes that the Tyres-County contract is an agreement by County to buy its tire requirements from Tyres, Tyres probably will

   (A) recover under the contracts clause of the United States Constitution.
   (B) recover under the provisions of the Uniform Commercial Code.
   (C) not recover, because the agreement lacks mutuality of obligation.
   (D) not recover, because the agreement is indefinite as to quantity.

18. Supermarket is in a section of town where there are sometimes street fights and where pedestrians are occasionally the victims of pickpockets and muggers. In recognition of the unusual number of robberies in the area, the supermarket posted signs in the store and in its parking lot that read:

Warning: There are pickpockets and muggers at work in this part of the city. Supermarket is not responsible for the acts of criminals.

One evening, Lorner drove to Supermarket to see about a special on turkeys that Supermarket was advertising. She decided that the turkeys were too large and left the store without purchasing anything. In the parking lot, she was attacked by an unknown man who raped her and then ran away.

If Lorner sues Supermarket, the result should be for the

(A) plaintiff, if Supermarket failed to take reasonable steps to protect customers against criminal attack in its parking lot.

(B) plaintiff, because Supermarket is liable for harm to business invitees on its premises.

(C) defendant, if the warning signs were plainly visible to Lorner.

(D) defendant, because the rapist was the proximate cause of Lorner's injuries.

19. Jones wanted to kill Adams because he believed Adams was having an affair with Jones's wife. Early one morning, armed with a pistol, he crouched behind some bushes on a park hillside overlooking a path upon which Adams frequently jogged. On this morning, however, Jones saw Adams jogging on another path about a half mile away. Nonetheless, Jones fired five shots at Adams. None of the five shots came anywhere close to Adams as he was well out of the range of the pistol Jones was using.

Jones is

(A) guilty of attempted murder, if he was not aware of the limited range of his pistol.

(B) guilty of attempted murder, if a reasonable person would not have been aware of the limited range of his pistol.

(C) not guilty of attempted murder, or any lesser included offense, because, under the circumstances, it was impossible for him to have killed Adams.

(D) not guilty of attempted murder, but guilty of assault.

20. Widgets are manufactured wholly from raw materials mined and processed in the state of Green. The only two manufacturers of widgets in the United States are also located in that state. However, their widgets are purchased by retailers located in every state. The legislature of the state of Green is considering the adoption of a statute that would impose a tax solely on the manufacture of widgets. The tax is to be calculated at 3% of their wholesale value.

Which of the following arguments would be LEAST helpful to the state in defending the constitutionality of this proposed state tax on widgets?

(A) At the time widgets are manufactured and taxed they have not yet entered the channels of interstate commerce.

(B) The economic impact of this tax will be passed on to both in-state and out-of-state purchasers of widgets and, therefore, it is wholly nondiscriminatory in its effect.

(C) Because of the powers reserved to them by the Tenth Amendment, states have plenary authority to construct their tax system in any manner they choose.

(D) A tax on the manufacture of widgets may be imposed only by the state in which the manufacturing occurs and, therefore, it is not likely to create the danger of a multiple tax burden on interstate commerce.

21. Blackacre is a large tract of land owned by a religious order known as The Seekers. On Blackacre, The Seekers erected a large residential building where its members reside. Blackacre is surrounded by rural residential properties and its only access to a public way is afforded by an easement over a strip of land 30 feet wide. The easement was granted to The Seekers by deed from Sally, the owner of one of the adjacent residential properties. The Seekers built a driveway on the strip, and the easement was used for 20 years without incident or objection.

Last year, as permitted by the applicable zoning ordinance, The Seekers constructed a 200-bed nursing home and a parking lot on Blackacre, using all of Blackacre that was available for such development. The nursing home was very successful, and on Sundays visitors to the nursing home overflowed the parking facilities on Blackacre and parked all along the driveway from early in the morning through the evening hours. After two Sundays of the resulting congestion and inconvenience, Sally erected a barrier across the driveway on Sundays preventing any use of the driveway by anyone seeking access to Blackacre. The Seekers objected.

Sally brought an appropriate action to terminate the easement.

The most likely result in this action is that the court will hold for

(A)   Sally, because The Seekers excessively expanded the use of the dominant tenement.
(B)   Sally, because the parking on the driveway exceeded the scope of the easement.
(C)   The Seekers, because expanded use of the easement does not terminate the easement.
(D)   The Seekers, because Sally's use of self-help denies her the right to equitable relief.

22.   Ralph and Sam were engaged in a heated discussion over the relative merits of their favorite professional football teams when Ralph said, "You have to be one of the dumbest persons around." Sam slapped Ralph. Ralph drew a knife and stabbed Sam in the stomach. Other persons then stepped in and stopped any further fighting. Despite the pleas of the other persons, Sam refused to go to a hospital or to seek medical treatment About two hours later, he died as the result of a loss of blood. Ralph was charged with the murder of Sam. At trial, medical evidence established that if Sam had been taken to a hospital, he would have survived.

At the end of the case, Ralph moves for a judgment of acquittal or, in the alternative, for an instruction on the elements of voluntary manslaughter.

The court should

(A)   grant the motion for acquittal.
(B)   deny the motion for acquittal, but instruct on manslaughter because there is evidence of adequate provocation.
(C)   deny both motions, because Ralph failed to retreat.
(D)   deny both motions, because malice may be proved by the intentional use of a deadly weapon on a vital part of the body.

23.   Three months ago, Bert agreed in writing to buy Sam's single-family residence, Liveacre, for $110,000. Bert paid Sam a $5,000 deposit to be applied to the purchase price. The contract stated that Sam had the right at his option to retain the deposit as liquidated damages in the event of Bert's default. The closing was to have taken place last week.

Six weeks ago, Bert was notified by his employer that he was to be transferred to another job 1,000 miles away. Bert immediately notified Sam that he could not close, and therefore he demanded the return of his $5,000. Sam refused, waited until after the contract closing date, listed with a broker, and then conveyed Liveacre for $108,000 to Conner, a purchaser found by the real estate broker. Conner paid the full purchase price and immediately recorded his deed. Conner knew of the prior contract with Bert. In an appropriate action, Bert seeks to recover the $5,000 deposit from Sam.

The most probable result will be that Sam

(A)   must return the $5,000 to Bert, because Sam can no longer carry out his contract with Bert.
(B)   must return the $5,000 to Bert, because Bert was legally justified in not completing the contract.
(C)   must return $3,000 to Bert, because Sam's damages were only $2,000.
(D)   may keep the $5,000 deposit, because Bert breached the contract.

24.   Rollem, an automobile retailer, had an adult daughter, Betsy, who needed a car in her employment but had only $3,000 with which to buy one. Rollem wrote to her, "Give me your $3,000 and I'll give you the car on our lot that we have been using as a demonstrator." Betsy thanked her father and paid him the $3,000. As both Rollem and Betsy knew, the demonstrator was reasonably worth $10,000. After Betsy had paid the $3,000, but before the car had been delivered to her, one of Rollem's sales staff sold and delivered the same car to a customer for $10,000. Neither the salesperson nor the customer was aware of the transaction between Rollem and Betsy.

Does Betsy, after rejecting a tendered return of the $3,000 by Rollem, have an action against him for breach of contract?

(A)   Yes, because Rollem's promise was supported by bargained–for consideration.
(B)   Yes, because Rollem's promise was supported by the moral obligation a father owes his child as to the necessities of modern life.

(C) No, because the payment of $3,000 was inadequate consideration to support Rollem's promise.

(D) No, because the salesperson's delivery of the car to the customer made it impossible for Rollem to perform.

25. Peter, who was 20 years old, purchased a new, high-powered sports car that was marketed with an intended and recognized appeal to youthful drivers. The car was designed with the capability to attain speeds in excess of 100 miles per hour. It was equipped with tires designed and tested only for a maximum safe speed of 85 miles per hour. The owner's manual that came with the car stated that "continuous driving over 90 miles per hour requires high-speed capability tires," but the manual did not describe the speed capability of the tires sold with the car.

Peter took his new car out for a spin on a straight, smooth country road where the posted speed limit was 55 miles per hour. Intending to test the car's power, he drove for a considerable distance at over 100 miles per hour. While he was doing so, the tread separated from the left rear tire, causing the car to leave the road and hit a tree.

Peter sustained severe injuries.

Peter has brought a strict product liability action in tort against the manufacturer of the car. You should assume that pure comparative fault principles apply to this case.

Will Peter prevail?

(A) No, because Peter's driving at an excessive speed constituted a misuse of the car.

(B) No, because the car was not defective.

(C) Yes, if the statement in the manual concerning the tires did not adequately warn of the danger of high-speed driving on the tires mounted on the car.

(D) Yes, unless Peter's driving at a speed in excess of the posted speed limit was negligence *per se* that, by the law of the jurisdiction, was not excusable.

26. In a federal court diversity action by Plant against Decord on an insurance claim, a question arose whether the court should apply a presumption that, where both husband and wife were killed in a common accident, the husband died last.

Whether this presumption should be applied is to be determined according to

(A) traditional common law.
(B) federal statutory law.
(C) the law of the state whose substantive law is applied.
(D) the federal common law.

27. Plagued by neighborhood youths who had been stealing lawn furniture from his back yard, Armando remained awake nightly watching for them. One evening Armando heard noises in his backyard. He yelled out, warning intruders to leave. Receiving no answer, he fired a shotgun filled with nonlethal buckshot into bushes along his back fence where he believed the intruders might be hiding. A six-year-old child was hiding in the bushes and was struck in the eye by some of the pellets, causing loss of sight.

If Armando is charged with second degree assault, which is defined in the jurisdiction as "maliciously causing serious physical injury to another," he is

(A) not guilty, because the child was trespassing and he was using what he believed was nondeadly force.
(B) not guilty, because he did not intend to kill or to cause serious physical injury.

(C) guilty, because he recklessly caused serious physical injury.
(D) guilty, because there is no privilege to use force against a person who is too young to be criminally responsible.

28. Twenty percent of the residents of Green City are members of minority racial groups. These residents are evenly distributed among the many different residential areas of the city. The five city council members of Green City are elected from five single-member electoral districts that are nearly equally populated. No candidate has ever been elected to the city council who was a member of a minority racial group.

A group of citizens who are members of minority racial groups file suit in federal district court seeking a declaratory judgment that the single-member districts in Green City are unconstitutional. They claim that the single-member distracting system in that city diminishes the ability of voters who are members of minority racial groups to affect the outcome of city elections.

They seek an order from the court forcing the city to adopt an at-large election system in which the five candidates with the greatest vote totals would be elected to the city council. No state or federal statutes are applicable to the resolution of this suit.

Which of the following constitutional provisions provides the most obvious basis for plaintiffs' claim in this suit?

(A) The Thirteenth Amendment.
(B) The due process clause of the Fourteenth Amendment.
(C) The privileges and immunities clause of the Fourteenth Amendment.
(D) The Fifteenth Amendment.

29. Loomis, the owner and operator of a small business, encourages "wellness" on the part of his employees and supports various physical-fitness programs to that end. Learning that one of his employees, Graceful, was a dedicated jogger, Loomis promised to pay her a special award of $100 if she could and would run one mile in less than six minutes on the following Saturday. Graceful thanked him, and did in fact run a mile in less than six minutes on the day specified. Shortly thereafter, however, Loomis discovered that for more than a year Graceful had been running at least one mile in less than six minutes every day as a part of her personal fitness program. He refused to pay the $100.

In an action by Graceful against Loomis for breach of contract, which of the following best summarizes the probable decision of the court?

(A) Loomis wins, because it is a compelling inference that Loomis's promise did not induce Graceful to run the specified mile.
(B) Loomis wins, because Graceful's running of the specified mile was beneficial, not detrimental, to her in any event.
(C) Graceful wins, because running a mile in less than six minutes is a significantly demanding enterprise.
(D) Graceful wins, because she ran the specified mile as requested, and her motives for doing so are irrelevant.

30. Able was the owner of Blackacre, an undeveloped city lot. Able and Baker executed a written document in which Able agreed to sell Blackacre to Baker and Baker agreed to buy Blackacre from Able for $100,000; the document did not provide for an earnest money down payment. Able recorded the document, as authorized by statute.

Able orally gave Baker permission to park his car on Blackacre without charge prior to the closing. Thereafter, Baker frequently parked his car on Blackacre.

Another property came on the market that Baker wanted more than Blackacre. Baker decided to try to escape any obligation to Able.

Baker had been told that contracts for the purchase and sale of real property require consideration and concluded that because he had made no earnest money down payment, he could refuse to close and not be liable. Baker notified Able of his intention not to close and, in fact, did refuse to close on the date set for the closing. Able brought an appropriate action to compel specific performance by Baker.

If Able wins, it will be because

(A) Baker's use of Blackacre for parking constitutes part performance.

(B) general contract rules regarding consideration apply to real estate contracts.

(C) the doctrine of equitable conversion applies.

(D) the document was recorded.

Questions 31–32 are based on the following fact situation.

Under the terms of a written contract, Karp agreed to construct for Manor a garage for $10,000. Nothing was said in the parties' negotiations or in the contract about progress payments during the course of the work.

31. For this question only, assume the following facts. After completing 25% of the garage strictly according to Manor's specifications, Karp demanded payment of $2,000 as a "reasonable progress payment." Manor refused, and Karp abandoned the job.

If each party sues the other for breach of contract, which of the following will the court decide?

(A) Both parties are in breach, and each is entitled to damages, if any, from the other.

(B) Only Karp is in breach, and liable for Manor's damages, if any.

(C) Only Manor is in breach and liable for Karp's damages, if any.

(D) Both parties took reasonable positions, and neither is in breach.

32. For this question only, assume the following facts. After completing 25% of the garage strictly according to Manor's specifications, Karp assigned his rights under the contract to Banquo as security for an $8,000 loan. Banquo immediately notified Manor of the assignment. Karp thereafter, without legal excuse, abandoned the job before it was half-complete. Karp subsequently defaulted on the loan from Banquo. Karp has no assets. It will cost Manor at least $8,000 to get the garage finished by another builder.

If Banquo sues Manor for $8,000, which of the following will the court decide?

(A) Banquo wins, because the Karp-Manor contract was in existence and Karp was not in breach when Banquo gave Manor notice of the assignment.

(B) Banquo wins, because Banquo as a secured creditor over Karp is entitled to priority over Manor's unsecured claim against Karp.

(C) Manor wins, because his right to recoupment on account of Karp's breach is available against Banquo as Karp's assignee.

(D) Manor wins, because his claim against Karp arose prior to Karp's default on his loan from Banquo.

33. The Sports Championship Revenue Enhancement Act is a federal statute that was enacted as part of a comprehensive program to eliminate the federal budget deficit. That act imposed, for a period of five years, a 50% excise tax on the price of tickets to championship sporting events. Such events included the World Series, the Super Bowl, major college bowl games, and similar championship sports events.

This federal tax is probably

(A) constitutional, because the compelling national interest in reducing the federal budget deficit justifies this tax as a temporary emergency measure.

(B) constitutional, because an act of Congress that appears to be a revenue raising measure on its face is not rendered invalid because it may have adverse economic consequences for the activity taxed.

(C) unconstitutional, because a 50% tax is likely to reduce attendance at championship sporting events and, therefore, is not rationally related to the legitimate interest of Congress in eliminating the budget deficit.

(D) unconstitutional, because Congress violates the equal protection component of the Fifth Amendment by singling out championship sporting events for this tax while failing to tax other major sporting, artistic, or entertainment events to which tickets are sold.

34. On June 1, Topline Wholesale, Inc., received a purchase-order form from Wonder-Good, Inc., a retailer and new customer, in which the latter ordered 1,000 anti-recoil widgets for delivery no later than August 30 at a delivered total price of $10,000, as quoted in Topline's current catalog. Both parties are merchants with respect to widgets of all types. On June 2, Topline mailed to Wonder-Good its own form, across the top of which Topline's president had written, "We are pleased to accept your order." This form contained the same terms as Wonder-Good's form except for an additional printed clause in Topline's form that provided for a maximum liability of $100 for any breach of contract by Topline.

As of June 5, when Wonder-Good received Topline's acceptance form, which of the following is an accurate statement concerning the legal relationship between Topline and Wonder-Good?

(A) There is no contract, because the liability-limitation clause in Topline's form is a material alteration of Wonder-Good's offer.

(B) There is no contract, because Wonder-Good did not consent to the liability-limitation clause in Topline's form.

(C) There is an enforceable contract whose terms include the liability limitation clause in Topline's form, because liquidation of damages is expressly authorized by the Uniform Commercial Code.

(D) There is an enforceable contract whose terms do not include the liability–limitation clause in Topline's form.

35. Electco operates a factory that requires the use of very high voltage electricity. Paul owns property adjacent to the Electco plant where he has attempted to carry on a business that requires the use of sensitive electronic equipment. The effectiveness of Paul's electronic equipment is impaired by electrical interference arising from the high voltage currents used in Electco's plant. Paul has complained to Electco several times, with no result. There is no way that Electco, by taking reasonable precautions, can avoid the interference with Paul's operation that arises from the high voltage currents necessary to Electco's operation.

In Paul's action against Electco to recover damages for the economic loss caused to him by the electrical interference, will Paul prevail?

(A) Yes, because Electco's activity is abnormally dangerous.

(B) Yes, for loss suffered by Paul after Electco was made aware of the harm its activity was causing to Paul.

(C) No, unless Electco caused a substantial and unreasonable interference with Paul's business.

(D) No, because Paul's harm was purely economic and did not arise from physical harm to his person or property.

36. Les leased a barn to his neighbor, Tom, for a term of three years. Tom took possession of the barn and used it for his farming purposes. The lease made Les responsible for structural repairs to the barn, unless they were made necessary by actions of Tom.

One year later, Les conveyed the barn and its associated land to Lottie "subject to the lease to Tom." Tom paid the next month's rent to Lottie. The next day a portion of an exterior wall of the barn collapsed because of rot in the interior structure of the wall.

The wall had appeared to be sound, but a competent engineer, on inspection, would have discovered its condition. Neither Lottie nor Tom had the barn inspected by an engineer. Tom was injured as a result of the collapse of the wall.

Les had known that the wall was dangerously weakened by rot and needed immediate repairs, but had not told Tom or Lottie. There is no applicable statute.

Tom brought an appropriate action against Les to recover damages for the injuries he sustained. Lottie was not a party.

Which of the following is the most appropriate comment concerning the outcome of this action?

(A)   Tom should lose, because Lottie assumed all of Les's obligations by reason of Tom's attornment to her.
(B)   Tom should recover, because there is privity between lessor and lessee and it cannot be broken unilaterally.
(C)   Tom should recover, because Les knew of the danger but did not warn Tom.
(D)   Tom should lose, because he failed to inspect the barn.

37.   Dahle is charged with possession of heroin. Prosecution witness Walker, an experienced dog trainer, testified that he was in the airport with a dog trained to detect heroin. As Dahle approached, the dog immediately became alert and pawed and barked frantically at Dahle's briefcase. Dahle managed to run outside and throw his briefcase into the river, from which it could not be recovered. After Walker's experience is established, he is asked to testify as an expert that the dog's reaction told him that Dahle's briefcase contained heroin.

Walker's testimony is

(A)   admissible, as evidence of Dahle's guilt.
(B)   admissible, because an expert may rely on hearsay.
(C)   inadmissible, because it is based on hearsay not within any exception.
(D)   inadmissible, because of the unreliability of the reactions of an animal.

38.   Doe negligently caused a fire in his house, and the house burned to the ground. As a result, the sun streamed into Peter's yard next door, which previously had been shaded by Doe's house.

The sunshine destroyed some delicate and valuable trees in Peter's yard that could grow only in the shade. Peter has brought a negligence action against Doe for the loss of Peter's trees. Doe has moved to dismiss the complaint.

The best argument in support of this motion would be that

(A)   Doe's negligence was not the active cause of the loss of Peter's trees.

(B)   Doe's duty to avoid the risks created by a fire did not encompass the risk that sunshine would damage Peter's trees.

(C)   the loss of the trees was not a natural and probable consequence of Doe's negligence.

(D)   Peter suffered a purely economic loss, which is not compensable in a negligence action.

39.   Phillips bought a new rifle and wanted to try it out by doing some target shooting. He went out into the country to an area where he had previously hunted. Much to his surprise, he noticed that the area beyond a clearing contained several newly constructed houses that had not been there before. Between the houses there was a small playground where several children were playing. Nevertheless, Phillips nailed a paper target to a tree and went to a point where the tree was between himself and the playground. He then fired several shots at the target. One of the shots missed the target and the tree and hit and killed one of the children in the playground.

Phillips was convicted of murder. He appealed, contending that the evidence was not sufficient to support a conviction of murder.

The appellate court should

(A)   affirm the conviction, as the evidence is sufficient to support a conviction of murder.

(B)   reverse the conviction and remand for a new trial, because the evidence is not sufficient for murder but will support a conviction of voluntary manslaughter.

(C)   reverse the conviction and remand for a new trial, because the evidence is not sufficient for murder but will support a conviction of involuntary manslaughter.

(D) reverse the conviction and order the case dismissed, because the evidence is sufficient only for a finding of negligence and negligence alone cannot support a criminal conviction.

Questions 40-41 are based on the following fact situation.

Dominique obtained a bid of $10,000 to tear down her old building and another bid of $90,000 to replace it with a new structure in which she planned to operate a sporting goods store. Having only limited cash available, Dominique asked Hardcash for a $100,000 loan. After reviewing the plans for the project, Hardcash in a signed writing promised to lend Dominique $100,000 secured by a mortgage on the property and repayable over ten years in equal monthly installments at 10% annual interest. Dominique promptly accepted the demolition bid and the old building was removed, but Hardcash thereafter refused to make the loan. Despite diligent efforts, Dominique was unable to obtain a loan from any other source.

40. Does Dominique have a cause of action against Hardcash?

(A) Yes, because by having the building demolished, she accepted Hardcash's offer to make the loan.
(B) Yes, because her reliance on Hardcash's promise was substantial,

reasonable, and foreseeable.
(C) No, because there was no bargained-for exchange of consideration for Hardcash's promise to make the loan.
(D) No, because Dominique's inability to obtain a loan from any other source demonstrated that the project lacked the financial soundness that was a constructive condition to Hardcash's performance.

41. For this question only, assume that Dominique has a cause of action against Hardcash.

If she sues him for monetary relief, what is the probable measure of her recovery?
(A) Expectancy damages, measured by the difference between the value of the new building and the old building, less the amount of the proposed loan ($100,000).

(B) Expectancy damages, measured by the estimated profits from operating the proposed sporting goods store for ten years, less the cost of repaying a $100,000 loan at 10% interest over ten years.

(C) Reliance damages, measured by the $10,000 expense of removing the old building, adjusted by the decrease or increase in the market value of Dominique's land immediately thereafter.

(D) Nominal damages only, because both expectancy and reliance damages are speculative, and there is no legal or equitable basis for awarding restitution.

42. Dan, an eight-year-old, rode his bicycle down his driveway into a busy highway and Driver had to stop her car suddenly to avoid colliding with the bike. Because of the sudden stop, Driver's two-year-old son, Peter, who was sitting on the seat without any restraint, was thrown into the dashboard and injured. Had Peter been properly restrained in a baby car seat, as required by a state safety statute of which his mother was a ' ware, he would not have been injured.

In an action brought on Peter's behalf against Dan's parents to recover for Peter's injuries, Peter will

(A) not prevail, because parents are not vicariously liable for the negligent acts of their children.

(B) not prevail, because Peter's injury was attributable to his mother's knowing violation of a safety statute.

(C) prevail, if Dan's parents knew that he sometimes drove into the highway, and they took no steps to prevent it.

(D) prevail, if Dan's riding into the highway was negligent and the proximate cause of Peter's injuries.

43. While Hill was in her kitchen, she heard the screech of automobile tires. She ran to the window and saw a tricycle flying through the air. The tricycle had been hit by a car driven by Weber, who had been speeding. She also saw a child's body in the grass adjacent to the street. As a result of her shock from this experience, Hill suffered a heart attack.

In a claim by Hill against Weber, the issue on which Hill's right to recover will depend is whether

(A) a person can recover damages based on the defendant's breach of a duty owed to another.

(B) it is foreseeable that a person may suffer physical harm caused solely by an injury inflicted on another.

(C) a person can recover damages caused by shock unaccompanied by bodily impact.

(D) a person can recover damages for harm resulting from shock caused solely by another's peril or injury.

44. Suffering from painful and terminal cancer, Willa persuaded Harold, her husband, to kill her to end her misery. As they reminisced about their life together and reaffirmed their love for each other, Harold tried to discourage Willa from giving up. Willa insisted, however, and finally Harold held a gun to her head and killed her.

The most serious degree of criminal homicide of which Harold can be legally convicted is

(A) no degree of criminal homicide.

(B) involuntary manslaughter.

(C) voluntary manslaughter.

(D) murder.

45. Peterson sued Dylan for libel. After Peterson testified that Dylan wrote to Peterson's employer that Peterson was a thief, Dylan offers evidence that Peterson once stole money from a former employer.

The evidence of Peterson's prior theft is

(A) admissible, as substantive evidence to prove that Peterson is a thief.

(B) admissible, but only to impeach Peterson's credibility.

(C) inadmissible, because character may not be shown by specific instances of conduct.

(D) inadmissible, because such evidence is more unfairly prejudicial than probative.

46. The Federal Computer Abuse Act establishes the Federal Computer Abuse Commission, authorizes the Commission to issue licenses for the possession of computers on terms that are consistent with the purposes of the act, and makes the unlicensed possession of a computer a crime.

The provisions of the Federal Computer Abuse Act are inseverable.

User applied to the Federal Computer Abuse Commission for a license to possess a computer. The Commission held, and User participated in, a trial type proceeding on User's license application. In that proceeding it was demonstrated that User repeatedly and intentionally used computers to introduce secret destructive computer programs (computer viruses) into electronic data banks without the consent of their owners. As a result, the Commission denied User's application for a license. The license denial was based on a Commission rule authorized by the Computer Abuse Act that prohibited the issuance of computer licenses to persons who had engaged in such conduct. Nevertheless, User retained and continued to use his computer. He was subsequently convicted of the crime of unlicensed possession of a computer. On appeal, he challenges the constitutionality of the licensing provision of the Federal Computer Abuse Act. In this case, the reviewing court would probably hold that act to be

(A)   constitutional, because the Constitution generally authorizes Congress to enact all laws that are necessary and proper to advance the general welfare, and Congress could reasonably believe that possession of computers by people like User constitutes a threat to the general welfare.

(B)   constitutional, because Congress may use the authority vested in it by the commerce clause to regulate the possession of computers and the provisions of this act do not violate any prohibitory provision of the Constitution.

(C)   unconstitutional, because Congress may not impose a criminal penalty on action that is improper only because it is inconsistent with an agency rule.

(D)   unconstitutional, because the mere possession of a computer is a wholly local matter that is beyond the regulatory authority of Congress.

47.   Defendant left her car parked on the side of a hill. Two minutes later, the car rolled down the hill and struck and injured Plaintiff.

In Plaintiff's negligence action against Defendant, Plaintiff introduced into evidence the facts stated above, which are undisputed. Defendant testified that, when she parked her car, she turned the front wheels into the curb and put on her emergency brakes, which were in good working order. She also introduced evidence that, in the weeks before this incident, juveniles had been seen tampering with cars in the neighborhood. The jury returned a verdict in favor of Defendant, and Plaintiff moved for a judgment notwithstanding the verdict.

Plaintiff's motion should be

(A)   granted, because it is more likely than not that Defendant's negligent conduct was the legal cause of Plaintiff's injuries.
(B)   granted, because the evidence does not support the verdict.
(C)   denied, because, given Defendant's evidence, the jury was not required to draw an inference of negligence from the circumstances of the accident.
(D)   denied, if Defendant was in no better position than Plaintiff to explain the accident.

48.   Able conveyed Blackacre to Baker by a warranty deed.

Baker recorded the deed four days later. After the conveyance but prior to Baker's recording of the deed, Smollett properly filed a judgment against Able.

The two pertinent statutes in the jurisdiction provide the following: 1) any judgment properly filed shall, for ten years from filing, be a lien on the real property then owned or subsequently acquired by any person against whom the judgment is rendered, and 2) no conveyance or mortgage of real property shall be good against subsequent purchasers for value and without notice unless the same be recorded according to law.

The recording act has no provision for a grace period.

Smollett joined both Able and Baker in an appropriate action to foreclose the judgment lien against Blackacre.

If Smollett is unsuccessful, it will be because

(A)   Able s warranty of title to Baker defeats Smollett's claim.
(B)   Smollett is not a purchaser for value.
(C)   any deed is superior to a judgment lien.

(D)   four days is not an
        unreasonable delay in
        recording a deed.

49.   The United States Department
        of Energy regularly transports
        nuclear materials through
        Centerville on the way to a
        nuclear weapons processing
        plant it operates in a nearby
        state. The city of Centerville
        recently adopted an
        ordinance prohibiting the
        transportation of any nuclear
        materials in or through the
        city. The ordinance declares
        that its purpose is to protect
        the health and safety of the
        residents of that city.
        May the Department of
        Energy continue to transport
        these nuclear materials
        through the city of
        Centerville?

(A)   No, because the
        ordinance is rationally
        related to the public
        health and safety of
        Centerville residents.
(B)   No, because the Tenth
        Amendment reserves
        to the states certain
        enumerated sovereign
        powers.
(C)   Yes, because the
        Department of Energy
        is a federal agency
        engaged in a lawful
        federal function and,
        therefore, its activities
        may not be regulated
        by a local government
        without the consent of
        Congress.
(D)   Yes, because the
        ordinance enacted by
        Centerville is invalid
        because it denies
        persons transporting
        such materials the
        equal protection of the
        laws.

50.   Dart is charged with the
        statutory offense of
        "knowingly violating a
        regulation of the State
        Alcoholic Beverage Control
        Board" and specifically that
        he knowingly violated
        regulation number 345-90
        issued by the State Alcoholic
        Beverage Control Board. That
        regulation prohibits the sale
        of alcoholic beverages to any
        person under the age of 18
        and also prohibits the sale of
        any alcoholic beverage to a
        person over the age of 17
        and under the age of 22
        without the presentation of
        such person's driver's license
        or other identification
        showing the age of the
        purchaser to be 18 or older.

        The evidence showed that
        Dart was a bartender in a
        tavern and sold a bottle of
        beer to a person who was 17
        years old and that Dart did
        not ask for or see the
        purchaser's driver's license or
        any other identification.

        Which of the following, if
        found by the jury, would be
        of the most help to Dart?

(A) The purchaser had a driver's license that falsely showed his age to be 21.

(B) Dart had never been told he was supposed to check identification of persons over 17 and under 22 before selling them alcohol.

(C) Dart did not know that the regulations classified beer as an alcoholic beverage.

(D) Dart mistakenly believed the purchaser to be 24 years old.

Questions 51–52 are based on the following 52. fact situation.

In a writing signed by both parties on December 1, Kranc agreed to buy from Schaff a gasoline engine for $1,000, delivery to be made on the following February 1. Through a secretarial error, the writing called for delivery on March 1, but neither party noticed the error until February 1. Before signing the agreement, Kranc and Schaff orally agreed that the contract of sale would be effective only if Kranc should notify Schaff in writing not later than January 2 that Kranc had arranged to resell the engine to a third person. Otherwise, they agreed orally, "There is no deal." On December 15, Kranc entered into a contract with Trimota to resell the engine to Trimota at a profit.

51. For this question only, assume the following facts. Kranc did not give Schaff notice of the resale until January 25, and Schaff received it by mail on January 26. Meantime, the value of the engine had unexpectedly increased about 75% since December 1, and Schaff renounced the agreement.

If Kranc sues Schaff on February 2 for breach of contract, which of the following is Schaff's best defense?

(A) The secretarial error in the written delivery-term was a mutual mistake concerning a basic fact, and the agreement is voidable by either party.

(B) Kranc's not giving written notice by January 2 of his resale was a failure of a condition precedent to the existence of a contract.

(C) In view of the unexpected 75% increase in value of the engine after December 1, Schaff's performance is excused by the doctrine of commercial frustration.

(D) The agreement, if any, is unenforceable because a material term was not included in the writing.

52. For this question only, assume the following facts. On December 16, Kranc notified Schaff by telephone of Kranc's resale agreement with Trimota, and explained that a written notice was unfeasible because Kranc's secretary was ill. Schaff replied, "That's okay. I'll get the engine to you on February 1, as we agreed." Having learned, however, that the engine had increased in value about 75% since December 1, Schaff renounced the agreement on February 1. If Kranc sues Schaff on February 2 for breach of contract, which of the following concepts best supports Kranc's claim?

(A) Substantial performance.
(B) Nonoccurrence of a condition subsequent.
(C) Waiver of condition.
(D) Novation of buyers.

53. David owned a shotgun that he used for hunting. David knew that his old friend, Mark, had become involved with a violent gang that recently had a shootout with a rival gang. David, who was going to a farm to hunt quail, placed his loaded shotgun on the back seat of his car. On his way to the farm, David picked up Mark to give him a ride to a friend's house. After dropping off Mark at the friend's house, David proceeded to the farm, where he discovered that his shotgun was missing from his car. Mark had taken the shotgun and, later in the day, Mark used it to shoot Paul, a member of the rival gang. Paul was severely injured. Paul recovered a judgment for his damages against David, as well as Mark, on the ground that David was negligent in allowing Mark to obtain possession of the gun, and was therefore liable jointly and severally with Mark for Paul's damages. The jurisdiction has a statute that allows contribution based upon proportionate fault and adheres to the traditional common-law rules on indemnity.

If David fully satisfies the judgment, David then will have a right to recover from Mark

(A) indemnity for the full amount of the judgment, because Mark was an intentional tortfeasor.
(B) contribution only, based on comparative fault, because David himself was negligent.
(C) one-half of the amount of the judgment.
(D) nothing, because David's negligence was a substantial proximate cause of the shooting.

54. The legislature of the state of Chetopah enacted a statute requiring that all law enforcement officers in that state be citizens of the United States. Alien, lawfully admitted to permanent residency five years before the enactment of this statute, sought employment as a forensic pathologist in the Chetopah coroner's office. He was denied such a job solely because he was not a citizen. Alien thereupon brought suit in federal district court against appropriate Chetopah officials seeking to invalidate this citizenship requirement on federal constitutional grounds.

The strongest ground upon which to attack this citizenship requirement is that it

(A) constitutes an ex post facto law as to previously admitted aliens.

(B) deprives an alien of a fundamental right to employment without the due process of law guaranteed by the Fourteenth Amendment.

(C) denies an alien a right to employment in violation of the privileges and immunities clause of the Fourteenth Amendment.

(D) denies an alien the equal protection of the laws guaranteed by the Fourteenth Amendment.

55. Olwen owned 80 acres of land, fronting on a town road. Two years ago, Olwen sold to Buck the back 40 acres. The 40 acres sold to Buck did not adjoin any public road. Olwen's deed to Buck expressly granted a right-of-way over a specified strip of Olwen's retained 40 acres, so Buck could reach the town road. The deed was promptly and properly recorded.

Last year, Buck conveyed the back 40 acres to Sam. They had discussed the right-of-way over Olwen's land to the road, but Buck's deed to Sam made no mention of it. Sam began to use the right-of-way as Buck had, but Olwen sued to enjoin such use by Sam.

The court should decide for

(A) Sam, because he has an easement by implication.

(B) Sam, because the easement appurtenant passed to him as a result of Buck's deed to him.

(C) Olwen, because Buck's easement in gross was not transferable.

(D) Olwen, because Buck's deed failed expressly to transfer the right-of-way to Sam.

56. Dickinson was charged with possession of cocaine. At Dickinson's trial, the prosecution established that, when approached by police on a suburban residential street corner, Dickinson dropped a plastic bag and ran, and that when the police returned to the corner a few minutes later after catching Dickinson, they found a plastic bag containing white powder. Dickinson objects to introduction of this bag (the contents of which would later be established to be cocaine), citing lack of adequate identification.

The objection should be

(A) overruled, because there is sufficient evidence to find that the bag was the one Dickinson dropped.

(B) overruled, because the objection should have been made on the basis of incomplete chain of custody.

(C) sustained, because Dickinson did not have possession of the bag at the time he was arrested.

(D) sustained, unless the judge makes a finding by a preponderance of the evidence that the bag was the one dropped by Dickinson.

57. Chemco manufactured a liquid chemical product known as XRX. Some XRX leaked from a storage tank on Chemco's property, seeped into the groundwater, flowed to Farmer's adjacent property, and Polluted Farmer's well. Several of Farmer's cows drank the Polluted well water and died. If Farmer brings an action against Chemco to recover the value of the cows that died, Farmer will

(A) prevail, because a manufacturer is strictly liable for harm caused by its products.

(B) prevail, because the XRX escaped from Chemco's premises.

(C) not prevail, unless Farmer can establish that the storage tank was defective.

(D) not prevail, unless Chemco failed to exercise reasonable care in storing the XRX.

58. A threatening telephone call that purports to be from Defendant to Witness is most likely to be admitted against Defendant if

(A) the caller identified himself as Defendant.

(B)   Witness had previously given damaging testimony against Defendant in another lawsuit.

(C)   Witness had given his unlisted number only to Defendant and a few other persons.

(D)   Witness believes that Defendant is capable of making such threats.

59.   The open-air amphitheater in the city park of Rightville has been utilized for concerts and other entertainment programs. Until this year, each of the groups performing in that city facility was allowed to make its own arrangements for sound equipment and sound technicians.

After recurring complaints from occupants of residential buildings adjacent to the city park about intrusive noise from some performances held in the amphitheater, the Rightville City Council passed an ordinance establishing city control over all sound amplification at all programs held there. The ordinance provided that Rightville's Department of Parks would be the sole provider in the amphitheater of sound amplification equipment and of the technicians to operate the equipment "to ensure a proper balance between the quality of the sound at such performances and respect for the privacy of nearby residential neighbors."

Which of the following standards should a court use to determine the constitutionality on its face of this content neutral ordinance?

(A)   The ordinance is narrowly tailored to serve a substantial government interest, and does not unreasonably limit alternative avenues of expression.

(B)   The ordinance is rationally related to a legitimate government interest, and does not unreasonably limit alternative avenues of expression.

(C)   The ordinance is rationally related to a legitimate government interest and restricts the expressive rights involved no more than is reasonable under the circumstances.

(D)   The ordinance is substantially related to a legitimate governmental interest and restricts the expressive rights involved no more than is reasonable in light of the surrounding circumstances.

60. Smith and Penn were charged with murder. Each gave a confession to the police that implicated both of them. Smith later retracted her confession, claiming that it was coerced.

Smith and Penn were tried together. The prosecutor offered both confessions into evidence. Smith and Penn objected. After a hearing, the trial judge found that both confessions were voluntary and admitted both into evidence. Smith testified at trial. She denied any involvement in the crime and claimed that her confession was false and the result of coercion. Both defendants were convicted.

On appeal, Smith contends her conviction should be reversed because of the admission into evidence of Penn's confession.

Smith's contention is

(A)   correct, unless Penn testified at trial.
(B)   correct, whether or not Penn testified at trial.
(C)   incorrect, because Smith testified in her own behalf.
(D)   incorrect, because Smith's own confession was properly admitted into evidence.

61. The state of Orrington wanted to prevent its only major league baseball team, the privately owned and operated Orrington Opossums, from moving to the rival state of Atrium. After a heated political debate in the legislature, Orrington enacted legislation providing for a one-time grant of $10 million in state funds to the Opossums to cover part of the projected income losses the team would suffer during the next five years if it remained in that state. The legislation required that the team remain in the state for at least ten years if it accepted the grant.

After accepting the grant, the owners of the Opossums decided to build a new $150 million stadium in Orrington. As plans for the construction of the new stadium proceeded, it became evident that all of the contractors and subcontractors would be white males, and that they had been chosen by the owners of the Opossums without any public bids because these contractors and subcontractors had successfully built the only other new baseball stadium in the region.

Several contractors who were females or members of minority racial groups filed suit against the owners of the Opossums in federal district court to compel public solicitation of bids for the construction of its new stadium on an equal opportunity basis, and to enjoin construction of the stadium until compliance was ensured. Their only claim was that the contracting practices of the owners of the Opossums denied them the equal protection of the laws in violation of the Fourteenth Amendment.

In this suit, the court will probably rule that

(A) the nexus between the actions of the owners of the Opossums and the one-time grant of monies to them by the state is sufficiently substantial to subject their actions to the limitations of the Fourteenth Amendment.

(B) the intense public preoccupation with the activities of major league baseball teams coupled with the fact that baseball is considered to be our national pastime is sufficient to justify application of the Fourteenth Amendment to the activities of major league teams.

(C) in the absence of additional evidence of state involvement in the operations or decisions of the owners of the Opossums, a onetime grant of state monies to them is insufficient to warrant treating their actions as subject to the limitations of the Fourteenth Amendment.

(D) the issues presented by this case are nonjusticiable political questions because there is a lack of judicially manageable standards to resolve them and they are likely to be deeply involved in partisan politics.

Questions 62-63 are based on the following 63. fact situation.

Walker, who knew nothing about horses, inherited Aberlone, a thoroughbred colt whose disagreeable behavior made him a pest around the barn. Walker sold the colt for $1,500 to Sherwood, an experienced racehorse-trainer who knew of Walker's ignorance about horses. At the time of sale, Walker said to Sherwood, "I hate to say it, but this horse is bad-tempered and nothing special."

62. For this question only, assume that soon after the sale, Aberlone won three races and earned $400,000 for Sherwood.

Which of the following additional facts, if established by Walker, would best support his chance of obtaining rescission of the sale to Sherwood?

(A) Walker did not know until after the sale that Sherwood was an experienced racehorse-trainer.

(B) At a pre-sale exercise session of which Sherwood knew that Walker was not aware, Sherwood clocked Aberlone in record-setting time, far surpassing any previous performance.

(C) Aberlone was the only thoroughbred that Walker owned, and Walker did not know how to evaluate young and untested racehorses.

(D) At the time of the sale, Walker was angry and upset over an incident in which Aberlone had reared and thrown a rider.

63. Which one of the following scenarios would best support an action by Sherwood, rather than Walker, to rescind the sale?

(A) In his first race after the sale, Aberlone galloped to a huge lead but dropped dead 100 yards from the finish line because of a rare congenital heart defect that was undiscoverable except by autopsy.

(B) Aberlone won $5 million for Sherwood over a three-year racing career but upon being retired was found to be incurably sterile and useless as a breeder.

(C) After Aberlone had won three races for Sherwood, it was discovered that by clerical error, unknown to either party, Aberlone's official birth registration listed an undistinguished racehorse as the sire rather than the famous racehorse that in fact was the sire.

(D) A week after the sale, Aberlone went berserk and inflicted injuries upon Sherwood that required his hospitalization for six months and a full year for his recovery.

64. Sixty years ago by a properly executed and recorded deed, Albert conveyed Greenacre, a tract of land: "To Louis for life, then to Louis's widow for her life, then to Louis's child or children in equal shares." At that time, Louis, who was Albert's grandson, was six years old.

Shortly thereafter, Albert died testate. Louis was his only heir at law. Albert's will left his entire estate to First Church.

Twenty-five years ago, when he was 41, Louis married Maria who was then 20 years old; they had one child, Norman. Maria and Norman were killed in an automobile accident three years ago when Norman was 21. Norman died testate, leaving his entire estate to the American Red Cross. His father, Louis, was Norman's sole heir at law.

Two years ago, Louis married Zelda. They had no children. This year, Louis died testate, survived by his widow, Zelda, to whom he left his entire estate.

The common-law Rule Against Perpetuities is unchanged by statute in the jurisdiction.
In an appropriate action to determine the ownership of Greenacre, the court should find that title is vested in

(A) First Church, because the widow of Louis was unborn at the time of conveyance and, hence, the remainder violated the Rule Against Perpetuities.

(B) Zelda, because her life estate and her inheritance from Louis (who was Albert's sole heir at law and who was Norman's sole heir at law) merged the entire title in her.

(C) the American Red Cross, because Norman had a vested remainder interest (as the only child of Louis) that it inherited, the life estate to Louis's widow being of no force and effect.

(D) Zelda for life under the terms of Albert's deed, with the remainder to the American Red Cross as the successor in interest to Norman, Louis's only child.

65. In an automobile collision case brought by Poe against Davies, Poe introduced evidence that Ellis made an excited utterance that Davies ran the red light.

Davies called Witt to testify that later Ellis, a bystander, now deceased, told Witt that Davies went through a yellow light.

Witt's testimony should be

(A)   excluded, because it is hearsay not within any exception.

(B)   excluded, because Ellis is not available to explain or deny the inconsistency.

(C)   admitted only for the purpose of impeaching Ellis.

(D)   admitted as impeachment and as substantive evidence of the color of the light.

66.   Plaintiff, a jockey, was seriously injured in a race when another jockey, Daring, cut too sharply in front of her without adequate clearance. The two horses collided, causing Plaintiff to fall to the ground, sustaining injury. The State Racetrack Commission ruled that, by cutting in too sharply, Daring committed a foul in violation of racetrack rules requiring adequate clearance for crossing lanes. Plaintiff has brought an action against Daring for damages in which one count is based on battery.

Will Plaintiff prevail on the battery claim?

(A)   Yes, if Daring was reckless in cutting across in front of Plaintiff's horse.

(B)   Yes, because the State Racetrack Commission determined that Daring committed a foul in violation of rules applicable to racing.

(C)   No, unless Daring intended to cause impermissible contact between the two horses or apprehension of such contact by Plaintiff.

(D)   No, because Plaintiff assumed the risk of accidental injury inherent in riding as a jockey in a horse race.

67.   Able entered into a written contract with Baker to sell Greenacre. The contract was dated June 19 and called for a closing date on the following August 19. There was no other provision in the contract concerning the closing date. The contract contained the following clause: "subject to the purchaser, Baker, obtaining a satisfactory mortgage at the current rate." On the date provided for closing, Baker advised Able that he was unable to close because his mortgage application was still being processed by a bank. Able desired to declare the contract at an end and consulted his attorney in regard to his legal position.

Which of the following are relevant in advising Able of his legal position?

I.   Is time of the essence?
II.   Parol evidence rule.
III. Statute of Frauds.
IV.   Specific performance.

(A)   I and III only.
(B)   II and IV only.
(C)   II, III, and IV only.
(D)   I, II, III, and IV.

68. Lester was engaged to marry Sylvia. One evening, Lester became enraged at the comments of Sylvia's eight-year-old daughter, Cynthia, who was complaining, in her usual fashion, that she did not want her mother to marry Lester. Lester, who had had too much to drink, began beating her. Cynthia suffered some bruises and a broken arm. Sylvia took Cynthia to the hospital. The police were notified by the hospital staff. Lester was indicted for felony child abuse. Lester pleaded with Sylvia to forgive him and to run away with him. She agreed. They moved out of state and took Cynthia with them. Without the testimony of the child, the prosecution was forced to dismiss the case.

Some time later, Sylvia returned for a visit with her family and was arrested and indicted as an accessory-after-the-fact to child abuse.

At her trial, the court should

(A)   dismiss the charge, because Lester had not been convicted.

(B)   dismiss the charge, because the evidence shows that any aid she rendered occurred after the crime was completed.

(C)   submit the case to the jury, on an instruction to convict only if Sylvia knew Lester had been indicted.

(D)   submit the case to the jury, on an instruction to convict only if her purpose in moving was to prevent Lester's conviction.

69. In response to massive layoffs of employees of automobile assembly plants located in the state of Ames, the legislature of that state enacted a statute which prohibits the parking of automobiles manufactured outside of the United States in any parking lot or parking structure that is owned or operated by the state or any of its instrumentalities. This statute does not apply to parking on public streets.

Which of the following is the strongest argument with which to challenge the constitutionality of this statute?

(A) The statute imposes an undue burden on foreign commerce.

(B) The statute denies the owners of foreign-made automobiles the equal protection of the laws.

(C) The statute deprives the owners of foreign-made automobiles of liberty or property without due process of law.

(D) The statute is inconsistent with the privileges and immunities clause of the Fourteenth Amendment.

70. Pate sued Dr. Doke for psychiatric malpractice and called Dr. Will as an expert witness. During Will's direct testimony, Will identified a text as a reliable authority in the field. He seeks to read to the jury passages from this book on which he had relied in forming his opinion on the proper standard of care.

The passage is
(A) admissible, as a basis for his opinion and as substantive evidence of the proper standard of care.

(B) admissible, as a basis for his opinion but not as substantive evidence of the proper standard of care.

(C) inadmissible, because a witness's credibility cannot be supported unless attacked.

(D) inadmissible, because the passage should be received as an exhibit and not read to the jury by the witness.

71. The Daily Sun, a newspaper, printed an article that stated:

Kitchen, the popular restaurant on the town square, has closed its doors. Kitchen employees have told the Daily Sun that the closing resulted from the owner's belief that Kitchen's general manager has embezzled thousands of dollars from the restaurant over the last several years. A decision on reopening the restaurant will be made after the completion of an audit of Kitchen's books.

Plaintiff, who is Kitchen's general manager, brought a libel action against the Daily Sun based on the publication of this article. The parties stipulated that Plaintiff never embezzled any funds from Kitchen. They also stipulated that Plaintiff is well known among many people in the community because of his job with Kitchen.

The case went to trial before a jury.

The defendant's motion for a directed verdict in its favor, made at the close of the evidence, should be granted if the

(A) record contains no evidence that Plaintiff suffered special harm as a result of the publication.

(B) record contains no evidence that the defendant was negligent as to the truth or falsity of the charge of embezzlement.

(C) evidence is not clear and convincing that the defendant published the article with "actual malice."

(D) record contains uncontradicted evidence that the article accurately reported what the employees told the Daily Sun.

72. Surgeon performed a sterilization operation on Patient. After the surgery, Surgeon performed a test that showed that Patient's fallopian tubes were not severed, as was necessary for sterilization. Surgeon did not reveal the failure of the operation to Patient, who three years later became pregnant and delivered a baby afflicted with a severe birth defect that will require substantial medical care throughout its life. The birth defect resulted from a genetic defect unknown to, and undiscoverable by, Surgeon. Patient brought an action on her own behalf against Surgeon, seeking to recover the cost of her medical care for the delivery of the baby, and the baby's extraordinary future medical expenses for which Patient will be responsible.

Which of the following questions is relevant to the lawsuit and currently most difficult to answer?

(A) Did Surgeon owe a duty of care to the baby in respect to medical services rendered to Patient three years before the baby was conceived?

(B) Can a person recover damages for a life burdened by a severe birth defect based on a physician's wrongful failure to prevent that person's birth from occurring?

(C) Did Surgeon owe a duty to Patient to inform her that the sterilization operation had failed?

(D) Is Patient entitled to recover damages for the baby's extraordinary future medical expenses?

73. Robert walked into a store that had a check-cashing service and tried to cash a $550 check which was payable to him. The attendant on duty refused to cash the check because Robert did not have two forms of identification, which the store's policies required. Robert, who had no money except for the check and who needed cash to pay for food and a place to sleep, became agitated. He put his hand into his pocket and growled, "Give me the money or I'll start shooting." The attendant, who knew Robert as a neighborhood character, did not believe that he was violent or had a gun. However, because the attendant felt sorry for Robert, he handed over the cash. Robert left the check on the counter and departed. The attendant picked up the check and found that Robert had failed to endorse it.

If Robert is guilty of any crime, he is most likely guilty of

(A) robbery.
(B) attempted robbery.
(C) theft by false pretenses.
(D) larceny by trick.

Questions 74-75 are based on the following fact situation.

Kabb, the owner of a fleet of taxis, contracted with Petrol, a dealer in petroleum products, for the purchase and sale of Kabb's total requirements of gasoline and oil for one year. As part of that agreement, Petrol also agreed with Kabb that for one year Petrol would place all his advertising with Ada Artiste, Kabb's wife, who owned her own small advertising agency. When Artiste was informed of the Kabb-Petrol contract, she declined to accept an advertising account from the Deturgid Soap Company because she could not handle both the Petrol and Deturgid accounts during the same year.

74. For this question only, assume the following facts. During the first month of the contract, Kabb purchased substantial amounts of his gasoline from a supplier other than Petrol, and Petrol thereupon notified Artiste that he would no longer place his advertising with her agency.

In an action against Petrol for breach of contract, Artiste probably will

(A) succeed, because she is a third-party beneficiary of the Kabb-Petrol contract.
(B) succeed, because Kabb was acting as Artiste's agent when he contracted with Petrol.

(C)   not succeed, because the failure of constructive condition precedent excused Petrol's duty to place his advertising with Artiste.

(D)   not succeed, because Artiste did not provide any consideration to support Petrol's promise to place his advertising with her.

75.   For this question only, make the following assumptions. Artiste was an intended beneficiary under the Kabb-Petrol contract. Kabb performed his contract with Petrol for six months, and during that time Petrol placed his advertising with Artiste. At the end of the six months, Kabb and Artiste were divorced, and Kabb then told Petrol that he had no further obligation to place his advertising with Artiste. Petrol thereupon notified Artiste that he would no longer place his advertising with her.

In an action against Petrol for breach of contract, Artiste probably will

(A)   succeed, because, on the facts of this case, Petrol and Kabb could not, without Artiste's consent, modify their contract so as to discharge Petrol's duties to Artiste.

(B)   succeed, because Kabb acted in bad faith in

releasing Petrol from his duty with respect to Artiste.

(C)   not succeed, because, absent a provision in the contract to the contrary, the promisor and promisee of a third-party beneficiary contract retain by law the right to modify or terminate the contract.

(D)   not succeed, because the agency relationship, if any, between Kabb and Artiste terminated upon their divorce.

76.   Drew, the owner of a truck leasing company, asked Pat, one of Drew's employees, to deliver $1,000 to the dealership's main office. The following week, as a result of a dispute over whether the money had been delivered, Drew instructed Pat to come to the office to submit to a lie detector test.

When Pat reported to Drew's office for the test, it was not administered. Instead, without hearing Pat's story, Drew shouted at him, "You're a thief!" and fired him. Drew's shout was overheard by several other employees who were in another office, which was separated from Drew's office by a thin partition.

The next day, Pat accepted another job at a higher salary. Several weeks later, upon discovering that the money had not been stolen, Drew offered to rehire Pat.

In a suit for slander by Pat against Drew, Pat will

    (A)   prevail, because Pat was fraudulently induced to go to the office for a lie detector test, which was not, in fact, given.

    (B)   prevail, if Drew should have foreseen that the statement would be overheard by other employees.

    (C)   not prevail, if Drew made the charge in good faith, believing it to be true.

    (D)   not prevail, because the statement was made to Pat alone and intended for his ears only.

77.   Adam owns his home, Blackacre, which was mortgaged to Bank by a duly recorded purchase money mortgage. Last year, Adam replaced all of Blackacre's old windows with new windows.

Each new window consists of a window frame with three inserts: regular windows, storm windows, and screens. The windows are designed so that each insert can be easily inserted or removed from the window frame without tools to adjust to seasonal change and to facilitate the cleaning of the inserts.

The new windows were expensive. Adam purchased them on credit, signed a financing statement, and granted a security interest in the windows to Vend, the supplier of the windows. Vend promptly and properly filed and recorded the financing statement before the windows were installed. Adam stored the old windows in the basement of Blackacre.

This year, Adam has suffered severe financial reverses and has defaulted on his mortgage obligation to Bank and on his obligation to Vend.

Bank brought an appropriate action to enjoin Vend from its proposed repossession of the window inserts.

In the action, the court should rule for

    (A)   Bank, because its mortgage was recorded first.

    (B)   Bank, because windows and screens, no matter their characteristics, are an integral part of a house.

    (C)   Vend, because the inserts are removable.

(D)   Vend, because the availability of the old windows enables Bank to return Blackacre to its original condition.

78.   In a suit by Palmer against Denby, Palmer sought to subpoena an audiotape on which Denby had narrated his version of the dispute for his attorney. Counsel for Denby moves to quash the subpoena on the ground of privilege.

The audiotape is most likely to be subject to subpoena if

(A)   Denby played the audiotape for his father to get his reactions.

(B)   the lawsuit involved alleged criminal behavior by Denby.

(C)   Denby has been deposed and there is good reason to believe that the audiotape may contain inconsistent statements.

(D)   Denby is deceased and thus unavailable to give testimony in person.

79.   The National Ecological Balance Act prohibits the destruction or removal of any wild animals located on lands owned by the United States without express permission from the Federal Bureau of Land Management. Violators are subject to fines of up to $1,000 per offense.

After substantial property damage was inflicted on residents of the state of Arkota by hungry coyotes, the state legislature passed the Coyote Bounty Bill, which offers $25 for each coyote killed or captured within the state. The Kota National Forest, owned by the federal government, is located entirely within the state of Arkota. Many coyotes live in the Kota National Forest.

Without seeking permission from the Bureau of Land Management, Hunter shot several coyotes in the Kota National Forest and collected the bounty from the state of Arkota. As a result, he was subsequently tried in federal district court, convicted, and fined $1,000 for violating the National Ecological Balance Act. Hunter appealed his conviction to the United States Court of Appeals.

On appeal, the Court of Appeals should hold the National Ecological Balance Act, as applied to Hunter, to be

(A)   constitutional, because the property clause of Article IV, Section 3, of the Constitution authorizes such federal statutory controls and sanctions.

(B) constitutional, because Article I, Section 8, of the Constitution authorizes Congress to enact all laws necessary and proper to advance the general welfare.

(C) unconstitutional, because Congress may not use its delegated powers to override the Tenth Amendment right of the state of Arkota to legislate in areas of traditional state governmental functions, such as the protection of the property of its residents.

(D) unconstitutional, because Congress violates the full faith and credit clause of Article IV when it punishes conduct that has been authorized by state action.

80. A kidnapping statute in State A makes it a crime for a person, including a parent, to "take a child from the custody of his custodial parent, knowing he has no privilege to do so."

After a bitter court battle Ann and Dave were divorced and Ann was given custody of their daughter, Maria. Dave later moved to State B where he brought an action to obtain custody of Maria. A local judge awarded him custody. His attorney incorrectly advised him that, under this award, he was entitled to take Maria away from Ann. Dave drove to State A, picked Maria up at her preschool, and took her back to State B with him.

He was indicted for kidnapping in State A, extradited from State B, and tried. At trial, he testified that he had relied on his attorney's advice in taking Maria, and that at the time he believed his conduct was not illegal.

If the jury believes his testimony, Dave should be

(A) acquitted, because he acted on the advice of an attorney.

(B) acquitted, because he lacked a necessary mental element of the crime.

(C) convicted, because reliance on an attorney's advice is not a defense.

(D) convicted, provided a reasonable person would have known that the attorney's advice was erroneous.

81. Owen, the owner of Greenacre, a tract of land, mortgaged Greenacre to ABC Bank to secure his preexisting obligation to ABC Bank.

The mortgage was promptly and properly recorded. Owen and Newton then entered into a valid written contract for the purchase and sale of Greenacre, which provided for the transfer of "a marketable title, free of encumbrances." The contract did not expressly refer to the mortgage.

Shortly after entering into the contract, Newton found another property that much better suited her needs and decided to try to avoid her contract with Owen. When Newton discovered the existence of the mortgage, she asserted that the title was encumbered and that she would not close. Owen responded by offering to provide for payment and discharge of the mortgage at the closing from the proceeds of the closing. Newton refused to go forward, and Owen brought an appropriate action against her for specific performance.
If the court holds for Owen in this action, it will most likely be because

(A)   the mortgage is not entitled to priority because it was granted for preexisting obligations.

(B)   the doctrine of equitable conversion supports the result.

(C)   Owen's arrangements for the payment of the mortgage fully satisfied Owen's

obligation to deliver marketable title.

(D)   the existence of the mortgage was not Newton's real reason for refusing to close.

82.   Pawn sued Dalton for injuries received when she fell down a stairway in Dalton's apartment building. Pawn, a guest in the building, alleged that she caught the heel of her shoe in a tear in the stair carpet. Pawn calls Witt, a tenant, to testify that Young, another tenant, had said to him a week before Pawn's fall: "When I paid my rent this morning, I told the manager he had better fix that torn carpet."

Young's statement, reported by Witt, is

(A)   admissible, to prove that the carpet was defective.

(B)   admissible, to prove that Dalton had notice of the defect.

(C)   admissible, to prove both that the carpet was defective and that Dalton had notice of the defect.

(D)   inadmissible, because it is hearsay not within any exception.

83. A law of the state of Wonatol imposed a generally applicable sales tax payable by the vendor. That law exempted from its provisions the sale of "all magazines, periodicals, newspapers, and books." In order to raise additional revenue, the state legislature eliminated that broad exemption and substituted a narrower exemption. The new, narrower exemption excluded from the state sales tax only the sale of those "magazines, periodicals, newspapers, and books that are published or distributed by a recognized religious faith and that consist wholly of writings sacred to such a religious faith."

Magazine is a monthly publication devoted to history and politics. Magazine paid under protest the sales tax due on its sales according to the amended sales tax law. Magazine then filed suit against the state in an appropriate state court for a refund of the sales taxes paid. It contended that the state's elimination of the earlier, broader exemption and adoption of the new, narrower exemption restricted to sacred writings of recognized religious faiths violates the First and Fourteenth Amendments to the Constitution.

In this case, the court will probably rule that

(A) Magazine lacks standing to sue for a refund of sales taxes imposed by a generally applicable state law because Article III of the Constitution precludes taxpayers from bringing such suits.

(B) the Eleventh Amendment bars the state court from exercising jurisdiction over this suit in the absence of a law of Wonatol expressly waiving the state's immunity.

(C) the new, narrower exemption from the state sales tax law violates the establishment clause of the First and Fourteenth Amendments by granting preferential state support to recognized religious faiths for the communication of their religious beliefs.

(D) the new, narrower exemption from the state sales tax law violates the freedom of the press guaranteed by the First and Fourteenth Amendments because it imposes a prior restraint on nonreligious publications that are required to pay the tax.

84. For five years, Rancher had kept his horse in a ten-acre field enclosed by a six-foot woven wire fence with six inches of barbed wire on top. The gate to the field was latched and could not be opened by an animal. Rancher had never had any trouble with people coming onto his property and bothering the horse, and the horse had never escaped from the field. One day, however, when Rancher went to the field, he found that the gate was open and the horse was gone. Shortly before Rancher's discovery, Driver was driving with due care on a nearby highway when suddenly Rancher's horse darted in front of his car. When Driver attempted to avoid hitting the horse, he lost control of the car, which then crashed into a tree. Driver was injured.

Driver sued Rancher to recover damages for his injuries and Rancher moved for summary judgment.

If the facts stated above are undisputed, the judge should

(A) deny the motion, because, pursuant to the doctrine of *res ipsa loquitur*, a jury could infer that Rancher was negligent.
(B) deny the motion, because an animal dangerous to highway users escaped from Rancher's property and caused the collision.
(C) grant the motion, because there is no evidence that Rancher was negligent.
(D) grant the motion, because Rancher did not knowingly permit the horse to run at large.

85. Defendant was prosecuted for bankruptcy fraud. Defendant's wife, now deceased, had testified adversely to Defendant during earlier bankruptcy proceedings that involved similar issues. Although the wife had been cross-examined, no serious effort was made to challenge her credibility despite the availability of significant impeachment information.

At the fraud trial, the prosecutor offers into, evidence the testimony given by Defendant's wife at the bankruptcy proceeding.

This evidence should be

(A)   admitted, under the hearsay exception for former testimony.
(B)   admitted, because it is a statement by a person identified with a party.
(C)   excluded, because it is hearsay not within any exception.
(D)   excluded, because Defendant has the right to prevent use of his spouse's testimony against him in a criminal case.

Questions 86–87 are based on the following fact situation.

Mermaid owns an exceptionally seaworthy boat that she charters for sport fishing at a $500 daily rate. The fee includes the use of the boat with Mermaid as the captain, and one other crew member, as well as fishing tackle and bait. On May 1, Phinney agreed with Mermaid– that Phinney would have the full-day use of the boat on May 15 for himself and his family for $500. Phinney paid an advance deposit of $200 and signed an agreement that the deposit could be retained by Mermaid as liquidated damages in the event Phinney canceled or failed to appear.

86.   For this question only, assume the following facts. At the time of contracting,

Mermaid told Phinney to be at the dock at 5 a.m. on May 15. Phinney and his family, however, did not show up on May 15 until noon.

Meantime, Mermaid agreed at 10 a.m. to take Tess and her family out fishing for the rest of the day. Tess had happened to come by and inquire about the possibility of such an outing. In view of the late hour, Mermaid charged Tess $400 and stayed out two hours beyond the customary return time. Phinney's failure to appear until noon was due to the fact that he had been trying to charter another boat across the bay at a lower rate and had gotten lost after he was unsuccessful in getting such a charter.

Which of the following is an accurate statement concerning the rights of the parties?

(A)   Mermaid can retain the $200 paid by Phinney, because it would be difficult for Mermaid to establish her actual damages and the sum appears to have been a reasonable forecast in light of anticipated loss of profit from the charter.

(B) Mermaid is entitled to retain only $50 (10% of the contract price) and must return $150 to Phinney.

(C) Mermaid must return $100 to Phinney in order to avoid her own unjust enrichment at Phinney's expense.

(D) Mermaid must return $100 to Phinney, because the liquidated–damage clause under the circumstances would operate as a penalty.

87. For this question only, assume the following facts. On May 15 at 1 a.m., the Coast Guard had issued offshore "heavy weather" warnings and prohibited all small vessels the size of Mermaid's from leaving the harbor. This prohibition remained in effect throughout the day. Phinney did not appear at all on May 15, because he had heard the weather warnings on his radio.

Which of the following is an accurate statement?

(A) The contract is discharged because of impossibility, and Phinney is entitled to return of his deposit.

(B) The contract is discharged because of mutual mistake concerning an essential fact, and Phinney is entitled to return of his deposit.

(C) The contract is not discharged, because its performance was possible in view of the exceptional seaworthiness of Mermaid's boat, and Phinney is not entitled to return of his deposit.

(D) The contract is not discharged, and Phinney is not entitled to return of his deposit, because the liquidated–damage clause in effect allocated the risk of bad weather to Phinney.

88. Eight years ago, Orben, prior to moving to a distant city, conveyed Blackacre, an isolated farm, to his son, Sam, by a quitclaim deed. Sam paid no consideration. Sam, who was 19 years old, without formal education, and without experience in business, took possession of Blackacre and operated the farm but neglected to record his deed. Subsequently, Orben conveyed Blackacre to Fred by warranty deed. Fred, a substantial land and timber promoter, paid valuable consideration for the deed to him.

He was unaware of Sam's possession, his quitclaim deed, or his relationship to Orben. Fred promptly and properly recorded his deed and began removing timber from the land. Immediately upon learning of Fred's actions, Sam recorded his deed and brought an appropriate action to enjoin Fred from removing the timber and to quiet title in Sam. The recording act of the jurisdiction provides:

"No conveyance or mortgage of real property shall be good against subsequent purchasers for value and without notice unless the same be recorded according to law."

In this actions Fred should

(A)   prevail, because a warranty deed for valuable consideration takes priority over a quitclaim deed without consideration.

(B)   prevail, because Orben's subsequent conveyance to Fred revoked the gift to Sam.

(C)   lose, because Sam's possession charged Fred with notice.

(D)   lose, because the equities favor Sam.

89.   Brown owned Blackacre, a tract of undeveloped land. Blackacre abuts Whiteacre, a tract of land owned by Agency, the state's governmental energy agency.

At Whiteacre, Agency has operated a waste-to-electricity recycling facility for 12 years. Blackacre and Whiteacre are in a remote area and Whiteacre is the only developed parcel of real estate within a ten-mile radius. The boundary line between Blackacre and Whiteacre had never been surveyed or marked on the face of the earth.

During the past 12 years, some of the trucks bringing waste to the Agency facility have dumped their loads so that the piles of waste extend from Whiteacre onto a portion of Blackacre. However, prior to the four-week period during each calendar year when the Agency facility is closed for inspection and repairs, the waste piles are reduced to minimal levels so that during each of the four-week closures no waste was, in fact, piled on Blackacre. Neither Brown nor any representative of Agency knew the facts about the relation of the boundary line to the waste piles.

The time for acquiring title by adverse possession in the jurisdiction is ten years.

Last year, Brown died, and his son, Silas, succeeded him as the owner of Blackacre. Silas became aware of the facts, demanded that Agency stop using Blackacre for the piling of waste, and, when Agency refused his demand, brought an appropriate action to enjoin any such use of Blackacre in the future.

If Agency prevails in that action, it will be because

(A) the facts constitute adverse possession and title to the portion of Blackacre concerned has vested in Agency.

(B) Brown's failure to keep himself informed as to Agency's use of Blackacre and his failure to object constituted implied consent to the continuation of that use.

(C) the interest of the public in the conversion of waste to energy overrides any entitlement of Silas to equitable remedies.

(D) the power of eminent domain of the state makes the claim of Silas moot.

90. Defendant was charged with possession of cocaine with intent to distribute. He had been stopped while driving a car and several pounds of cocaine were found in the trunk. In his opening statement, defendant's counsel asserted that his client had no key to the trunk and no knowledge of its contents. The prosecutor offers the state motor vehicle registration, shown to have been found in the glove compartment of the car, listing Defendant as the owner.

The registration should be

(A) admitted, as a statement against interest.

(B) admitted, as evidence of Defendant's close connection with the car and, therefore, knowledge of its contents.

(C) excluded, unless authenticated by testimony of or certification by a state official charged with custody of vehicle registration records.

(D) excluded, as hearsay not within any exception.

91. Donald was arrested in Marilyn's apartment after her neighbors had reported sounds of a struggle and the police had arrived to find Donald bent over Marilyn's prostrate body. Marilyn was rushed to the hospital where she lapsed into a coma.

Despite the explanation that he was trying to revive Marilyn after she suddenly collapsed, Donald was charged with attempted rape and assault after a neighbor informed the police that she had heard Marilyn sobbing, "No, please no, let me alone."

At trial, the forensic evidence was inconclusive. The jury acquitted Donald of attempted rape but convicted him of assault. While he was serving his sentence for assault, Marilyn, who had never recovered from the coma, died. Donald was then indicted and tried on a charge of felony murder. In this common-law jurisdiction, there is no statute that prevents a prosecutor from proceeding in this manner, but Donald argued that a second trial for felony murder after his original trial for attempted rape and assault would violate the double jeopardy clause.

His claim is

(A) correct, because he was acquitted of the attempted rape charge.

(B) correct, because he was convicted of the assault charge.

(C) incorrect, because Marilyn had not died at the-time of the first trial and he was not placed in jeopardy for murder.

(D) incorrect, because he was convicted of the assault charge.

92. Ogle owned Greenacre, a tract of land, in fee simple. Five years ago, he executed and delivered to Lilly an instrument in the proper form of a warranty deed that conveyed Greenacre to Lilly "for and during the term of her natural life." No other estate or interest or person taking an interest was mentioned. Lilly took possession of Greenacre and has remained in possession.

Fifteen months ago, Ogle died, leaving a will that has been duly admitted to probate. The will, inter alia, had the following provision:

"I devise Greenacre to Mina for her natural life and from and after Mina's death to Rex, his heirs and assigns, forever."

Administration of Ogle's estate has been completed. Mina claims the immediate right to possession of Greenacre. Rex also asserts a right to immediate possession.

In an appropriate lawsuit to which Lilly, Mina, and Rex are parties, who should be adjudged to have the right to immediate possession?

(A) Lilly, because no subsequent act of Ogle would affect her life estate.

(B) Mina, because Ogle's will was the final and definitive expression of his intent.

(C) Mina, because Lilly's estate terminated with the death of Ogle.

(D) Rex, because Lilly's estate terminated with Ogle's death and all that Ogle had was the right to transfer his reversion in fee simple.

93. Devlin was charged with murder. Several witnesses testified that the crime was committed by a person of Devlin's general description who walked with a severe limp. Devlin in fact walks with a severe limp. He objected to a prosecution request that the court order him to walk across the courtroom in order to display his limp to the jury to assist it in determining whether Devlin was the person that the witnesses had seen.

Devlin's objection will most likely be

(A) sustained, because the order sought by the prosecution would violate Devlin's privilege against self-incrimination.

(B) sustained, because the order sought by the prosecution would constitute an illegal search and seizure.

(C) denied, because the order sought by the prosecution is a legitimate part of a proper courtroom identification process.

(D) denied, because a criminal defendant has no legitimate expectation of privacy.

94. A statute of the state of Kiowa provided state monetary grants to private dance, theater, and opera groups located in that state.

The statute required recipients of such grants to use the granted monies for the acquisition, construction, and maintenance of appropriate facilities for the public performance of their performing arts. The last section of the statute conditioned the award of each such grant on the recipient's agreement to refrain from all kinds of political lobbying calculated to secure additional tax support for the performing arts.

The strongest constitutional basis for an attack upon the validity of the last section of the statute would be based upon the

(A)   commerce clause.
(B)   obligation of contracts clause.
(C)   Fifth Amendment.
(D)   First and Fourteenth Amendments.

95.   Penkov suffered a severe loss when his manufacturing plant, located in a shallow ravine, was flooded during a sustained rainfall. The flooding occurred because City had failed to maintain its storm drain, which was located on City land above Penkov's premises, and because Railroad had failed to maintain its storm drain, which was located on Railroad land below Penkov's premises. The flooding would not have occurred if either one of the two storm drains had been maintained properly.

Penkov sued Railroad to recover compensation for his loss. The evidence in the case established that the failures of the two drains were caused by the respective negligence of City and Railroad. There is no special rule insulating City from liability.

In his action against Railroad, Penkov should recover

(A)   nothing, because he should have joined City, without whose negligence he would have suffered no loss.
(B)   nothing, unless he introduces evidence that enables the court reasonably to apportion responsibility between City and Railroad.
(C)   one-half his loss, in the absence of evidence that enables the court to allocate responsibility fairly between City and Railroad.
(D)   all of his loss, because but for Railroad's negligence none of the flooding would have occurred.

96.   Smith asked Jones if he would loan him $500, promising to repay the amount within two weeks. Jones loaned him the $500. The next day Smith took the money to the race track and lost all of it betting on horse races. He then left town for six months. He has not repaid Jones.

Smith has committed

(A)   both larceny by trick and obtaining money by false pretenses (although he can only be convicted of one offense).
(B)   larceny by trick only.

(C) obtaining money by false pretenses only.

(D) neither larceny by trick nor obtaining money by false pretenses.

97. Assume that Congress passed and the President signed the following statute:

"The appellate jurisdiction of the United States Supreme Court shall not extend to any case involving the constitutionality of any state statute limiting the circumstances in which a woman may obtain an abortion, or involving the constitutionality of this statute."

The strongest argument against the constitutionality of this statute is that

(A) Congress may not exercise its authority over the appellate jurisdiction of the Supreme Court in a way that seriously interferes with the establishment of a supreme and uniform body of federal constitutional law.

(B) Congress may only regulate the appellate jurisdiction of the Supreme Court over cases initially arising in federal courts.

(C) the appellate jurisdiction of the Supreme Court may only be altered by constitutional amendment.

(D) the statute violates the equal protection clause of the Fourteenth Amendment.

98. The federal statute admitting the state of Blue to the Union granted Blue certain public lands, and established some very ambiguous conditions on the subsequent disposition of these lands by Blue. This federal statute also required the new state to write those exact same conditions into its state constitution.

One hundred years later, a statute of Blue dealing with the sale of these public lands was challenged in a state court lawsuit on the ground that it was inconsistent with the conditions contained in the federal statute, and with the provisions of the Blue Constitution that exactly copy the conditions contained in the federal statute. The trial court decision in this case was appealed to the Blue Supreme Court. In its opinion, the Blue Supreme Court dealt at length with the ambiguous language of the federal statute and with cases interpreting identical language in federal statutes admitting other states to the union.

The Blue Supreme Court opinion did not discuss the similar provisions of the Blue Constitution, but it did hold that the challenged Blue statute is invalid because it is "Inconsistent with the language of the federal statute and therefore is inconsistent with the identical provisions of our state constitution."

If the losing party in the Blue Supreme Court seeks review of the decision of that court in the United States Supreme Court, the United States Supreme Court should

(A) accept the case for review and determine the validity and interpretation of the federal statute if it is an important and substantial question.

(B) ask the Blue Supreme Court to indicate more clearly whether it relied on the state constitutional provision in rendering its decision.

(C) decline to review the case on the ground that the decision of the Blue Supreme Court rests on an adequate and independent state ground.

(D) decline to review the case because a decision by a state supreme court concerning the proper disposition of state public lands is not reviewable by the United States Supreme Court.

99. Trawf, the manager of a state fair, contracted with Schweinebauch, a renowned hog breeder, to exhibit Schweinebauch's world champion animal, Megahawg, for the three weeks of the annual fair, at the conclusion of which Schweinebauch would receive an honorarium of $300. Two days before the opening of the fair, Megahawg took sick with boarsitis, a communicable disease among swine, and, under the applicable state quarantine law, very probably could not be exhibited for at least a month.

Upon learning this, Trawf can legally pursue which of the following courses of action with respect to his contract with Schweinebauch?

(A) Suspend his own performance, demand assurances from Schweinebauch, and treat a failure by Schweinebauch to give them as an actionable repudiation.

(B) Suspend his own performance and recover damages from Schweinebauch for breach of contract unless Schweinebauch at once supplies an undiseased hog of exhibition quality as a substitute for Megahawg.

(C) Terminate his own performance and treat Megahawg's illness as discharging all remaining duties under the contract.

(D) Terminate the contract, but only if he (Trawf) seeks promptly to obtain for the exhibit a suitable substitute for Megahawg from another hog owner.

100. The manager of a department store noticed that Paula was carrying a scarf with her as she examined various items in the blouse department. The manager recognized the scarf as an expensive one carried by the store. Paula was trying to find a blouse that matched a color in the scarf, and, after a while, found one. The manager then saw Paula put the scarf into her purse, pay for the blouse, and head for the door. The manager, who was eight inches taller than Paula, blocked Paula's way to the door and asked to see the scarf in Paula's purse. Paula produced the scarf, as well as a receipt for it, showing that it had been purchased from the store on the previous day. The manager then told Paula there was no problem, and stepped out of her way.

If Paula brings a claim against the store based on false imprisonment, the store's best defense would be that

(A) by carrying the scarf in public view and then putting it into her purse, Paula assumed the risk of being detained.

(B) the manager had a reasonable belief that Paula was shoplifting and detained her only briefly for a reasonable investigation of the f acts.

(C) Paula should have realized that her conduct would create a reasonable belief that facts existed warranting a privilege to detain.

(D) Paula was not detained, but was merely questioned about the scarf.

STOP
IF YOU FINISH BEFORE TIME IS CALLED, CHECK YOUR WORK ON THIS TEST.

Time-3 hours

Directions: Each of the questions or incomplete statements below is followed by four suggested answers or completions. You are to choose the best of the stated alternatives. Answer all questions according to the generally accepted view, except where otherwise noted.

For the purposes of this test, you are to assume that Articles 1 and 2 of the Uniform Commercial Code have been adopted. You are also to assume relevant application of Article 9 of the UCC concerning fixtures. The Federal Rules of Evidence are deemed to control. The terms "Constitution," "constitutional," and "unconstitutional" refer to the federal Constitution unless indicated to the contrary. You are also to assume that there is no applicable community property law, no guest statute, and no No-Fault Insurance Act unless otherwise specified. In negligence cases, if fault on the claimant's part is or may be relevant, the statement of facts for the particular question will identify the contributory or comparative negligence rule that is to be applied.

101. A proposed federal statute would prohibit all types of discrimination against black persons on the basis of their race in every business transaction executed anywhere in the United States by any person or entity, governmental or private.

Is this proposed federal statute likely to be constitutional?

(A) Yes, because it could reasonably be viewed as an exercise of Congress's authority to enact laws for the general welfare.

(B) Yes, because it could reasonably be viewed as a means of enforcing the provisions of the Thirteenth Amendment.

(C) No, because it would regulate purely local transactions that are not in interstate commerce.

(D) No, because it would invade the powers reserved to the states by the Tenth Amendment.

102. Sam told Horace, his neighbor, that he was going away for two weeks and asked Horace to keep an eye on his house. Horace agreed. Sam gave Horace a key to use to check on the house. Horace decided to have a party in Sam's house. He invited a number of friends.

One friend, Lewis, went into Sam's bedroom, took some of Sam's rings, and put them in his pocket.

Which of the following is true?

    (A)   Horace and Lewis are guilty of burglary.

    (B)   Horace is guilty of burglary and Lewis is guilty of larceny.

    (C)   Horace is guilty of trespass and Lewis is guilty of larceny.

    (D)   Lewis is guilty of larceny and Horace is not guilty of any crime.

103.   John's father, Jeremiah, died in Hospital. Hospital maintains a morgue with refrigerated drawers a bit larger than a human body. Jeremiah's body was placed in such a drawer awaiting pickup by a mortician. Before the mortician called for the body, a Hospital orderly placed two opaque plastic bags in the drawer with Jeremiah's body. One bag contained Jeremiah's personal effects, and the other contained an amputated leg from some other Hospital patient. It is stipulated that Hospital was negligent to allow the amputated leg to get into Jeremiah's drawer. The mortician delivered the two opaque plastic bags to John, assuming both contained personal effects. John was shocked when he opened the bag containing the amputated leg. John sued Hospital to recover for his emotional distress. At the trial, John testified that the experience had been extremely upsetting that he had had recurring nightmares about it, and that his family and business relationships had been adversely affected for a period of several months. He did not seek medical or psychiatric treatment for his emotional distress.

Who should prevail?

    (A)   John, because of the sensitivity people have regarding the care of the bodies of deceased relatives.

    (B)   John, because hospitals are strictly liable for mishandling dead bodies.

    (C)   Hospital, because John did not require medical or psychiatric treatment.

    (D)   Hospital, because John suffered no bodily harm.

104.   Able was the owner of Greenacre, a large tract of land. Able entered into a binding written contract with Baker for the sale and purchase of Greenacre for $125,000. The contract required Able to convey marketable record title.

Baker decided to protect his interest and promptly and properly recorded the contract.

Thereafter, but before the date scheduled for the closing, Charlie obtained and properly filed a final judgment against Able in the amount of $1 million in a personal injury suit. A statute in the jurisdiction provides: "Any judgment properly filed shall, for ten years from filing, be a lien on the real property then owned or subsequently acquired by any person against whom the judgment is rendered."

The recording act of the jurisdiction authorizes recording of contracts and also provides: "No conveyance or mortgage of real property shall be good against subsequent purchasers for value and without notice unless the same be recorded according to law."

There are no other relevant statutory provisions.

At the closing, Baker declined to accept the title of Able on the ground that Charlie's judgment lien encumbered the title he would receive and rendered it unmarketable. Able brought an appropriate action against Baker for specific performance of the contract and joined Charlie as a party.

In this action, the judgment should be for

(A)   Able, because in equity a purchaser takes free of judgment liens.
(B)   Able, because the contract had been recorded.
(C)   Baker, because Able cannot benefit from Baker's action in recording the contract.
(D)   Baker, because the statute creating judgment liens takes precedence over the recording act.

105.   Post sued Dint for dissolution of their year-long partnership. One issue concerned the amount of money Post had received in cash. It was customary for Dint to give Post money from the cash register as Post needed it for personal expenses. Post testified that, as he received money, he jotted down the amounts in the partnership ledger. Although Dint had access to the ledger, he made no changes in it. The ledger was admitted into evidence. Dint seeks to testify to his memory of much larger amounts he had given Post.

Dint's testimony is

(A)   admissible, because it is based on Dint's firsthand knowledge.

(B)   admissible, because the ledger entries offered by a party opponent opened the door.

(C)   inadmissible, because the ledger is the best evidence of the amounts Post received.

(D)   inadmissible, because Dint's failure to challenge the accuracy of the ledger constituted an adoptive admission.

106.   In a signed writing, Nimrod contracted to purchase a 25-foot travel trailer from Trailco for $15,000, cash on delivery no later than June 1. Nimrod arrived at the Trailco sales lot on Sunday, May 31, to pay for and take delivery of the trailer, but refused to do so when he discovered that the spare tire was missing.

Trailco offered to install a spare tire on Monday when its service department would open, but Nimrod replied that he did not want the trailer and would purchase another one elsewhere.

Which of the following is accurate?

(A)   Nimrod had a right to reject the trailer, but Trailco was entitled to a reasonable

opportunity to cure the defect.

(B)   Nimrod had a right to reject the trailer and terminate the contract under the perfect tender rule.

(C)   Nimrod was required to accept the trailer, because the defect could be readily cured.

(D)   Nimrod was required to accept the trailer, because the defect did not substantially impair its value.

107.   Oker owned in fee simple two adjoining lots, Lots 1 and 2. He conveyed in fee simple Lot 1 to Frank. The deed was in usual form of a warranty deed with the following provision inserted in the appropriate place:

"Grantor, for himself, his heirs and assigns, does covenant and agree that any reasonable expense incurred by grantee, his heirs and assigns, as the result of having to repair the retaining wall presently situated on Lot 1 at the common boundary with Lot 2, shall be reimbursed one-half the costs of repairs; and by this provision the parties intend a covenant running with, the land."

Frank conveyed Lot 1 in fee simple to Sara by warranty deed in usual and regular form. The deed omitted any reference to the retaining wall or any covenant. Fifty years after Oker's conveyance to Frank, Sara conveyed Lot 1 in fee simple to Tim by warranty deed in usual form; this deed omitted any reference to the retaining wall or the covenant.

There is no statute that applies to any aspect of the problems presented except a recording act and a statute providing for acquisition of title after ten years of adverse possession.

All conveyances by deeds were for a consideration equal to fair market value.

The deed from Oker to Frank was never recorded. All other deeds were promptly and properly recorded.

Lot 2 is now owned by Henry, who took by intestate succession from Oker, now dead.

Tim expended $3,500 on the retaining wall. Then he obtained all of the original deeds in the chain from Oker to him. Shortly thereafter, Tim discovered the covenant in Oker's deed to Frank. He demanded that Henry pay $1,750, and when Henry refused, Tim instituted an appropriate action to recover that sum from Henry. In such action, Henry asserted all defenses available to him.

If judgment is for Henry, it will be because

(A) Tim is barred by adverse possession.

(B) Frank's deed from Oker was never recorded.

(C) Tim did not know about the covenant until after he had incurred the expenses and, hence, could not have relied on it.

(D) Tim's expenditures were not proved to be reasonable and customary.

108. While Prudence was leaving an elevator, it suddenly dropped several inches, causing her to fall. An investigation of the accident revealed that the elevator dropped because it had been negligently maintained by the Acme Elevator Company. Acme had a contract with the owner of the building to inspect and maintain the elevator. Prudence's fall severely aggravated a preexisting physical disability.

If Prudence sues Acme Elevator Company for damages for her injuries, she should recover

(A)   nothing, if Acme could not reasonably have been expected to foresee the extent of the harm that Prudence suffered as a result of the accident.

(B)   nothing, if the accident would not have caused significant harm to an ordinarily prudent elevator passenger.

(C)   damages for the full amount of her disability, because a tortfeasor must take its victim as it finds her.

(D)   damages for the injury caused by the falling elevator, including the aggravation of her preexisting disability.

109.   Dix is on trial for killing Vetter. prosecutor calls Winn to testify that after being shot, Vetter said, "Dix did it." Before the testimony is given, Dix's lawyer asks for a hearing on whether Vetter believed his death was imminent when he made the statement.

Before permitting evidence of the dying declaration, the judge should hear evidence on the issue from

(A)   both sides, with the jury not present, and decide whether Winn may testify to Vetter's statement.

(B)   both sides, with the jury present, and decide whether Winn

may testify to Vetter's statement.

(C)   both sides, with the jury present, and allow the jury to determine whether Winn may testify to Vetter's statement.

(D)   the prosecutor only, with the jury not present, and if the judge believes a jury could reasonably find that Vetter knew he was dying, permit Winn to testify to the statement, with Dix allowed to offer evidence on the issue as a part of the defendant's case.

110.   Police received an anonymous tip that Tusitala was growing marijuana in her backyard, which was surrounded by a 15-foot high, solid wooden fence. Officer Boa was unable to view the yard from the street, so he used a police helicopter to fly over Tusitala's house. Boa identified a large patch of marijuana plants growing right next to the house and used this observation to obtain a search warrant.

Tusitala is prosecuted for possession of marijuana and moves to suppress use of the marijuana in evidence.

The court should

(A) grant the motion, because the only purpose of Boals flight was to observe the yard.

(B) grant the motion, because Tusitala had a reasonable expectation of privacy in the curtilage around her house and the police did not have a warrant.

(C) deny the motion, because a warrant is not required for a search of a residential yard.

(D) deny the motion, because Tusitala had no reasonable expectation of privacy from aerial observation.

111. Buyem faxed the following signed message to Zeller, his long-time widget supplier: "Urgently need blue widgets. Ship immediately three gross at your current list price of $600." Upon receipt of the fax, Zeller shipped three gross of red widgets to Buyem, and faxed to Buyem the following message: "Temporarily out of blue. In case red will help, am shipping three gross at the same price. Hope you can use them."

Upon Buyem's timely receipt of both the shipment and Zeller's fax, which of the following best describes the rights and duties of Buyem and Zeller?

(A) Buyem may accept the shipment, in which case he must pay Zeller the list price, or he must reject the shipment and recover from Zeller for total breach of contract.

(B) Buyem may accept the shipment, in which case he must pay Zeller the list price, or he may reject the shipment, in which case he has no further rights against Zeller.

(C) Buyem may accept the shipment, in which case he must pay Zeller the list price, less any damages sustained because of the nonconforming shipment, or he may reject the shipment and recover from Zeller for total breach of contract, subject to Zeller's right to cure.

(D) Buyem may accept the shipment, in which case he must pay Zeller the list price, less any damages sustained because of the nonconforming shipment, or he may reject the shipment provided that he promptly covers by obtaining conforming widgets from another supplier.

112. Members of a religious group calling itself the Friends of Lucifer believe in Lucifer as their Supreme Being. The members of this group meet once a year on top of Mt. Snow, located in a U.S. National Park, to hold an overnight encampment and a midnight dance around a large campfire. They believe this overnight encampment and all of its rituals are required by Lucifer to be held on the top of Mt. Snow. U.S. National Park Service rules that have been consistently enforced prohibit all overnight camping and all campfires on Mt. Snow because of the very great dangers overnight camping and campfires would pose in that particular location. As a result, the park Superintendent denied a request by the Friends of Lucifer for a permit to conduct these activities on top of Mt. Snow. The park Superintendent, who was known to be violently opposed to cults and other unconventional groups had, in the past, issued permits to conventional religious groups to conduct sunrise services in other areas of that U.S. National Park.

The Friends of Lucifer brought suit in Federal Court against the U.S. National Park Service and the Superintendent of the park to compel issuance of the requested permit.

As a matter of constitutional law, the most appropriate result in this suit would be a decision that denial of the permit was

(A) invalid, because the free exercise clause of the First Amendment prohibits the Park Service from knowingly interfering with religious conduct.

(B) invalid, because these facts demonstrate that the action of the Park Service purposefully and invidiously discriminated against the Friends of Lucifer.

(C) valid, because the establishment clause of the First Amendment prohibits the holding of religious ceremonies on federal land.

(D) valid, because religiously motivated conduct may be subjected to nondiscriminatory time, place, and manner restrictions that advance important public interests.

113. Park sued Davis Co. for injuries suffered in the crash of Park's dune buggy, allegedly caused by a defective auto part manufactured by Davis Co. Davis Co. claims that the part was a fraudulent imitation, not produced by Davis Co.

Which of the following is NOT admissible on the issue of whether the part was manufactured by Davis Co.?

(A) The fact that the defective part bears Davis Co.'s insignia or trademark.

(B) Testimony that the part was purchased from a parts house to which Davis Co. regularly sold parts.

(C) The part itself and a concededly genuine part manufactured by Davis Co. (for the jury's comparison).

(D) A judgment for another plaintiff against Davis Co. in another case involving substantially similar facts.

114. Anna entered into a valid written contract to purchase Blackacre, a large tract of land, from Jones for its fair market value of $50,000. The contract was assignable by Anna. Anna duly notified Jones to convey title to Anna and Charles, Charles being Annals friend whom Anna had not seen for many years. When Anna learned that Charles would have to sign certain documents in connection with the closing, she prevailed upon her brother, Donald, to attend the closing and pretend to be Charles. Anna and Donald attended the closing, and Jones executed an instrument in the proper form of a deed, purporting to convey Blackacre to Anna and Charles, as tenants in common. Donald pretended that he was Charles, and he signed Charles's name to all the required documents. Anna provided the entire $50,000 consideration for the transaction. The deed was promptly and properly recorded.

Unknown to Anna or Donald, Charles had died several months before the closing. Charles's will, which was duly probated, devised "All my real estate to my nephew, Nelson" and the residue of his estate to Anna.

Anna and Nelson have been unable to agree as to the status or disposition of Blackacre. Nelson brought an appropriate action against Jones and Anna to quiet legal title to an undivided one-half interest in Blackacre.

The court should hold that legal title to Blackacre is vested

(A) all in Jones.
(B) all in Anna.
(C) one-half in Anna and one-half in Jones.
(D) one-half in Anna and one-half in Nelson.

Questions 115–116 are based on the following fact situation.

Staff, Inc., a flour wholesaler, contracted to deliver to Eclaire, a producer of fine baked goods, her flour requirements for a one-year period. Before delivery of the first scheduled installment, Staff sold its business and "assigned" all of its sale contracts to Miller, Inc., another reputable and long-time flour wholesaler. Staff informed Eclaire of this transaction.

115. For this question only, assume that when Miller tendered the first installment to Eclaire in compliance with the Staff–Eclaire contract, Eclaire refused to accept the goods.

Which of the following arguments, if any, legally support(s) Eclaire's rejection of the goods?

I. Executory requirements contracts are nonassignable.
II. Duties under an executory bilateral contract are assumable only by an express promise to perform on the part of the delegates.

III. Language of "assignment" in the transfer for value of a bilateral sale-of-goods contract effects only a transfer of rights, not a delegation of duties.

(A) I only.
(B) II and III only.
(C) I and II and III.
(D) Neither I nor II nor III.

116. For this question only, assume that Eclaire accepted Miller's delivery of the first installment under the Staff–Eclaire contract, but that Eclaire paid the contract price for that installment to Staff and refused to pay anything to Miller.

In an action by Miller against Eclaire for the contractual amount of the first installment, which of the following, if any, will be an effective defense for Eclaire?

I. Eclaire had not expressly agreed to accept Miller as her flour supplier.
II. Eclaire's payment of the contractual installment to Staff discharged her obligation.
III. Staff remained obligated to Eclaire even though Staff had assigned the contract to Miller.

(A) I only.
(B) II only.
(C) I and III only.
(D) Neither I nor II nor III.

117. On October 22, Officer Jones submitted an application for a warrant to search 217 Elm Street for cocaine. In the application, Officer Jones stated under oath that he believed there was cocaine at that location because of information supplied to him on the morning of October 22 by Susie Schultz. He described Schultz as a cocaine user who had previously supplied accurate information concerning the use of cocaine in the community and summarized what Schultz had told him as follows: the previous night, October 21, Schultz was in Robert Redd's house at 217 Elm Street. Redd gave her cocaine. She also saw three cellophane bags containing cocaine in his bedroom.

The warrant was issued and a search of 217 Elm Street was conducted on October 22. The search turned up a quantity of marijuana but no cocaine. Robert Redd was arrested and charged with possession of marijuana. Redd moved to suppress the use of the marijuana as evidence contending that Susie Schultz was not in 217 Elm Street on October 21 or at any other time.
If, after hearing evidence, the judge concludes that the statement in the application attributed to Susie Schultz is incorrect, the judge should grant the motion to suppress

(A) because the application contains a material statement that is false.
(B) because of the false statement and because no cocaine was found in the house.
(C) only if he also finds that Susie Schultz's statement was a deliberate lie.
(D) only if he also finds that Officer Jones knew the statement was false.

118. The Personnel Handbook of Green City contains all of that city's personnel policies. One section of the handbook states that "where feasible and practicable supervisors are encouraged to follow the procedures specified in this Handbook before discharging a city employee." Those specified procedures include a communication to the employee of the reasons for the contemplated discharge and an opportunity for a pretermination trial-type hearing at which the employee may challenge those reasons.

After a year of service, Baker, the secretary to the Green City Council, was discharged without receiving any communication of reasons for her contemplated discharge and without receiving an opportunity for a pretermination trial-type hearing. Baker files suit in federal district court to challenge her discharge solely on constitutional grounds.

Which of the following best describes the initial burden of persuasion in that suit?

(A) The Green City Council must demonstrate that its personnel handbook created no constitutionally protected interest in city employment or in the procedures by which such employment is terminated.

(B) The Green City Council must demonstrate that Baker's termination was for good cause.

(C) Baker must demonstrate that state law creates a constitutionally protected interest in her employment or in the procedures by which her employment is terminated.

(D) Baker must demonstrate that she reasonably believed that she could work for Green City for as long as she wished.

119. Dean was prosecuted in federal court for making threats against the President of the United States. Dean was a voluntary patient in a private psychiatric hospital and told a nurse, shortly before the President came to town, that Dean planned to shoot the President. The nurse reported the threat to FBI agents.

Dean's motion to prevent the nurse's testifying is likely to be

(A) successful, because the statement was made in a medical setting.

(B) successful, because the nurse violated a confidence in reporting the statement.

(C) unsuccessful, because the statement was not within any privilege.

(D) unsuccessful, because Dean had not been committed involuntarily by court order.

120. Able, who owned Blackacre, a residential lot improved with a dwelling, conveyed it for a valuable consideration to Baker.

The dwelling had been constructed by a prior owner. Baker had inspected Blackacre prior to the purchase and discovered no defects. After moving in, Baker became aware that sewage seeped into the basement when the toilets were flushed. Able said that this defect had been present for years and that he had taken no steps to hide the facts from Baker. Baker paid for the necessary repairs and brought an appropriate action against Able to recover his cost of repair.

If Baker wins, it will be because

    (A)   Able failed to disclose a latent defect.

    (B)   Baker made a proper inspection.

    (C)   the situation constitutes a health hazard.

    (D)   Able breached the implied warranty of habitability and fitness for purpose.

121. Gardner's backyard, which is landscaped with expensive flowers and shrubs, is adjacent to a golf course. While Driver was playing golf on the course, a thunderstorm suddenly came up. As Driver was returning to the clubhouse in his golf cart, lightning struck a tree on the course, and the tree began to fall in Driver's direction. In order to avoid being hit by the tree, Driver deliberately steered his cart onto Gardner's property, causing substantial damage to Gardner's expensive plantings.

In an action by Gardner against Driver to recover damages for the harm to his plantings, Gardner will

    (A)   prevail, because, although occasioned by necessity, Driver's entry onto Gardner's property was for Driver's benefit.

    (B)   prevail, for nominal images only, because Driver was privileged to enter Gardner's property.

    (C)   not prevail, because the lightning was an act of God.

    (D)   not prevail, because Driver's entry onto Gardner's property was occasioned by necessity and therefore privileged.

122. Steve, in desperate need of money, decided to hold up a local convenience store. Determined not to harm anyone, he carried a toy gun that resembled a real gun. In the store, he pointed the toy gun at the clerk and demanded money.

A customer who entered the store and saw the robbery in progress pulled his own gun and fired at Steve. The bullet missed Steve but struck and killed the clerk.

Steve was charged with felony murder.

His best argument for being found NOT guilty is that he

- (A) did not intend to kill.
- (B) did not commit the robbery because he never acquired any money from the clerk.
- (C) did not intend to create any risk of harm.
- (D) is not responsible for the acts of the customer.

123. Client consulted Lawyer about handling the sale of Client's building, and asked Lawyer what her legal fee would be. Lawyer replied that her usual charge was $100 per hour, and estimated that the legal work on behalf of Client would cost about $5,000 at that rate. Client said, "Okay; let's proceed with it," and Lawyer timely and successfully completed the work. Because of unexpected title problems, Lawyer reasonably spent 75 hours on the matter and shortly thereafter mailed Client a bill for $7,500, with a letter itemizing the work performed and time spent. Client responded by a letter expressing his good-faith belief that Lawyer had agreed to a total fee of no more than $5,000. Client enclosed a check in the amount of $5,000 payable to Lawyer and conspicuously marked, "Payment in full for legal services in connection with the sale of Client's building." Despite reading the "Payment in full ... " language, Lawyer, without any notation of protest or reservation of rights, endorsed and deposited the check to her bank account. The check was duly paid by Client's bank. A few days later, Lawyer unsuccessfully demanded payment from Client of the $2,500 difference between the amount of her bill and the check, and now sues Client for that difference.

What, if anything, can Lawyer recover from Client?

- (A) Nothing, because the risk of unexpected title problems in a real-property transaction is properly allocable to the seller's attorney and thus to Lawyer in this case.
- (B) Nothing, because the amount of Lawyer's fee was disputed in good faith by Client, and Lawyer impliedly agreed to an accord and satisfaction.

(C) $2,500, because Client agreed to an hourly rate for as many hours as the work reasonably required, and the sum of $5,000 was merely an estimate.

(D)   The reasonable value of Lawyer's services in excess of $5,000, if any, because there was no specific agreement on the total amount of Lawyer's fee.

124. Pauline and Doris own adjacent parcels of land. On each of their parcels was a low-rise of f ice building. The two office buildings were of the same height. Last year Doris decided to demolish the low-rise office building on her parcel and to erect a new high-rise office building of substantially greater height on the parcel as permitted by the zoning and building ordinances. She secured all the governmental approvals necessary to pursue her project.

As Doris's new building was in the course of construction, Pauline realized that the shadows it would create would place her (Pauline's) building in such deep shade that the rent she could charge for space in her building would be substantially reduced.

Pauline brought an appropriate action against Doris to enjoin the construction in order to eliminate the shadow problem and for damages. Pauline presented uncontroverted evidence that her evaluation as to the impact of the shadow on the fair rental value of her building was correct. There is no statute or ordinance (other than the building and zoning ordinances) that is applicable to the issues before the court.

The court should

(A)   grant to Pauline the requested injunction.

(B)   award Pauline damages measured by the loss of rental value, but not an injunction.

(C)   grant judgment for Doris, because she had secured all the necessary governmental approvals for the new building.

(D)   grant judgment for Doris, because Pauline has no legal right to have sunshine continue to reach the windows of her building.

Questions 125-126 are based on the following fact situation.

Dumont, a real estate developer, was trying to purchase land on which he intended to build a large commercial development. Perkins, an elderly widow, had rejected all of Dumont's offers to buy her ancestral home, where she had lived all her life and which was located in the middle of Dumont's planned development. Finally, Dumont offered her $250,000.

He told her that it was his last offer and that if she rejected it, state law authorized him to have her property condemned.

Perkins then consulted her nephew, a law student, who researched the question and advised her that Dumont had no power of condemnation under state law. Perkins had been badly frightened by Dumont's threat, and was outraged when she learned that Dumont had lied to her.

125. If Perkins sues Dumont for damages for emotional distress, will she prevail?

    (A)   Yes, if Dumont's action was extreme and outrageous.

    (B)   Yes, because Perkins was frightened and outraged.

    (C)   No, if Perkins did not suffer emotional distress that was severe.

    (D)   No, if it was not Dumont's purpose to cause emotional distress.

126. If Perkins asserts a claim based on misrepresentation against Dumont, will she prevail?

    (A)   Yes, if Dumont knew he had no legal power of condemnation.

    (B)   Yes, if Dumont tried to take unfair advantage of a gross difference between himself and Perkins in commercial knowledge and experience.

    (C)   No, if Dumont's offer of $250,000 equaled or exceeded the market value of Perkins's property.

    (D)   No, because Perkins suffered no pecuniary loss.

127. State Y employs the Model Penal Code or American Law Institute test for insanity, and requires the state to prove sanity, when it is in issue, beyond a reasonable doubt. At Askew's trial for murder, he pleaded insanity. The state put on an expert psychiatrist who had examined Askew. He testified that, in his opinion, Askew was sane at the time of the murder.

Askew's attorney did not introduce expert testimony on the question of sanity. Rather, he presented lay witnesses who testified that, in their opinion, Askew was insane at the time of the murder. At the end of the trial, each side moves for a directed verdict on the question of sanity.

Which of the following correctly describes the judge's situation?

(A) She may grant a directed verdict for the defense if she believes that the jury could not find the prosecution to have proved sanity beyond a reasonable doubt.

(B) She may grant a directed verdict for the prosecution if she believes that Askew's witnesses on the insanity question are not believable.

(C) She may not grant a directed verdict for the defense, because the state had expert testimony and the defense only lay witnesses.

(D) She may grant a directed verdict for the prosecution if she is convinced by their experts that Askew was sane beyond a reasonable doubt.

128. Trelawney worked at a day-care center run by the Happy Faces Day Care Corporation.

At the center, one of the young charges, Smith, often arrived with bruises and welts on his back and legs. A statute in the jurisdiction requires all day-care workers to report to the police cases where there is probable cause to suspect child abuse and provides for immediate removal from the home of any suspected child abuse victims. Trelawney was not aware of this statute. Nevertheless, he did report Smith's condition to his supervisor, who advised him to keep quiet about it so the day-care center would not get into trouble for defaming a parent. About two weeks after Trelawney first noticed Smith's condition, Smith was beaten to death by his fat' her. Trelawney has been charged with murder in the death of Smith. The evidence at trial disclosed, in addition to the above, that the child had been the victim of beatings by the father for some time, and that these earlier beatings had been responsible for the marks that Trelawney had seen. Smith's mother had been aware of the beatings but had not stopped them because she was herself afraid of Smith's father.

Trelawney's best argument that he is NOT guilty of murder is

(A) he was not aware of the duty-to-report statute.

(B) he lacked the mental state necessary to the commission of the crime.

(C) his omission was not the proximate cause of death.

(D) the day-care corporation, rather than Trelawney, was guilty of the omission, which was sanctioned by its supervisory-level agent.

Questions 129-130 are based on the following fact situation.

Perkins and Morton were passengers sitting in adjoining seats on a flight on Delval Airline. There were many empty seats on the aircraft.

During the flight, a flight attendant served Morton nine drinks. As Morton became more and more obviously intoxicated and attempted to engage Perkins in a conversation, Perkins chose to ignore Morton. This angered Morton, who suddenly struck Perkins in the face, giving her a black eye.

129. If Perkins asserts a claim for damages against Delval Airline based on negligence, Perkins will

(A) not recover, because a person is not required by law to come to the assistance of another who is imperiled by a third party.

(B) not recover, if Perkins could easily have moved to another seat.

(C) recover, because a common carrier is strictly liable for injuries suffered by a passenger while aboard the carrier.

(D) recover, if the flight attendants should have perceived Morton's condition and acted to protect Perkins before the blow was struck.

130. If Perkins asserts a claim for damages against Delval Airline based on battery, she will

(A) prevail, because she suffered an intentionally inflicted harmful or offensive contact.

(B) prevail, if the flight attendant acted recklessly in continuing to serve liquor to Morton.

(C) not prevail, because Morton was not acting as an agent or employee of Delval Airline.

(D) not prevail, unless she can establish some permanent injury from the contact.

131. Terrorists in the foreign country of Ruritania kidnapped the United States ambassador to that country. They threatened to kill her unless the President of the United States secured the release of an identified person who was a citizen of Ruritania and was held in a prison of the state of Aurora in the United States pursuant to a valid conviction by that state.

The President responded by entering into an agreement with Ruritania which provided that Ruritania would secure the release of the United States ambassador on a specified date in return for action by the President that would secure the release of the identified person held in the Aurora prison. The President then ordered the governor of Aurora to release the prisoner in question. The governor refused. No federal statutes are applicable.

Which of the following is the strongest constitutional argument for the authority of the President to take action in these circumstances requiring the governor of Aurora to release the Aurora prisoner?

(A) The power of the President to conduct the foreign affairs of the United States includes a plenary authority to take whatever action the President deems wise to protect the safety of our diplomatic agents.

(B) The power of the President to appoint ambassadors authorizes him to take any action that he may think desirable to protect them from injury because, upon appointment, those officials become agents of the President.

(C) The power of the President to negotiate with foreign nations impliedly authorizes the President to make executive agreements with them which prevail over state law.

(D) The duty of the President to execute faithfully the laws authorizes him to resolve finally any conflicts between state and federal interests, making the determination of such matters wholly nonjusticiable.

132. Damson was charged with murder, and Wagner testified for the prosecution. On cross-examination of Wagner, Damson seeks to elicit an admission that Wagner was also charged with the same murder and that the prosecutor told her,

"If you testify against Damson, we will drop the charges against you after the conclusion of Damson's trial."

The evidence about the prosecutor's promise is

(A) admissible, as proper impeachment of Wagner.
(B) admissible, as an admission by an agent of a party-opponent.
(C) inadmissible, because the law encourages plea-bargaining.
(D) inadmissible, because the evidence is hearsay not within any exception.

Questions 133-134 are based on the following fact situation.

On November 1, Debbit, an accountant, and Barrister, a lawyer, contracted for the sale by Debbit to Barrister of the law books Debbit had inherited from his father. Barrister agreed to pay the purchase price of $10,000 when Debbit delivered the books on December 1.

On November 10, Barrister received a signed letter from Debbit that stated: "I have decided to dispose of the book stacks containing the law books you have already purchased. If you want the stacks, I will deliver them to you along with the books on December 1 at no additional cost to you. Let me know before November 15 whether you want them. I will not sell them to anyone else before then." On November 14, Barrister faxed and Debbit received the following message: "I accept your offer of the stacks." Debbit was not a merchant with respect to either law books or book stacks.

133. Debbit is contractually obligated to deliver the stacks because

(A) Barrister provided a new bargained-for exchange by agreeing to take the stacks.
(B) Debbit's letter (received by Barrister on November 10) and Barrister's fax-message of November 14 constituted an effective modification of the original sale-of-books contract.
(C) Barrister's tax-message of November 14 operated to rescind unilaterally the original sale-of-books contract.
(D) Debbit's letter (received by Barrister on November 10) waived the bargained-for consideration that would otherwise be required.

134. For this question only assume that on November 12 Debbit told Barrister that he had decided not to part with the stacks.

Will this communication operate as a legally effective revocation of his offer to deliver the stacks?

(A)   Yes, because Barrister had a pre-existing obligation to pay $10,000 for the law books.

(B)   Yes, because Debbit was not a merchant with respect to book stacks.

(C)   No, because Debbit had given a signed assurance that the offer would be held open until November 15.

(D)   No, because by delaying his acceptance until November 14, Barrister detrimentally relied on Debbit's promise not to sell the stacks to anyone else in the meantime.

135.   Seller owned Blackacre, improved with an aging four-story warehouse. The warehouse was built to the lot lines on all four sides. On the street side, recessed loading docks permitted semi trailers to be backed in. After the tractors were unhooked, the trailers extended into the street and occupied most of one lane of the street. Over the years, as trailers became larger, the blocking of the street became more severe. The municipality advised Seller that the loading docks could not continue to be used because the trailers blocked the street; it gave Seller 90 days to cease and desist.

During the 90 days, Seller sold and conveyed Blackacre by warranty deed for a substantial consideration to Buyer. The problem of the loading docks was not discussed in the negotiations.

Upon expiration of the 90 days, the municipality required Buyer to stop using the loading docks. This action substantially reduced the value of Blackacre.

Buyer brought an appropriate action against Seller seeking cancellation of the deed and return of all monies paid.

Such action should be based upon a claim of

(A)   misrepresentation.
(B)   breach of the covenant of warranty.
(C)   failure of consideration.
(D)   mutual mistake.

136.   Prescott sued Doxie for fraud. After verdict for Prescott, Doxie talked with juror Wall about the trial.

Doxie's motion for a new trial would be most likely granted if Wall is willing to testify that he voted for Prescott because he

(A)   misunderstood the judge's instructions concerning the standard of proof in a fraud case.

(B) was feeling ill and needed to get home quickly.

(C) relied on testimony that the judge had stricken and ordered the jury to disregard.

(D) learned from a court clerk that Doxie had been accused of fraud in several recent lawsuits.

137. Despondent over losing his job, Wilmont drank all night at a bar. While driving home, he noticed a car following him and, in his intoxicated state, concluded he was being followed by robbers. In fact, a police car was following him on suspicion of drunk driving. In his effort to get away, Wilmont sped through a stop sign and struck and killed a pedestrian. He was arrested by the police.
Wilmont is prosecuted for manslaughter.

He should be

(A) acquitted, because he honestly believed he faced an imminent threat of death or severe bodily injury.

(B) acquitted, because his intoxication prevented him from appreciating the risk he created.

(C) convicted, because he acted recklessly and in fact was in no danger.

(D) convicted, because he acted recklessly and his apprehension of

danger was not reasonable.

138. Ody, owner of Profitacre, executed an instrument in the proper form of a deed, purporting to convey Profitacre "to Leon for life, then to Ralph in fee simple." Leon, who is Ody's brother and Ralph's father, promptly began to manage Profitacre, which is valuable income producing real estate. Leon collected all rents and paid all expenses, including real estate taxes. Ralph did not object, and this state of affairs continued for five years until 1987. In that year, Leon executed an instrument in the proper form of a deed, purporting to convey Profitacre to Mona. Ralph, no admirer of Mona, asserted his right to ownership of Profitacre. Mona asserted her ownership and said that if Ralph had an) rights he was obligated to pay real estate taxes, even though Leon had beef kind enough to pay them in the past.

Income from Profitacre is ample to cover expenses, including real estate taxes.

In an appropriate action to determine the rights of the parties, the court should decide

(A)   Leon's purported deed forfeited his life estate, so Ralph owns Profitacre in fee simple.

(B)   Mona owns an estate for her life, entitled to all income, and must pay real estate taxes; Ralph owns the remainder interest.

(C)   Mona owns an estate for the life of Leon and is entitled to all income, and must pay real estate taxes; Ralph owns the remainder interest.

(D)   Mona owns an estate for the life Leon and is entitled to all income; Ralph owns the remainder interest, and must pay real estate taxes.

139.   Homer Ethel were jointly in possession of Greenacre in fee simple as tenants in common. They joined in a mortgage of Greenacre to Fortunoff Bank. Homer erected a fence along what he considered to be the true boundary between Greenacre and the adjoining property, owned by Mitchell. Shortly thereafter, Homer had an argument with Ethel and gave up his possession to Greenacre. The debt secured by the mortgage had not been paid.

Mitchell surveyed his land and found that the fence erected a year earlier by Homer did not follow the true boundary. Part of the fence was within Greenacre. Part of the fence encroached on Mitchell's land. Mitchell and Ethel executed an agreement fixing the boundary line in accordance with the fence constructed by Homer. The agreement, which met all the formalities required in the jurisdiction, was promptly and properly recorded.

A year after the agreement was recorded, Homer temporarily reconciled his differences with Ethel and resumed joint possession of Greenacre. Thereafter, Homer repudiated the boundary line agreement and brought an appropriate action against Mitchell and Ethel to quiet title along the original true boundary.

In such action, Homer will

(A)   win, because Fortunoff Bank was not a party to the agreement.

(B)   win, because one tenant in common; cannot bind another tenant in common to a boundary line agreement.

(C) lose, because the agreement, as a matter of law, was mutually beneficial to Ethel and Homer.

(D) lose, because Ethel was in sole possession of said premises at the time the agreement was signed.

140. At the trial of an action against Grandmother on behalf of Patrick, the following evidence has been introduced. Grandson and his friend, Patrick, both aged eight, were visiting at Grandmother's house when, while exploring the premises, they discovered a hunting rifle in an unlocked gun cabinet. They removed it from the cabinet and were examining it when the rifle, while in Grandson's hands, somehow discharged. The bullet struck and injured Patrick. The gun cabinet was normally locked. Grandmother had opened it for dusting several days before the boys' visit, and had then forgotten to relock it. She was not aware that it was unlocked when the boys arrived.

If the defendant moves for a directed verdict in her favor at the end of the plaintiff's case, that motion should be

(A) granted, because Grandmother is not legally responsible for the acts of Grandson.

(B) granted, because Grandmother did not recall that the gun cabinet was unlocked.

(C) denied, because a firearm is an inherently dangerous instrumentality.

(D) denied, because a jury could find that Grandmother breached a duty of care she owed to Patrick.

Questions 141–142 are based on the following fact situation.

On November 15, Joiner in a signed writing contracted with Galley for an agreed price to personally remodel Galley's kitchen according to specifications provided by Galley, and to start work on December 1. Joiner agreed to provide all materials for the job in addition to all of the labor required.

141. For this question only, assume that on November 26 Joiner without legal excuse repudiated the contract and that Galley, after a reasonable and prolonged effort, could not find anyone to remodel his kitchen for a price approximating the price agreed to by Joiner.

If one year later Galley brings an action for specific performance against Joiner, which of the following will provide Joiner with the best defense?

(A)   An action for equitable relief not brought within a reasonable time is barred by laches.

(B)   Specific performance is generally not available as a remedy to enforce a contractual duty to perform personal services.

(C)   Specific performance is generally not available as a remedy in the case of an anticipatory repudiation.

(D)   Specific performance is not available as a remedy where even nominal damages could have been recovered as a remedy at law.

142.   For this question only, assume the following facts. On November 26, Galley without legal excuse repudiated the contract. Notwithstanding Galley's repudiation, however, Joiner subsequently purchased for $5,000 materials that could only be used in remodeling Galley's kitchen, and promptly notified Galley, "I will hold you to our contract." If allowed to perform, Joiner would have made a profit of $3,000 on the job.

If Galley refuses to retract his repudiation, and Joiner sues him for damages, what is the maximum that Joiner is entitled to recover?

(A)   Nothing, because he failed to mitigate his damages.

(B) $3,000, his expectancy damages.

(C) $5,000, on a restitutionary theory.

(D) $5,000, his reliance damages, plus $3,000, his expectancy damages.

Questions 143–144 are based on the following fact situation.

The police suspected that Yancey, a 16-year-old high school student, had committed a series of burglaries. Two officers went to Yancey's high school and asked the principal to call Yancey out of class and to search his backpack. While the officers waited, the principal took Yancey into the hall where she asked to look in his backpack. When Yancey refused, the principal grabbed it from him, injuring Yancey's shoulder in the process. In the backpack, she found jewelry that she turned over to the officers.

The officers believed that the jewelry had been taken in one of the burglaries. They arrested Yancey, took him to the station, and gave him Miranda warnings. Yancey asked to see a lawyer. The police called Yancey's parents to the station. When Yancey's parents arrived, the police asked them to speak with Yancey. They put them in a room and secretly recorded their conversation with a concealed electronic device.

Yancey broke down and confessed to his parents that he had committed the burglaries.

Yancey was charged with the burglaries.

143. Yancey moves to suppress the use of the jewelry.

The court should

(A) deny the motion on the ground that the search was incident to a lawful arrest.

(B) deny the motion on the ground that school searches are reasonable if conducted by school personnel on school grounds on the basis of reasonable suspicion.

(C) grant the motion on the ground that the search was conducted with excessive force.

(D) grant the motion on the ground that the search was conducted without probable cause or a warrant.

144. Assume for this question only that the court denied the motion to suppress the jewelry. Yancey moves to suppress the use of the statement Yancey made to his parents.

The best argument for excluding it would be that

(A) Yancey was in custody at the time the statement was recorded.

(B) the police did not comply with Yancey's request for a lawyer.

(C) once Yancey had invoked his right to counsel, it was improper for the police to listen to any of his private conversations.

(D) the meeting between Yancey and his parents was arranged by the police to obtain an incriminating statement.

145. A newly enacted federal statute appropriates $100 million in federal funds to support basic research by universities located in the United States. The statute provides that "the ten best universities in the United States" will each receive $10 million. It also provides that "the ten best universities" shall be "determined by a poll of the presidents of all the universities in the nation, to be conducted by the United States Department of Education." In responding to that poll, each university president is required to apply the well-recognized and generally accepted standards of academic quality that are specified in the statute. The provisions of the statute are inseverable.

Which of the following statements about this statute is correct?

(A) The statute is unconstitutional, because the reliance by Congress on a poll of individuals who are not federal officials to determine the recipients of its appropriated funds is an unconstitutional delegation of legislative power.

(B) The statute is unconstitutional, because the limitation on recipients to the ten best universities is arbitrary and capricious and denies other high quality universities the equal protection of the laws.

(C) The statute is constitutional, because Congress has plenary authority to determine the objects of its spending and the methods used to achieve them, so long as they may reasonably be deemed to serve the general welfare and do not violate any prohibitory language in the Constitution.

(D) The validity of the statute is nonjusticiable, because the use by Congress of its spending power necessarily involves political considerations that must be resolved finally by those branches of the government that are closest to the political process.

146. Which of the following fact patterns most clearly suggests an implied-in-fact contract?

(A) A county tax assessor mistakenly bills Algernon for taxes on Bathsheba's property, which Algernon, in good faith, pays.

(B) Meddick, a physician, treated Ryder without Ryder's knowledge or consent, while Ryder was unconscious as the result of a fall from his horse.

(C) Asphalt, thinking that he was paving Customer's driveway, for which Asphalt had an express contract, mistakenly paved Nabor's driveway while Nabor looked on without saying anything or raising any objection.

(D) At her mother's request, Iris, an accountant, filled out and filed her mother's "E-Z" income-tax form (a simple, short form).

147. Ashton owned Woodsedge, a tract used for commercial purposes, in fee simple and thereafter mortgaged it to First Bank. She signed a promissory note secured by a duly executed and recorded mortgage. There was no "due on sale" clause, that is, no provision that, upon sale, the whole balance then owing would become due and owing. Ashton conveyed Woodsedge to Beam "subject to a mortgage to First Bank, which the grantee assumes and agrees to pay." Beam conveyed Woodsedge to Carter it subject to an existing mortgage to First Bank." A copy of the note and the mortgage that secured it had been exhibited to each grantee.

After Carter made three timely payments, no further payments were made by any party. In fact, the real estate had depreciated to a point where it was worth less than the debt.

There is no applicable statute or regulation.
In an appropriate foreclosure action, First Bank joined Ashton, Beam, and Carter as defendants. At the foreclosure sale, although the fair market value for Woodsedge in its depreciated state was obtained, a deficiency resulted.

First Bank is entitled to collect a deficiency judgment against

(A)   Ashton only.
(B)   Ashton and Beam only.
(C)   Beam and Carter only.
(D)   Ashton, Beam, and Carter.

148. Landco purchased a large tract of land intending to construct residential housing on it. Landco hired Poolco to build a large in-ground swimming pool on the tract. The contract provided that Poolco would carry out blasting operations that were necessary to create an excavation large enough for the pool. The blasting caused cracks to form in the walls of Plaintiff Is home in a nearby residential neighborhood.

In Plaintiff's action for damages against Landco, Plaintiff should

(A)   prevail, only if Landco retained the right to direct and control Poolco's construction of the pool.
(B)   prevail, because the blasting that Poolco was hired to perform damaged Plaintiff's home.
(C)   not prevail, if Poolco used reasonable care in conducting the blasting operations.

(D)   not prevail, if Landco used reasonable care to hire a competent contractor.

149.   The state of Atlantica spends several million dollars a year on an oyster conservation program. As part of that program, the state limits, by statute, oyster fishing in its coastal waters to persons who have state oyster permits. In order to promote conservation, it issues only a limited number of oyster permits each year. The permits are effective for only one year from the date of their issuance and are awarded on the basis of a lottery, in which there is no differentiation between resident and nonresident applicants. However, each nonresident who obtains a permit is charged an annual permit fee that is $5 more than the fee charged residents.

Fisher, Inc., is a large fishing company that operates from a port in another state and is incorporated in that other state. Each of the boats of Fisher, Inc., has a federal shipping license that permits it "to engage in all aspects of the coastal trade, to fish and to carry cargo from place to place along the coast, and to engage in other lawful activities along the coast of the United States." These shipping licenses are authorized by federal statute. Assume no other federal statutes or administrative rules apply.

Although it had previously held an Atlantica oyster permit, Fisher, Inc., did not obtain a permit in that state's lottery this year.

Which of the following is the strongest argument that can be made in support of a continued right of Fisher, Inc., to fish for oysters this year in the coastal waters of Atlantica?

(A)   Because the Atlantica law provides higher permit charges for nonresidents, it is an undue burden on interstate commerce.
(B)   Because the Atlantica law provides higher permit charges for nonresidents, it denies Fisher, Inc., the privileges and immunities of state citizenship.
(C)   Because it holds a federal shipping license, Fisher, Inc., has a right to fish for oysters in Atlantica waters despite the state law.

(D) Because Fisher, Inc., previously held an Atlantica oyster permit and Atlantica knows that company is engaged in a continuing business operation, the refusal to grant Fisher, Inc., a permit this year is a taking of its property without due process of law.

150. The United States Department of the Interior granted Concessionaire the food and drink concession in a federal park located in the state of New Senora. Concessionaire operated his concession out of federally owned facilities in the park. The federal statute authorizing the Interior Department to grant such concessions provided that the grantees would pay only a nominal rental for use of these federal facilities because of the great benefit their concessions would provide to the people of the United States.

The legislature of the state of New Senora enacted a statute imposing an occupancy tax on the occupants of real estate within that state that is not subject to state real estate taxes. The statute was intended to equalize the state tax burden on such occupants with that on people occupying real estate that is subject to state real estate taxes. Pursuant to that statute, the New Senora Department of Revenue attempted to collect the state occupancy tax from Concessionaire because the federal facilities occupied by Concessionaire were not subject to state real estate taxes. Concessionaire sued to invalidate the state occupancy tax as applied to him.

The strongest ground upon which Concessionaire could challenge the occupancy tax is that it violates the

(A) commerce clause by unduly burdening the interstate tourist trade.
(B) privileges and immunities clause of the Fourteenth Amendment by interfering with the fundamental right to do business on federal property.
(C) equal protection of the laws clause of the Fourteenth Amendment because the tax treats him less favorably than federal concessionaires in other states who do not have to pay such occupancy taxes.
(D) supremacy clause of Article VI and the federal statute authorizing such concessions.

151. Davis has a small trampoline in his backyard which, as he knows, is commonly used by neighbor children as well as his own. The trampoline is in good condition, is not defective in any way, and normally is surrounded by mats to prevent injury if a user should fall off. Prior to leaving with his family for the day, Davis leaned the trampoline up against the side of the house and placed the mats in the garage.

While the Davis family was away, Philip, aged 11, a new boy in the neighborhood, wandered into Davis's yard and saw the trampoline. Philip had not previously been aware of its presence, but, having frequently used a trampoline before, he decided to set it up, and started to jump. He lost his balance on one jump and took a hard fall on the bare ground, suffering a serious injury that would have been prevented by the mats.

An action has been brought against Davis on Philip's behalf to recover damages for the injuries Philip sustained from his fall. In this jurisdiction, the traditional common-law rules pertaining to contributory negligence have been replaced by a pure comparative negligence rule.

In his action against Davis, will Philip prevail?

(A) No, if children likely to be attracted by the trampoline would normally realize the risk of using it without mats.

(B) No, if Philip failed to exercise reasonable care commensurate with his age, intelligence, and experience.

(C) No, because Philip entered Davis's yard and used the trampoline without Davis's permission.

(D) No, because Philip did not know about the trampoline before entering Davis's yard and thus was not "lured" onto the premises.

152. Deben was charged with using a forged prescription from a Dr. Kohl to obtain Percodan from Smith's Drugstore on May 1. At trial, Smith identified Deben as the customer, but Deben testified that he had not been in the store.

In rebuttal, the prosecutor calls Wallman and Witler to testify that on May 1 a man they identified as Deben had presented prescriptions for Percodan from a Dr. Kohl at, respectively, Wallman's Drugs and Witler's Drugstore.

Wallman's and Witler's testimony is

(A) admissible, to prove a pertinent trait of Deben's character and Deben's action in conformity therewith.

(B) admissible, to identify the man who presented the prescription at Smith's Drugstore.

(C) inadmissible, because it proves specific acts rather than reputation or opinion.

(D) inadmissible, because other crimes may not be used to show propensity.

153. An ordinance of the city of Green requires that its mayor must have been continuously a resident of the city for at least five years at the time he or she takes office. Candidate, who is thinking about running for mayor in an election that will take place next year, will have been a resident of Green for only four and one-half years at the time the mayor elected then takes office. Before he decides whether to run for the position of mayor, Candidate wants to know whether he could lawfully assume that position if he were elected. As a result, Candidate files suit in the local federal district court for a declaratory judgment that the Green five-year-residence requirement is unconstitutional and that he is entitled to a place on his political party's primary election ballot for mayor. He names the chairman of his political party as the sole defendant but does not join any election official. The chairman responds by joining Candidate in requesting the court to declare the Green residence requirement invalid.

In this case, the court should

(A) refuse to determine the merits of this suit, because there is no case or controversy.

(B) refuse to issue such a declaratory judgment, because an issue of this kind involving only a local election does not present a substantial federal constitutional question.

(C) issue the declaratory judgment, because a residency requirement of this type is a denial of the equal protection of the laws.

(D) issue the declaratory judgment, because Candidate will have substantially complied with the residency requirement.

154. Oliver, owner of Blackacre, needed money. Blackacre was fairly worth $100,000, so Oliver tried to borrow $60,000 from Len on the security of Blackacre. Len agreed, but only if Oliver would convey Blackacre to Len outright by warranty deed, with Len agreeing orally to reconvey to Oliver once the loan was paid according to its terms. Oliver agreed, conveyed Blackacre to Len by warranty deed, and Len paid Oliver $60,000 cash. Len promptly and properly recorded Oliver's deed.

Now, Oliver has defaulted on repayment with $55,000 still due on the loan. Oliver is still in possession.

Which of the following best states the parties' rights in Blackacre?

(A) Len's oral agreement to reconvey is invalid under the Statute of Frauds, so Len owns Blackacre outright.

(B) Oliver, having defaulted, has no further rights in Blackacre, so Len may obtain summary eviction.

(C) The attempted security arrangement is a creature unknown to the law, hence a nullity; Len has only a personal right to $55,000 from Oliver.

(D) Len may bring whatever foreclosure proceeding is appropriate under the laws of the jurisdiction.

155. Big City High School has had a very high rate of pregnancy among its students : In order to assist students who keep their babies to complete high school, Big City High School has established an infant day-care center for children of its students, and also offers classes in childcare. Because the child-care classes are always overcrowded, the school limits admission to those classes solely to Big City High School students who are the mothers of babies in the infant day-care center.

Joe, a student at Big City High School, has legal custody of his infant son. The school provides care for his son in its infant day-care center, but will not allow Joe to enroll in the child-care classes. He brings suit against the school challenging, on constitutional grounds, his exclusion from the childcare classes.

Which of the following best states the burden of persuasion in this case?

(A) Joe must demonstrate that the admission requirement is not rationally related to a legitimate governmental interest.

(B) Joe must demonstrate that the admission requirement is not as narrowly drawn as possible to achieve a substantial governmental interest.

(C) The school must demonstrate that the admission policy is the least restrictive means by which to achieve a compelling governmental interest.

(D) The school must demonstrate that the admission policy is substantially related to an important governmental interest.

156. Defendant was upset because he was going to have to close his liquor store due to competition from a discount store in a new shopping mall nearby. In desperation, he decided to set fire to his store to collect the insurance. While looking through the basement for flammable material, he lit a match to read the label on a can. The match burned his finger and, in a reflex action, he dropped the match. It fell into a barrel and ignited some paper. Defendant made no effort to put out the fire but instead left the building. The fire spread and the store was destroyed by fire. Defendant was eventually arrested and indicted for arson.

Defendant is

(A) guilty, if he could have put out the fire before it spread and did not do so because he wanted the building destroyed.

(B) guilty, if he was negligent in starting the fire.

(C) not guilty, because even if he wanted to burn the building there was no concurrence between his *mens rea* and the act of starting the fire.

(D) not guilty, because his starting the fire was the result of a reflex action and not a voluntary act.

157. In his employment, Grinder operates a grinding wheel. To protect his eyes, he wears glasses, sold under the trade name "Safety Glasses," manufactured by Glassco. The glasses were sold with a warning label stating that they would protect only against small, flying objects. One day, the grinding wheel Grinder was using disintegrated and fragments of the stone wheel were thrown off with great force.

One large fragment hit Grinder, knocking his safety glasses up onto his forehead. Another fragment then hit and injured his eye. Grinder brought an action against Glassco for the injury to his eye. The jurisdiction adheres to the traditional common-law rule pertaining to contributory negligence.

In this action, will Grinder prevail?

(A) Yes, because the safety glasses were defective in that they did not protect him from the disintegrating wheel.

(B) Yes, because the glasses were sold under the trade name "Safety Glasses."

(C) No, because the glasses were not designed or sold for protection against the kind of hazard Grinder encountered.

(D) No, if Grinder will be compensated under the workers' compensation law.

Questions 158-160 are based on the following Fact situation.

Oscar purchased a large bottle of NoFlake dandruff shampoo, manufactured by Shampoo Company. The box containing the bottle stated in part: "CAUTION--Use only 1 capful at most once a day. Greater use may cause severe damage to the scalp." Oscar read the writing on the box, removed the bottle, and threw the box away. Oscar's roommate, Paul, asked to use the No-Flake, and Oscar said, "Be careful not to use too much." Paul thereafter used No-Flake twice a day, applying two or three capfuls each time, notwithstanding the label statement that read: "Use no more than one capful per day. See box instructions." The more he used NoFlake, the more inflamed his scalp became, the more it itched, and the more he used. After three weeks of such use, Paul finally consulted a doctor who diagnosed his problem as a serious and irreversible case of dermatitis caused by excessive exposure to the active ingredients in No-Flake. These ingredients are uniquely effective at controlling dandruff, but there is no way to remove a remote risk to a small percentage of persons who may contract dermatitis as the result of applying for prolonged periods of time amounts of NoFlake substantially in excess of the directions. This jurisdiction adheres to the traditional common-law rules pertaining to contributory negligence and assumption of risk.

158. Based upon the foregoing facts, if Paul sues Shampoo Company to recover damages for his dermatitis, his most promising theory of liability will be that the No-Flake shampoo

(A) had an unreasonably dangerous manufacturing defect.

(B)   had an unreasonably
      dangerous design
      defect.
(C)   was inherently
      dangerous.
(D)   was inadequately
      labeled to warn of its
      dangers.

159. If Paul asserts a claim for his
      injuries against Shampoo
      Company based on strict
      liability in tort, which of the
      following would constitute a
      defense?

      I.   Paul misused the No-
            Flake shampoo.
      II.   Paul was contributorily
            negligent in continuing
            to use No-Flake
            shampoo when his
            scalp began to hurt
            and itch.
      III. Paul was a remote user
            and not in privity with
            Shampoo Company.

      (A)   I only.
      (B)   I and II only.
      (C)   II and III only.
      (D)   Neither I, nor II, nor III.

160. If Paul asserts a claim against
      Oscar for his dermatitis
      injuries, Oscar's best defense
      will be that

      (A)   Paul was contributorily
            negligent.
      (B)   Paul assumed the risk.
      (C)   Oscar had no duty
            toward Paul, who was
            a gratuitous donee.
      (D)   Oscar had no duty
            toward Paul, because
            Shampoo Company
            created the risk and

had a nondelegable
duty to foreseeable
users.

161. Unprepared for a final
      examination, Slick asked his
      girlfriend, Hope, to set off the
      fire alarms in the university
      building 15 minutes after the
      test commenced. Hope did
      so. Several students were
      injured in the panic that
      followed as people were
      trying to get out of the
      building. Slick and Hope are
      prosecuted for battery and
      for conspiracy to commit
      battery.
      They are

      (A)   guilty of both crimes.
      (B)   guilty of battery but
            not guilty of
            conspiracy.
      (C)   not guilty of battery
            but guilty of
            conspiracy.
      (D)   not guilty of either
            crime.

162. A statute of the state of
      Wasminia prohibits the use of
      state-owned or state-
      operated facilities for the
      performance of abortions
      that are not "necessary to
      save the life of the mother."
      That statute also prohibits
      state employees from
      performing any such
      abortions during the hours
      they are employed by the
      state.

Citizen was in her second month of pregnancy. She sought an abortion at the Wasminia State Hospital, a state-owned and state-operated facility. Citizen did not claim that the requested abortion was necessary to save her life. The officials in charge of the hospital refused to perform the requested abortion solely on the basis of the state statute. Citizen immediately filed suit against those officials in an appropriate federal district court. She challenged the constitutionality of the Wasminia statute and requested the court to order the hospital to perform the abortion she sought.

In this case, the court will probably hold that the Wasminia statute is

(A) unconstitutional, because a limit on the availability of abortions performed by state employees or in state-owned or state-operated facilities to situations in which it is necessary to save the life of the mother impermissibly interferes with the fundamental right of Citizen to decide whether to have a child.

(B) unconstitutional, because it impermissibly discriminates against poor persons who cannot afford to pay for abortions in privately owned and operated facilities and against persons who live far away from privately owned and operated abortion clinics.

(C) constitutional, because it does not prohibit a woman from having an abortion or penalize her for doing so, it is rationally related to the legitimate governmental goal of encouraging childbirth, and it does not interfere with the voluntary performance of abortions by private physicians in private facilities.

(D) constitutional, because the use of state-owned or state-operated facilities and access to the services of state employees are privileges and not rights and, therefore, a state may condition them on any basis it chooses.

163. Oscar, owner of Greenacre, conveyed Greenacre by quitclaim deed as a gift to Ann, who did not then record her deed.

Later, Oscar conveyed Greenacre by warranty deed to Belle, who paid valuable consideration, knew nothing of Ann's claim, and promptly and properly recorded.

Next, Ann recorded her deed. Then Belle conveyed Greenacre by quitclaim deed to her son Cal as a gift. When the possible conflict with Ann was discovered Cal recorded his deed.

Greenacre at all relevant times has been vacant unoccupied land.

The recording act of the jurisdiction provides: "No unrecorded conveyance or mortgage of real property shall be good against subsequent purchasers for value without notice, who shall first record." No other statute is applicable.

Cal has sued Ann to establish who owns Greenacre.

The court will hold for

(A)   Cal, because Ann was a donee.
(B)   Cal, because Belle's purchase cut off Ann's rights'
(C)   Ann, because she recorded before Cal.
(D)   Ann, because Cal was a subsequent donee.

164.   While Driver was taking a leisurely spring drive, he momentarily took his eyes off the road to look at some colorful trees in bloom. As a result, his car swerved a few feet off the roadway, directly toward Walker, who was standing on the shoulder of the road waiting for a chance to cross. When Walker saw the car bearing down on him, he jumped backwards, fell, and injured his knee.

Walker sued Driver for damages, and Driver moved for summary judgment. The foregoing facts are undisputed.

Driver's motion should be

(A)   denied, because the record shows that Walker apprehended an imminent, harmful contact with Driver's car.
(B)   denied, because a jury could find that Driver negligently caused Walker to suffer a legally compensable injury.
(C)   granted, because the proximate cause of Walker's injury was his own voluntary act.
(D)   granted, because it is not unreasonable for a person to be distracted momentarily.

165. In which of the following situations is the defendant most likely to be convicted, even though he did not intend to bring about the harm that the statute defining the offense is designed to prevent?

(A) Defendant was the president of an aspirin manufacturing company. A federal inspector discovered that a large number of aspirin tablets randomly scattered through several bottles in a carton ready for shipment were laced with arsenic. Defendant is charged with attempted introduction of adulterated drugs into interstate commerce.

(B) Defendant struck Victim in the face with a baseball bat, intending to inflict a serious injury. Victim died after being hospitalized for three days. Defendant is charged with murder.

(C) Defendant burglarized a jewelry store, intending to steal some diamonds. As he entered the store, he short-circuited the store's burglar alarm system, thereby preventing a warning of his entry to police. The smoldering wires eventually caused a fire that destroyed the store. Defendant is charged with arson.

(D) Defendant wanted to frighten Victim's friend by placing a plastic rattlesnake in his lunch box. When Victim mistakenly took the lunch box and opened it, believing it to be his own, the plastic rattlesnake popped out. As a result of the fright, Victim suffered a heart attack and died. Defendant is charged with manslaughter.

166. Happy-Time Beverages agreed in writing with Fizzy Cola Company to serve for three years as a distributor in a six-county area of Fizzy Cola, which contains a small amount of caffeine. Happy-Time promised in the contract to "promote in good faith the sale of Fizzy Cola" in that area; but the contract said nothing about restrictions on the products that Happy-Time could distribute.

Six months later, Happy-Time agreed with the Cool Cola Company to distribute its caffeine-free cola beverages in the same six-county area.

If Fizzy Cola Company sues Happy-Time for breach of their distribution contract, which of the following facts, if established, would most strengthen Fizzy's case?

(A)   Cool Cola's national advertising campaign disparages the Fizzy Cola product by saying, "You don't need caffeine and neither does your cola."

(B)   Since Happy-Time began to distribute Cool Cola, the sales of Fizzy Cola have dropped 3% in the six-county area.

(C)   Prior to signing the contract with Fizzy Cola Company, a representative of Happy-Time said that the deal with Fizzy would be "an exclusive."

(D)   For many years in the soft-drink industry, it has been uniform practice for distributors to handle only one brand of cola.

167.   Dove is on trial for theft. At trial, the prosecutor called John and May Wong. They testified that, as they looked their apartment window, they saw thieves across the street break the window of a jewelry store, take jewelry, and leave in a car. Mrs. Wong telephoned the police and relayed to them the license number of the thieves' car as Mr. Wong looked out the window with binoculars and read it to her. Neither of them has any present memory of the number. The prosecutor offers as evidence a properly authenticated police tape recording of May Wong's telephone call with her voice giving the license number, which is independently shown to belong to Dovel's car.

The tape recording of May Wong's stating the license number is

(A)   admissible, under the hearsay exception for present sense impressions.

(B)   admissible, as nonhearsay circumstantial evidence.

(C)   inadmissible, because it is hearsay not within any exception.

(D)   inadmissible, because May Wong never had firsthand knowledge of the license number.

168.   Diggers Construction Company was engaged in blasting operations to clear the way for a new road. Diggers had erected adequate barriers and posted adequate warning signs in the vicinity of the blasting.

Although Paul read and understood the signs, he entered the area to walk his dog. As a result of the blasting, Paul was hit by a piece of rock and sustained head injuries. The jurisdiction follows the traditional common-law rules governing the defenses of contributory negligence, assumption of risk, and last clear chance.

In an action by Paul against Diggers to recover damages for his injuries, Paul will

(A)   not prevail, if Diggers exercised reasonable care to protect the public from harm.

(B)   not prevail, because Paul understood the signs and disregarded the warnings.

(C)   prevail, because Paul was harmed by Diggers's abnormally dangerous activity.

(D)   prevail, unless Paul failed to use reasonable care to protect himself from harm.

169.   Pike sued Day City Community Church for damages he suffered when Pike crashed his motorcycle in an attempt to avoid a cow that had escaped from its corral' The cow and corral belonged to a farm that had recently been left by will to the church. At trial, Pike seeks to ask Defendant's witness, Winters, whether she is a member of that church.

The question is

(A)   improper, because evidence of a witness's religious beliefs is not admissible to impeach credibility.

(B)   improper, because it violates First Amendment and privacy rights.

(C)   proper, for the purpose of ascertaining partiality or bias.

(D)   proper, for the purpose of showing capacity to appreciate the nature and obligation of an oath.

170.   Radon is a harmful gas found in the soil of certain regions of the United States. A statute of the state of Magenta requires occupants of residences with basements susceptible to the intrusion of radon to have their residences tested for the presence of radon and to take specified remedial steps if the test indicates the presence of radon above specified levels. The statute also provides that the testing for radon may be done only by testers licensed by a state agency.

According to the statute, a firm may be licensed to test for radon only if it meets specified rigorous standards relating to the accuracy of its testing. These standards may easily be achieved with current technology; but the technology required to meet them is 50% more expensive than the technology required to measure radon accumulations in a slightly less accurate manner.

The United States Environmental Protection Agency (EPA) does not license radon testers. However, a federal statute authorizes the EPA to advise on the accuracy of various methods of radon testing and to provide to the general public a list of testers that use methods it believes to be reasonably accurate.

WeTest, a recently established Magenta firm, uses a testing method that the EPA has stated is reasonably accurate. WeTest is also included by the EPA on the list of testers using methods of testing it believes to be reasonably accurate. WeTest applies for a Magenta radon testing license, but its application is denied because WeTest cannot demonstrate that the method of testing for radon it uses is sufficiently accurate to meet the rigorous Magenta statutory standards. WeTest sues appropriate Magenta officials in federal court claiming that Magenta may not constitutionally exclude WeTest from performing the required radon tests in Magenta.

In this suit, the court will probably rule in favor of

(A)   WeTest, because the full faith and credit clause of the Constitution requires Magenta to respect and give effect to the action of the EPA in including WeTest on its list of testers that use reasonably accurate methods.

(B)   WeTest, because the supremacy clause of the Constitution requires Magenta to respect and give effect to the action of the EPA in including WeTest on its list of testers that use reasonably accurate methods.

(C)   Magenta, because the federal statute and the action of the EPA in including WeTest on its list of testers that use reasonably accurate methods are not inconsistent with the more rigorous Magenta licensing requirement, and that requirement is reasonably related to a legitimate public interest.

(D) Magenta, because radon exposure is limited to basement areas, which, by their very nature, cannot move in interstate commerce.

171. Bitz, an amateur computer whiz, agreed in writing to design for the Presskey Corporation, a distributor of TV game systems, three new games a year for a five-year period. The writing provided, in a clause separately signed by Bitz, that "No modification shall be binding on Presskey unless made in writing and signed by Presskey's authorized representative."

Because of family problems, Bitz delivered and Presskey accepted only two game-designs a year for the first three years; but the games were a commercial success and Presskey made no objection. Accordingly, Bitz spent substantial sums on new computer equipment that would aid in speeding up future design work. In the first quarter of the fourth year, however, Presskey terminated the contract on the ground that Bitz had breached the annual quantity term.

In Bitz's suit against Presskey for damages, the jury found that the contract had been modified by conduct and the trial court awarded Bitz substantial compensatory damages.

Is this result likely to be reversed on appeal?

(A) Yes, because the contract's no-oral-modification clause was not expressly waived by Presskey.

(B) Yes, because the contract's no-oral-modification clause was a material part of the agreed exchange and could not be avoided without new consideration.

(C) No, because the contract's no-oral-modification clause was unconscionable as against an amateur designer.

(D) No, because Presskey by its conduct waived the annual-quantity term and Bitz materially changed his position in reasonable reliance on that waiver.

172. Test owned Blackacre, a vacant one-acre tract of land in State. Five years ago, he executed a deed conveying Blackacre to "Church for the purpose of erecting a church building thereon." Three years ago, Test died leaving Sonny as his sole heir at law. His duly probated will left Hall my Estate, both real and personal, to my friend Fanny."

Church never constructed a church building on Blackacre and last month Church, for a valid consideration, conveyed Blackacre to Developer.

Developer brought an appropriate action to quiet title against Sonny, Fanny, and Church, and joined the appropriate state official. Such official asserted that a charitable trust was created which has not terminated.

In such action, the court should find that title is now in

(A) Developer.
(B) Sonny.
(C) Fanny.
(D) the state official.

173. Mr. Denby was charged with the sale of narcotics. The federal prosecutor arranged with Mrs. Denby for her to testify against her husband in exchange for leniency in her case. At trial, the prosecution calls Mrs. Denby, who had been granted immunity from prosecution, to testify, among other things, that she saw her husband sell an ounce of heroin.

Which of the following statements is most clearly correct in the federal courts?

(A) Mrs. Denby cannot be called as a witness over her husband's objection.
(B) Mrs. Denby can be called as a witness but cannot testify, over Mr. Denby's objection, that she saw him sell heroin.
(C) Mrs. Denby can refuse, to be a witness against her husband.
(D) Mrs. Denby can be required to be a witness and to testify that she saw her husband sell heroin.

174. Freund, a U.S. west-coast manufacturer, gave Wrench, a hardware retailer who was relocating to the east coast, the following "letter of introduction" to Tuff, an east-coast hardware wholesaler.

This will introduce you to my good friend and former customer, Wrench, who will be seeking to arrange the purchase of hardware inventory from you on credit. If you will let him have the goods, I will make good any loss up to $25,000 in the event of his default.

/Signed/Freund

Wrench presented the letter to Tuff, who then sold and delivered $20,000 worth of hardware to Wrench on credit. Tuff promptly notified Freund of this sale.

Which of the following is NOT an accurate statement concerning the arrangement between Freund and Tuff?

(A) It was important to enforceability of Freund's promise to Tuff that it be embodied in a signed writing.

(B) By extending the credit to Wrench, Tuff effectively accepted Freund's offer for a unilateral contract.

(C) Although Freund received no consideration from Wrench, Freund's promise is enforceable by Tuff.

(D) Freund's promise is enforceable by Tuff whether or not Tuff gave Freund seasonable notice of the extension of credit to Wrench.

175. The legislature of the state of Gray recently enacted a statute forbidding public utilities regulated by the Gray Public Service Commission to increase their rates more than once every two years. Economy Electric Power Company, a public utility regulated by that commission, has just obtained approval of the commission for a general rate increase. Economy Electric has routinely filed for a rate increase every ten to 14 months during the last 20 years. Because of uncertainties about future fuel prices, the power company cannot ascertain with any certainty the date when it will need a further rate increase; but it thinks it may need such an increase sometime within the next 18 months.

Economy Electric files an action in the federal district court in Gray requesting a declaratory judgment that this new statute of Gray forbidding public utility rate increases more often than once every two years is unconstitutional.

Assume no federal statute is relevant.

In this case, the court should

(A) hold the statute unconstitutional, because such a moratorium on rate increases deprives utilities of their property without due process of law.

(B) hold the statute constitutional, because the judgment of a legislature on a matter involving economic regulation is entitled to great deference.

(C) dismiss the complaint, because this action is not ripe for decision.

(D)   dismiss the complaint, because controversies over state-regulated utility rates are outside of the jurisdiction conferred on federal courts by Article III of the Constitution.

176.   Daniel is on trial for evading $100,000 in taxes. The prosecution offers in evidence an anonymous letter to the IRS, identified as being in Daniel's handwriting, saying, "I promised my mother on her deathbed I would try to pay my back taxes. Here is $10,000. I'll make other payments if you promise not to prosecute. Answer yes by personal ad saying, 'OK on tax deal.'

The letter is

(A)   admissible, as a statement of present intention or plan.
(B)   admissible, as an admission of a party opponent.
(C)   inadmissible, because it is an effort to settle a claim.
(D)   inadmissible, because the probative value is substantially outweighed by the risk of unfair prejudice.

Questions 177–178 are based on the following fact situation.

Broker needed a certain rare coin to complete a set that he had contracted to assemble and sell to Collecta. On February 1, Broker obtained such a coin from Hoarda in exchange for $1,000 and Broker's signed, written promise to re-deliver to Hoarda "not later than December 31 this year" a comparable specimen of the same kind of coin without charge to Hoarda. On February 2, Broker consummated sale of the complete set to Collecta.

On October 1, the market price of rare coins suddenly began a rapid, sustained rise; and on October 15 Hoarda wrote Broker for assurance that the latter would timely meet his coin-replacement commitment. Broker replied, "In view of the surprising market, it seems unfair that I should have to replace your coin within the next few weeks."

177.   For this question only, assume the following facts. Having received Broker's message on October 17, Hoarda sued Broker on November 15 for the market value of a comparable replacement-coin as promised by Broker in February. The trial began on December 1.

If Broker moves to dismiss Hoarda's complaint, which of the following is Broker's best argument in support of the motion?

(A) Broker did not repudiate the contract on October 17, and may still perform no later than the contract deadline of December 31.

(B) Even if Broker repudiated on October 17, Hoarda's only action would be for specific performance because the coin is a unique chattel.

(C) Under the doctrine of impossibility, which includes unusually burdensome and unforeseen impracticability, Broker is temporarily excused by the market conditions from timely performance of his coin-replacement obligation.

(D) Even if Broker repudiated on October 17, Hoarda has no remedy without first demanding in writing that Broker retract his repudiation.

178. For this question only, assume the following facts. After receiving Broker's message on October 17, Hoarda telephoned Broker, who said, "I absolutely will not replace your coin until the market drops far below its present level." Hoarda then sued Broker on November 15 for the market value of a comparable replacement-coin as promised by Broker in February. The trial began on December 1.

If Broker moves to dismiss Hoarda's complaint, which of the following is Hoarda's best argument in opposing the motion?

(A) Hoarda's implied duty of good faith and fair dealing in enforcement of the contract required to mitigate her losses on the rising market by suing promptly, as she did, after becoming reasonably apprehensive of a prospective breach by Broker.

(B) Although the Joetrine of anticipatory breach is not applicable under the prevailing view if, at the time of repudiation, the repudiates owes the repudiator no remaining duty of performance, the doctrine applies in this case because Hoarda, the repudiates, remains potentially liable under an implied warranty that the coin advanced to Broker was genuine.

(C) When either party to a sale-of-goods contract repudiates with respect to a performance not yet due, the loss of which will substantially impair the value of the contract to the other, the aggrieved party may in good faith resort to any appropriate remedy for breach.

(D) Anticipatory repudiation, as a deliberate disruption without legal excuse of an ongoing contractual relationship between the parties, may be treated by the repudiates at her election as a present tort, actionable at once.

179. Alice owned a commercial property, Eastgate, consisting of a one-story building rented to various retail stores and a very large parking lot. Two years ago, Alice died and left Eastgate to her nephew, Paul, for life, with remainder to her godson, Richard, his heirs and assigns. Paul was 30 years old and Richard was 20 years old when Alice died. The devise of Eastgate was made subject to any mortgage on Eastgate in effect at the time of Alice's death.

When Alice executed her will, the balance of the mortgage debt on Eastgate was less than $5,000. A year before her death, Alice suffered financial reverses; and in order to meet her debts, she had mortgaged Eastgate to secure a loan of $150,000. The entire principal of the mortgage remained outstanding when she died. As a result, the net annual income from,. Eastgate was reduced not only by real estate taxes and regular maintenance costs, but also by the substantial mortgage interest payments that were due each month.

Paul was very dissatisfied with the limited benefit that he was receiving from the life estate. When, earlier this year, Acme, Inc., proposed to purchase Eastgate, demolish the building, pay off the mortgage, and construct a 30-story office building, Paul was willing to accept Acme's offer. However, Richard adamantly refused the offer, even though Richard, as the remainderman, paid the principal portion of each monthly mortgage amortization payment. Richard was independently wealthy and wanted to convert Eastgate into a public park when he became entitled to possession.

When Acme realized that Richard would not change his mind, Acme modified its proposal to a purchase of the life estate of Paul. Acme was ready to go ahead with its building plans, relying upon a large life insurance policy on Paul's life to protect it against the economic risk of Paul's death. Paul's life expectancy was 45 years.

When Richard learned that Paul had agreed to Acme's modified proposal, Richard brought an appropriate action against them to enjoin their carrying it out.

There is no applicable statute.

The best argument for Richard is that

(A) Acme cannot purchase Paul's life estate, because life estates are not assignable.
(B) the proposed demolition of the building constitutes waste.
(C) Richard's payment of the mortgage principal has subrogated him to Paul's rights as a life tenant and bars Paul's assignment of the life estate without Richard's consent.
(D) continued existence of the one-story building is more in harmony with the ultimate use as a park than the proposed change in use.

180. Doppler is charged with aggravated assault on Vezy, a game warden. Doppler testified that, when he was confronted by Vezy, who was armed and out of uniform, Doppler believed Vezy was a robber and shot in self-defense. The state calls Willy to testify that a year earlier, he had seen Doppler shoot a man without provocation and thereafter falsely claim self-defense.

Wilay's testimony is

(A) admissible, as evidence of Doppler's untruthfulness.
(B) admissible, as evidence that Doppler did not act in self-defense on this occasion.
(C) inadmissible, because it is improper character evidence.

(D) inadmissible, because it is irrelevant to the defense Doppler raised.

181. Eddie worked as the cashier in a restaurant. One night after the restaurant had closed, Eddie discovered that the amount of cash in the cash register did not match the cash register receipt tapes.

He took the cash and the tapes, put them in a bag, gave them to Rita, the manager of the restaurant, and reported the discrepancy. Rita immediately accused him of taking money from the register and threatened to fire him if he did not make up the difference. Rita placed the bag in the office safe. Angered by what he considered to be an unjust accusation, Eddie waited until Rita left the room and then reached into the still open safe, took the bag containing the cash, and left.

Eddie is guilty of

(A)   larceny.
(B)   embezzlement.
(C)   either larceny or embezzlement but not both.
(D)   neither larceny nor embezzlement.

182.   A grand jury returned an indictment charging Daniels with bank robbery, and when he could not make bond he was jailed pending trial. He had received Miranda warnings when arrested and had made no statement at that time. The prosecutor arranged to have Innis, an informant, placed as Daniels's cellmate and instructed Innis to find out about the bank robbery without asking any direct questions about it. Innis, once in the cell, constantly boasted about the crimes that he had committed. Not to be outdone, Daniels finally declared that he had committed the bank robbery with which he was charged.

A Daniels's trial, his attorney moved to exclude any testimony from Innis concerning Daniels's boast.

The motion should be

(A)   granted, because Daniels's privilege against self-incrimination was violated.
(B)   granted, because Daniels's right to counsel was violated.
(C)   denied, because Daniels had received Miranda warnings.
(D)   denied, because Daniels was not interrogated by Innis.

183.   Pamela sued Driver for damages for the death of Pamela's husband Ronald, resulting from an automobile collision. At trial, Driver calls Ronald's doctor to testify that the day before his death, Ronald, in great pain, said, "It was my own fault; there's nobody to blame but me."

The doctor's testimony should be admitted as

(A)   a statement against interest.
(B)   a dying declaration.

(C)   a statement of Ronald's then existing state of mind.

(D)   an excited utterance.

184.   Clerk is a clerical worker who has been employed for the past two years in a permanent position in the Wasmania County Public Records Office in the state of Orange. Clerk has been responsible for copying and filing records of real estate transactions in that office. Clerk works in a nonpublic part of the office and has no contact with members of the public. However, state law provides that all real estate records in that office are to be made available for public inspection.

On the day an attempted assassination of the governor of Orange was reported on the radio, Clerk remarked to a coworker, "Our governor is such an evil man, I am sorry they did not get him." Clerk's coworker reported this remark to Clerk's employer, the county recorder. After Clerk admitted making the remark, the county recorder dismissed him stating that "there is no room in this office for a person who hates the governor so much."

Clerk sued for reinstatement and back pay. His only claim is that the dismissal violated his constitutional rights.

In this case, the court should hold that the county recorder's dismissal of Clerk was

(A)   unconstitutional, because it constitutes a taking without just compensation of Clerk's property interest in his permanent position with the county.

(B)   unconstitutional, because in light of Clerk's particular employment duties his right to express himself on a matter of public concern outweighed any legitimate interest the state might have had in discharging him.

(C)   constitutional, because the compelling interest of the state in having loyal and supportive employees outweighs the interest of any state employee in his or her job or in free speech on a matter of public concern.

(D)   nonjusticiable, because public employment is a privilege rather than a right and, therefore, Clerk lacked standing to bring this suit.

185. Slalome, a ski-shop operator, in a telephone conversation with Mitt, a glove manufacturer, ordered 12 pairs of vortex-lined ski gloves at Mitt's list price of $600 per dozen "for delivery in 30 days." Mitt orally accepted the offer, and immediately faxed to Slalome this signed memo: "Confirming our agreement today for your purchase of a dozen pairs of vortex-lined ski gloves for $600, the shipment will be delivered in 30 days." Although Slalome received and read Mitt's message within minutes after its dispatch, she changed her mind three weeks later about the purchase and rejected the conforming shipment when it timely arrived.

On learning of the rejection, does Mitt have a cause of action against Slalome for breach of contract?

(A) Yes, because the gloves were identified to the contract and tendered to Slalome.

(B) Yes, because Mitt's faxed memo to Slalome was sufficient to make the agreement enforceable.

(C) No, because the agreed price was $600 and Slalome never signed a writing evidencing a contract with Mitt.

(D) No, because Slalome neither paid for nor accepted any of the goods tendered.

186. A burglar stole Collecta's impressionist painting valued at $400,000. Collecta, who had insured the painting for $300,000 with Artistic Insurance Co., promised to pay $25,000 to Snoop, a full-time investigator for Artistic, if he effected the return of the painting to her in good condition. By company rules, Artistic permits its investigators to accept and retain rewards from policyholders for the recovery of insured property. Snoop, by long and skillful detective work, recovered the picture and returned it undamaged to Collecta.

If Collecta refuses to pay Snoop anything, and he sues her for $25,000, what is the probable result under the prevailing modern rule?

(A) Collecta wins, because Snoop owed Artistic a preexisting duty to recover the picture if possible.

(B) Collecta wins, because Artistic, Snoop's employer, had a preexisting duty to return the recovered painting to Collecta.

(C) Snoop wins, because Collecta will benefit more from return of the $400,000 painting than from receiving the $300,000 policy proceeds.

(D) Snoop wins, because the preexisting duty rule does not apply if the promisee's (Snoop's) duty was owed to a third person.

187. Oren owned Purpleacre, a tract of land, in fee simple. By will duly admitted to probate after his death, Oren devised Purpleacre to "any wife who survives me with remainder to such of my children as are living at her death."

Oren was survived by Well, his wife, and by three children, Cynthia, Cam, and Camelia. Thereafter, Cam died and by will duly admitted to probate devised his entire estate to David. Cynthia and Camelia were Cam's heirs at law.

Later Well died. In appropriate lawsuit to which Cynthia, Camelia, and David are parties, title to Purpleacre is at issue.

In such lawsuit, judgment should be that title to Purpleacre is in

(A) Cynthia, Camelia, and David, because the earliest vesting of remainders is favored and reference to Well's death should be construed as relating to time of taking possession.

(B) Cynthia, Camelia, and David, because the provision requiring survival of children violates the Rule Against Perpetuities since the surviving wife might have been a person unborn at the time of writing of the will.

(C) Cynthia and Camelia, because Cam's remainder must descend by intestacy and is not devisable.

(D) Cynthia and Camelia, because the remainders were contingent upon surviving the life tenant.

188. Allen and Bradley were law school classmates who had competed for the position of editor of the law review. Allen had the higher grade point average, but Bradley was elected editor, largely in recognition of a long and important note that had appeared in the review over her name.

During the following placement interview season, Allen was interviewed by a representative of a nationally prominent law firm. In response to the interviewer's request for information about the authorship of the law review note, Allen said that he had heard that the note attributed to Bradley was largely the work of another student.

The firm told Bradley that it would not interview her because of doubts about the authorship of the note. This greatly distressed Bradley. In fact the note had been prepared by Bradley without assistance from anyone else.

If Bradley asserts a claim against Allen based on defamation, Bradley will

(A)   recover, because Allen's statement was false.

(B)   recover, if Allen had substantial doubts about the accuracy of the information he gave the interviewer.

(C)   not recover, unless Bradley proves pecuniary loss.

(D)   not recover,– because the statement was made by Allen only after the interviewer inquired about the authorship of the note.

Questions 189–190 are based on the following fact situation.

Sue Starr, a minor both in fact and appearance, bought on credit and took delivery of a telescope from 30-year-old Paul Prism for an agreed price of $100. Upon reaching her majority soon thereafter, Starr encountered Prism and said, "I am sorry for not having paid you that $100 for the telescope when the money was due, but I found out it was only worth $75. So I now promise to pay you $75." Starr subsequently repudiated this promise and refused to pay Prism anything.

189.   In an action for breach of contract by Prism against Starr, Prism's probable recovery is

(A)   nothing, because Starr was a minor at the time of the original transaction.

(B)   nothing, because there was no consideration for the promise made by Starr after reaching majority.

(C) $75.

(D) $100.

190.   For this question only, assume that Starr bought the telescope from Prism after reaching her majority and promised to pay $100 "as soon as I am able."

What effect does this quoted language have on enforceability of the promise.

(A)   None.

(B)   It makes the promise illusory.

(C)   It requires Starr to prove her inability to pay.

(D)   It requires Prism to prove Starr's ability to pay.

191.   Beach owned a tract of land called Blackacre. An old road ran through Blackacre from the abutting public highway. The road had been used to haul wood from Blackacre. Without Beach's permission and with no initial right, Daniel, the owner of Whiteacre, which adjoined Blackacre, traveled over the old road for a period of 15 years to obtain access to Whiteacre, although Whiteacre abutted another public road. Occasionally, Daniel made repairs to the old road.

The period of time to acquire rights by prescription in the jurisdiction is ten years.

After the expiration of 15 years, Beach conveyed a portion of Blackacre to Carrol. The deed included the following clause: "together with the right to pass and repass at all times and for all purposes over the old road." Carrol built a house fronting on the old road.

The road was severely damaged by a spring flood, and Carrol made substantial repairs to the road.

Carrol asked Daniel and Beach to contribute one-third each to the cost of repairing the flood damage. They both refused, and Carrol brought an appropriate action to compel contribution from Beach and Daniel.

In this action, Carrol will

(A)   lose as to both defendants.

(B)   win as to both defendants.

(C)   win as to Beach, but lose as to Daniel.

(D)   win as to Daniel, but lose as to Beach.

192.   Prine sued Dover for an assault that occurred March 5 in California. To support his defense that he was in Utah on that date, Dover identifies and seeks to introduce a letter he wrote to his sister a week before the assault in which he stated that he would see her in Utah on March 5.

The letter is

(A)   admissible, within the state of mind exception to the hearsay rule.

(B)   admissible, as a prior consistent statement to support Dover's credibility as a witness.

(C) inadmissible, because it lacks sufficient probative value.

(D) inadmissible, because it is a statement of belief to prove the fact believed.

193. Maple City has an ordinance that prohibits the location of "adult theaters and bookstores" (theaters and bookstores presenting sexually explicit performances or materials) in residential or commercial zones within the city. The ordinance was intended to protect surrounding property from the likely adverse secondary effects of such establishments. "Adult theaters and bookstores" are freely permitted in the areas of the city zoned industrial, where those adverse secondary effects are not as likely. Storekeeper is denied a zoning permit to open an adult theater and bookstore in a building owned by him in an area zoned commercial. As a result, Storekeeper brings suit in an appropriate court challenging the constitutionality of the zoning ordinance.
Which of the following statements regarding the constitutionality of this Maple City ordinance is most accurate?

(A) The ordinance is valid, because a city may enforce zoning restrictions on speech-related businesses to ensure that the messages they disseminate are acceptable to the residents of adjacent property.

(B) The ordinance is valid, because a city may enforce this type of time, place, and manner regulation on speech-related businesses, so long as this type of regulation is designed to serve a substantial governmental interest and does not unreasonably limit alternative avenues of communication.

(C) The ordinance is invalid, because a city may not enforce zoning regulations that deprive potential operators of adult theaters and bookstores of their freedom to choose the location of their businesses.

(D) The ordinance is invalid, because a city may not zone property in a manner calculated to protect property from the likely adverse secondary effects of adult theaters and bookstores.

194. Kingsley was prosecuted for selling cocaine to an undercover police agent. At his trial, he testified that he only sold the drugs to the agent, whom Kingsley knew as "Speedy," because Speedy had told him that he (Speedy) would be killed by fellow gang members unless he supplied them with cocaine. The prosecution did not cross-examine Kingsley. As rebuttal evidence, however, the prosecutor introduced records, over Kingsley's objection, showing that Kingsley had two prior convictions for narcotics-related offenses. The court instructed the jury concerning the defense of entrapment and added, also over Kingsley's objection but in accord with state law, that it should acquit on the ground of entrapment only if it found that the defendant had established the elements of the defense by a preponderance of the evidence. Kingsley was convicted.

On appeal, Kingsley's conviction should be

(A) reversed, because it was an error for the court to admit the evidence of his prior convictions as substantive evidence.

(B) reversed, because it was a violation of due process to impose on the defense a burden of persuasion concerning entrapment.

(C) reversed, for both of the above reasons.

(D) affirmed, because neither of the above reasons constitutes a ground for reversal.

Questions 195–196 are based on the following fact situation.

Pat sustained personal injuries in a three-car collision caused by the concurrent negligence of the three drivers, Pat, Donald, and Drew. In Pat's action for damages against Donald and Drew, the jury apportioned the negligence 30% to Pat, 30% to Donald, and 40% to Drew. Pat's total damages were $100,000.

195. Assume for this question only that a state statute provides for a system of pure comparative negligence, joint and several liability of concurrent tortfeasors, and contribution based upon proportionate fault.

If Pat chooses to execute against Donald alone, she will be entitled to collect at most

(A) $70,000 from Donald, and then Donald will be entitled to collect $40,000 from Drew.

(B) $30,000 from Donald, and then Donald will be entitled to collect $10,000 from Drew.

(C) $30,000 from Donald, and then Donald will be entitled to collect nothing from Drew.

(D) nothing from Donald, because Donald's percentage of fault is not greater than that of Pat.

196. Assume for this question only that the state has retained the common-law rule pertaining to contribution and that the state's comparative negligence statute provides for a system of pure comparative negligence but abolishes joint and several liability.

If Pat chooses to execute against Donald alone, she will be entitled to collect at most

(A) $70,000 from Donald, and then Donald will be entitled to collect $40,000 from Drew.

(B) $30,000 from Donald, and then Donald will be entitled to collect $10,000 from Drew.

(C) $30,000 from Donald, and then Donald will be entitled to collect nothing from Drew.

(D) nothing from Donald, because Donald's percentage of fault is not greater than that of Pat.

197. Tess Traviata owed Dr. Paula Pulmonary, a physician, $25,000 for professional services. Dr. Pulmonary orally assigned this claim to her adult daughter, Bridey, as a wedding gift. Shortly thereafter, on suffering sudden, severe losses in the stock market, Dr. Pulmonary assigned by a signed writing the same claim to her stockbroker, Margin, in partial satisfaction of advances legally made by Margin in Dr. Pulmonary's previous stock-market transactions. Subsequently, Traviata, without knowledge of either assignment, paid Dr. Pulmonary the $25,000 then due, which Dr. Pulmonary promptly lost at a horse track, although she remains solvent.

Assuming that Article 9 of the Uniform Commercial Code does NOT apply to either of the assignments in this situation, which of the following is a correct statement of the parties' rights and liabilities?

(A) As the assignee prior in time, Bridey can recover $25,000 from Traviata, who acted at her peril in paying Dr. Pulmonary.

(B)   As the sole assignee for value, Margin can recover $25,000 from Traviata, who acted at her peril in paying Dr. Pulmonary.

(C)   Neither Bridey nor Margin can recover from Traviata, but Bridey, though not Margin, can recover $25,000 from Dr. Pulmonary.

(D)   Neither Bridey nor Margin can recover from Traviata, but Margin, though not Bridey, can recover $25,000 from Dr. Pulmonary.

198.   Patten suffered from a serious, though not immediately life–threatening, impairment of his circulatory system. Patten's cardiologist recommended a cardiac bypass operation and referred Patten to Dr. Cutter. Cutter did not inform Patten of the 2% risk of death associated with this operation. Cutter defended his decision not to mention the risk statistics to Patten because "Patten was a worrier and it would significantly lessen his chances of survival to be worried about the nonsurvival rate."

Cutter successfully performed the bypass operation and Patten made a good recovery. However, when Patten learned of the 2% risk of death associated with the operation, he was furious

that Cutter had failed to disclose this information to him.

If Patten asserts a claim against Cutter based on negligence, will Patten prevail?

(A)   No, if Cutter used his best personal judgment in shielding Patten from the risk statistic.

(B)   No, because the operation was successful and Patten suffered no harm.

(C)   Yes, if Patten would have refused the operation had he been informed of the risk.

(D)   Yes, because a patient must be told the risk factor associated with a surgical procedure in order to give an informed consent.

199.   A statute of the state of Orrington provides that assessments of real property for tax purposes must represent the "actual value" of the property. The Blue County Tax Commission, in making its assessments, has uniformly and consistently determined the "actual value" of real property solely by reference to the price at which the particular property was last sold.

In recent years, the market values of real property in Blue County have been rising at the rate of 15% per year.

Owner is required to pay real estate taxes on her home in Blue County that are 200% to 300% higher than those paid by many other owners of similar homes in similar neighborhoods in that county, even though the current market values of their respective homes and Owner's home are nearly identical. The reason the taxes on Owner's home are higher than those imposed on the other similar homes In similar neighborhoods is that she bought her home much more recently than the other owners and therefore, it Is assessed at a much higher "actual value" than their homes. Persistent efforts by Owner to have her assessment –reduced or the assessments of the others raised by the Blue County Tax Commission have failed.

Owner has now filed suit against the Blue County Tax Commission, charging only that the tax assessment on her property is unconstitutional.

The strongest constitutional argument to support Owner's claim is that the comparative overvaluation of Owner's property by the Blue County Tax Commission in making tax assessments over time

(A)   deprives Owner of the equal protection of the laws.

(B)   deprives Owner of a privilege or immunity of national citizenship.

(C)   constitutes a taking of private property for public use without just compensation.

(D)   constitutes an ex post facto law.

200.   Plaza Hotel sued Plaza House Hotel for infringement of its trade name. To establish a likelihood of name confusion, Plaintiff Plaza Hotel offers a series of memoranda which it had asked its employees to prepare at the end of each day listing instances during the day in which telephone callers, cab drivers, customers, and others had confused the two names.

The memoranda should be

(A)   excluded, because they are more unfairly prejudicial and confusing than probative.

(B)   excluded, because they are hearsay not within any exception.

(C)   admitted, because they are records of regularly conducted business activity.

(D)   admitted, because they are past recollection recorded.

STOP
IF YOU FINISH BEFORE TIME IS
CALLED, CHECK YOUR WORK ON
THIS TEST.

If you use the questions in this publication as a practice exam, you should not rely on your raw score to identify how well you are doing. MBE raw scores are converted to scaled scores through an equating procedure that is designed to ensure that the level of difficulty of the examination remains consistent from administration to administration. The Raw Score Conversion Table following the Answer Key will help you determine where your performance would have placed you had you taken the test in 1991.

Item	Answer	Subject	Item	Answer	Subject
001	C	REAL PROP	054	D	CONST LAW
002	C	TORTS	055	B	REAL PROP
003	A	TORTS	056	A	EVIDENCE
004	C	CONTRACTS	057	B	TORTS
005	D	CONTRACTS	058	C	EVIDENCE
006	A	CRIM LAW	059	A	CONST LAW
007	A	EVIDENCE	060	A	CRIM LAW
008	C	CONST LAW	061	c	CONST LAW
009	B	CRIM LAW	062	B	CONTRACTS
010	B	EVIDENCE	063	A	CONTRACTS
011	C	TORTS	064	D	REAL PROP
012	D	EVIDENCE	065	C	EVIDENCE
013	D	REAL PROP	066	C	TORTS
014	B	TORTS	067	D	REAL PROP
015	B	EVIDENCE	068	D	CRIM LAW
016	A	CONTRACTS	069	A	CONST LAW
017	B	CONTRACTS	070	A	EVIDENCE
018	A	TORTS	071	B	TORTS
019	A	CRIM LAW	072	D	TORTS
020	C	CONST LAW	073	B	CRIM LAW
021	C	REAL PROP	074	C	CONTRACTS
022	A,B,D*	CRIM LAW	075	A	CONTRACTS
023	D	REAL PROP	076	B	TORTS
024	A	CONTRACTS	077	C	REAL PROP
025	C	TORTS	078	A	EVIDENCE
026	C	EVIDENCE	079	A	CONST LAW
027	C	CRIM LAW	080	B	CRIM LAW
028	D	CONST LAW	081	c	REAL PROP
029	D	CONTRACTS	082	D	EVIDENCE
030	B	REAL PROP	083	C	CONST LAW
031	B	CONTRACTS	084	A,C*	TORTS
032	C	CONTRACTS	085	A	EVIDENCE
033	B	CONST LAW	086	A	CONTRACTS
034	D	CONTRACTS	087	A	CONTRACTS

035	C	TORTS		088	C	REAL PROP
036	C	REAL PROP		089	A	REAL PROP
037	A	EVIDENCE		090	B	EVIDENCE
038	B	TORTS		091	A	CRIM LAW
039	A	CRIM LAW		092	A	REAL PROP
040	B	CONTRACTS		093	C	CRIM LAW
041	C	CONTRACTS		094	D	CONST LAW
042	C	TORTS		095	D	TORTS
043	D	TORTS		096	D	CRIM LAW
044	D	CRIM LAW		097	A	CONST LAW
045	A	EVIDENCE		098	A	CONST LAW
046	B	CONST LAW		099	C	CONTRACTS
047	C	TORTS		100	B	TORTS
048	B	REAL PROP		101	B	CONST LAW
049	C	CONST LAW		102	D	CRIM LAW
050	B	CRIM LAW		103	A	TORTS
051	B	CONTRACTS		104	B	REAL PROP
052	C	CONTRACTS		105	A	EVIDENCE
053	A	TORTS		106	A	CONTRACTS
107	D	REAL PROP		154	D	REAL PROP
108	D	TORTS		155	D	CONST LAW
109	A	EVIDENCE		156	A	CRIM LAW
110	D	CRIM LAW		157	C	TORTS
111	B	CONTRACTS		158	D	TORTS
112	D	CONST LAW		159	D	TORTS
113	D	EVIDENCE		160	A	TORTS
114	C	REAL PROP		161	B,D*	CRIM LAW
115	D	CONTRACTS		162	C	CONST LAW
116	D	CONTRACTS		163	B	REAL PROP
117	D	CRIM LAW		164	B	TORTS
118	C	CONST LAW		165	B	CRIM LAW
119	C	EVIDENCE		166	D	CONTRACTS
120	A	REAL PROP		167	A	EVIDENCE
121	A	TORTS		168	B	TORTS
122	D	CRIM LAW		169	C	EVIDENCE

123	B	CONTRACTS	170	C	CONST LAW
124	D	REAL PROP	171	D	CONTRACTS
125	C	TORTS	172	A	REAL PROP
126	D	TORTS	173	C	EVIDENCE
127	A	CRIM LAW	174	D	CONTRACTS
128	B	CRIM LAW	175	C	CONST LAW
129	D	TORTS	176	B	EVIDENCE
130	C	TORTS	177	A	CONTRACTS
131	C	CONST LAW	178	C	CONTRACTS
132	A	EVIDENCE	179	B	REAL PROP
133	B	CONTRACTS	180	C	EVIDENCE
134	B	CONTRACTS	181	A	CRIM LAW
135	A	REAL PROP	182	D	CRIM LAW
136	D	EVIDENCE	183	A	EVIDENCE
137	D	CRIM LAW	184	B	CONST LAW
138	C	REAL PROP	185	B	CONTRACTS
139	B	REAL PROP	186	D	CONTRACTS
140	D	TORTS	187	D	REAL PROP
141	B	CONTRACTS	188	B	TORTS
142	B	CONTRACTS	189	C	CONTRACTS
143	D	CRIM LAW	190	D	CONTRACTS
144	D	CRIM LAW	191	A	REAL PROP
145	C	CONST LAW	192	A	EVIDENCE
146	C	CONTRACTS	193	B	CONST LAW
147	B	REAL PROP	194	D	CRIM LAW
148	B	TORTS	195	A	TORTS
149	C	CONST LAW	196	C	TORTS
150	D	CONST LAW	197	D	CONTRACTS
151	A	TORTS	198	B	TORTS
152	B	EVIDENCE	199	A	CONST LAW
153	A	CONST LAW	200	B	EVIDENCE

*Immediately following the administration of an MBE, preliminary scoring is conducted to identify any unanticipated item functioning or unusual response patterns.

For example, an item might be flagged if a large number of applicants who did well on the test overall selected an option other than the key on that item. Flagged items are then reviewed by the MBE Drafting Committees to assure there are no ambiguities and that they have been keyed correctly. If a content problem is identified, an item may be double-keyed, triple-keyed, or eliminated from scoring by having all four options keyed correct. In a typical administration of the MBE, more than one option may be scored as correct on one or more of the 200 items.

RAW SCORE CONVERSION TABLE

RAW SCORE	SCALED SCORE	PERCENTILE RANK
161–167	170–175	97.6–99.4
154–160	163–169	92.2–97.1
147–153	157–162	82.6–91.1
140–146	151–156	68.7–80.8
133–139	145–150	53.3–66.6
126–132	139–144	38.0–51.1
119–125	133–138	25.0–35.9
112–118	126–132	15.0–23.5
105–111	120–126	8.3–13.9

The raw score is the total number of correct answers given by an examinee. A statistical procedure is used to convert raw scores to scaled scores to provide comparison of scores across test forms. The scaled score represents a comparable level of achievement for all forms of the MBE and scaled scores on one test form can be used interchangeable with the scaled scores on another test form.

The percentile rank shows an examinee's relative position in a group of examinees in terms of the percentage of
examinees scoring below the specified score. On this exam, those examinees who obtained a raw score of 153 scored better than 91 percent of all examinees who took the exam initially. Likewise, a raw score of 119 placed an examinee at the 25th percentile, indicating that the examinee scored higher than only 25 percent of the group. A raw score of 132 converted to a scaled score of 144 and placed an applicant at the 51st percentile.

Multistate Bar Examination Answers

1.   This question deals with the termination of a joint tenancy in real property by a conveyance during a joint tenant's lifetime. A joint tenant may convey her interest in jointly owned property by deed before her death, so Beth's conveyance to Eugenio is valid. There is no reversion to the joint tenants' grantor upon this event, nor will the property pass to Beth's heirs. (B) and (D) are incorrect.

After the conveyance by Beth, Christine and Eugenio held the property as tenants in common. Christine was free to convey her interest to Darin. Darin and Eugenio now hold as tenants in common, so (C) is correct.

2.   (A) is incorrect because the law of torts generally requires merely that the defendant have intended to commit the act, not that he have understood it was wrongful.

(B) is incorrect because the intent required for a battery is merely to bring about an unpermitted touching. No actual harm must have been intended.

(D) is incorrect because the defense of self-defense requires a reasonable belief that the force used was needed to repel an attack. Dorwin could not reasonably have believed that he was under attack by Peavey.

(C) is correct because intent to bring about the nonconsensual touching of a person is a required element of a battery.

3.   (B) is incorrect because it is irrelevant when, or whether, Drury knew he was committing a trespass.

(C) is incorrect because harm to the plaintiff's property is not an element of trespass. The tort of trespass involves merely an interference with the plaintiff's possessory interest.

(D) is incorrect because the intent required for a trespass is merely the intent to enter the property. The defendant need not have known it was the plaintiff's property; a good faith mistake about the ownership of the property will not excuse the defendant.

(A) is correct because nominal damages may be recovered for interference with the plaintiff's right to possession, even where there was no actual harm to the land and the defendant did not know he was trespassing.

4.   (A) is incorrect because a contract may be modified where there is an unforeseen hardship making it difficult for the promisor to complete the work. The additional work required for Structo to overcome the hardship caused by the unanticipated presence of the rock constituted consideration for Bailey's promise to pay an additional $20,000.

(B) is incorrect. There was no duress because there was no wrongful act by Structo that deprived Bailey of a meaningful choice.

(D) is incorrect because there was consideration for Bailey's promise to pay $20,000; Structo need not prove the reasonable value of the total performance.

(C) is correct; it states the standard for modification of an existing contract for unforeseen hardship.

5.   (A) is incorrect because Structo's expectancy damages would be the contract price *minus* the market value of his services. There are no benefit of the bargain damages to be recovered by the seller where the value of his goods or services exceeds the contract price.

(B) is incorrect because fixing the driveway so that it can safely be used would not constitute "economic waste."

(C) is incorrect because it assumes no breach of contract by Structo. While Structo might have been justified in demanding additional consideration to complete the contract in light of the unforeseen hardship, he was not entitled to perform in a way that did not meet Bailey's requirements.

(D) is correct because Bailey has paid the contract price minus the cost of correcting the driveway, which is the measure of consequential damages from Structo's breach.

6.   The "good faith" exception to the exclusionary rule involves police officers reasonably relying on a facially valid search warrant. There was no warrant to search Larson's home, so (B) is incorrect.

(C) is incorrect because the nature of Larson's neurological problem would not per se make him incapable of giving consent; mental condition alone does not vitiate consent unless there was also official coercion, of which there is no evidence on these facts.

The diary entry discloses incriminating evidence but is not protected by the privilege against self-incrimination because it was voluntarily prepared. The Fifth Amendment protects against compelled self-incrimination only, so (D) is incorrect.

(A) states the correct result under the applicable standards of both the Fourth and Fifth Amendments.

7.   A court *may* take judicial notice of its own volition; the court *must* take judicial notice of facts for which counsel provides the proper means of verification. (B) is incorrect because it does not recognize that the court may take judicial notice even when the proof is not provided by counsel.

The burden of proof does not shift to the other party. In fact, no evidentiary proof is permitted to contradict a judicially noticed fact. Thus, (C) is incorrect.

A judicially noticed fact is conclusive in a civil case, so (D) is incorrect.

(A) is correct.

8.   (B) is incorrect. The statute imposes no undue burden on interstate commerce because the same requirements apply to policies offered by all companies, whether local or out-of-state.

Federal courts should abstain from hearing cases that might be decided on adequate and independent state grounds in a way that avoids the federal question. However, the basis for challenge here seems to be the federal constitution, not the state constitution or other state law, so the federal courts need not abstain. The presence of a federal basis for jurisdiction lowers the likelihood of abstention. (D) is incorrect.

(A) is incorrect because questions of substantive due process involve merely whether the statute has a rational basis. The statute presumably has a rational basis, and (C) is correct.

9.   Robbery is a serious felony giving rise to the felony-murder rule when someone dies as a result of the commission or attempted commission of the robbery. Dawson may be punished as an accomplice to the felony murder because he was an accessory before the fact to the bank robbery. (C) is incorrect.

Going home did not constitute withdrawal; to avoid liability, Dawson would have had to attempt to thwart the commission of the crime as well as communicate his withdrawal to Smith. Thus, (D) is incorrect.

Although he may be convicted of felony murder, it would violate the Eighth Amendment to impose the death penalty on one who aids and abets a felony in the course of which murder is committed by others but who does not himself kill, attempt to kill, or intend to kill. *Enmund v. Florida*, 458 U.S. 782 (1982).

(B) is correct because Dawson may be convicted of felony murder but may not receive the death penalty.

10.   It is permissible to attack the credibility of any witness, so (D) is incorrect.

Watts was called to the stand to testify to Juilliard's reputation for truthfulness; Watts' standard of judgment as to Juilliard's reputation is not at issue, so (A) is incorrect.

Federal Rule 608(b) permits questions on cross-examination about specific instances of the witness's conduct that involve honesty or dishonest, so (C) is incorrect, and (B) is correct.

11.   This question deals with a continuing trespass to land. For damages in trespass, the defendant's entry onto the land must have been intentional, but he need not have known he was committing a trespass. Thus, (A) is incorrect.

Where the initial trespass was tortious, not pursuant to a license or privilege, the original trespasser remains liable for damages under a continuing trespass theory even though it has subsequently become impossible or impracticable for him to terminate the intrusion on the plaintiff's land. *Rest.2d, Torts,* § 161, Comment *e.* Prudence may proceed against David even though David no longer owns the garage, so (B) is incorrect.

Where ownership of the thing that was tortiously placed on the land is transferred, the transferee comes under a duty to the possessor to remove the thing upon acquiring knowledge that the thing is wrongfully on the land. *Rest.2d, Torts,* § 161, Comment *f.* Even if Drake has become liable for the trespass, however, David is not relieved of responsibility. Thus, (D) is incorrect.

(C) is correct because David's liability for trespass was established by his knowledge of where the garage was being built, regardless of whether he knew it was encroaching onto Prudence's property, and his liability is not relieved by his sale of the property to Drake, regardless of whether Drake had knowledge of the encroachment.

12.   If the piece of evidence involved were a writing, recording, or photograph, the best evidence rule would require the original to be produced unless it were shown to be unavailable for some reason other than the serious fault of the proponent. Duplicates, including photographs of the original, may be introduced if the original is shown to be unavailable, unless a genuine question is raised as to the authenticity of the original. If the original has been destroyed and no copies exist, oral testimony may be admitted to describe the lost item. However, the requirements of the best evidence rule do not apply to physical evidence, such as the model in question. (D) is correct, and the other answers are incorrect.

13.   (D) is correct. The rule on which courts are split is whether options to purchase contained in a lease can be assigned separately from the lease. If they cannot be assigned, then Jones takes the property subject only to Teri's lease.

14.   (A) is not Daniel's best argument because "danger invites rescue," meaning that rescue attempts are foreseeable when a person places himself or others in danger.

     Policemen and firemen entering under authority of law, but without any element of business dealings with the landholder, are commonly held to stand on the same footing as licensees, *i.e.*, they have a privilege to enter but are not owed a duty of reasonable care as to conditions on the land because they may enter at unforeseeable times and under emergency circumstances under which careful preparation for their visit cannot reasonably be expected. *Rest.2d, Torts*, § 345, Comment *c*. As a licensee, Officer would be owed only a duty to be warned of dangerous conditions on the land known to the possessor of the land. Although (D) states a true principle of law, the sort of danger Officer faced did not arise from the condition of the property, so (D) is incorrect.

     Daniel's conduct could be considered the proximate cause of Officer's injury despite the tortious nature of the guests' behavior. When the defendant's conduct creates a situation which is utilized by a third person to inflict intentional harm upon another, but the defendant had no reason to expect that the third person would so act, the defendant is not responsible for the harm thus inflicted unless he has special reasons for anticipating criminal action by the third person. *Rest.2d, Torts*, § 448, Comment *a*. However, if the likelihood that a third person may act in a particular manner is the very hazard which makes the defendant negligent, the third person's act, even if intentionally tortious or criminal, does not prevent the defendant from being liable for harm caused thereby. *Rest.2d, Torts*, §§ 302B, 449. Thus, (C) is incorrect. Even though Daniel's conduct could be considered the proximate cause of Officer's injury, Officer will not be able to recover because he assumes these risks in his job. (B) is correct.

15.   The professor's statement is offered to establish West's expert qualifications, not for any substantive purpose in the lawsuit. Thus, it is not hearsay. (C) is incorrect. The qualification of an expert is a preliminary evidentiary issue which should be determined by the judge, not the jury. (B) is correct.

16.   A requirements contract involves a promise to purchase all of the buyer's needs for particular goods from a particular seller. The consideration is the promise not to purchase those goods from others; if the promisor may buy only as much as he wants under the contract, his promise may be deemed illusory. County may attempt to show that the contract was illusory for this reason, so (D) is incorrect.

Although the advertisement was in writing, the question of whether or not it can be admitted as an expression of the parties' intent is governed by the parol evidence rule. It is not admissible solely because it is in writing, so (B) is incorrect. The parol evidence rule permits evidence outside the written contract to show the meaning of terms when there is an ambiguity on the face of the written agreement. Here there is an ambiguity as to the meaning of "all tires," so (A) is correct and (C) is incorrect.

17.   The Contracts Clause of the U.S. Constitution prohibits the states from passing any law impairing contract obligations. The Supreme Court has applied a stricter scrutiny when the state is attempting to avoid its own contractual obligations than when it is invalidating the obligations of third parties. (A) is incorrect because there was no state law involved in County's breach of its agreement with Tyres, leaving Tyres to a private means of enforcing its contract rights.

The U.C.C. favors enforcement of a requirements contract to the extent of the quantity of goods actually required by the buyer, rather than finding the agreement illusory for indefiniteness of quantity or mutuality of obligation. (B) is correct, and (C) and (D) are incorrect.

18.   Where the defendant can be found negligent for failure to take reasonable measures to protect against the act of a third party, the third person's act, even if intentionally tortious or criminal, does not cut off the defendant's liability. *Rest.2d, Torts,* §§ 302B, 449. (D) is incorrect.

A possessor of land who holds it open to the public for entry for business purposes is subject to liability to members of the public, while they are upon the land for such a purpose, for physical harm caused by the accidental, negligent, or intentionally harmful acts of third persons. The landholder has a duty to exercise reasonable care to discover that such acts are being done or likely to be done and give adequate warnings or otherwise protect visitors from such harm. *Rest.2d, Torts,* § 344.

The landholder is not an insurer of the visitor's safety, so (B) is incorrect because it is too broad a statement, but if he knows or has reason to know from past experience that there is a likelihood of criminal conduct by third persons, he has a duty to take precautions against it, not only to warn visitors but also to provide a "sufficient number of servants to afford a reasonable protection." *Id.*, Comment *f*. (C) is incorrect, and (A) is correct.

19.   An attempt requires a substantial step in the direction of committing a crime, coupled with an intention to commit that crime and the apparent ability to complete it. Factual impossibility to commit the crime is not a defense, so (C) is incorrect. However, an attempt to commit murder requires an intent to kill, which would be negated if Jones knew he could not hit Adams with that gun. The standard is subjective, not what a reasonable person would have known. (A) is correct and (B) is incorrect.
        Assault itself is an attempt (to commit a battery). The same question of intent arises, so (D) is incorrect.

20.   (A), (B), and (D) represent reasonable arguments in favor of the validity of the tax under a Commerce Clause analysis, and thus none of these is the correct answer.
        The Tenth Amendment does not give states plenary authority to construct their tax systems without limitation. State taxes are subject to various federal constitutional limitations, including those imposed under the Commerce Clause. (C) is the correct answer because it is the least helpful argument.

21.   Where an easement is created by express grant, courts will allow for a reasonable expansion to preserve the usefulness of the easement to the dominant estate. An easement may not be terminated by expanded use that is reasonably related to the purpose for which the easement was granted. (B) is incorrect, and (C) is correct.

22.   The Multistate Bar Examiners accepted (A), (B), and (D) as answers to this question, all but throwing it away.

23.   Bert's transfer would not have made it impossible for him to purchase Sam's home, merely more difficult, so his refusal to perform constitutes breach of the contract and (B) is incorrect.
        Pursuant to the liquidated damages provision of the contract, Sam may keep the deposit and had no duty to mitigate damages. (C) is incorrect.

Where the contract for sale provides for the deposit to serve as liquidated damages, the seller may keep the deposit if the buyer fails to perform. (D) is correct.

24.   Even though the car has been delivered to another customer, this is not a case for Rollem to claim impossibility of performance. The doctrine is usually applied where a unique property that was the subject of the contract was unforeseeably destroyed without fault by the promisor. Here Rollem's own agent caused the breach of contract. Even though a specific car was named in the contract, Rollem could have provided a similar car that would meet Betsy's needs. (D) is incorrect.

Courts rarely find a contract supported by "moral consideration" and these facts present an unlikely case. Betsy is an adult, and her father has no legal or even moral obligation to continue to support her. Furthermore, Betsy has a much sounder argument for an enforceable contract based on bargained-for consideration. (B) is incorrect.

Courts of law generally do not look into the adequacy of consideration. Betsy gave value for the automobile, and it is irrelevant that she paid $3,000 for a car worth $10,000. (C) is incorrect, and (A) is correct.

25.   (A) is incorrect because a manufacturer may have a duty to warn of known dangers from foreseeable uses of the product, even an abnormal or unintended use or misuse such as driving at excessive speeds.

(B) is incorrect because the discrepancy between the speed capability of the car and of its tires constitutes a design defect or at least a foreseeable danger against which the manufacturer has a duty to warn the consumer.

Contributory negligence is not a complete bar to recovery in a comparative fault jurisdiction, so (D) is incorrect.

(C) is correct because the failure to warn of a foreseeable danger or defect may be the basis of liability in this case.

26.   Although this case is being tried in federal court, it does not arise under the federal Constitution or federal statutes. This type of issue is traditionally resolved by state courts, and does not require nationwide uniformity. The issue is not one to be resolved by either federal statute or federal common law. (B) and (D) are incorrect.

The applicability of the presumption should be decided under the law of the state under which other substantive issues in the case will be determined, including the common law but also any applicable statutes. (C) is a more complete answer than (A).

27.   Nondeadly force may be used to prevent unlawful trespass and carrying away of the defendant's personal property. However, the use of force must be reasonable under the circumstances and necessary to prevent the crime. This is not a subjective standard, and (A) is incorrect. Although Armando may thus have exceeded his privilege, or had no privilege due to the age of the child, (D) is incorrect because (C), stating the basis for Armando's liability, is a better answer. The absence of a privilege does not in itself make Armando guilty.

     The mental state required by the statute is "malice," which does not require an intent to kill or to cause serious physical injury. (B) is incorrect. Reckless conduct posing a high risk of substantial harm to others may constitute malice. (C) is correct.

28.   The 13th Amendment outlaws slavery and gives Congress the power to pass any law necessary and proper to eliminate all badges and incidents of slavery. It applies to actions by individuals and the states, but the 13th Amendment has generally been applied to support the federal Civil Rights Acts barring private acts of discrimination in housing and employment. It has not been invoked in voting rights cases, for which there are other bases for authority. (A) is incorrect.

     Most challenges to voting districts are waged under the Equal Protection Clause rather than the Due Process Clause, which requires a showing of a deprivation of life, liberty or property. (B) is incorrect.

     The Privileges and Immunities Clause of the 14th Amendment protects rights of national citizenship, not state citizenship. It would not be implicated in a city council election issue. (C) is incorrect.

     The 15th Amendment provides that the right to vote shall not be denied or abridged by the United States or by any State on account of race, color, or previous condition of servitude. Various voting rights issues have been addressed under this Amendment. (D) is the correct answer.

29.   The basic definition of consideration is legal detriment plus a bargained-for exchange. Legal detriment does not mean that the performance must be detrimental to the actor, but merely something that the actor was under no legal requirement to do. (B) is incorrect. The required action may be minimal; it need not be "significantly demanding." (C) reaches the right result for the wrong reason. Running the mile at the time requested by Loomis was something Graceful was under no obligation to do, and her act thus constituted legal detriment even if it was relatively easy for her to do.

     It seems clear from the facts that Graceful's performance and Loomis's payment of the $100 were a bargained-for exchange, so (A) is incorrect.

(D) best summarizes the court's probable decision, although the reference to "motives" is unclear. If she ran to collect on Loomis's promise to pay her $100, she was entitled to the payment even if she did not reveal to Loomis her prior experience in this activity.

30.   Part performance is a doctrine that might allow Baker to obtain specific performance from Able if Baker has substantially performed. Baker's performance involves payment of the purchase price; his parking his car on Blackacre does not constitute substantial performance. Even if it did, Baker would have a right to specific performance against Able, not vice versa. (A) is incorrect.
        Equitable conversion is a doctrine that treats the purchaser as the owner for certain purposes, such as risk of loss, between the date of the contract and the date of the closing. Equitable conversion requires that the purchaser's obligation to buy be specifically enforceable; it is not a doctrine that independently supports an action for specific performance. (C) is incorrect.
        Recordation of an instrument for the sale of real property does not affect the enforceability of the contract for sale. General contract rules determine the enforceability of the contract. (D) is incorrect, and (B) is correct.

31.   The basic rule under the doctrine of constructive conditions of exchange in a bilateral contract is that a party who is to perform work must substantially perform before he is entitled to payment. Periodic "progress" payments are not implied. By demanding such payments before finishing the work, Karp has anticipatorily breached the contract. Manor is not in breach for refusing to pay before the work is complete. (B) is correct.

32.   An assignee (here, Banquo) obtains whatever rights his assignor (Karp) had under the contract, and the assignee takes subject to any defenses the obligor (Manor) could have raised against the assignor. If the obligor has a right of set-off, it can be raised against the assignee if the alleged set-off arises out of the same transaction as the original contract. It is not a question of priority between secured and unsecured claims or the date of the breach versus the date of the assignment, so (C) is correct and the other responses are incorrect.

33.   Congress's power to raise revenues is broad and plenary, subject only to due process and certain requirements of geographical uniformity. Due process challenges to taxes are rarely successful, however, and Congress need not "justify" a tax, so (A), (C), and (D) are incorrect.

   Congress may determine which activities should bear the burden of taxation. (B) is the correct answer.

34.   This is a contract between merchants, so Article 2 of the Uniform Commercial Code applies. Unlike the common law, the U.C.C. does not treat a proposal for additional terms as a rejection of the offer. UCC § 2-207 would treat Topline's form as an acceptance of Wonder-Good's offer, even though it contained an additional term, and even if deemed a material alteration, because Topline's acceptance was not made conditional on assent to the additional term. (A) and (B) are incorrect.

   The additional terms do not automatically become part of the contract, however, if they materially alter it; Wonder-Good would have to assent. While liquidated damages clauses may be negotiated in U.C.C. contracts, they are not necessarily a part of any contract. (C) is incorrect, and (D) is correct.

35.   (A) is incorrect. Electco's activity was probably not abnormally dangerous because the value and apprpriateness of the activity to the community in which it is located is a factor that weighs against a finding that it is abnormally dangerous.

   (D) is incorrect because economic harm is compensable. However, Paul must show that Electco caused a substantial and unreasonable interference with Paul's business. Electco's knowledge of Paul's harm is not at issue, so (B) is incorrect.

   (C) is correct. Paul must prove a substantial and unreasonable interference.

36.   If the landlord knows of a dangerous condition on the property and has reason to believe that the condition is not readily discoverable by the tenant in an ordinary inspection, the landlord has a duty to disclose it or be liable for injuries to the tenant. The tenant does not have a duty to hire an engineer to inspect the premises. (D) is incorrect, and (C) is correct.

37.   An expert witness is allowed greater latitude than a lay witness to base his opinion testimony on reports of others that are not admissible as evidence, so long as such reports are of a type reasonably upon by experts in the particular field in forming opinions on the subject.

(B) is incorrect because it is too broad a statement of the rule, and because the dog's behavior was not hearsay. Hearsay is a verbal or nonverbal assertion of a person. FRE 801. (C) is also incorrect because the dog's behavior was not hearsay.

(D) is incorrect because a properly qualified expert could testify regarding the degree of reliability of animal behavior.

(A) is correct.

38. The traditional rule does not permit recovery in negligence by a plaintiff who suffers purely intangible economic loss, but Peter in fact has suffered tangible property damage in the loss of the trees. Even under the traditional rule, this is compensable, so (D) is incorrect.

(A) is incorrect because Doe was the active cause of the loss (the sunshine being the "passive" cause). (C) is incorrect because the loss of the trees was a natural consequence (there was no supervening cause). Whether it was a "probable" consequence, however, is debatable.

(B) is the best answer because this is an issue of foreseeability and the scope of the risk created by Doe's negligence.

39. Criminal negligence can support a conviction for manslaughter. (D) is incorrect. Phillips' actions went beyond negligence, however, since he knew of the presence of children within range of his rifle. (C) is incorrect. Voluntary manslaughter involves either provocation or imperfect use of a defense. (B) is incorrect.

Phillips could not be convicted of first-degree murder because he lacked premeditation/deliberation, but the evidence is sufficient to support a conviction of second-degree murder on the basis of a willful and wanton disregard of an unreasonable risk to human life. (A) is correct.

40. Having the building demolished was not an acceptance of Hardcash's offer; Hardcash was bargaining for the payment of interest after the loan funds were granted, not the demolition of the building or proof that the project was financially sound. (A) and (D) are incorrect.

Even though the contract is not enforceable on the basis of bargained-for consideration, it may be at least partially enforceable on the basis of promissory estoppel. The doctrine of promissory estoppel applies where substantial reliance on a promise was foreseeable and in fact occurred, as here. (C) is incorrect, and (B) is correct.

41.   Since Dominique's cause of action is based on promissory estoppel, she is entitled to reliance damages only to the extent of her loss related to such reliance. (C) is correct. Some damages clearly are provable, so (D) is incorrect. There are no expectancy or benefit-of-the-bargain damages since that is not the basis of Dominique's action, so (A) and (B) are incorrect.

42.   (B) is incorrect because Peter's mother's negligence will not be imputed to Peter. A child who suffers physical harm is not barred from recovery by the negligence of his parent. *Rest.2d, Torts,* § 488.
        (D) is incorrect because Dan's negligence would not support a cause of action against his parents. The common law does not recognize vicarious liability of parents for torts committed by their children.
        (A) is true so far as it goes with respect to the lack of vicarious liability, but that is not the end of the analysis. The parents may be held liable for negligent supervision of the child, *i.e.*, failing to take corrective measures when they had reason to know of the child's propensity for dangerous conduct. (C) is correct.

43.   (A) is incorrect because it is too broad a statement of the potential liability of a negligent tortfeasor to third parties. The other three answers all attempt to state a narrower basis for any liability of Weber to Hill. The question does not ask whether Hill will recover, and in fact she probably will not. Hill was inside her kitchen and not in personal danger from the speeding vehicle; moreover, she was apparently not related to the child. The traditional rule allows recovery for purely emotional distress at observing harm to others if the plaintiff was also in the zone of danger (or if the victim was a close relative). *Rest.2d, Torts,* § 436, 436A. (D) is correct because it is the most precise statement of the issue.

44.   Under the Model Penal Code and some state statutes, assisting in suicide is at most a manslaughter offense. However, this is not the majority rule. At common law, which is still the majority rule, Harold could be convicted of murder because he deliberately killed Willa, regardless of his motives in doing so. (D) is correct.

45.   Truth is a defense to libel, making the proffered evidence relevant and admissible substantively. (A) is correct.

46.   (A) makes an incorrect statement of the "necessary and proper" clause. Congress has no general power to legislate for the general welfare, but does have the power to enact laws that are appropriate to the exercise of legislative powers that are specifically delegated to Congress. The "necessary and proper" clause would be a good answer only if the power Congress was attempting to exercise did not appear to be directly authorized by one of the Constitution's direct grants of legislative power. In this case, the Commerce Clause provides a basis for Congressional action.

The Federal Computer Abuse Act itself provides for criminal penalties for unlicensed use, and it was proper for Congress to delegate to a federal agency the authority to define the terms on which such licenses would be issued. (C) is incorrect.

The possession and use of a computer without a license, unlike the possession of a firearm in a school zone in *United States v. Lopez* (1995), is an activity with potential economic implications for interstate commerce and thus is not a "wholly local matter" beyond the regulatory authority of Congress. (D) is incorrect.

(B) is the correct answer. The activity that Congress is attempting to regulate could have a substantial effect on economic activity in interstate commerce.

47.   The theory of *res ipsa loquitur* permits an inference that harm suffered by the plaintiff was caused by the defendant's negligence when the event is of a kind which ordinarily does not occur in the absence of negligence, other responsible causes are sufficiently eliminated, and the negligence falls within the scope of the defendant's duty to the plaintiff. The inference can support a verdict, so (B) is incorrect.

The majority rule today does not require the defendant to be in a better position than the plaintiff to explain the occurrence. *Rest.2d, Torts,* § 328D, Comment *b.* Thus, (D) is incorrect. However, potential third party causes must be sufficiently eliminated, so (A) is incorrect and (C) is correct.

48.   There is no rule that a deed is always superior to a judgment lien. When a judgment lien is properly recorded against property, subsequent purchasers of the property (even purchasers for value) take subject to the lien if it is not satisfied at the time of the transfer. (C) is incorrect.

Neither is there a rule that forgives "reasonable delay" in recording a deed. Absent a statutory grace period or notice requirements, the "first in time, first in right" rule applies. (D) is incorrect.

Breach of a warranty of title could make Able liable to Baker for damages caused by Smollett's claim; the warranty would not defeat Smollett's claim. (A) is incorrect.

The only possible defense against Smollett is (B). Some jurisdictions might look at the timing and basis for Smollett's claim to determine whether he should be treated as a purchaser for value under the statute. This defense is not likely to be successful since in most jurisdictions an unrecorded deed is void as to docketed judgment creditors, whether the debt was contracted before or after the date of the unrecorded deed.

49.   The ordinance may be rationally related to local interests, but that is not the end of the analysis when federal interests are also involved. (A) is incorrect. Persons transporting dangerous materials are not a suspect class, and the ordinance has a rational basis. (D) is incorrect. The Tenth Amendment reserves powers to the states when they do not conflict with federal powers. Here, the Supremacy Clause rules. (B) is incorrect. (C) is the correct answer.

50.   The regulation involved creates a strict liability "public welfare offense." Mistake of law, *i.e.*, the actor does not know that the particular act is criminal, does not constitute a defense to a strict liability crime. (C) is incorrect. Even a reasonable mistake of fact is not a defense. One who sells liquor to a minor cannot defend on the ground that he believed the minor was of age. Both (A) and (D) are incorrect.

(B) would be the most helpful to Dart because, even if his employer's culpability does not relieve Dart of liability, Dart may be able to obtain partial or full indemnity from his employer, who should have trained Dart to comply with the law.

51.   A contract is voidable for a mutual mistake that goes to a basic assumption on which the contract was made and that has a material effect on the bargain. That is not the case here, however. This is a proper case for reformation of the written contract to reflect the mutual understanding and agreement of the parties, and where reformation is available, neither party can void the contract. (A) is incorrect.

Frustration of purpose is seldom applied to excuse performance. The doctrine is generally applied only when the property subject to the contract is destroyed through an unforeseeable event. Price increases do not rise to this level of frustration, so (C) is incorrect.

A condition precedent to the existence of a contract may be shown by parol evidence. This does not mean that a material term was missing from the written contract, but rather that the parties agreed that no binding effect would be given to the contract terms unless the pre-condition occurred. (D) is incorrect.

(B) is correct. Although Kranc's contract with Trimota might appear to have affirmed his intent to perform the contract, he did not give written notice in the form required before January 2.

52. Kranc has not substantially performed, since his required performance is the payment of the purchase price. (A) is incorrect.

Nor has there been a novation. Schaff did not agree to release Kranc from his payment obligation, so (D) is incorrect.

The written notice was a condition precedent, not a condition subsequent, and it was waived by Schaff's oral agreement. (B) is incorrect, and (C) is correct.

53. David's negligence was a proximate cause of Paul's injury since David knew or should have known of the likelihood that his conduct would create an opportunity for Mark to harm someone. *Rest.2d, Torts,* § 448. However, Mark's intentional act means that David may seek full indemnification from Mark. The Restatement notes that indemnity may be sought where the two parties are guilty of different types of tortious conduct or are held to different standards of care, e.g., one is negligent and the other is guilty of reckless or intentional misconduct. *Rest.2d, Torts,* § 886B, Comment *k.* One who has been found liable but who was not an active wrongdoer may seek indemnification for the entire amount against the actual wrongdoer, not merely contribution for a portion of the harm, so (A) is incorrect.

54. An ex post facto law criminalizes conduct that was not criminal when committed. It is not an ex post facto law merely to change Alien's job prospects. (A) is incorrect.

The Due Process Clause protects property rights that have vested in some way, not merely job prospects. (B) is incorrect.

The Privileges and Immunities Clause of the 14th Amendment protects rights of "citizens of the United States." It does not apply to non-citizens. (C) is incorrect.

Aliens who are lawful residents of the United States are "persons" within the protection of the Equal Protection Clause, alienage is a protected status, and the right to earn a living is a fundamental interest, making the Equal Protection Clause Alien's strongest ground to challenge the state law. (D) is the correct answer.

55. An easement by implication is created at the time commonly owned property is divided. Since the ownership of the two parcels had previously been separated before Sam acquired his land, he does not hold an easement by implication and (A) is incorrect.

Sam has an easement appurtenant. An easement is appurtenant if the easement owner holds it only by virtue of his status as the owner or possessor of land that is benefited by the easement. Such an easement is useless without concurrent ownership of the land, and the appurtenant easement is automatically transferred with the land benefited, regardless of whether the easement is mentioned in the instrument of conveyance. (D) is incorrect. An easement in gross, by contrast, benefits no particular parcel of land and is generally not transferable. The right to use a strip of land to reach the road obviously benefited the owner of the land, not Buck personally, so (C) is incorrect. (B) is correct.

56. The foundation required to admit a piece of physical evidence is a showing of reasonable certainty that the item offered into evidence may be identified with the defendant and has not been exchanged, contaminated or tampered with. Chain of custody is a way of providing adequate identification, so (B) is incorrect. The chain of custody requirement is not absolute; it merely must be sufficiently complete to render it reasonably probable that the offered item is the original item at issue. The police need not have taken the bag from Dickinson directly, and (C) is incorrect. The location of the bag in the same place where the police saw Dickinson drop it, and the fact that only a few minutes had passed, in the absence of evidence showing a likelihood of someone tampering with the bag, should be sufficient evidence of the connection to Dickinson. (A) is correct. The standard is reasonable probability, not a preponderance of the evidence, so (D) is incorrect.

57. A manufacturer's liability extends to those who purchase or use products obtained through the marketplace. The product in question had not reached the market, so (A) is incorrect. Farmer will prevail on a strict liability theory relating to the escape of a dangerous substance from Chemco's premises under the theory of *Rylands v. Fletcher*. It is not necessary for the plaintiff to show negligence, because one who carries on an abnormally dangerous activity is liable for resulting harm even though he has exercised the utmost care to prevent the harm. *Rest.2d, Torts,* § 519. (C) and (D) are incorrect, and (B) is correct.

58.   When the relevancy of a voice communication depends on identification of the owner of the voice, the identification must be authenticated. Authentication can be provided by a witness who is familiar with the caller's voice. Identification of a party to a telephone call can also be authenticated by the witness's testimony that he called the party's number and the party identified himself.

It is not necessarily authenticated if the owner of the voice called the witness and identified himself, so (A) is incorrect. Other facts may also logically identify the caller, such as if the communication reveals that the speaker had knowledge of facts that only the caller would be likely to know. *Santora, McKay & Ranieri v. Franklin*, 339 S.E.2d 799 (1986). Limited access to the witness's phone number makes the identification substantially more certain, so (C) is correct. Witness's motive is tangential to authentication and can be addressed on cross-examination, so (A) and (D) are incorrect.

59.   The Court will uphold time, place or manner restrictions on speech if they are content-neutral, narrowly tailored to serve a substantial government interest, and leave open ample alternative channels of communication. *United States v. Grace*, 461 U.S. 171 (1983).

(A) is the correct statement of the test. The other statements are incorrect because they refer only to a "legitimate" rather than a "substantial" government interest and do not contain the "narrowly tailored" standard.

60.   The use of a non-testifying co-defendant's confession against the accused at trial presumptively violates the accused's Sixth Amendment right of confrontation. It is thus significant whether or not Penn testified at trial to provide a right to confrontation. (A) is the correct answer.

61.   The fact that partisan politics are involved does not render an issue a nonjusticiable political question. (D) is incorrect.

The question turns on a nexus with the state sufficient to constitute state action. The fact that baseball is "the national pastime" clearly does not render everything involving baseball subject to the 14th Amendment.

A one-time grant of state funds is not a sufficient nexus to evidence state involvement in the operations of the team. Building sports facilities is not traditionally or exclusively a government function within the state action concept. (A) is incorrect, and (C) is correct.

62.   This is a case of unilateral mistake. Walker's misconception about the value of his own horse will not, without some affirmative overreaching on Sherwood's part, give Walker a right to rescind the contract. Sherwood was under no duty to inform Walker of the value of Walker's horse, and (C) is incorrect.

         Likewise, Sherwood was under no duty to disclose the extent of his own experience with horses, so long as he made no affirmative misrepresentations in this regard. (A) is incorrect.

         (D) is clearly not an argument for rescission because it involves a fact known to Walker only and could have legitimately affected the value of the horse to Walker on the ground that the horse was "bad tempered."

         (B) is the best answer because Sherwood might have a duty to disclose facts solely within his knowledge affecting a basic assumption of Walker's, *i.e.*, that the horse was "nothing special."

63.   In each of these instances, the event leading Sherwood to seek rescission occurred after the sale, so presumably he needs restitution of the price he paid. Generally, rescission and restitution of the price paid or the value of services performed is allowed when a party that has partially performed finds the remainder of his performance excused by impossibility or frustration of purpose. See *Rest.2d, Torts,* § 377. The requirements for excuse on the grounds of frustration of purpose are that an event have occurred "the non-occurrence of which was a basic assumption on which the contract was made." *Rest.2d, Torts,* § 265. The purpose that is frustrated must have been a principal purpose of the party in making the contract, without which the transaction would make little sense, and the frustration must be substantial, not merely causing the party some disappointment or loss. Sherwood may have hoped that Aberlone would make him additional money for stud services, but after earning $5 million over three years (many times what Sherwood paid for the horse), it could not be said that the value of the contract to Sherwood was substantially impaired. The principal purpose of the contract, to provide Sherwood with a competitive racehorse, was fulfilled. (B) is incorrect.

         The clerical error in (C) can probably be corrected and does not go to the underlying assumption that Aberlone was sired by a famous racehorse. The frustration must be so severe that it is not fairly regarded as within the risks that the party assumed under the contract.

         (D) is incorrect because, although Sherwood's injuries were severe, Sherwood was warned that the horse was bad-tempered and assumed the risk of this type of problem. Furthermore, Aberlone's attack on Sherwood does not go to his basic qualities as a racehorse.

The death of the horse in his first race would frustrate the purpose of the contract as none of the other problems would. Walker could argue that Sherwood assumed the risk of undiscoverable health problems and might win on this point, but (A) would be Sherwood's strongest scenario for rescission. A party seeking restitution must return or offer to return any property he received in exchange in substantially as good condition as when he received it.

However, this requirement does not apply if the property was worthless when received or has been destroyed as a result of its own defects. *Rest.2d, Torts,* § 384. Such would be the case with Aberlone's heart defect in the first scenario, so (A) is correct.

64. Under the common-law Rule Against Perpetuities, the "unborn widow" rule does not void the life interest in Louis's widow because her interest was certain to vest within the period of the Rule (at Louis's death). Maria never became Louis's widow, since she predeceased him. Louis's widow is Zelda and Zelda's life estate is valid. The MBE published (D) as the correct answer, but (B) appears more likely, since Norman's interest under the deed would be voided by the unborn widow problem, and Norman predeceased Louis.

65. When a hearsay statement has been admitted into evidence, the credibility of the declarant may be attacked by his inconsistent statements or conduct. FRE 806. Availability of the declarant is not required. (B) is incorrect, and (C) is correct.

66. Under the majority rule, a willing participant in a normally dangerous professional sport may recover only for intentional attacks, not for negligent or even reckless rule violations because a professional athlete is deemed to understand the usual incidents of competition resulting from the foreseeable carelessness or roughness of other players. (C) is correct. This is a close question because there is a judicial trend toward deeming *some* reckless rule violations outside the scope of a participant's consent, and *Rest.2d, Torts,* § 50, Comment *b* treats *any* violation of a safety rule as outside the scope of a participant's consent. Courts often look at the circumstances with reference to the way each particular sport is played, *i.e.*, the rules and customs that shape the participants' ideas of foreseeable conduct in the course of the game. Whether a sport is normally contact or non-contact may not be determinative.

In the game of golf, for example, "a golfer accepts the risk of coming in contact with wayward golf shots on the links," but "a player who hurls a club into the air in a moment of pique and injures another golfer should be held accountable." *Thompson v. McNeill,* 559 N.E.2d 705 (Ohio 1990). In a hockey game, "[b]utt-ending [the practice of taking the end of the stick which does not come into contact with the puck and driving this part of the stick into another player's body] is unexpected and unsportsmanlike conduct for a hockey game" and has been found actionable as a "reckless disregard of safety." *Gauvin v. Clark,* 537 N.E.2d 94 (Mass. 1989). In horse racing, the violation of rules prohibiting "foul riding" or failure to control a horse does not necessarily give rise to liability since such dangers are "inherent in the sport." *Turcotte v. Fell,* 502 N.E.2d 964 (N.Y. 1986).

Thus, (B) is incorrect. [The case said the violation does not, without more, constitute recklessness, but said that if a showing of recklessness could be made the court would find liability.]

67.   Whether time is of the essence (I) will affect whether or not Baker is in breach. A reasonable delay will not constitute a breach unless time is of the essence, either as stated in the contract or as inferred from the circumstances.

The parol evidence rule (II) could be involved with respect to the question of whether the condition was a condition precedent to the activation of the contract.

Of course, a contract for the sale of land is subject to the Statute of Frauds (III), but it may be supplemented or reformed in appropriate cases so long as the essential terms are stated with reasonable certainty. Baker may attempt to enforce the contract in an action for specific performance (IV) if he can show there is a contract and he is not in breach of the contract. (D) is correct because all of these issues may be involved.

68.   At common law, an accessory could be convicted only if the principal had been apprehended, charged and convicted. This is not a requirement, however, where the accessory's acts prevented apprehension or conviction. (A) is incorrect.

An accessory after the fact must have known of the commission of the felony (not of the felon's indictment, so (C) is incorrect) and have given aid to the felon for the purpose of hindering the felon's apprehension, conviction, or punishment. As the name suggests, such aid is typically given after the commission of the felony, and (B) is incorrect. (D) is correct.

69. The owners of foreign-made autos are not a suspect class, so the Equal Protection Clause is not a strong argument. (B) is incorrect.

A prohibition or limitation on parking does not deprive auto owners of their property, so the Due Process Clause is not a likely argument. (C) is incorrect.

The Privileges and Immunities Clause of the 14th Amendment is seldom invoked and is not generally a good answer. It protects incidents of national citizenship, which automobile ownership is not. (D) is incorrect.

Congress holds plenary power to regulate commerce with foreign nations, but there may be room for state regulation where Congress has not acted and there is little need for national uniformity.

However, as under the interstate Commerce Clause, a court examining a state's action in the area of foreign commerce should first look at whether the state had a discriminatory purpose or intent, which was clearly the case here. (A) is the strongest argument and thus the correct answer.

70. (A) is correct. FRE 803 permits a learned treatise to be relied upon in direct examination as a basis for the expert's opinion; it is not being used as extraneous evidence to support the witness's credibility.

(D) is incorrect because a published treatise must be admitted by being read to the jury. It is not admissible as an exhibit.

71. Defamatory statements in a printed newspaper article may be actionable as libel, which, unlike slander, does not require proof of special damages. (A) is incorrect.

A showing of malice is required with respect to the publication of defamatory statements about public figures, and the standard of proof in such cases is clear and convincing evidence on the issue of malice, but merely being well known in certain circles is not enough to make a private citizen a public figure unless the plaintiff has "thrust [himself] to the forefront of particular public controversies." *Gertz v. Robert Welch, Inc.,* 418 U.S. 323 (1974). Since that does not appear to be the case with Kitchen's general manager, he should not be required to show malice, so (C) is incorrect.

The defendant's motion for a directed verdict should be granted if the plaintiff has produced no evidence of the defendant's negligence. The defendant need not show "uncontradicted evidence" of accurate reporting, and merely reporting accurately what the employees said would not necessarily discharge the defendant's duty of care with respect to the truth or falsity of the charge of embezzlement. (D) is incorrect, and (B) is correct.

72.   It seems clear that Surgeon owed Patient a disclosure about the failure of the operation so that Patient could take corrective action if so desired. Thus, (C), while relevant, is not the most difficult question to answer.

(A) and (B) would argue a duty of care toward the baby to prevent its "wrongful life." Courts do not accept this cause of action, and Patient is not seeking such recovery.

(D) is the best answer, seeking medical damages for "wrongful birth." Some courts allow parents to recover for medical expenses from a child's unintended or damaged birth.

73.   Larceny by trick involves obtaining possession of another's property by lying or trickery, and theft by false pretenses involves obtaining title by such means. Here there were no misrepresentations or false pretenses, so (C) and (D) are incorrect.

Robbery is a larceny from the person by violence or intimidation. Here, no violence or intimidation actually occurred because the attendant was not alarmed by Robert's actions. (A) is incorrect.

(B) is correct because Robert intended to commit the crime of robbery and took a substantial step toward it when he threatened to shoot.

74.   Kabb was a principal to the contract with Petrol, not merely Artiste's agent, so (B) is incorrect.

Artiste is an intended beneficiary of the Kabb–Petrol contract because Kabb intended to give Artiste the benefit of Petrol's performance. Her rights vested when she changed her position in justifiable reliance on Petrol's promise by declining the Detrugid account. She need not have provided consideration, so (D) is incorrect.

As an intended beneficiary with vested rights under the contract, Artiste may have a cause of action against Petrol, but Petrol can raise any defenses against Artiste that he could raise against Kabb on their contract, including the failure of a condition precedent. Kabb breached the requirements contract by purchasing substantial amounts from another supplier. Petrol can raise this breach by Kabb to excuse his duty to Artiste. (A) is incorrect and (C) is correct.

75.   Artiste's rights are not based upon an agency relationship with Kabb, so (D) is incorrect.

Artiste has enforceable legal rights under the contract, not merely an equitable argument of "bad faith," so (D) is incorrect.

The original parties to a third-party beneficiary contract may modify the contract after the beneficiary's rights have vested only with the beneficiary's consent. Artiste's rights vested when she relied upon the Petrol contract to turn down the Deturgid contract, so her consent was required to any modification that would alter or discharge Petrol's performance to her. (A) is correct, and (C) is incorrect.

76.   (A) is incorrect because these facts are not relevant to the issues in a suit for slander.

Pat is not a public figure, so negligence, not malice, is the basis of liability and Drew's state of mind is not relevant to his negligence. (C) is incorrect.

Publication of defamatory matter is its communication intentionally or by a negligent act to one other than the person defamed. *Rest.2d, Torts,* § 577(1). Calling Pat a thief in a loud voice when Drew knew or should have known other people in the office could overhear him constituted publication of the defamation, so (B) is the correct answer.

77.   The windows are fixtures. Fixtures may be the subject of security interests separate from a mortgage on the real property unless they become an unremovable part of the property such as bricks and cement. The windows are removable, so (B) is incorrect and (C) is correct. A purchase-money security interest in fixtures takes priority over a prior mortgage on the real property if the PMSI is recorded within a statutory period (10 or 20 days) after annexation of the fixture to the property. Vend recorded its PMSI before the windows were installed, so (A) is incorrect.

78.   This question involves the scope of, and exceptions to, the attorney-client privilege. The privilege applies to confidential communications between an attorney and his client for the purpose of facilitating the rendition of professional legal services to the client.

Discussions of past crimes are generally within the privilege, so (B) is not the most likely basis for allowing a subpoena.

Prior inconsistent statements may be admissible for certain purposes under the hearsay rules, but this is not an exception to the attorney-client privilege. (C) is incorrect.

Death does not terminate the attorney-client privilege, nor permit disclosure on the ground that the client is unavailable. (D) is incorrect.

The tape is no longer confidential if Denby played it for one who does not fall within the attorney-client relationship. His father is not a person within the privilege because he is not a representative of either Denby or his lawyer. (A) is the correct answer.

79.   The Article IV, Section 3 power of Congress over federal property such as wild animals on federal lands is plenary and not subject to state action. *Kleppe v. New Mexico*, 426 U.S. 529 (1976) (state could not round up wild burros on federal land protected by federal law). (C) and (D), which would leave room for state action involving federal property, are incorrect.

     On the other hand, the federal power in Article I, Section 8 is overstated in (B), which confuses the power to tax and spend for the general welfare with the power to make laws necessary and proper to execute Congress's enumerated powers. (A) is the correct answer.

80.   The kidnapping statute requires knowledge of lack of privilege to take the child and thus creates a specific intent crime. Reliance on erroneous advice from a private attorney does not establish a mistake of law defense, so (A) is incorrect. This is true even if such reliance was reasonable and in good faith. (D) is incorrect.

     It might thus seem that (C) is the correct answer, but the knowledge requirement is subjective. If the defendant's lack of knowledge is bona fide, the reason for his ignorance does not matter. (B) is correct.

81.   Although a purchase-money mortgage may take priority over a mortgage to secure a preexisting obligation, Owen was selling the property to Newton, not mortgaging it. Newton's purchase of the property would have been subject to the mortgage if the sale had proceeded without satisfaction of the mortgage obligation. (A) is incorrect.

     Under the doctrine of equitable conversion the buyer is treated as holding title for some purposes between the date of the contract of sale and the closing, e.g., risk of loss. However, if the seller's title is unmarketable, equitable conversion will not take place In other words, the seller must prove he is entitled to specific performance before claiming that the risk of loss has passed to the buyer or that equitable conversion otherwise applies, so (B) begs the question.

     (C) is correct. Marketable title does not contemplate any encumbrances on the property, whether or not specifically named, but a mortgage is not an encumbrance if the seller pays it off before the closing. Owen has offered to do so, and Newton is in breach by refusing to close. It is not necessary to examine Newton's "real reason" for the refusal (D), only her behavior, to find her in breach of the contract.

82.   Young's statement is hearsay because it was made by an out-of-court declarant whether it is offered to prove that the carpet was defective or that Dalton knew of the defect. (D) is the correct answer.

83.   *Flast v. Cohen* recognized that taxpayers had standing to bring suit to challenge federal taxing and spending where there is a logical nexus between the taxpayer status and the claim sought to be adjudicated. Magazine as a payer of the disputed tax could allege competitive disadvantages, and (A) is incorrect.

The 11th Amendment prohibits suits by citizens of one state against another state in federal court. This case was brought in Wonatol state court, so the 11th Amendment is not implicated, and (B) is incorrect.

(C) is the correct answer. In *Texas Monthly, Inc. v. Bullock*, 489 U.S. 1 (1989), a state statute exempting religious publications from sales taxes was held to violate the Establishment Clause. The reason was that the exemption in effect provided a subsidy for those promoting religious beliefs, not that it was a prior restraint on nonreligious publications that had to pay the tax, and (D) is incorrect.

84.   The liability of an owner for harm done by his livestock and other domestic animals is for negligence (*Rest.2d, Torts,* § 518), unless the owner knows of a dangerous propensity of the animal giving rise to strict liability (*Rest.2d, Torts,* § 509), or the animal trespasses off the owner's land (*Rest.2d, Torts,* § 504) . Here the horse had no dangerous propensities and had not been known to escape before. Nor did the horse commit a trespass in this instance, since the harm occurred on the highway and did not involve entry on or harm to Driver's land. The relevant standard is not strict liability in this case, so (B) is incorrect.

Rancher need not be shown to have intentionally let the horse run at large, so (D) is incorrect. The applicable standard is negligence, but the NCBE accepted both (A) and (C) as correct answers to this question.

85.   Spousal immunity belongs to the witness spouse, not the defendant spouse, so (D) is incorrect.

FRE 804(b)(1) recognizes a hearsay exception, when the declarant is unavailable for testimony, for testimony given under oath in another proceeding at which the declarant was available for cross-examination, whether or not that opportunity was effectively used at the time. (A) is the correct answer.

86.   A liquidated damages clause is enforceable if the amount of damages stipulated is reasonable in relation to either the actual damages suffered or the damages reasonably anticipated at the time the contract was made. Even though Mermaid actually lost only $100 because she was able to find a late rental at a reduced rate, the reasonable anticipation at the time she made the contract with Phinney was that Mermaid might not be able to find a substitute rental prospect.

There is no general rule that liquidated damages clauses are penalties unless limited to 10% or 20% of the contract price. (B) and (D) are incorrect. Nor must Mermaid refund any amount in excess of her actual damages. (C) is incorrect.

(A) correctly states the standards for validity of a liquidated damages clause.

87.	The contract is discharged due to impossibility. The liquidated damages clause is intended to cover a breach of contract, not discharge due to impossibility, in which circumstances the parties should be returned to the status quo ante. (D) is incorrect. The storm warnings were an supervening event that could not be predicted at the time the contract was made, not a mistake as to a fact that could have been ascertained by one or both parties. (B) is incorrect, and (A) is correct.

88.	There is no rule that a warranty deed takes priority over a quitclaim deed. Whether the deed was conveyed for consideration is relevant only when a subsequent deed is delivered as a gift, in which case it cannot defeat a prior deed. The fact that Orben's subsequent deed to Fred was for consideration does not automatically defeat Sam's prior deed, even though it was a gift. Thus, (A) and (B) are incorrect.

The public interest in certainty with respect to land titles generally forecloses results based solely on equitable considerations. (D) is incorrect.

(C) is correct because Sam's possession put Fred on "inquiry notice," meaning that he had a duty to investigate Sam's rights to the property. A purchaser generally has a duty to inspect the property before buying it and cannot claim lack of notice of obvious facts giving rise to questions about ownership interests.

89.	(C) is a broad public policy argument that can be eliminated preliminarily on the ground that such arguments are rarely the correct answer.

(D) is incorrect because the exercise of eminent domain requires that the state pay just compensation

The use of Brown's land by Agency constitutes adverse possession because the use has been open and notorious for the statutory period, and the periodic breaks in the use while the facility was closed would not be deemed to interrupt Agency's "continuous" possession. Brown's acquiescence permitted adverse possession to occur, but all the elements of adverse possession are also present, so (B) is incorrect and (A) is correct.

90.   The vehicle registration statement is not hearsay because the document has operative legal effect. Since it is not hearsay, no exception need be found. (A) and (D) are incorrect.

   A certified copy of a public record is self-authenticating without testimony of a state official under FRE 902(4). (C) is incorrect.

   The evidence is relevant to a material issue in the case and is admissible. (B) is correct.

91.   The Double Jeopardy Clause would not prevent Donald from later being tried for murder if the victim of a felony for which he was convicted subsequently died. Although Donald was convicted of assault, he was acquitted of the greater offense of attempted rape. Assault is a misdemeanor at common law, so it could not provide a basis for felony-murder liability, and he was acquitted of the potential felony charge. (A) is correct.

92.   An inter vivos grant is not revoked by a subsequent testamentary provision for the property. On the contrary, a testamentary gift lapses if the property has already been disposed of and is no longer in the decedent's estate. Thus, (B) is incorrect.

   (C) and (D) are incorrect because Lilly's life estate lasts for her life, not Ogle's. The lack of a remainderman would cause a reversion to Ogle's estate only after Lilly's death.

   (A) is correct. Lilly has a life estate that could not subsequently be affected by Ogle.

93.   It is not the law that a criminal defendant has no privacy expectations merely because he is on trial. (D) is incorrect. However, there is no reasonable expectation of privacy in one's physical characteristics, so requiring Devlin to display his limp would not be a Fourth Amendment search. (B) is incorrect.

   The Fifth Amendment privilege against self-incrimination protects only testimonial evidence, not physical evidence or physical characteristics. His limp is not intended to make an assertion. (A) is incorrect.

   (C) is correct. Requiring Devlin to walk across the room would be a legitimate part of the courtroom identification process.

94.   The strongest argument would be that the prohibition on lobbying would be an unconstitutional condition, denying the recipients their First Amendment rights to free speech and association, as applied to the states through the 14th Amendment.

The law permits some restrictions in this area. For example, *Regan v. Taxation with Representation of Washington,* 461 U.S. 540 (1983), upheld Internal Revenue Code Section 501(C)(3), which grants special tax exempt status to organizations that are prohibited from using their tax-deductible contributions for lobbying activities. In this question, however, the state of Kiowa's grant would prevent the recipient from all lobbying activities of a specified type, regardless of whether the organization receives additional funding for such activities. (D) is the correct answer.

95.   City and Railroad are jointly and severally liable to Penkov because their concurrent negligence brought about Penkov's harm and it is not possible to separate portions of the harm as attributable to each defendant. An inability to apportion the harm does not relieve joint tortfeasors of liability, so (B) is incorrect.

The effect of joint and several liability is that each defendant is liable for the entire amount of the plaintiff's damages, so (C) is incorrect. The plaintiff is not required to join them both in the same action, so (A) is incorrect.

Railroad's negligence was a "but for" cause of Penkov's harm because if Railroad had properly maintained its storm drain, the flooding would not have occurred. (D) is correct. Under joint and several liability, Penkov may recover all of his loss from Railroad, which may then attempt to obtain contribution from City.

96.   Obtaining property by false pretenses requires that the defendant know that his representation is false, and thereby intends to defraud the owner. Smith made no false representations of fact to Jones at the time he borrowed the money. A false promise to return the money would not constitute a false representation in most jurisdictions, and it is not apparent that Smith had no intention to return the money at the time he borrowed it. (A) and (C) are incorrect.

Larceny by trick involves obtaining mere possession of another's property by lying or trickery. Smith merely asked to borrow the money, which is more consistent with obtaining possession than title, but again, there is no evidence that Smith lied or made a misrepresentation in that he had no intent to return the money when he borrowed it; few people gamble with the intention to lose money. (B) is incorrect, and (D) is correct.

97.   Congress may make "exceptions" to Supreme Court jurisdiction without constitutional amendment, so (C) is incorrect. Congress can limit Supreme Court jurisdiction over cases arising in state courts, so (B) is incorrect.

The strongest argument is that Congress cannot alter federal court jurisdiction in a way that would violate individual rights guaranteed by the Constitution or otherwise interfere with the establishment of a supreme and uniform body of federal constitutional law. (A) is the correct answer.

98.   Although involving state lands, the case also involved a federal statute; it could be and in fact was decided under federal law. The United States Supreme Court may review by certiorari state court decisions in cases involving matters of federal law, in order to ensure uniform interpretation of such laws. (D) is incorrect. It is unimportant whether the Blue Supreme Court also relied on the state law, so (B) is incorrect.
       The issues involved are the same under the state statute and the federal statute it was patterned after. Thus, the state grounds would not be "independent" of the federal issues that are proper for Supreme Court review, and (C) is incorrect.
       (A) is the correct answer.

99.   Megahawg appears to be a unique property, the unavailability of which effectively makes the contract impossible or impracticable to perform. Trawf need not demand assurances or accept another hog from Schweinebauch before terminating his own performance. (C) is the correct answer.

100.   Paula was detained if the manager was blocking her only reasonable exit without her consent, so (D) is incorrect.
       (A) and (C) are difficult to distinguish, and both are incorrect. A merchant has a privilege to detain a person whom the merchant has reasonable grounds to believe is stealing or attempting to steal his property, and Paula's behavior may have contributed to the reasonableness of the manager's belief. However, the reasonableness of such belief is not the only requirement for the merchant's privilege. The detention must be conducted in a reasonable manner and last only for a reasonable period of time. Thus, (B) is the store's best defense.

101.   Congress has power under Article I, § 8, cl. 1 to *spend* for the general welfare, not to *legislate* for the general welfare. (A) is incorrect.
       An exercise of legislative power under the Commerce Clause may regulate some purely local transactions of a type that also affect interstate commerce. A broad attempt to prohibit discrimination in all business transactions throughout the country could be justified under an expansive interpretation of the Commerce Clause. (C) is incorrect.

(D) is incorrect because the 10th Amendment merely preserves to the states powers not specifically granted to the federal government.

The 13th Amendment specifically grants Congress the power to legislate against the badges and incidents of slavery, including private, individual acts of discrimination. *Jones v. Alfred H. Mayer Co.,* 392 U.S. 409 (1968). (B) is correct.

102. Neither Horace nor Lewis is guilty of burglary because there was no breaking. Horace had a key and permission to enter any time during the two weeks Sam was away, and Horace gave Lewis ingress. (A) and (B) are incorrect.

Lewis is clearly guilty of larceny in taking the rings. Horace is not guilty of trespass because he had permission to enter the property. (D) is correct.

103. Liability for infliction of emotional distress is based on the outrageousness of the conduct and the severity of the distress, but severe emotional distress is presumed from the mishandling of a dead relative's remains. (Even though the leg was not Jeremiah's, John would not have known that.) Proof of bodily harm or medical or psychiatric treatment is not required. (C) and (D) are incorrect.

Hospital is not strictly liable; its liability is based on a showing of recklessness or intent. (B) is incorrect, and (A) is correct.

104. The judgment lien statute does not take precedence over the recording act; priority is determined by the time of filing under one statute or the other. (D) is incorrect.

The conveyance from Able to Baker will not be encumbered by Charlie's judgment lien, not because such liens are not enforced in equity but because Baker recorded the conveyance prior to entry of the judgment lien, making Baker a purchaser for value without notice. (A) is incorrect, and (B) is correct.

105. Even if Dint's failure to challenge the ledger is treated as an adoptive admission, that would not prevent Dint from introducing evidence to contradict the inferences to be drawn from the admission. (D) is incorrect.

The best evidence rule applies when the document itself has operative legal effect and its contents must be proven. It does not apply to contemporaneously made records of events where the event and not the record is in issue, particularly where the witness has personal knowledge and present memory of the event in question. (C) is incorrect, and (A) is correct.

106. The law of contracts recognizes the doctrine of substantial performance, but in contracts for the sale of goods by a merchant under Article 2 there is a "perfect tender" rule that gives Nimrod the right to reject nonconformance, even if insubstantial. The UCC allows the seller to cure the defect before his time for performance has expired, however. Trailco should have the opportunity to cure the defect on June 1, the latest delivery date under the contract. (A) is correct.

107. The covenant to pay for repairs to the retaining wall meets all of the requirements for a covenant to run with the land. For Tim to enforce the covenant, it is not necessary for Tim to have relied on it when making the expenditures, but it is necessary for him to show that his expenditures were reasonable and customary. (D) is correct.

108. So long as damages to a passenger were foreseeable as a result of Acme's negligence, Acme must "take the plaintiff as it finds her" and foreseeability of the extent of the harm is not required. (A) is incorrect.

Acme is liable for injuries related to the fall, including the aggravation of Prudence's disability, but is not liable "for the full amount of her disability" to the extent of problems unrelated to the falling elevator. (C) is incorrect, and (D) is correct.

109. Preliminary questions concerning the admissibility of evidence are determined by the judge, out of the hearing of the jury when clearly prejudicial, with both parties present to argue the issues related to admissibility. (A) is correct.

110. There is no reasonable expectation of privacy from aerial observation of one's yard. In *Florida v. Riley,* 488 U.S. 445 (1989), the Supreme Court held that an officer's observation, with his naked eye from a helicopter, of the interior of a greenhouse in a residential backyard did not constitute a "search" because the accused could not reasonably have expected that his greenhouse was protected from public or official observation from a helicopter that was not violating the law or FAA regulations. (D) is correct.

111. This contract is governed by UCC Article 2, which allows the buyer to accept a nonconforming tender or reject it. If he accepts the goods, he must pay the list price and may not seek damages for the nonconformance. If he rejects, he has no further rights against Zeller. (B) is the correct answer.

112.   It is not discriminatory for the Park Service to distinguish between traditional sunrise services and an overnight stay involving a campfire in a fire-sensitive area of a national park. (B) is incorrect.

The Establishment Clause would not be offended by permitting religious groups to hold ceremonies on federal land so long as any group with a similar request is treated similarly. (C) is incorrect.

The substantial government interest in protecting the park and its visitors would provide adequate justification for placing some restrictions on the time, place and manner of this form of religious expression. (A) is incorrect, and (D) is correct.

113.   (A), (B), and (C) all represent relevant and legitimate ways to identify the defective part as one manufactured by Davis Co. (D), on the other hand, is the correct answer because evidence of similar transactions, accidents, or lawsuits is generally not admissible since it is most likely to be found more prejudicial than relevant, except on certain limited issues.

114.   The attempted conveyance by Jones to Anna and Charles was ineffective as to Charles, since he was not living at the time and did not sign the required documents. The grantor, Jones, retains the interest that was not effectively conveyed, leaving Jones a co-owner of the property with Anna. (C) is correct.

115.   There is no general rule that requirements contracts are nonassignable, and the facts here do not show a material change to the detriment of Eclaire, so (I) is not a good choice.

Whether Miller had expressly agreed to perform the contract for Staff would affect Staff or Eclaire's right to sue Miller for non-performance but would not give Eclaire a right to reject conforming goods tendered by Miller. (II) is incorrect.

The modern rule under the *Restatement (Second)* § 328 and Article 2 (§ 2-210(4)) is that language attempting to "assign the contract" presumptively intends not only to assign the rights but also to delegate the duties, so (III) is incorrect.

Since none of these arguments would support Eclaire's rejection of the goods, (D) is correct.

116.   Whether or not Eclaire agreed to accept Miller's performance would affect whether there is a novation releasing Staff from further performance, but not whether Eclaire must pay Miller for his conforming performance. (I) will not be an effective defense.

Once notice of the assignment is given, payment to the assignor is no defense. Since Eclaire had notice, her payment to Staff did not discharge her obligation to Miller. (II) is incorrect.

Although it may be true that Staff remains obligated on the contract, that argument is not a defense available to Eclaire in an action by Miller for the first installment.

(D) is the correct answer.

117.   The validity of the search warrant is based on a police officer's personal knowledge or reliance on reasonably trustworthy information from a reliable informant. Since Susie had previously been reliable, Officer Jones was justified in relying on her statements in this case, and the inaccuracy of her statement, whether deliberate or not, does not invalidate the warrant unless Jones knew her statement to be false. (D) is correct.

118.   The initial burden in a government employment termination case is for the employee to show that the nature of her employment agreement created a constitutionally protected interest giving rise to certain due process protections. The basis is not her reasonable belief, but objectively verifiable terms of employment as found in state law and employee handbooks. (D) is incorrect. (C) is correct and (A) is incorrect because the initial burden on this issue is not on the government. Green City Council need not demonstrate cause for the termination unless Baker first shows that she had a right to hear and contest such reasons at a pretermination hearing. (B) is incorrect.

119.   (A) is too broad a statement of the physician–patient privilege. It does not apply to every statement made in "a medical setting," but only to those made for purposes of diagnosis or treatment.

It is not relevant to the privilege whether Dean was voluntarily or involuntarily committed. (D) is incorrect. It might be relevant whether the hospital personnel were under some legal duty to report further threats by Dean, but this is not specified in the facts.

Dean's statement was not within the psychotherapist–patient privilege because the statement was apparently not made for purposes of diagnosis or treatment but merely because Dean felt compelled to make another threat against the President. Statements made to a nurse may or may not be subject to the privilege, depending on whether the nurse was or was not under the direction of Dean's doctors and more significantly whether the conversation was related to diagnosis or treatment. (C) is the most likely answer.

120.   A seller of a used home has no liability based on an implied warranty of habitability, so (C) and (D) are incorrect. However, the seller may be liable for misrepresentation if he knowingly makes any false statements of material facts or conceals conditions that would substantially change the value of the property to the buyer.

The modern rule extends such liability not only to active concealment but also to failure to disclose known defects that are not readily discoverable by the buyer, i.e., "latent defects." The bar examiners chose (A) as the correct answer. (B) is a close call because it seems to prove the defect was not discoverable by an ordinary inspection, but the basis of liability is the failure to disclose.

121.   The privilege to enter onto someone's land without permission in an emergency is complete (i.e., no damages are compensable) if the actor was attempting to protect the public generally.
     If the actor who entered onto the land was attempting to protect his own person or property, he is not technically considered a trespasser, but must pay the owner for any damage done to the property. Gardner can collect for the damage to his plantings. (A) is correct.

122.   Robbery is an inherently dangerous felony that may give rise to liability for felony murder. It is inherent in the nature of the act that it creates a risk of harm. (C) is not a viable argument. So long as the death was foreseeable, it does not matter that the defendant had no actual intent to kill. (A) is incorrect.
     It is irrelevant whether or not the underlying felony was completed, so long as the death occurred during the commission or attempted commission of such felony. (B) is incorrect.
     The only issue on which Steve could make an argument for non-liability for the death would be the foreseeability of the customer's actions. It is unlikely that he would be successful, but (D) is the best answer.

123.   If a drawer of a check tenders the check "in full satisfaction" of a claim, there is an offer of an accord and satisfaction as to the compromise amount of the check. If the payee endorses the check, she will likely be bound by the accord and satisfaction, even if she attempts a "reservation of rights." UCC § 1-207(2). (B) is correct.

124.   Absent an ordinance creating rights to sunshine, Pauline has no legal rights. An easement by implication will not be created for light and air, nor does the blockage of light create an easement by necessity. (D) is correct. *See, e.g., Fontainbleau Hotel Corp. v. Forth-Five Twenty-Five, Inc.,* 114 So.2d 357 (Fla. 1959).

125.   The *Restatement* allows recovery for damages for emotional distress caused by the defendant's intentional or willful conduct that is "extreme and outrageous." It is not enough that the defendant's conduct have been extreme, however.

There is also a requirement that the plaintiff's emotional distress have been severe. *Rest.2d, Torts* § 46, Comment *j.* (C) is correct.

126. Knowledge of the falsity of the representation (A), and intent to induce reliance (B), are elements of an action for misrepresentation, but Perkins did not in fact rely on it or suffer any damages. (D) is correct.

127. The function of the judge on a motion for a directed verdict is to determine whether the case hinges on a question of law. The judge must not determine questions of fact, such as evaluating the relative credibility of witnesses, unless the evidence presented on the critical issues is so deficient as to be inadequate as a matter of law. (A) is correct and the others are incorrect for that reason.

128. Ignorance of a statute that creates a strict liability offense is no defense to a prosecution under the statute. (A) is incorrect. However, violation of the statute in itself does not make Trelawney liable for murder, for which the common law requirements include premeditation and deliberation. He lacked this mental state. This is a stronger argument than lack of causation, since the statute contemplates that some person or persons other than the day-care worker will ultimately cause the harm to the child. (B) is correct and (C) is incorrect.

   Finding vicarious liability on the part of Trelawney's employee would not relieve Trelawney of his own responsibility. (D) is incorrect.

129. A common carrier is not strictly liable for the safety of its passengers but has a duty of due care toward them. (C) is incorrect and (D) is correct.

   Even a common carrier is not "required by law" to rescue its passenger from an assault by a third party. (A) is incorrect.

   Perkins was under no obligation to take action to prevent the unexpected injury to herself. (B) is incorrect.

130. Battery is an intentional tort, for which vicarious liability is seldom applied. It does not state a cause of action against Delval Airline that Perkins suffered a harmful or offensive contact on the airline, or that she sustained permanent injury at the hands of Morton. (A) and (D) are incorrect. There is no reason to hold Delval liable for Morton's battery.

   Vicarious liability could be imposed on the airline for acts of its agents. A battery is generally considered by be outside the scope of an agent's employment unless the employer knew of the agent's propensity to use violence and of the opportunity to do so on the job, but (C) was the answer chosen by the Bar Examiners.

Many courts, however, might find liability either under the theory that a common carrier owes a special duty to its passengers to protect them from assault, or under the theory in (B) that the serving of liquor must be done responsibly. *See, Figueroa v. Evangelical Covenant Church,* 879 F.2d 1427 (7th Cir. 1989); *Toombs v. Manning,* 835 F.2d 453 (3rd Cir. 1987); *Matin v. Nelson,* 741 F. Supp. 690 (N.D. Ill. 1990); *Worcester Ins. Co. v. Fells Acres Day School, Inc.,* 558 N.E.2d 958 (Mass. 1990).

131.   The presidential power of appointment does not give the President plenary power to protect his appointees. The appointees become officials of the United States government, not agents of the President, and are protected by federal and other laws. (B) is incorrect.

The U.S. Constitution explicitly provides for the division of authority between the state and federal governments and establishes procedures for resolving conflicts, so these matters are not nonjusticiable. (D) is incorrect.

The President's broadest power is his power to conduct foreign affairs, but it is not plenary. (A) is incorrect. The President may enter into executive agreements without ratification by Congress, and these have the force of federal law, including supremacy over state law. (C) is correct.

132.   A plea bargain is admissible as impeachment because it shows the witness's interest or bias in favor of the prosecution. (A) is correct. This is a non-hearsay purpose, so (B) and (D) are incorrect.

133.   (B) is correct. The contract was effectively modified.

134.   Barrister's pre-existing promise to pay $10,000 for the books does not support Debbit's promise of the stacks or prevent Debbit from revoking this new offer. (A) is incorrect.

Holding an offer open requires consideration unless the offeror is a merchant who makes the promise in a signed writing. Debbit is not a merchant with respect to these goods. (C) is incorrect, and (B) is correct.

This is not a proper case for detrimental reliance. Under § 90 of the *Rest.2d, Contracts,* the reliance must be "substantial" and there must be "injustice" which can only be avoided by enforcing the promise. There was no substantial reliance or injustice to Barrister. (D) is incorrect.

135.   A seller of property may be held liable on certain implied warranties, but these generally relate to buildings on the land, not to uses extending outside the property. A failure to disclose a matter substantially affecting the value of the land may be actionable in an action for misrepresentation. (A) is correct.

136.   A new trial for juror misconduct may be only based on influences external to the courtroom proceedings, not matters such as misunderstanding instructions or reliance on stricken testimony. (D), which involves the entry of extraneous information not filtered through the courtroom admission process, is the correct answer.

To be successful in winning a new trial, Doxie will be required to show not only juror misconduct of this nature but also that the extraneous information colored the decision-making process and likely affected the outcome of the trial. *See, e.g., St. Louis Southwestern Railway Co. v. White,* 788 S.W.2d 483 (Ark. 1990).

137.   Mistake of fact is a defense only when it negates the specific intent required for a particular crime and the defendant's mistake belief was reasonable. The standard is not a purely subjective belief, so (A) is incorrect.

Voluntary intoxication might have prevented Wilmont from forming the specific intent necessary for murder, but it will not prevent his prosecution for manslaughter on the ground that he was engaged in reckless and dangerous behavior. (B) is incorrect.

Wilmont should be convicted because of his recklessness. (D) is a better statement of the requirement as to his state of mind and mistake of fact than (C), so (D) is the correct answer.

138.   A life tenant may convey his interest in the property, and a purported conveyance of Profitacre by Leon to Mona would be interpreted as a conveyance of Leon's life interest only, leaving Ralph's remainder interest undisturbed. The life tenant has a right to all rents and profits during his/her life but is also obligated to pay real estate taxes out of such income. (C) is the correct answer.

139.   One co-tenant cannot bind another with respect to a boundary line dispute. Homer remained a tenant in common even during the period in which he was not exercising his right to possession. (D) is incorrect, and (B) is correct.

140.   Merely owning guns and having them on one's property is not an inherently dangerous activity, so Grandmother will not be held strictly liable. (C) is incorrect.

Grandmother will not be held vicariously liable for the actions of her grandson, but she had a duty to supervise him and take due care to prevent him from harming others. (A) is incorrect.

Grandmother's duty of care toward Patrick was that of a landowner to a social guest/licensee. Generally, the duty to a licensee is to warn of known dangers, with no duty to inspect and discover dangers. However, the duty to a child visitor may be greater because one is charged with anticipating careless or dangerous conduct on the part of children, who are not expected to be capable of exercising the same degree of care as the average adult. (B) is incorrect, and (D) is correct.

141. Equity does not permit a party to "sleep on his rights" where the delay causes prejudice to the other party. Nonprejudicial delay, however does not bar equitable relief. Here there is no evidence of prejudice. (A) is incorrect.

Specific performance is available when the damage remedy is inadequate, which includes many cases where only nominal damages could be recovered at law. (D) is incorrect.

(B) is correct. The best defense is that specific performance is not available to enforce a contract to perform personal services and Joiner agreed to "personally" remodel Galley's kitchen.

142. Joiner may recover his expectancy damages of $3,000. However, he had a duty to mitigate damages after notice of the breach by Galley, and is not entitled to recover the $5,000 on either a reliance or restitutionary theory. (B) is correct.

143. The search occurred prior to the arrest and was the cause of the arrest; it was not "incident to" the arrest. (A) is incorrect.

Use of excessive force might give rise to police liability, but does not invalidate the arrest. (C) is incorrect.

Although the Supreme Court has found in recent years that public school children have lesser expectations of privacy on school grounds, this rationale has been used to uphold random searches, not searches targeted at a specific individual already under suspicion. (B) is incorrect, and (D) is correct.

144. The fact that Yancey was in custody triggered the *Miranda* rule, but Yancey received his *Miranda* warnings. (A) is incorrect.

The *Miranda* rule prohibits police interrogation after a custodial suspect has requested a lawyer, but Yancey was not subjected to police questioning beyond that point. (B) is incorrect.

The fact that Yancey invoked his right to counsel prohibits the police from listening in on conversations with his counsel, but not necessarily conversations with others. (B) and (C) are incorrect.

Yancey's parents were apparently not agents of the police and it is unclear whether they interrogated Yancey or just let him talk. However, the police arranged the meeting and taped it secretly, distinguishing this case from *Arizona v. Mauro*, 485 U.S. 520 (1987), in which the defendant's wife insisted on speaking with her husband over the objections of the police and the taping of the conversation was done openly. (D) is the correct answer.

145.   It is not arbitrary or capricious to make an award based on merit, nor is it a denial of equal protection. (B) is incorrect. Congress may delegate the decision making with respect to the appropriate recipients of the award. (A) is incorrect.
Exercise of the spending power is not nonjusticiable, but it is subject to review only to see that it reasonably serves the general welfare and does not violate any specific constitutional prohibitions. (D) is incorrect, and (C) is correct.

146.   An implied-in-fact contract involves conduct indicating assent or agreement. Agreement is not implied where the facts show the individual was unaware of the nature of the obligation. (A) is incorrect because Algernon was not aware he had been wrongly billed for taxes on Bathsheba's property. (B) is incorrect because Ryder was unconscious.
(D) is incorrect because helping one's mother with a relatively simple chore would not ordinarily imply a right to payment.
(C) is correct because Nabor was aware he was receiving a benefit to which he was not entitled without payment.

147.   If mortgaged property is conveyed "subject to" the mortgage, the purchaser will lose his land if the mortgage is not paid, but he is not personally liable on the note. On the other hand, a purchaser who assumes the mortgage becomes personally liable to pay the mortgage and for any deficiency at a foreclosure sale. The original mortgagor also remains liable on the mortgage unless released by the mortgagee. In this case, Beam assumed and agreed to pay the mortgage but Carter did not. Ashton and Beam are liable for the deficiency, but Carter is not. (B) is the correct answer.

148.   The *Restatement* provides that one who carries on an abnormally dangerous activity such as blasting is subject to liability for harm to the person or property of another resulting from the activity, even if he has exercised the utmost care to prevent the harm. (C) and (D) are incorrect, and (B) is correct.

Landco's liability arises from ownership of the land on which the abnormally dangerous activity is carried out, not its supervision and control of Poolco, so (A) is incorrect.

149. Higher usage charges for nonresidents are permitted under the Commerce Clause. (A) is incorrect.

Under the Article IV Privileges and Immunities Clause which requires comity for the rights of state citizenship, the interest protected must be fundamental. A hunting or fishing license is not a fundamental right. (B) is incorrect.

Due process is not implicated if the recipient of a government license is granted only a temporary permit and is given no reason to expect that the license will be renewed after its initial term. In such cases, the license does not create a property right beyond the period of its term. (D) is incorrect. (C) is correct.

150. Taxes on interstate commerce may be upheld unless discriminatory or unduly burdensome. This could be a valid "compensatory tax" designed to make interstate commerce share a burden already borne by intrastate commerce. (A) is incorrect.

The Privileges and Immunities Clause of the 14th Amendment is narrowly construed to protect only incidents of national citizenship, which include the right to enter public lands, but not all citizens have a right to do business on public lands, so the interest is not "fundamental." (B) is incorrect.

The Equal Protection Clause is not implicated because there is no discrimination based on a suspect category. (C) is incorrect.

The Supremacy Clause is the best argument. (D) is correct.

151. The attractive nuisance doctrine assumes that the child entered the property without the landowner's permission, so (C) is incorrect. The doctrine places a duty of reasonable care on the landowner, Davis, not on the child. The duty applicable to the landowner looks at such factors as whether he had reason to know that children were likely to trespass, and whether the burden of eliminating the danger was slight as compared to the risk to children involved.

The doctrine, despite its name, does not require that the child have been lured onto the property by the nuisance. (D) is incorrect. The doctrine does require, however, that the child's youth have prevented his realization of the danger. *Restatement 2d, Torts,* § 339(c). The age of the child and the nature of the hazard are relevant in this respect; most cases involve children between the ages of six and twelve, but there is no fixed age limit.

The injured child will be barred from recovery if he could have been expected to apprehend the risk. (A) is correct. (B) is incorrect because it states the standard of care imposed on children generally, not in the attractive nuisance situation.

152.   Wallman's and Witler's testimony is admissible, if at all, only to support Smith's identification. (A) is incorrect and (B) is correct.

153.   Issues related to voting rights, including residency requirements, generally do present constitutional issues because they are fundamental interests protected by the due process and equal protection clauses. (B is incorrect.

Lengthy residency requirements for voters have been found unjustified, but substantial residency requirements for candidates may be justified on the basis that the state has a legitimate or even compelling interest in requiring that candidates understand and have a stake in the community. It is unclear how long a period may be justified on this basis. Five years may or may not be too long. *See, Hatcher v. Bell,* 521 S.W.2d 799 (Tenn.); *cf., Bay Area Women's Coalition v. San Francisco,* 78 Cal. App.3d 961, 144 Ca. Rptr. 591 (1978). There is a clearer basis for challenge, however.

A controversy that is appropriate for judicial determination must be "real and substantial," allowing for specific and conclusive relief, as distinguished from an advisory opinion on a hypothetical set of facts. Declaratory judgments are permitted where there is an actual controversy between adverse litigants. This case is not ripe, and presents no case or controversy at this time. It presents a hypothetical question concerning what would happen if Candidate were elected. If Candidate attempted to run and were not elected, a court would not have to decide the issue. Furthermore, Candidate has not named any specific adverse litigants who could vigorously present the case against Candidate's claim. (A) is correct.

154.   The agreement between Oliver and Len was in substance a security agreement. Courts have found a deed to a lender with a promise to reconvey when the loan is repaid an "equitable mortgage." Extrinsic evidence may be admitted to show the intent of the parties despite the Statute of Frauds. To obtain possession, Len must bring a foreclosure proceeding. (D) is correct.

155.   (A) states the rational basis test, which applies to statutes and regulations not implicating a fundamental right or protected class of persons.

(C), at the other extreme, states the strict scrutiny test. Classifications based on race are traditionally the only ones involving a suspect category requiring the strict scrutiny test.

Classifications based on sex are reviewed under an intermediate scrutiny standard. *Craig v. Boren*, 429 U.S. 190 (1976), held that gender classifications must serve important governmental objectives and be substantially related to those objectives. (D) is correct.

156. Even though the actual starting of the fire was not intentional, Defendant can be found guilty if he could have stopped the fire and intentionally did not do so. The fact that he started the fire imposed a duty on him to take corrective action. (C) and (D) are incorrect. Arson is a general intent crime, requiring either intent to burn or a wanton and reckless disregard for human safety. Simple negligence would not be enough. (B) is incorrect. (A) is correct.

157. A manufacturer may be liable for the manufacture and sale of a product that is suitable for its intended use but unreasonably dangerous if handled differently. Here the critical issue is whether proper warnings accompanied the sale of the product. The glasses, whether or not called "Safety Glasses," did not have to protect Grinder from all harm, so long as the warnings about their limitations were clear. (A) and (B) are incorrect, and (C) is correct. The glasses were not unreasonably dangerous when used for their intended, clearly specified use.

Workers' compensation laws would prevent Grinder from suing his employer for injuries resulting from this work-related accident, but would not prevent him from recovering from Glassco. Workers' compensation would not reduce or eliminate Glassco's liability. (D) is incorrect.

158. The *Restatement* recognizes that certain products are unavoidably unsafe for certain people while providing significant benefits for the majority of users. Such products are not deemed unreasonably dangerous if accompanied by adequate warnings of the risk and directions for use to minimize the risk. (D) is correct because Paul must show inadequate labeling in order to establish liability by Shampoo Company.

159. The plaintiff's misuse of a product may be a defense to a product liability claim. Where misuse of a product is foreseeable, however, strict liability may still apply. Paul's misuse was not unforeseeable, so (I) is not a defense.

(II) is incorrect because contributory negligence is not a defense to a strict liability claim unless the plaintiff knew of the danger and assumed the risk, which Paul did not.

(III) is incorrect because any user or consumer may be protected by strict liability rules; privity is not required.

Since neither (I), (II), nor (III) is a defense for Shampoo, (D) is correct.

160.   Oscar and Paul were roommates, not strangers, and Oscar undertook to give Paul the shampoo. He cannot claim he had no duty not to behave negligently toward Paul regardless of the nature of Shampoo Company's liability, so (C) and (D) are incorrect.

Since Oscar is not the manufacturer, he need not prove that Paul knowingly and voluntarily assumed the risk. (B) is correct.

(A) is correct. Contributory negligence is Oscar's best defense.

161.   To be guilty of conspiracy to commit battery or battery itself, the defendants need not have intended to hurt anyone. Battery is not a specific intent crime, and the general criminal intent required can be met by the commission of criminal negligence or the doing of an act that is malum in se. Pulling the fire alarm was probably one of these, and it set in motion forces that physically harmed people. The defendant need not have touched the plaintiff(s) directly so long as he was the cause of the indirect touching. However, the NCBE apparently thought this was a close call because they accepted both (B) and (D) as correct answers.

If there was a battery, there would also appear to have been a conspiracy here. The requirements of a plurality, an agreement for an unlawful purpose, and an overt act are met on these facts. Conspiracy does not merge into the crime that is the object of the conspiracy when that crime is completed.

162.   *Webster v. Reproductive Health Services*, 492 U.S. 469 (1989), permitted the states to limit or prohibit the use of public funds and public facilities or employees to provide abortion services. (C) is a much more precise statement of the holding and rationale of *Webster* than (D). (C) is correct.

163.   The recording act is a race–notice type statute. Belle's purchase cut off Ann's rights because Belle was a purchaser for value without notice of the deed to Ann, and Belle recorded first. Belle then had full power to convey to Cal, despite the recordation of Ann's deed. (B) is correct.

164.   (A) is incorrect because Driver did not intend to cause an imminent harmful contact or the apprehension thereof.

Walker's defensive action was not independent of Driver's act, so (C) is incorrect.

The issue of Driver's negligence should go to the jury, not be decided on a motion for summary judgment. (D) is incorrect, and (B) is correct.

165.   A strict liability crime occurs, despite a lack of intent, when the prohibited act takes place. There is no liability for "attempt" to commit a strict liability crime; there can be no attempt to commit a crime that does not require intent. (A) is incorrect.

Arson requires an intent to burn the dwelling of others or a reckless disregard for the safety of their place of habitation. (C) is incorrect because the jewelry store was not a dwelling, and Defendant had no intent to burn or reason to expect that his actions would cause a fire.

(D) is incorrect because attempting to frighten someone by playing a prank of this nature is not ordinarily a life-endangering act that is *malum in se*, leading to manslaughter liability.

Murder requires malice aforethought, but a person who acts without an intent to kill but with an intent to do great bodily injury and thereby causes another's death possesses malice aforethought. Defendant can be charged with murder. (B) is correct.

166.   Happy Time's "good faith" promise does not require Happy Time to guarantee that sales won't decline or that another client of Happy Time's won't disparage Fizzy Cola. (A) and (B) are incorrect.

The parol evidence rule might bar evidence of an oral agreement for an exclusive distribution arrangement that should have been included in the written contract. (C) is incorrect.   However, under the UCC, a written contract may be supplemented by evidence of trade usage. (D) is correct.

167.   FRE 803(1) permits testimony regarding statement made by persons who were observing some event at the exact time there were making the statement, whether or not the declarant is unavailable at trial. This is a present sense impression. (A) is the correct answer.

168.   Strict liability applies because Diggers was involved in an ultrahazardous activity, so neither Digger's care nor Paul's lack of care would decide the case. (A) and (D) are incorrect. A defense to strict liability is assumption of the risk, where the plaintiff knowingly and voluntarily proceeded in disregard of the danger, as Paul did. (C) is incorrect and (B) is correct.

169.   Winters' testimony as to her affiliation with the church, like membership in any other organization, can be admitted where relevant to show bias. Her credibility is not being impeached because of her religious beliefs but rather because her church has an interest in the litigation. Her First Amendment rights will not be offended. (C) is correct.

170.   The Full Faith and Credit Clause requires each state to recognize the public acts, records and judicial proceedings of every other state. This issue involves federal law, not the law of another state. (A) is incorrect.
     The federal law does not attempt to regulate the field of radon testing, so Magenta does not have a basis to challenge the federal statute on Commerce Clause grounds. (D) is incorrect.
     The correct analysis is under the Supremacy Clause. Because the federal statute does not require the use of testers on the EPA-approved list, there is no direct conflict with the Magenta licensing standards, and the state law promotes, rather than inhibits, the policy behind the federal law. (B) is incorrect.
     (C) is correct.

171.   The common law rule is that even if the contract states that no oral modifications will be recognized, the parties may alter their agreement by parol. If the contract is between a merchant and a non-merchant, a no-oral-modification clause on the merchant's form must be separately signed by the non-merchant. Bitz separately signed the clause, so the clause is valid. (C) is incorrect.
     Despite the no-oral-modification clause, the Code allows the merchant to waive the requirement for modifications to be in writing. The waiver may be by conduct but is retractable upon reasonable notification "unless the retraction would be unjust in view of a material change of position in reliance on the waiver." (D) is correct.

172.   Charitable trusts are liberally construed and may be reformed under the *cy pres* doctrine as necessary to ensure that the donor's charitable intent will be carried out. *Restatement, 2d, Trusts* § 399. Test apparently did not create a charitable trust, however, since the grant was by deed to the Church rather than into a trust. If there is no trust, the state official does not have a say in the disposition of the property. (D) is incorrect. Test in fact granted Blackacre to Church by deed, and Church had full rights to convey to Developer. (A) is correct.

173.   Spousal immunity in a criminal case is a privilege in the witness spouse not to testify against her spouse. *Trammel v. California*, 445 U.S. 40 (1980). The privilege does not lie with the criminal defendant spouse. (C) is correct.

174. (A) is an accurate statement and thus the wrong answer because a promise to pay the debt of another is within the Statute of Frauds and requires a signed writing.

(B) is a correct statement of law and therefore the wrong answer.

(C) is an accurate statement and thus the wrong answer because consideration is required to make the contract enforceable.

(D) is correct because it is wrong.

175. Utility companies do not have a property right to rate increases, so the due process clause is not offended by the moratorium. (A) is incorrect.

(B) makes a true statement as a matter of general principles of law, but is too broad to apply specifically to this case, and there is a preliminary issue of justiciability.

The case is not ripe for judicial decision because Economy Electric is many months away from needing a rate increase and various factors such as future fuel prices are unknown. There is no specific and immediate set of facts for the decision-maker. (C) is correct.

176. Daniel's statement might be admitted as a statement of present intention or plan if the issue were whether he in fact subsequently made payments in accordance with his plan. That does not seem to be the reason for admitting this letter, however; the purpose is to prove that he owed back taxes. The exception does not serve to admit backward-looking statements such as Daniel's promise to his mother. (A) is incorrect.

Daniel's statement is an admission of his liability. (B) is correct. If the admission of liability is voluntary, not preceded by any claim or dispute or threat thereof, the rule excluding settlement offers or plea negotiations is not applicable. (C) is not the best answer because it is not clear that the authorities were aware of Daniel's tax liability and intended to prosecute before his statement was made

177. The answer to this question may depend on whether UCC Article 2 applies because Article 2 gives a right to demand assurances. Hoarda had reasonable grounds for insecurity because of the condition of the market, and was within his rights to request assurances on October 15 if the Code applies. U.C.C. § 2-609. Failure by Broker to supply adequate assurances with a reasonable time, not exceeding 30 days, could create an anticipatory repudiation, giving rise to all the remedies for repudiation. Broker's statement on October 17, while not an outright repudiation under other circumstances, probably falls short of providing assurances under these circumstances. If not covered by the Code, however, Broker has not repudiated and may perform within the contract term. (A) is the correct answer.

178. (C) is the best argument because it states the Code rule on anticipatory repudiation in § 2-610: "When either party repudiates the contract with respect to a performance not yet due the loss of which will substantially impair the value of the contract to the other, the aggrieved party may (a) for a commercially reasonable time await performance by the repudiating party; or (b) resort to any remedy for breach even though he has notified the repudiating party that he would await the latter's performance and has urged retraction; and (c) in either case suspend his own performance or proceed in accordance with the provisions of this Article on the seller's right to identify goods to the contract notwithstanding breach or to salvage unfinished goods."

179. A life estate may be conveyed or assigned. (A) is incorrect.
Since the property was mortgaged before the conveyance to Paul and Richard, Paul as the life tenant was obliged to pay only the mortgage interest, not the principal. (C) is incorrect.
The life tenant has a duty not to commit waste, which at common law included substantial changes in the use of the property even if such changes increased the value of the property. Ironically, Paul could be enjoined from committing "waste" under the common law rule even though Paul's purpose in building the larger office building was to make the property more profitable and even if Richard's proposed use of the property would also involve demolition of the current building. (B) is Richard's best argument.

180. FRE 608 permits opinion evidence about another witness's reputation for truth or veracity, or a direct opinion based on personal observation. Character may be impeached by specific instances of conduct only when character is directly is issue. Doppler has not put his character in issue here. (C) is correct.

181. Larceny is a taking from a person with a superior possessory interest in the property. Rita as manager had taken possession of the money, and Eddie no longer had the right to possession, as required for embezzlement. He had the intent to convert the property and physically carried it away as required for larceny. (A) is correct.

182. A criminal defendant is entitled to his *Miranda* rights when he is in custody and is questioned by the police or their agents or informers, but there must be interrogation, not merely a voluntary statement by the defendant. *Illinois v. Perkins,* 496 U.S. 292 (1990). Here there was no interrogation by the police informer. (D) is correct.

183.   This was not a dying declaration unless there is a showing that Ronald believed he was dying imminently. (B) is incorrect.

A statement concerning a past act does not come under the existing state of mind exception. (C) is incorrect.

This statement was not an excited utterance because not made in the heat of the moment during the reported event. (D) is incorrect.

The statement was against the declarant's pecuniary interest. (A) is correct.

184.   A public employee may not be dismissed for the exercise of First Amendment rights so long as the speech was not unduly disruptive of the workplace, i.e., the danger to the employer's functions from the employee's remarks was minimal. *Rankin v. McPherson*, 483 U.S. 378 (1987). (B) is correct.

185.   Both parties are merchants, so the contract is governed by UCC Article 2, which contains a statute of frauds provision for contracts involving goods with a price over $500.. Thus, Mitt will need to show a memorandum signed by the party to be charged, Slalome. Slalome's order was placed orally, and the only memorandum was signed by Mitt. However, § 2-201(2) contains an exception between merchants if within a reasonable time a writing in confirmation of the contract, sufficient against the sender, is received and the party receiving it has reason to know its contents and does not object to its contents within 10 days after it is received. (B) is correct, and (C) is incorrect for this reason. There are other exceptions to the writing requirement for specially manufactured goods and goods for which payment has been made and accepted or which have been received and accepted, but it is not necessary to fit the case within these exceptions because Mitt's memo, received and uncontested by Slalome, will suffice.

186.   The preexisting duty rule does not apply here because Snoop had a duty to work for Artistic, not for Collecta. Snoop may collect on Collecta's promise, an offer that he accepted by performance. (D) is correct.

187.   Cam's interest, like Cynthia's and Camelia's, was contingent upon surviving Well. Since he did not survive, his contingent interest was neither devisable nor inheritable. (B) recognizes the unborn widow problem, it does not deal with the fact that invalidating the remainder would apply equally to all Oren's children since none of these interests would vest until the end of Well's life. (D) is correct.

188.   A false statement is a necessary element of defamation, but fault is also required. (C) is incorrect. Defamation is not a strict liability tort, so (A) is incorrect.

A defamation action by a private plaintiff requires proof of negligence, which could be shown by Allen having doubts but not verifying the accuracy of his statement. It is not relevant that Allen was prompted to make the statement by the interviewer's question. (D) is incorrect, and (B) is correct.

Slander is not actionable without proof of damages, unless it falls into the category of slander per se. Allen's statement does, because it related to Bradley's livelihood.

189.   Prism may recover $75 because an infant has a right to avoid a contract made before the age of majority, or may ratify the contract in whole or in part by showing assent in any form after reaching majority. Once made as an adult, Starr's promise could not be repudiated without breach of contract. Starr will be required to pay the amount she agreed to, or the fair value of the goods (if this were a necessity). (C) is correct.

190.   The contract will be enforced according to the terms agreed to by Starr after reaching her majority. Prism must prove that the condition precedent has been met. (D) is correct.

191.   Carrol will lose as to both Beach and Daniel. As the easement holder, Carrol has an obligation to keep the easement in repair and does not have a right to contribution from either of the adjoining owners. (A) is correct.

192.   A statement regarding one's intentions at the time the statement was made is admissible under the state of mind exception to the hearsay rule. This question is similar to *Mutual Life Insurance v. Hillmon,* 45 U.S. 285 (1891), in which a letter expressing intent to make a trip was found admissible to support the inference that the declarant's conduct was in accord with his intentions. (A) is correct.

193.   (A) is incorrect because it proposes an impermissible content–based restriction on speech.

In *Renton v. Playtime Theatres, Inc.,* 475 U.S. 41 (1986), the Supreme Court held that communities could apply time, place and manner–type zoning restrictions on adult bookstores in order to protect the community from the "secondary effects" of such businesses. (C) and (D) are incorrect.

Zoning for adult theaters and bookstores is evaluated under the tests for content–neutral time, place and manner restrictions, i.e., "narrowly tailored to serve a significant governmental interest" and Leaving open "ample alternative channels for communication of the information." (B) is correct.

194. When the entrapment defense is raised, the defendant's past criminal record becomes relevant to prove predisposition under the majority rule. (A) is incorrect.

  The defendant bears the burden of persuasion on an affirmative defense such as entrapment, although the ultimate burden of proof remains on the prosecution. (B) is incorrect. (D) is correct.

195. Under pure comparative negligence, Pat's $100,000 in damages will be reduced by her own 30% fault, but she can sue either of the other responsible drivers for the full amount remaining ($70,000) because this jurisdiction allows joint and several liability. By requesting contribution from Drew, Donald can recover Drew's $40,000 share he paid Pat. (A) is correct.

  Pat's equal fault with Donald might be a problem under a "modified" comparative negligence statute, depending on whether the statute provided that the plaintiff cannot recover anything if her fault is *equal to or greater than* that of the defendant or if her negligence is *less than* that of the defendant, and whether her fault is compared to all the defendants in the aggregate or to each defendant individually. These problems need not be addressed in a pure comparative negligence jurisdiction.

196. Without joint and several liability, Pat may hold each defendant liable only for the percent of total damages attributable to that defendant's fault. (C) is correct.

197. An oral assignment for no consideration is valid. and Margin does not necessarily obtain an advantage over Bridey because his assignment was in writing and for value. However, when the obligor (Traviata) has paid the assignor (Dr. Pulmonary), payment is a defense against the assignee(s) unless the obligor had notice of the assignment. Traviata did not have notice of either assignment, so (A) and (B) are incorrect.

  Both Bridey and Margin retain any rights they previously had against Dr. Pulmonary. Bridey has no right to sue to recover a gift, but Margin may seek to enforce his legal rights against Dr. Pulmonary. (D) is correct.

198.   (D) provides a true statement about the nature of informed consent, but does not deal with the basis of liability.

   (C) would be correct under the older battery theory of informed consent cases. However, negligence principles apply today in most informed consent cases. Both (A) and (B) relate to negligence issues, but (B) is the better answer because ultimately negligence cases turn on whether or not there was any compensable harm.

199.   Home ownership is not an incident of national citizenship, so (B) is incorrect.

   There has been no "taking" of her property for public use, so (C) is incorrect.

   This is not an *ex post facto* law, which makes criminal an act that was not criminal when performed. (D) is incorrect.

   Owner's best argument, although it is not strong, would be based on equal protection. An equal protection challenge would be difficult because the Constitution requires merely that classifications made for tax purposes by rationally related to a legitimate government objective and that the tax be applied equally to persons or property of the same class. Owner may attempt to show that she is being treated differently than other property owners in the same category. *See, e.g., Minnegasco, Inc. v. County of Carver,* 447 N.W.2d 878 (Minn. 1989).

200.   This information was compiled for purposes of litigation, not as part of a regularly conducted business activity. (C) is incorrect.

   The exception for past recollection recorded requires that the declarant be available and testify that he made the record and has no present memory of the facts recorded. Even if Plaza Hotel could produce the employees who made the records, the memoranda themselves would not be admissible under this exception unless the adverse party requested their admission. (B) is correct.

Made in the USA
Columbia, SC
24 May 2018